A Fragmented La

Protest, Culture and Society

General editors:
Kathrin Fahlenbrach, Institute for Media and Communication, University of University of Hamburg, Germany.
Martin Klimke, New York University Abu Dhabi.
Joachim Scharloth, Technical University Dresden, Germany.

Protest movements have been recognized as significant contributors to processes of political participation and transformations of culture and value systems, as well as to the development of both a national and transnational civil society.

This series brings together the various innovative approaches to phenomena of social change, protest and dissent which have emerged in recent years, from an interdisciplinary perspective. It contextualizes social protest and cultures of dissent in larger political processes and socio-cultural transformations by examining the influence of historical trajectories and the response of various segments of society, political and legal institutions on a national and international level. In doing so, the series offers a more comprehensive and multi-dimensional view of historical and cultural change in the twentieth and twenty-first century.

For a full volume listing, please see back matter

A Fragmented Landscape
Abortion Governance and Protest Logics in Europe

Edited by Silvia De Zordo, Joanna Mishtal
and Lorena Anton

berghahn
NEW YORK · OXFORD
www.berghahnbooks.com

Published in 2017 by
Berghahn Books
www.berghahnbooks.com

© 2017, 2018 Silvia De Zordo, Joanna Mishtal and Lorena Anton

Library of Congress Cataloging-in-Publication Data
A C.I.P. cataloging record is available from the Library of Congress
LCCN: 2016052931. https://lccn.loc.gov/2016052931

British Library Cataloguing in Publication Data
A catalogue record for this book is available from the British Library

ISBN 978-1-78533-427-6 hardback
ISBN 978-1-78920-071-3 paperback
ISBN 978-1-78533-428-3 ebook

Contents

Introduction

by Silvia De Zordo, Joanna Mishtal, Lorena Anton

In an editorial dating December 2010,[1] *The Guardian* underscored the fact that in Europe abortion is – still – 'a right that isn't'. Even if the 'greatest achievement of Europe's human rights framework has been to banish the death penalty from its shores', in terms of other matters of life and death Europe presents a fragmented landscape. Is abortion a 'human right', according to the United Nations' definition of 1994, for women living in today's Europe? Or is this 'right to choose' a 'right that isn't', differently explained in local, national and historical backgrounds, but continentally accepted as such?

In March 2015, the European Parliament approved the Tarabella Report, recognising women's sexual and reproductive rights as fundamental rights, while simultaneously giving each member state the right to autonomously legislate abortion.[2] Women are therefore in principle entitled to sexual and reproductive rights in Europe, but not to abortion rights, or not everywhere in the same way. Most European countries have relatively liberal abortion laws and generally allow elective termination of pregnancy in the first trimester, while second trimester procedures are limited to cases of health or life risk to the woman or severe foetal health problems (Berer 2008; IPPF 2012). This uneven policy landscape leads women to seek abortion in countries with more liberal abortion legislations, like the Netherlands, Spain and the United Kingdom; however, even there women may face procedural/social barriers to abortion access due to shortages of providers offering abortion (Habiba et al. 2009), limited or poor training in abortion care (Lohr 2008), or conscientious objection among physicians. Such refusals have recently provoked an intense scientific and political debate (Campbell 2011; Cook and Dickens 2006; EU 2005). Finally, three European countries – Ireland, Poland and Malta – have very restrictive laws that force women to seek illegal abortion (in the case of Poland – see Mishtal 2009, 2015; Nowicka 2008) or to travel to other countries, like thousands of Irish women do every year (Best 2005; Irish Family Planning Association

2000; Rossiter 2009). Abortion is therefore still in most European penal codes, and continues to be a topic of scientific, ethical and political debate as timely and important, as it is vigorously debated and controversial.

In this volume we examine the struggles surrounding abortion in contemporary Europe from the perspective of multiple protest logics occurring in public and private spheres. A cursory review of European media reveals multiple sites of struggle around abortion. For example, in 2014 Bernadette Smyth, the head of the largest anti-abortion group in Northern Ireland, was found guilty of harassing a Marie Stopes clinic director and women entering the clinic in Belfast. The judge deemed Smyth's protest as 'vicious and malicious', and expressed that patients should enter family planning clinics unimpeded. This verdict amounted to a significant blow to the pro-life groups, in a nation where the anti-abortion position has practically defined Northern Irishness, but it was then overturned in 2015 on the grounds that the evidence of harassment was insufficient, thus emboldening the anti-abortion activists.[3]

In the Republic of Ireland similar struggles are taking place. Political and social debates about the right to abortion have been provoked by the death of Savita Halappanavar, who in 2012 was denied a life-saving abortion while in an Irish hospital in Galway (O'Toole 2012). This terrible case along with the 2010 ECHR ruling against Ireland in 2010 called on Ireland to make the Irish abortion law include life-saving exceptions and triggered a robust political debate. As a consequence, the law was modified in 2014 to allow abortion when the life of the woman is at risk, including the risk of a suicide.

Elsewhere in Europe other forms of protests are taking place, provoking legal and political controversy. In 2014, Warsaw doctor Bogdan Chazan was fired from a hospital for refusing to provide a lawful abortion to a woman for a severe foetal abnormality – one of only three circumstances under which Polish women can still seek legal abortion care. The popular protest by women's groups, progressive politicians, and much of the Polish public against Chazan's use of objection to deny the procedure forced Warsaw's president, Hanna Gronkiewicz-Waltz, to dismiss him from his post as the hospital director.[4] In October 2015, Poland took an extreme right turn politically when the parliamentary elections handed a victory to the Law and Justice Party, which campaigned on a platform that made economic promises to the rural poor and capitalised on anti-immigrant anxieties. Significantly for reproductive rights, the Law and Justice Party claims it will restore the 'moral order' by banning abortion altogether. This development in Poland is poorly understood by political analysts, particularly given that Poland has enjoyed relatively strong economic footing for almost a decade under the centrist Civic Platform.[5] It highlights political engagement and a strong voting participation of conservative groups in the Polish electorate, with meagre representation from other political positions (see Mishtal this volume).

The issue of conscientious objection to abortion services is ongoing in other parts of Europe as well. In the United Kingdom, the case of two midwives claiming conscientious objection went to the Supreme Court to debate the right of healthcare support staff to refuse to assist in terminations.[6] The Supreme Court ruled against the midwives, arguing that objection can only be claimed by providers directly performing abortions – a significant victory for the abortion rights advocates.[7] If objection were to include supporting staff, it would potentially disrupt services, as doctors providing abortion may be unable to do so without proper assistance. This actually occurs in Italian hospitals where up to 80 per cent of gynaecologists declare themselves to be objectors in the south and in key regions of the centre – Lazio and the north – Veneto (Italia, Ministero della Salute 2015), and high rates of objection are also registered among midwives and anaesthesiologists (see De Zordo this volume, and De Zordo 2015, 2016).

In France, the abortion law has been further liberalised since 2001, extending gestational age limit from ten to twelve weeks, and expanding the right to provide abortion care to general practitioners, who signed special protocols with gynaecological units at nearby hospitals. The Parliament also reaffirmed abortion as a fundamental woman's right[8] and eliminated the mandatory waiting week prior to the procedure. However, women still face barriers to access, and if the National Front (the right wing party that has recently been successful at regional elections) pursues its anti-abortion rights agenda,[9] women may face even more serious barriers in the future. A recent report on legal and procedural barriers in France, including conscientious refusal of care, shows that women are forced to travel to other regions of France as well as abroad (Haut Conseil à l'Egalité entre les Femmes et les Hommes 2013). Physicians sometimes refuse to provide abortion to specific categories of women, including those who have repeated terminations, and minors without parental authorisation. Furthermore, in some hospitals where the chief gynaecologist objects, most obstetricians/gynaecologists also object, but this may be out of fear of potential repercussions in the workplace, rather than based on conscience per se (ibid.: 62).

Over the last decade, the struggles around conscientious refusal of care, and questions of women's right to abortion v. providers' right to refuse, have been escalating to the EU level and subject to supranational governance (Mishtal 2014). The Council of Europe recognises that refusals make access to safe abortion difficult or impossible, particularly for rural and low income women (Council of Europe, The Parliamentary Assembly 2010). The European Court of Human Rights and the European Committee of Social Rights emphasise, addressing this issue in Poland and Italy, that states must organise their health services to ensure that health professionals' exercise of freedom of conscience does not prevent patients from obtaining access to services to which they are entitled under national laws (Council of Europe 2014; Lamačková 2014).

While EU legal bodies try to regulate conscientious objection in order to safeguard women's sexual and reproductive rights, the Vatican defends health professionals' absolute right to object to abortion and condemns 'voluntary interruption of pregnancy', as termination by women's choice is defined in neo-Latin languages. In 2014, Pope Francis pressed this issue on many occasions, including at a meeting with U.S. President Obama[10] and at an important meeting of the Association of Italian Catholic physicians.[11] The Vatican has become increasingly engaged in efforts to limit sexual and reproductive rights, and in embryo research. This partially explains why conscientious objection is targeted in heated European political debates and why in Catholic countries like Italy and Spain a shift has already occurred in abortion governance (Morgan and Roberts 2014 [2012]), from language of women's to foetal health and 'rights'. However, as this book demonstrates, the Vatican's political influence is contested by feminist and leftist groups, and by abortion providers, who defend women's right to choose and ask the state to regulate conscientious objection in order to safeguard access to care.

Contentious battles over abortion rights are also taking place in individual member states. In 2013, the conservative-Catholic wing of the Spanish Council of Ministers proposed a new law entitled 'Law of the Protection of the Conceived Life and of Pregnant Women's Rights' meant to reverse the 2010 progressive abortion law and criminalise first trimester abortion on women's request and second trimester procedures for foetal malformations. Due to massive demonstrations by feminist and leftist groups and protests by medical associations, the parliamentary debate was suspended and the Minister of Justice Alberto Ruiz-Gallardón, 'father' of the proposed law, resigned. Other attempts to restrict abortion have not always been stopped by protests. Russia, Slovakia and Hungary have introduced new restrictions, including mandatory and biased pre-abortion counselling, and waiting time (Lamačková 2014). Waiting times are of particular burden for rural and low income women, increasing travel time and cost, which delays gestational age at termination and increases risks to women's health (WHO 2012).

At the EU level, struggles for prenatal right to life are waged by the Catholic anti-abortion campaigns 'One of us' and 'Citizen go', which have petitioned to the Council of Europe to ban, respectively, abortion after twenty weeks, the use of EU funds for research, and foreign aid programmes and public health activities linked to the destruction of embryos.[12] In May 2014 the European Commission dismissed the 'One of us' campaign,[13] provoking protests among Catholic groups.[14]

As conflicts around abortion continue to mount in Europe under both progressive and conservative governments, it is clear that reproduction, and abortion specifically, is central and instrumental in a variety of 'moral regimes' and agendas, including religious, neoliberal, and demographic. In this volume, we take up the analysis of these struggles in Europe from the perspective of protest logics and explore them in different countries and historical periods, drawing on local, detailed ethnographic and historical accounts that allow a rich and fruitful international comparison.

Looking Back: National Legislations of Abortion in Europe after 1945

After the Second World War, European states developed new reproductive and sexual politics, and deep transformations occurred around long-established concepts like 'motherhood', 'family' and 'the role of women' in the society. Accompanying these political shifts were major changes in abortion legislation. These changes have largely occurred since 1955, when for the first time in postwar Europe, a state – namely the Soviet Union – permitted women to interrupt a pregnancy upon request.[15] Soon all Central and Eastern European communist nations, except Albania, passed similar legislation (David 1999). Thus, abortion was legalised first in communist states, and then on the other side of the Berlin Wall, starting with the United Kingdom, in 1968. However, as this volume shows, the legalisation of abortion in these regions resulted from different historical and political processes: while the mobilisation of feminist groups and their alliance with leftist political forces were essential to the success for the legalisation of abortion in 'capitalist' Europe, in 'communist' Europe abortion rights were implemented by the state as part of the political ideology of gender equality and to encourage female employment. These dominant state discourses varied, as this volume shows. In some countries abortion was legalised to grant women body autonomy, while in others to promote 'responsible' motherhood. Elsewhere public health concerns to reduce maternal mortality due to unsafe abortion also played a role in decriminalising abortion. Despite this wave of legalisation, abortion remained illegal in Ireland, Portugal, and Malta, while in Romania the right to abortion was initially granted in

1957, but then reversed in 1966 under Nicolae Ceauşescu's dictatorship until 1989, when it was legalised again (see Anton this volume).

Since the 1990s, three major social and politico-economic shifts have profoundly influenced abortion rights and shaped reproductive governance: 1) the fall of communist regimes in Central and Eastern Europe, 2) dramatic demographic changes, and 3) the embrace of neoliberal economic policies and – more recently – of 'austerity measures' across the New Europe. In a number of post-communist nations abortion rights have been restricted or nearly eliminated due to the political revitalisation of religious institutions, in particular the Catholic Church, and the general 'remasculinisation' of the region manifested in a backlash against the gender equality ideology presumably imposed by communism (Watson 1993). The decline of the welfare state evidenced by the neoliberal cuts in social services greatly affected women's reproductive experiences, especially in Eastern Europe where conversion to capitalism has been abrupt, as authors of part IV show. The 'austerity measures' adopted after the 2008 crisis resulted in further cuts in social services and healthcare, making women's reproductive choices, either to have children, or to limit births, even more difficult.

Most European countries have also experienced dramatic fertility declines to below replacement levels. These demographic changes are fuelling anti-reproductive rights backlash with inflammatory political and media rhetoric about women's 'irrational' decisions to limit childbearing (De Zordo and Marchesi 2014 [2012]; Krause and De Zordo 2014 [2012]), the dangers of population 'aging', and of higher fertility rates among some immigrant populations 'threatening' the survival of European, Christian nations (Krause and Marchesi 2007; Marchesi 2014 [2012]).

This volume also highlights the important shift in European reproductive governance through a new understanding of individual, human rights (Morgan and Roberts 2014 [2012]). In particular, the rights of 'the unborn' have become central in the public debate on abortion, resulting not only from the increasing political influence of the Church, but also from the growth of Assisted Reproductive Technologies (ARTs), and research on embryos and foetuses. Sophisticated prenatal screening and foetal surgery techniques have transformed the embryo/foetus into a 'patient', entitled to healthcare (Casper 1998; Morgan 2009), while new neonatal intensive care has transformed pregnant women and their partners into 'moral pioneers' at the frontier of science (Rapp 2000). Gynaecologists and obstetricians may also face 'moral dilemmas' around abortion, particularly regarding later gestational ages. Furthermore, they participate, more or less actively, in the national and transnational battles around women's reproductive rights and 'foetal rights' that are becoming central in public debates on abortion, with the use of new Internet technologies and social networks.

As the authors in this volume show, anti-abortion movements have appropriated the scientific language and developments to claim foetal 'personhood', and the human rights rhetoric to claim the rights of these 'new bio-political subjects' (Kaufman and Morgan 2005: 328). These shifts are threatening women's sexual and reproductive rights, which were defined as human rights at key international Conferences in Cairo and Beijing in the 1990s. In this contentious context, pro- and anti-abortion rights movements and groups are continuously changing and adapting their abortion protest logics.

Theorising Abortion Governance and Protest Logics: Between Discourses and Practices

In this volume, we are using abortion protest logics as an analytic tool for tracing, exploring and contextualising – both synchronically as well as diachronically – different political, moral and religious rationalities directed towards liberalising or curtailing the termination of pregnancy at the social and individual level. As we show, the forms as well as the effects of public, political actions – in favour of or against abortion rights – change depending on a number of complex, intertwined political as well as historical, social and cultural factors. A form of protest that was successful in the past, for instance, may not be envisaged as the most successful or viable in another historical and political period. At the same time, new forms of protest arise, like Internet campaigns in the twenty-first century, which may add a new degree of complexity to the more traditional protest strategies we have observed thus far.

The authors of this volume describe and examine three main kinds of protest: mass demonstrations, public acts of destruction or disruption, and public performances and civil disobedience. Each is associated with a different logic that can be defined, from the perspective of the social movements theory, as the logic of numbers, the logic of damage, and the logic of bearing witness (Cammaerts 2012: 121). As the anthropologist Joanna Mishtal suggests (this volume), a fourth protest logic should be acknowledged: 'the logic of clandestine civic disobedience, wherein more than just bearing witness, they (women/social actors) actively subvert established laws and controls'. This kind of 'quiet, individual' protest consists in showing dissent while avoiding public visibility, and, therefore, political engagement with the public debate on abortion rights. Several authors of this volume show that a similar logic of 'civic and/or clandestine disobedience' is often embraced by women facing legal, procedural, or social barriers to safe, legal abortion as well as by other social actors, who are involved in anti- or pro-abortion rights movements in different geopolitical and historical contexts. Individualised and privatised strategies of 'silent protest' may be considered as forms of resistance, following Foucault (1978), vis-à-vis the conservative reproductive governance launched by the religious and nationalist politics in the New Europe. This concept includes a number of subtle forms of protest, expressing dissent and forming resistance-like practices (Lock and Kaufert 1998:13), including deliberate inaction as a strategic, informed response to power (Halliburton 2011) and reproductive governance.

As elucidated by Morgan and Roberts, reproductive governance refers to the 'mechanisms through which different historical configurations of actors … use legislative controls, economic inducements, moral injunctions, direct coercion, and ethical incitements to produce, monitor, and control reproductive behaviours and population practices' (2014: 107 [2012: 243]). The authors of this volume show how in contemporary Europe, as in other parts of the world, reproductive governance or abortion governance, as we have renamed it, has drastically changed in recent years. With the renewed political power of the Church in post-communist Eastern Europe and the resurgence, in Western Europe, of public debates about European Christian roots and values, as a direct consequence of Islamophobia, old and new religious moralities are more than ever shaping abortion protest logics. These sentiments have been intensifying as a result of the major influx of migrants to Europe due to economic and political unrest in Africa and the Middle East, especially Syria, and the terrorist attacks that have taken place in 2015, in particular in France.[16] Xenophobia further fuels demographic angst, as anti-immigrant attitudes turn into nationalist calls to increase the 'native' population. These demographic anxieties are often used to justify calls to restrict abortion rights, eclipsing women's rights by morality discourses of 'rights of the family'. Thus, the authors of this volume show how reproductive governance, nationalism, religion and women's advocacy for reproductive rights comingle in many European countries, a trend that has been observed also in other geopolitical settings, including Latin America (De Zordo and Mishtal 2011; Morgan and Roberts 2014 [2012]).

Structure of the Volume

This volume offers analyses from several disciplinary perspectives, including anthropology, sociology, history, medicine, and legal studies. The first part of the book examines the pro-abortion rights activism, movements, strategies and protests that aim to either maintain abortion rights or counteract various forces seeking to restrict this right, both at the EU level and at national levels, focusing particularly on the cases of the United Kingdom, Switzerland, and Sweden. The second part of the book is centred on contemporary discourses and practices against abortion rights in Catholic Italy and Belgium, and in Orthodox Russia. The third part analyses health providers' participation in both pro- and anti-abortion rights movements in northern Protestant Norway, and in southern Catholic Italy, and Spain. Finally, the fourth part examines the key political rationalities and agendas underlying abortion policies, in particular pronatalism and nationalism, in three different countries: Romania, Poland and Northern Ireland.

Part I: Pro-abortion Rights Activism, Movements, Strategies, and Protest Logics

The authors here focus on fundamental issues about abortion as a right, including the relationship between abortion rights and women's movements, as well as the nature of the discourse upon which abortion rights have been built in different contexts and in the international arena. In particular, they investigate how different forms of protest against abortion restrictions have been formulated in the past and how such struggles are waged in the present, with further analysis of international European advocacy efforts. They consider protest as a function of different actors, including advocacy 'from below' by women's movements, or advocacy 'from above' by policymakers.

Christina Zampas opens this section with a careful review of legal cases since the 1990s, and shows how fundamental rights to non-discrimination and gender equality – both of which are the basis of abortion rights – are neither fully recognised as such at the regional policymaking level in member states, nor at the EU level. This chapter highlights the importance of human rights as a legal strategy to combat increasing restrictions on abortion in some parts of Europe, much of which is underwritten by religious institutions. Sociologists Annulla Linders and Danielle Bessett in their chapter examine the case of Sweden, by comparing and exploring two key events: the well-publicised abortion obtained by an American woman in Sweden, and the efforts to prosecute Swedish women seeking abortions in Poland. Linders and Bessett consider the discourses upon which abortion rights have been built in Sweden since the 1960s, and demonstrate the importance of particular rhetorical strategies to long-term conceptualisation of women's rights. The interesting case of Sweden juxtaposes the well-established Swedish right to abortion with the foundational discourse for this right as based on traditional notions of motherhood. Through this analysis the authors consider the relative implications of using a less radical strategy versus a liberal-feminist strategy in advocating for reproductive rights.

Finally, historians Kristina Schulz and Leena Schmitter in their chapter compare the genealogy of abortion rights vis-à-vis the women's movements in Switzerland and the United Kingdom. Using a careful historical analysis, the authors demonstrate that abortion rights do not necessarily emerge from women's rights movements. This analysis therefore considers the place of concepts such as 'body autonomy', 'self-determination', and 'pro-choice' in the wider women's rights struggles. Since feminist movements often sought to forge alliances with other grass-roots movements, such as labour or particular political parties and causes, the authors also bring attention to the abortion right as a uniting, or at times a fragmenting, element of these debates and strategies. Finally, focusing on Switzerland and the United Kingdom also offers an opportunity for an analysis of the variations between the political systems, such as direct democracy versus semi-direct democracy, and how these structural differences shape both the struggle for abortion rights as well as the laws themselves.

Part II: Anti-abortion Rights Activism, Movements, Strategies, and Protest Logics

This part examines anti-abortion activism that emerged in postwar Europe, first in Western Europe, where activists since the 1960s and 1970s have organised into strong, national movements in opposition to feminist struggles to legalise abortion; then in the 1990s in Eastern and Central Europe, where these movements did not exist until the end of the Soviet era. Chapters by anthropologists Claudia Mattalucci and Sonja Luehrmann and historians Karen Celis and Gily Coene offer an interesting comparison of Italy, Russia and Belgium, where important differences but also unexpected similarities and transnational links emerge. Luehrmann shows that contemporary pro-life groups have appropriated the transnational, dominant discourse of anti-abortion rights' groups, originated in the United States in the 1990s, in which abortion is depicted as a 'trauma' and women having abortions as victims of PAS (post abortion syndrome) needing moral and spiritual support (Lee 2003). In Russia, however, this discourse has assumed a specific historical and political meaning as a young anti-abortion rights' militant affirmed, referring to the 'traumatic' memory of the Soviet past when abortion was the main birth control method available and abortion rates were very high: 'all Russia has PAS'. This discourse of 'trauma' is also mobilised in Italy and in Belgium, where anti-abortion rights groups advertise moral and spiritual support at 'pro-life' or 'pregnancy crisis centres', where Catholic (in Belgium and Italy) or Orthodox (in Russia) volunteers focus their advocacy work on the concept of 'trauma'. These groups also organise public demonstrations, including in front of health facilities, both to prevent women from receiving abortion, which they believe will jeopardise their well-being, and defend 'Life' from conception.

Using rich ethnographic details and meticulous historical analysis, authors here describe forms of protest against abortion rights, from visible marches and funerals for aborted embryos and foetuses (in Italy), to private, 'invisible' confessions to Orthodox (in Russia) or Catholic (in Italy) priests, and spiritual retreats organised by Catholic groups, during which women are invited to overcome their 'trauma'. These chapters also examine how anti-abortion rights tactics vary in the use of imagery, from bloody foetal remains used in some contexts, like Belgium, to smiling newborns currently used by many 'pro-life' groups, or the biblical icons of 'abortion as mortal sin' used in Russia. Finally, the authors of this part reflect upon the actual political impact of anti-abortion rights groups. As Mattalucci, Celis, and Coene argue, in Italy and Belgium these groups formally do not aim to restrict abortion laws as they did in the past; instead they depict their advocacy as focusing on safeguarding human life. Nevertheless, their efforts are clear attacks on progressive abortion laws. In Russia, in contrast, these groups have only recently emerged and gained the increased political support of President Vladimir Putin and part of the political elite, who are concerned with Russia's dramatic fertility decline since the 1990s and the relatively high abortion rates. As a result, an important change was made to the abortion legislation in 2011, allowing health professionals to refuse to provide abortion care on the grounds of conscience and introducing a mandatory waiting period for the procedure. In this new context, Luehrmann argues, Russian anti-abortion rights activists can see themselves at once as anti- (Soviet) state and patriotic.

In the three countries anti-abortion rights groups implicitly contest the notion of 'voluntary interruption of pregnancy'. Abortion emerges, in fact, in these groups' dominant discourse, as an 'involuntary' choice of women, either as the result of the violence of the state (in Russia) and of gender norms that are criticised (the communist working mother), or as the result of past violence and traumas that women have experienced (Italy). Women are not recognised as full rational, moral and political subjects able to decide what is best for them and their families, if they have one, while the embryo/

foetus is represented as a 'child' whose life should be protected and whose 'death' will always haunt unless women engage in self-examination and/ or, in the case of Russia, public engagement in anti-abortion rights groups.

Part III: Health Professionals'/Providers' Involvement in the Pro- or Anti-abortion Rights Debate and Access to Services

Chapters in this section show how new antenatal screening techniques have contributed to making the embryo/foetus hyper-visible and constructing it as a 'child' and a 'person'. These new constructions create a tension between the foetus' rights and a woman's 'rights as a patient', increasing abortion stigma and making termination less acceptable than it was in the past. As the anthropologist Silvia De Zordo suggests, based on her research in four public Italian maternity hospitals providing abortion care, this may partially explain the increase in conscientious objection that was registered in the 2000s in countries such as Italy. A complex moral classification of abortions and of women having abortions emerges in this study, as well as in the context of Norway, examined by the physician and abortion provider Mette Løkeland. Terminations are considered more or less acceptable or stigmatised by health professionals, depending on their causes (unwanted pregnancy, foetal malformations, women's health problems) and on women's gestational age (first trimester or beyond). As the authors of this part show, the moral classification of abortions radically changes from one context to the other. For instance, in Norway, where the phantom of the Nazi, eugenic past is still strong (Melhuus 2012), termination for foetal malformation is called 'selective abortion' and is publicly condemned as women's 'selfish' decision and as a potentially discriminatory act vis-à-vis people with disabilities. In Italy, on the contrary, it is called 'therapeutic abortion' and obstetricians/gynaecologists consider it much more acceptable than a termination of an unwanted pregnancy that could and should be prevented via effective contraception that women are responsible for. At the same time, in both countries abortion around or beyond foetal viability is an object of scientific and political debate. In fact, tremendous innovations in neonatal intensive care have recently occurred, allowing the survival of a statistically relevant number of severely premature neonates starting from twenty-four weeks of gestation. This shift in the age of viability[17] has made abortion near or beyond this gestational time less morally acceptable to some health professionals than it was in the past. Consequently, some providers are becoming more actively involved in the political debate on abortion and conscientious objection both in Italy and Norway. Providers' participation in anti- and pro-abortion rights protests has provoked further debates at the EU level, particularly in the case of Italy, and has led, in some cases, to important changes in abortion regulations. In Norway, for instance, midwives' protests against late abortions have led to the reduction of legal abortion time limits, without the support of scientific evidence. The consequence of this change is, as Løkeland argues, that 'foetal rights' are increasing, while women's rights during pregnancy are decreasing.

As the physician and anthropologist Beatriz Aragón Martín highlights in her chapter about Spain, the abortion rights of immigrant women in particular are under threat in this contentious context. In Spain, immigrant women's access to safe, free abortion cannot be taken for granted, as these groups do not always have full access to the public health system because of their irregular or undocumented legal status. To circumvent this legal barrier, physicians working in primary care in Madrid have started to use a law that was originally aimed at protecting the rights to health of the 'unborn' as a child to be and not women's right to freely terminate their pregnancies. This law grants all women the right to public health coverage during pregnancy, regardless of their legal status, and physicians use it, instead, to grant immigrant women access to legal, free abortion. By 'transgressively' using this law, Martín Aragón argues, Spanish physicians are 'silently' protesting against migrant women's discrimination and their exclusion from free abortion care, and, at the same time, defending women's abortion rights.

Part IV: Pronatalism, Nationalism, and Resistance in Abortion Politics and Access to Abortion Services

The final part of the volume examines the debates on the 'morality aspect' of discourses on reproduction in Ceaușescu's Romania, post-socialist Poland, and Northern Ireland, and draws attention to how it is entangled with, and perhaps central to, political processes and agendas. This analysis of abortion politics is especially significant in geopolitical areas with demographic anxieties about declining birth rates, or, alternatively, demographic social imaginaries of an expanded and 'radiant' future nation. The authors of this part examine the key political rationalities and agendas underlying abortion policies, in particular pronatalism and nationalism, and consider how such rationalities affect access to abortion care, and the various forms of resistance that these power configurations generate. These chapters demonstrate that the right to abortion has been the key political tool used both in dictatorial power structures and in ostensibly democratic states, highlighting how reproduction and women's rights in general are key targets for governance by 'moral regimes', including religious, neoliberal, nationalist, and demographic.

Specifically, anthropologist Robin Whitaker and social policy researcher Goretti Horgan examine the case of Northern Ireland around the time of the 1998 Belfast Agreement – a critical historical moment widely perceived as ushering a new democratic era. However, Whitaker and Horgan show that the outcome was quite undemocratic. Based on discourse analysis of the public debates at that time in Northern Ireland, they argue that despite some rhetoric about gender equality, the Agreement's authorisation of ostensibly rival nationalisms in the end promoted the tightening of an already extremely restrictive abortion law as the quintessentially Catholic nationalist position. This case also shows how the meaning of 'peace' and political dealmaking resulted in sacrificing women's rights in this political game, as conservatives argued to unite former enemies – British-identified unionists and Irish nationalists – through the 'shared morality' of an anti-abortion stance. Whitaker and Horgan ultimately interrogate the nature of democracy in Northern Ireland, and identify an important disjuncture between the professed democracy based on rights and equality, and the kind of democracy that emerged from the Belfast Agreement.

Similarly, anthropologist Joanna Mishtal examines how the Catholic nationalist administration in post-socialist Poland severely restricted abortion after 1989. Mishtal's analysis focuses, however, on the responses to these restrictions, and argues that Polish women's extensive use of illegal abortion as a way to control reproduction not only circumvents the abortion ban but constitutes a distinct form of resistance against the Church and the state's religious governance of women's bodies. In particular, Mishtal focuses on the range of coping mechanisms employed by Polish women to access abortion and share knowledge about preventing pregnancy, and argues that the very low birth rate function de facto is a 'collective protest' against declining women's rights. However, she also questions the political utility of 'quietly beating the system' through individualised strategies, and poses questions, similar to Whitaker, about the role of women's rights in an ostensibly democratic state.

Historically, the Catholic Church's political power and its strict anti-abortion doctrine have had a wide-ranging effect on abortion restrictions in Europe. However, as anthropologist Lorena Anton argues in her chapter, equally powerful abortion restrictions were instituted under a nonreligious but politically dictatorial regime of Nicolae Ceauşescu between 1966 and 1989 in communist Romania. Using oral history and ethnographic analyses that trace the genealogy of the anti-abortion decree produced by Ceauşescu's regime, Anton highlights the nationalist nature of the abortion ban, depicting births as Romanian women's patriotic duty, and the foetus as a socialist property and a 'national good'. Anton's ultimate focus, however, is on how women in post-socialist Romania remember their ways of coping with these restrictions through illegal abortion. Because contraception was also illegal, women typically had multiple abortions, many in unsafe and dangerous conditions, but as Anton argues, this was the only form of protest available against one of the harshest and most criminalising pronatalist policies in European history.

Collectively, the four parts of the book bring attention to both the reproductive governance by powerful political actors, and the instrumental use of reproduction in the political dealmaking and nation-making. At the same time, they highlight some of the weapons of protest that different social actors – from feminist and leftist groups to anti-abortion rights groups, from women having terminations to health professionals – have used and currently use in different countries to defend or contest abortion rights in contemporary Europe, from the Second World War until the present.

Notes

1. 'Abortion: A Right That Isn't', *The Guardian*, 20 December 2010. Retrieved 1 August 2016 from http://www.theguardian.com/commentisfree/2010/dec/20/abortion-europe-right

2. See: http://www.europarl.europa.eu/sides/getDoc.do?pubRef=-//EP//NONSGML+REPORT+A8-2015-0015+0+DOC+PDF+V0//EN [retrieved 1 August 2016].

3. 'Bernadette Smyth: Anti-abortion Protester Wins Appeal', *BBC News*, 29 June 2015. Retrieved 1 August 2016 from http://www.bbc.com/news/uk-northern-ireland-33317597

4. Siedlecka, E. 2014. 'Chazan zwolniony – problem zostaje', *Gazeta Wyborcza*, 10 July 2014. Retrieved 1 August 2016 from http://wyborcza.pl/1,75968,16299596,Chazan_zwolniony___problem_zostaje.html

5. 'A Conservative Enigma', *The Economist*, 31 October 2015. Retrieved 28 July 2016 from http://www.economist.com/news/europe/21677216-right-savours-victory-people-wonder-how-far-it-will-go-conservative-enigma

6. 'Midwife Abortion Objection Case Heard at Supreme Court', *BBC News*, 11 November 2014. Retrieved 28 July 2016 from http://www.bbc.com/news/uk-scotland-glasgow-west-29993924

7. 'Catholic Midwives Must Supervise Abortions, Supreme Court Decides', *The Telegraph*, 17 December 2014. Retrieved 28 July 2016 from http://www.telegraph.co.uk/news/uknews/law-and-order/11298385/Catholic-midwives-lose-Supreme-Court-case-over-objection-to-abortions.html

8. 'L'Assemblée réaffirme le "droit fondamental" à l'IVG', *Reuters-France*, 26 November 2014. Retrieved 28 July 2016 from http://fr.reuters.com/article/topNews/idFRKCN0JA1RL20141126

9. See: http://leplus.nouvelobs.com/contribution/1458213-avortement-droits-humains-le-fn-est-un-danger-pour-les-femmes-engageons-nous.html [retrieved 1 August 2016].

10. See: http://en.radiovaticana.va/news/2014/03/27/vatican_statement_on_meeting_of_pope_francis_and_president_obama/en1-785409 [retrieved 1 August 2016].

11. 'Il Papa: obiezione coscienza medici è segno di fedeltà al Vangelo', *Repubblica*, 15 November 2014.

12. See: http://www.oneofus.eu/ [retrieved 1 August 2016]; http://citizengo.org/en/13831-condemn-neonatal-infanticide [retrieved 1 August 2016].

13. See: https://euobserver.com/news/124416 [retrieved 1 August 2016].

14. 'EU Rejects Pro-life Initiative', *Catholic Herald*, 29 May 2014. Retrieved 1 August 2016 from http://www.catholicherald.co.uk/news/2014/05/29/eu-rejects-pro-life-initiative/

15. Abortion was first legalised in Russia in 1920 by the Bolsheviks and then restricted again (though not made illegal) by Stalin in 1936. The tension between the dominant pronatalism of the Soviet Union and the communist ideal of the working mother led to different policies concerning contraception and abortion in different historical periods of the Soviet Union (See Rivkin-Fish 2003, 2010).

16. 'The Paris Terrorist Attacks Cast New Suspicion on Syria's Migrants', *Los Angeles Times*, 15 November 2015. Retrieved 1 August 2016 from http://www.latimes.com/world/europe/la-fg-paris-attacks-migrants-20151114-story.html

17. The limit of viability is defined as the stage of foetal maturity that ensures a reasonable chance of extrauterine survival with biomedical support. However, it remains uncertain which extremely preterm infants have a reasonable chance of survival. The gestational age and birth weight below which infants are too immature to survive, and thus provision of intensive care is unreasonable, appears to be at under twenty-three weeks and 500g (Seri and Evans 2008).

References

Berer, M. 2008. 'A Critical Appraisal of Laws on Second Trimester Abortion', *Reproductive Health Matters* 16(31S): 3–13.

Best, A. 2005. 'Abortion Rights along the Irish-English Border and the Liminality of Women's Experiences', *Dialectical Anthropology* 29: 423–37.

Cammaerts, B. 2012. 'Protest Logics and the Mediation Opportunity Structure', *European Journal of Communication* 27(2): 117–34.

Campbell, M. 2011. 'Conscientious Objection and the Council of Europe', *Medical Law Review* 19: 467–75.

Casper, M. 1998. *The Making of the Unborn Patient: A Social Anatomy of Fetal Surgery.* New Brunswick, NJ: Rutgers University Press.

Cook, R. and B. Dickens. 2006. 'The Growing Abuse of Conscientious Objection', *Ethics Journal of the American Medical Association* 8(5): 337–40.

Council of Europe, Committee of Social Rights. 2014. Decision on the Merits of: International Planned Parenthood Federation – European Network (IPPF EN) v. Italy, Complaint No. 87/2012.

Council of Europe, Parliamentary Assembly. 2010. *Resolution 1763: The Right to Conscientious Objection in Lawful Medical Care.* Brussels: Council of Europe.

David, H. 1999. *From Abortion to Contraception: A Resource to Public Policies and Reproductive Behavior in Central and Eastern Europe from 1917 to the Present.* Westport, CT: Greenwood Press.

De Zordo, S. 2016. 'Lo stigma dell'aborto e l'obiezione di coscienza: l'esperienza e le opinioni dei ginecologi in Italia e in Catalogna (Spagna)' in C. Lalli (ed.), 'Aborto: stigma, senso di colpa, silenzio. Si può parlare di aborto?', *Medicina nei Secoli* (Sup.) 28(1): 197–250.

———. 2015. 'Interruption volontaire de grossesse et clause de conscience en Italie et en Espagne, entre droits des femmes et "droits" du fœtus/patient', *Sociologie Santé* 38 (Special Issue: 'Santé reproductive: routines, normes, invisibilités'): 107–29.

De Zordo, S. and M. Marchesi. 2014. *Reproduction and Biopolitics: Ethnographies of Governance, "Irrationality" and Resistance.* London and New York: Routledge. Originally published as Special Issue in 2012, titled: 'Irrational Reproduction: New Intersections of Politics, Gender, Race, and Class across the North-South divide', *Anthropology and Medicine* 19(2).

De Zordo, S. and J. Mishtal. 2011. 'Physicians and Abortion: Provision, Political Participation and Conflicts on the Ground. The Cases of Brazil and Poland', *Women's Health Issues* 21 (35S): S32–S36.

EU Network of Independent Experts on Fundamental Rights. 2005. *Opinion No. 4-2005 The Right to Conscientious Objection and the Conclusion by EU Member States of Concordats With the Holy See.* Brussels: EU Commission.

Foucault, M. 1978. *The History of Sexuality.* New York: Vintage.

Habiba, M., M. Da Frè, D.J. Taylor, C. Arnaud, O. Bleker, G. Lingman, M.M. Gomez, P. Gratia, W. Heyl, C. Viafora; the EUROBS Study Group. 2009. 'Late Termination of Pregnancy: A Comparison of Obstetricians' Experience in Eight European Countries', *BJOG* 116:1340–49.

Halliburton, M. 2011. 'Resistance or Inaction? Protecting Ayurvedic Medical Knowledge and Problems of Agency', *American Ethnologist* 38(1): 86–101.

Haut Conseil à l'Egalité entre les Femmes et les Hommes (7 novembre 2013). 'Rapport n°2013-1104-SAN-009 relatif à l'accès a l'IVG. Volet 2: Accès à l'IVG dans les territoires'. Paris: HCE/FH.

IPPF. 2012. *Abortion Legislation in Europe.* Brussels: IPPF.

Irish Family Planning Association. 2000. *The Irish Journey: Women's Stories of Abortion.* Dublin: Irish Family Planning Association.

Italia, Ministero della Salute. 2015. *Relazione sull'attuazione della Legge contenente norme per la tutela della tutela sociale della maternità e per l'interruzione volontaria della gravidanza. Dati preliminari 2014. Dati definitivi 2013.* Roma: Ministero della Salute.

Kaufman, S.R. and L.M. Morgan. 2005. 'The Anthropology of the Beginnings and Ends of Life', *Annual Review of Anthropology* 34: 317–41.

Krause E.L. and S. De Zordo. 2014. 'Introduction. Ethnography and Biopolitics: Tracing "Rationalities" of Reproduction across the North-South divide', in S. De Zordo and M. Marchesi (eds), *Reproduction and Biopolitics: Ethnographies of Governance, "Irrationality" and Resistance*. London and New York: Routledge, pp. 1–15. Reprint from: *Anthropology and Medicine* 19(2): 137–51.

Krause E. and M. Marchesi. 2007. 'Fertility Politics as "Social Viagra": Reproducing Boundaries, Social Cohesion and Modernity in Italy', *American Anthropologist* 109(2): 350–62.

Lamačková, A. Center for Reproductive Rights. 2014. 'Task sharing in Abortion Care', *The 11th FIAPAC Conference, 3 October 2014*. Ljubljana (Slovenia).

Lee, E. 2003. *Abortion, Motherhood and Mental Health. Medicalizing Reproduction in the United States and Great Britain*. New York: Aldine de Gruyer.

Lock, M. and P.A. Kaufert. 1998. *Pragmatic Women and Body Politics*. Cambridge: Cambridge University Press.

Lohr, P. 2008. 'Surgical Abortion in the Second Trimester', *Reproductive Health Matters* 16(31, Supplement): 151–61.

Melhuus, M. 2012. *Problems of Conception. Issues of Law, Biotechnology, Individuals and Kinship*. New York and Oxford: Berghahn.

Marchesi, M. 2014. 'Reproducing Italians: Contested Biopolitics in the Age of "Replacement Anxiety"', in S. De Zordo and M. Marchesi, *Reproduction and Biopolitics: Ethnographies of Governance, "Irrationality" and Resistance*. London and New York: Routledge, pp. 35–52. Reprint from: *Anthropology and Medicine* 19(2):171–88.

Mishtal, J. 2009. 'Matters of Conscience: The Politics of Reproductive Healthcare in Poland', *Medical Anthropology Quarterly* 23(2): 161–83.

_____. 2014. 'Reproductive Governance in the New Europe: Competing Visions of Morality, Sovereignty, and Supranational Policy', *Anthropological Journal of European Cultures* 23(1): 59–76.

_____. 2015. *Politics of Morality: The Church, the State, and Reproductive Rights in Postsocialist Poland*. Athens, OH: Ohio University Press.

Morgan, L.M. 2009. *Icons of life. A Cultural History of Human Embryos*. Berkeley, Los Angeles, London: University of California Press.

Morgan, L.M. and E.F.S Roberts. 2014. 'Reproductive Governance in Latin America', in S. De Zordo and M. Marchesi (eds), *Reproduction and Biopolitics: Ethnographies of Governance, "Irrationality" and Resistance*. London and New York: Routledge, pp. 105–18. Reprint from: *Anthropology and Medicine* 19(2): 241–54.

Nowicka, W. 2008. 'The Anti-Abortion Act in Poland – The Legal and Actual State', in *Reproductive Rights in Poland: The Effects of the Anti-Abortion Law in Poland*. Warsaw, Federation for Women and Family Planning, pp. 17–44.

O'Toole, F. 2012. 'When is an abortion not an abortion?' *The Irish Times*: 1–4. http://www.irishtimes.com/newspaper/weekend/2012/1117/1224326695598.html Retrieved 1 August 2016.

Rapp, R. 2000. *Testing Women, Testing the Fetus: The Social Impact of Amniocentesis in America*. New York and London: Routledge.

Rivkin-Fish, M. 2003. 'Anthropology, Demography and the Search for a Critical Analysis of Fertility: Insights from Russia', *American Anthropologist* 105(2): 289–301.

———. 2010 'Pronatalism, Gender Politics, and the Renewal of Family Support in Russia: Toward a Feminist Anthropology of "Maternity Capital"', *Slavic Review* 69(3): 228–312.

Rossiter, A. 2009. *Ireland's Hidden Diaspora: The "Abortion Trail" and the Making of a London-Irish Underground, 1980–2000*. London: IASC Publishing.

Seri, I. and J. Evans. 2008. 'Limits of Viability: Definition of the Gray Zone', *Journal of Perinatology* 28(1S): S4.

Watson, P. 1993. 'The Rise of Masculinism in Eastern Europe', *New Left Review* 198: 71–82.

World Health Organization, Department of Reproductive Health and Research. 2012. *Safe Abortion: Technical and Policy Guidance for Health Systems*. Geneva: WHO.

Part I

Pro-abortion Rights Activism, Movements, Strategies, and Protest Logics

Chapter 1

Legal and Political Discourses on Women's Right to Abortion

by Christina Zampas

Introduction

Around the world, political and legal discourses supporting abortion rights have emphasised the impact that denying access to abortion has on women's physical health. There are approximately 22 million unsafe abortions occurring annually worldwide; 98 per cent of which occur in developing countries. Globally, unsafe abortion results in death for approximately 47,000 women, and disabilities for an additional five million (WHO 2014). This accounts for roughly 13 per cent of maternal mortalities, making it the third largest cause of maternal mortality globally (WHO 2011: 14). While abortion is a safe procedure when performed properly, clandestine and illegal abortions are generally unsafe and can lead to complications. The World Health Organization defines unsafe abortion as a procedure for terminating a pregnancy that is performed by an individual lacking the necessary skills or in an environment that does not conform to minimal medical standards or both (WHO 2012: 23, 47–49). World Health Organization estimates confirm that restrictive abortion laws do not reduce the number of induced abortions, as women will seek abortions regardless of its legal status and lawful availability, but restrictive laws push women to undergo illegal and unsafe abortion (WHO 2011: 6).

Recognising unsafe abortion as a major public health concern that states have an obligation to address has been the predominant discourse by advocates supporting access to safe and legal abortion across the globe. This is true at both international and regional intergovernmental levels, including the United Nations (UN), the European Union and Council of

Europe. While physical health arguments may resonate well in parts of the world with restrictive abortion laws and high maternal mortality rates, this discourse has less meaning in Europe. Europe has the most liberal abortion laws in the world and the lowest maternal mortality and morbidity rates in the world. Only a handful of the forty-seven member states of the Council of Europe have restrictive abortion laws that do not allow abortion on request or on broad social and economic grounds (Center for Reproductive Rights 2015a; WHO, UNICEF, UNFPA, World Bank 2010: 14). Yet, political discourses in support of abortion rights, aside from health arguments such as those on bodily autonomy and equality and non-discrimination, despite their critical importance in the debate, have not had the traction they need to keep restrictions on abortion at bay in Europe.

As I will discuss in this chapter, growing nationalism and populism in Europe, combined with the influence of the Catholic and Orthodox churches in some countries and misleading demographic arguments, have fuelled calls to restrict access to abortion and have been successful in erecting barriers to access abortion. The discourse against abortion in Europe, like much of the rest of the world, has focused on values placed on the life of the foetus and embryo and on false and misleading information on the harm abortion has on the physical and mental health of women. Such arguments have led to increased procedural and other barriers in countries with otherwise generally liberal grounds for abortion. Such barriers include mandatory waiting periods, and counselling or information requirements that seek to dissuade women from terminating their pregnancies (Center for Reproductive Rights 2015b).

Justification for such barriers is grounded in prejudicial and non-evidenced based notions of protecting women's health and helping to support women's decision-making. But at their heart, they reinforce deeply entrenched stereotypes and prejudices concerning women's primarily role as child bearers and women's decision-making ability. As Rebecca Cook and Susannah Howard argue (2007: 1039–40), 'differences in women's physiology have been used over the centuries to justify discrimination against women, neglect of health services that only women need, and discriminatory state enforcement of traditional roles for women as mothers and self-sacrificing caregivers'.

Laws and practices limiting women's reproductive choices and other discriminatory laws and practices based on gender stereotypes reinforce inequalities in society and negatively impact women's lives, throughout their life. For example, after childbirth, social custom, lack of equal pay with men, and lack of adequate day care force women to become the primary caretakers of their children (MacKinnon 1991: 1281). They reinforce the stereotype that women's main value is their physiological and 'social' capacity to bear and raise children (Cook and Howard 2007: 1050–51).

Women's exercise of their reproductive rights has been long recognised as a prerequisite to equal enjoyment of other rights enshrined in international and regional human rights instruments. The United Nations Committee on the Elimination of All Forms of Discrimination Against Women (CEDAW), which monitors compliance with the Convention by the same name, has addressed women's existing inequalities in the family as they relate to decisions on the number and spacing of children, noting that 'the responsibilities that women have to bear and raise children affect their right of access to education [and] employment[,] … impose inequitable burdens of work on women … and also affect their physical and mental health' (CEDAW 1994: 21). The Committee has emphasised the obligation of the state to eliminate prejudices and customary practices grounded in stereotypes about appropriate sex roles for men and women (Cook and Cusak 2010: 5). It has been noted that the Convention requires state parties to adopt measures towards 'a real transformation of opportunities, institutions and systems so that they are no longer grounded in historically determined male paradigms of power and life patterns' (CEDAW 2004: 10, Article 5(a)).

Emphasis on this connection between stereotyped roles and women's agency to make reproductive choices would ensure that reproductive rights are not separate from, but rather indispensable to, women's equality, and is necessary to ensure freedom from discrimination. All major international and regional human rights treaties prohibit discrimination based on sex. Recognising restrictions on reproductive choice and autonomous decision-making as discrimination against women is critical, as it gets to the root of the problem and under national and international law states have little room to justify discriminatory laws and practices (ICCPR 1977: 4), and, as such, governments must address these violations immediately (CESCR 2009: 7). Greater recognition in the European and UN political and legal arenas that the denial of reproductive rights is a form of discrimination against women would be an important step towards dismantling the legal and social barriers against abortion in Europe.

This chapter looks at discourses in both political and legal bodies used by those opposing abortion and those supporting abortion. The distinction between political and legal discourses has been made because political debate can often shape developments in legal discourses (Seigal 2012: ch. 52), and vice versa.

An example of this is the influence of the political consensus document agreed upon at the International Conference on Population and

Development (ICPD), the ICPD Programme of Action, where for the first time states explicitly recognised that 'reproductive rights are human rights' and articulated commitments to advancing the reproductive rights of women and girls. This consensus document has played an important role in influencing the development of national law and of international and regional human rights standards on reproductive rights, including on abortion (UNFPA and Center for Reproductive Rights 2013).

While the regional focus of this book is Europe, the chapter begins with a very brief discussion of the discourses at the UN level. In a globalised world, discourses on very politicised issues such as abortion know no boundaries. A country and a region can be influenced by what is happening within the region and also beyond it. The same is true for international regional human rights systems; what happens at a UN level influences and is influenced by what happens at the European level.

This section is followed by a discussion on national level legal developments on abortion in Europe and the various factors influencing those developments. The chapter ends with a look at the political and legal developments and discourses on abortion at the European regional level, particularly at the European Parliament and the Council of Europe.

The Emergence of Women's Right to Access Abortion in the UN Human Rights System: A Brief Summary

Political Level Discourse

Over the past two decades, promotion of women's reproductive rights has gained momentum, in part, due to the 1994 International Conference on Population and Development (ICPD) held in Cairo, and the 1995 Fourth World United Nations (UN) Conference on Women held in Beijing, where unprecedented numbers of women's civil society organisations took part in shaping and influencing the political commitments coming out of these conferences (Cook, Dickens and Fathalla 2003: 148). These conferences led to the formal recognition by UN member states that the protection of reproductive health is a matter of social justice and can and should be realised through the application of binding human rights protections contained in existing national laws and constitutions, and regional and international human rights treaties (ICPD 1994). The consensus documents – adopted by nearly all states across the globe, including all countries in Europe – address abortion, albeit in a limited way.

Within the 1994 ICPD Programme of Action (PoA), focus was placed on the consequences of unsafe abortion as a major public health concern. In response, states committed to reducing the incidence of abortion through expanding and improving access to family planning services. States also agreed within the PoA that where abortion is legal, the procedure should be safe and accessible (ICPD 1994: 8.25).

States also committed to ensuring women have access to quality services for the management of abortion-related complications, and access to post-abortion counselling, education and family planning services (ICPD 1994: 8.25). During the five-year review of the PoA's implementation, states agreed, among other things, to ensure that healthcare providers are trained and equipped to safeguard women's health, including in the context of lawful abortion services (ICPD 1999: 63).

While discourses in UN consensus documents have primarily focused on women's physical health to justify ensuring access to lawful abortion, citing high maternal mortality rates, and have not addressed access to abortion as an issue concerning women's equality and agency, the outcome documents are indicative of the world's growing support for reproductive rights. These documents have supported legislative and policy reform, as well as interpretations of national law, including in Europe, and the development of international human rights standards on this issue (UNFPA and Center for Reproductive Rights 2013).

Since ICPD, discourse on addressing abortion at the UN political level has continued to focus on women's health. The UN Human Rights Council's recent resolutions addressing maternal mortality and morbidity include lack of access to safe abortion as one of the main causes of maternal mortality (UN Human Rights Council 2011). The ability to get beyond the health impact of denial of abortion rights, despite how important that is, and address it is an issue of discrimination against women and women's equality, is an ongoing and ever-growing challenge at the UN political level. This is, in part, due to the influence of the Catholic Church hierarchy and related pushes by very conservative countries, who promote support for 'traditional values', including advocating at the UN for recognition of women's primary role as a mother and wife. Their aim is to prevent further progress on human rights, including equality and non-discrimination, of women or sexual minorities (Omang 2013: 19–21). The UN Special Rapporteur on cultural rights recognised in 2012 that: 'many practices and norms that discriminate against women are justified by reference to culture, religion and tradition', and recommended that states ensure: 'The freedom of women to refuse to participate in traditions, customs and practices that infringe upon human dignity and rights, to critique existing cultural norms and traditional practices and to create new cultural meanings and norms of behavior'.

UN Treaty Monitoring Bodies: Legal Discourse

Legal bodies at the UN level, particularly UN Treaty Monitoring Bodies' interpretations and jurisprudence on state compliance with international treaty obligations, are not as straddled with such political influences, and have played a major role in advancing women's sexual and reproductive rights (UNFPA and Center for Reproductive Rights 2013). However, they have still not robustly addressed restrictive abortion laws as a violation of equality and non-discrimination, despite continuous pushes by civil society.

Since the ICPD PoA was adopted, United Nations treaty monitoring bodies, which monitor state compliance with their international human rights treaty obligations, have increasingly applied human rights provisions to the abortion context, including through finding violations of human rights in denying access to lawful abortion and calling on countries to liberalise restrictive abortion laws (Zampas and Gher 2008: 249).

The underlying discourse at the UN legal level is similar to that at the political level; a heavy emphasis is placed on the connection between restrictive laws and high rates of unsafe abortion, leading to maternal mortality and morbidity, implicating the rights to life and health, protected by international law. However, treaty bodies have gone an important step further than UN political commitments by condemning very restrictive abortion laws and calling for their liberalisation so that women are not forced to seek clandestine, unsafe abortions. They have recommended that states ensure access to abortion at a minimum, in cases when a woman's life and physical and mental health is in danger, in cases of severe foetal impairment, as well as in cases of rape and incest. They have also urged states to decriminalise abortion, so as to eliminate punitive measures for women and girls who undergo abortions, and for healthcare providers who provide abortion services. While UN treaty bodies have not yet explicitly called on states to ensure access to abortion on request or on broad, social and economic grounds, they have praised countries that have liberalised their laws on these grounds, and have called on countries that have such liberal laws to remove barriers to their effective implementation. They have addressed barriers such as biased counselling requirements, waiting periods and the practice of conscientious objection.

Treaty monitoring bodies have found that laws and practices that deny women access to abortion can violate numerous rights, including the right to life, to health, to private life, to be free from cruel, inhuman and degrading treatment, and the right to non-discrimination. While recognising there are broad implications for the exercise of women's rights when women cannot access abortion, much of the legal discourse in finding such violations focuses on the physical, and more recently, mental health impact of how such restrictive laws and punitive measures push women to seek clandestine, unsafe abortions. The overwhelming discourse has been the negative impact of restrictions on abortion on maternal mortality and morbidity.

While the health implications of women's experiences are critically important, there has been less meaningful discourse on the impact of such laws and practices on women's equality and non-discrimination, including the disproportionate impact that restrictive laws and practices have on vulnerable women, especially women belonging to ethnic or racial minorities, migrant women, and the young and the poor (Cook and Howard 2007: 1039–40).

To date, there have been four individual complaints brought before UN Treaty bodies claiming violations resulting from restrictive abortion laws. Three of the cases have been before the Human Rights Committee (HRC) under the International Covenant on Civil and Political Rights and one at the CEDAW Committee under the Convention on the Elimination of All Forms of Discrimination Against Women. The Committees, in all of these cases, have ruled in favour of the complainants.

The case of K. L. v. Peru concerned a young woman pregnant with an anencephalic foetus – a fatal condition that medical science has well-established would not allow it to survive more than a few hours or days beyond birth – was denied an abortion. Instead, she was forced to carry the pregnancy to term until its inevitable death four days later. The HRC held that the denial of a therapeutic abortion caused K. L. substantial and foreseeable 'mental suffering' and amounted to a violation of the prohibition on torture or cruel, inhuman or degrading treatment or punishment, amongst other rights. The Committee, however, did not address how the restrictive law and its application was discriminatory (Human Rights Committee 2005, K. L. v. Peru). Eleven years later, in Mellet v. Ireland, another case of a woman carrying a fatal foetal pregnancy and being denied an abortion, the complainant was forced to travel out of the country to terminate her pregnancy. The Committee found that a violation of torture and ill-treatment, as well as a violation of the right to privacy, noting the criminalization of abortion, the restrictive law denying women access to abortion in cases of fatal foetal impairment and to information on safe abortion, as well as being forced to travel abroad to terminate her pregnancy were in violation of the Convention. The Committee again failed to find a violation of the right to be free from gender discrimination, but focused its non-discrimination finding on the disproportionate socio-economic burdens of travel that the Irish legal system imposes on women who decide not to carry a fetus to term, an important development, but lacking in recognition of the underlying basis for which such a restrictive law exists: discriminatory stereotypes towards women. A separate concurring opinion by a committee member, Prof. Sarah Cleveland, however, importantly noted that the criminalization of abortion subjected the complainant to a gender-based stereotype of the reproductive role of women primarily as mothers, and that stereotyping her as a reproductive instrument subjected her to discrimination. (Human Rights Committee 2016, Mellet v. Ireland) While not part of the majority views, it provides a critically important analysis of the gender discrimination inherent in restrictive abortion laws, and could positively influence future legal developments.

The two other cases concerned abortion restrictions in cases of rape. In addressing an Argentine law that only permits abortion in instances of rape where the woman is mentally disabled, the Human Rights Committee found numerous violations for erecting barriers to lawful abortion and also urged the state to amend its abortion laws to permit abortion in all cases of rape (Human Rights Committee 2007, LMR v. Argentina). In 2011, the CEDAW Committee decided a case involving a young woman who after becoming pregnant as a result of rape was denied an abortion. Under Peru's restrictive abortion laws, abortion is not permitted in cases of rape or incest. In its decision, the CEDAW Committee urged the state party to 'review its legislation with a view to decriminalizing abortion when the pregnancy results from rape or sexual abuse' (CEDAW 2011, L. C. v. Peru).

In these two cases, the Committees recognised the discriminatory aspect of the lack of access to abortion, but both decisions primarily connected the discrimination claims to the physical and mental health impact of denying needed health services, and not to women's and girls' autonomy in decision-making.

In articulating the experiences as a violation of non-discrimination, the CEDAW Committee referred to its general standards on eliminating discrimination in healthcare, including its important standard that 'it is discriminatory for a state party to refuse to legally provide for the performance of certain reproductive health services for women'. Additionally, while the CEDAW Committee found a violation of Article 5 of the Convention, which requires state parties to take measures '[t]o modify the social and cultural patterns of conduct of men and women, with a view to achieving the elimination of prejudices and customary and all other practices which are based on the idea of the inferiority or the superiority of either of the sexes or on stereotyped roles for men and women', they failed to adequately articulate the stereotype as one relating to imposing reproductive roles on women as mothers. Instead, they articulated the violation as one in relation to 'protection of the foetus over the health of the mother'. Not only does this articulation fail to adequately identify the stereotype that needs to be eliminated – the primary role of a woman as a mother, at all costs, even if raped – and hence its harm, but the Committee reinforced gender stereotypes by using the term 'mother' to describe a pregnant woman seeking an abortion. As legal scholars, Cook and Cusak have noted, '[n]aming the stereotype, identifying its form, exposing its harm are critical to making it recognizable, and therefore legally cognizable, able to be judicially examined. Naming a stereotype is necessary in much the same way that a medical diagnosis is required before treatment can be applied' (Cook and Cusak 2010: 175).

While these case judgements are immensely important in their recognition of the harm caused by denying women access to abortion, findings of violations of gender discrimination based on gender stereotypes are needed in order to address the underlying causes driving restrictive abortion laws. The concurring opinion in Mellet v. Ireland provides a strong basis for such legal developments.

While most of these cases are from Latin America, they are critically important to the development of international human rights law, to which all European countries are bound. Additionally, given the influence UN and regional human rights bodies have on the development of each other's standards (Forowicz 2010: 155; Opuz v. Turkey 2009), their potential to shape abortion standards in the most influential European-wide human rights body, the European Court of Human Rights, is very important.

European Political and Legal Discourse

National Level Discourses

Almost all of the forty-seven Council of Europe member states allow abortion on request ranging from ten to eighteen weeks of gestation, and others allow abortion on broad social and economic grounds. Almost all countries permit abortion when a woman's health and life is in danger until the end of pregnancy, and have extended periods for termination on grounds of foetal impairment. There are a handful of countries, however, with very restrictive regulations. The microstates of Andorra, Malta and San Marino have total bans on abortion with no explicit exceptions in the law, even when a woman's life is in danger. Ireland and Poland also have restrictive laws, the former criminalising abortion in all cases, except when a woman's life is in danger, and the latter in three circumstances: when a woman's life or health is threatened, in cases when pregnancy is a result of a crime, and in cases of severe foetal impairment (Center for Reproductive Rights 2015a). Both countries have failed to implement their laws.

Despite Europe's relatively liberal legal framework with regards to abortion, advancing abortion rights remains a formidable challenge across the continent; abortion laws are consistently under threat and in some countries there are significant challenges in accessing lawful abortions. Numerous factors have shaped these developments, including the increasing influence of religious institutions. This is especially so in Central and Eastern Europe where the Catholic and Orthodox Church hierarchies, staunch abortion opponents, have gained substantial political clout since the fall of communism. Non-governmental organisations opposed to abortion are also increasingly influential across the continent and employ various means of civic participation, such as protests, advocacy and litigation, to limit access to abortion. In addition, the recent economic crisis has fuelled populism, often grounded in 'traditional family values', which promotes and exacerbates gender stereotypes. Discourses and initiatives attacking the concept of gender and the principle of gender equality have spread throughout Central and Eastern Europe. Such initiatives, promoting 'traditional family values', advocate for discriminatory laws and practices in the area of sexual orientation and gender identity, promote harmful traditional stereotypes of women and men, dispute that violence against women is a form of discrimination against women, and advocate for restrictions on reproductive rights (Heinrich Böll Foundation 2015).

Use of foetal 'rights' arguments, misinformation and biased information seeking to dissuade women from undergoing an abortion, and the practice of conscience-based refusal (conscientious objection) are but three common strategic entry points used by the opposition to attempt to directly restrict access to abortion.

Undermining Women's Decision-Making Authority

Legislative and regulatory proposals to limit women's access to abortion have been met with mixed success. Such proposed restrictions include reducing grounds or gestational limits, and imposing procedural barriers such as mandatory delay periods, or biased counselling or information requirements. While barriers to lawful abortion are particularly pronounced in countries with already restrictive laws, such as in Ireland and Poland, women are increasingly facing such barriers in countries with more liberal legislation (PACE 2008). For example, Hungary, Latvia, Macedonia, Russia, and

Slovakia, in the past few years, have imposed mandated waiting periods before women can access abortion. Some countries in the region have also passed counselling or so called 'informed consent' requirements that promote stigmatising or medically inaccurate or misleading information about abortion with the intention to dissuade women from going through with the procedure (Center for Reproductive Rights 2015b).

The discourse used in supporting such requirements includes overemphasis on the risks involved in the abortion procedure, non-evidence-based information on the negative impact that abortion has on women's mental health, such as regret women have in undergoing abortion and the pseudoscience of 'post abortion syndrome', and describing abortion as the killing of an 'unborn child' (Academy of Medical Royal Colleges 2011; Center for Reproductive Rights 2015a).

Abortion rights proponents, advocating against such restrictions, base their arguments on the health and human rights impact of such restrictions. For example, that waiting periods and biased counselling and information requirements threaten women's health by pushing women to postpone the procedure, which increases the possibility of complications and jeopardises the ability to obtain an abortion within gestational limits required by law. Abortion supporters also note that such restrictions disproportionately impact marginalised women, such as poor women and women living in rural areas who, because of mandatory waiting periods, have to travel several times to a provider before undergoing the procedure. Discourse against such restrictions reflects that such requirements also undermine women's decision-making authority and autonomy and their right to quality health services that includes the right to accurate and evidence-based information. Despite almost universal support for gender equality in Europe and the continent having the world's lowest maternal mortality and morbidity rates, these latter arguments resonate less in the political sphere than the health arguments (Center for Reproductive Rights 2015b; WHO, UNICEF, UNFPA and World Bank 2010: 20).

Governments often hide behind the veil of low maternal mortality and morbidity rates to continue to justify restrictive laws, even in the face of concrete cases that reflect the severe impact of such laws (Amnesty International 2015; Failure in Basic Care of Savita Halappanavar 2013; Tysiac v. Poland 2007; ABC v. Ireland 2010). They fail to address the impact on mental health and social well-being that such abortion laws have, never mind the discrimination and equality issues they raise. They also fail to recognise that restrictive abortion laws do not stop women from having abortions, but force them to undergo clandestine abortions at home or, for those who can afford it and are not prohibited from travelling, to travel to nearby countries to undergo lawful abortions (Amnesty International 2015). The fact that most women are not prohibited from travelling abroad to undergo abortions is often used as justification for not addressing restrictive laws. The European Court of Human Rights, for example, recently relied on the fact that women can travel to other European countries from Ireland to get abortions to not address the country's restrictive abortion law (A., B. and C v. Ireland 2010). Such argumentation contradicts the foundation on which human rights law stands – that states have an obligation to respect, protect and fulfil human rights within their own borders.

While civil society in support of women's choice have included in their discourse the need to respect women's decision-making authority and that restrictions on abortion are discriminatory, much effort has been placed on responding to abortion opponents' argumentation. At both the regional and national level in Europe, such argumentation emphasises primarily two issues in addition to the already discussed biased counselling and information requirements: protecting foetal life and respecting the practice of conscience-based refusal at all costs, even to the detriment of women's lives. Both arguments have gained traction in recent years primarily due to the influence of the Catholic and Orthodox churches and to conservative and nationalist political parties gaining power, especially in Central and Eastern Europe.

The Practice of Conscience-Based Refusal

The practice of conscience-based refusal (conscientious objection) arises when health professionals refuse to provide certain services based on religious, moral or philosophical objections. Refusal to provide services often arises in the context of abortion and is an increasing barrier to women's access to timely abortion services across Europe where effective regulation of the practice is scant (Zampas and Andión-Ibañez 2012: 232). For example, despite laws requiring objecting healthcare providers to refer patients who are requesting to undergo an abortion to other, non-objecting physicians, some refuse to do so (Chavkin 2013; Dickens and Cook 2006: 337–40).

The situation is exacerbated by states failing to effectively require conscientious objectors to report their objection to their employer, thereby negatively impacting the availability and numbers of healthcare providers willing to perform abortions. Even when they do, the number of objecting providers appears to be increasing in some countries without effective responses to ensure access to lawful abortion services. For instance, in Italy, where there is a law requiring providers to register their refusal to provide abortions, the Ministry of Health has reported that between 2003 and 2007 the number of gynaecologists invoking conscience in their refusal to perform an abortion rose from 58.7 per cent to 69.2 per cent (IPPF-EN v. Italy 2014; Italian Ministry of Health 2008).

In addition, despite the practice of conscience-based refusal being limited to individuals, not institutions, in some countries, such as in Italy, Poland and Spain, entire public hospitals refuse to provide abortion on grounds of conscience, making it difficult for women to gain access to the procedure within reasonable distance of their residence.

Foetal Personhood

Another major strategy used to limit women's access to abortion across Europe, as well as in other parts of the world, is to gain legal recognition and to grant rights to the foetus on par with rights of the pregnant woman. This strategy is being used at both regional and national levels. At the national level, in addition to statutory or regulatory reform there have been calls for interpretation of human rights and constitutional right to life protections that would include an embryo or foetus. In some countries attempts have been made for constitutional reform to recognise all prenatal life as constitutionally protected, including from the moment of conception. The outcomes of these efforts have been mixed.

In Hungary, the governing far-right coalition was successful in introducing a provision to the new 2011 constitution guaranteeing that 'the life of the foetus shall be protected from the moment of conception' (Constitution of Hungary 2011: II). While the application of the provision remains to be seen and government officials supporting this provision noted that it would not restrict access to abortion or the existing abortion law, which allows abortion on broad grounds, the Hungarian Constitution could now be interpreted to support a ban on abortion. In Poland, while an attempt to recognise the right to life from conception through a constitutional amendment narrowly failed, attempts to restrict access to abortion continue unabated (Polish Federation for Women in Family Planning 2013). Abortion opponents are also filing constitutional court cases challenging liberal laws. For example, a group of conservative members of the Slovak Parliament sought to restrict abortion by filing a complaint with the Constitutional Court complaining that the country's abortion law, which allows abortion on request during the first twelve weeks of pregnancy, violated the right to life of the foetus. In other words, they claimed that foetuses have a constitutionally protected right to life that supersedes women's right to reproductive self-determination. The Constitutional Court disagreed. In 2007 it decided that Slovakia's abortion law does not violate the right to life but strikes a fair balance between women's rights and the state's duty to protect prenatal life. The Court relied, in part, on international and regional human rights law to do so (Lamačková 2014: ch. 3).

European national law and jurisprudence generally support the position that protecting life prenatally as a constitutionally protected right or fundamental human right would interfere significantly with women's basic human rights. They do, however, recognise state interest in protection of prenatal life as a legitimate one, but that it must be pursued through proportionate means that give due consideration for the human rights of pregnant women, and have thus upheld liberal abortion laws.

Addressing Abortion Rights at the European Regional Level

The European Parliament and the Parliamentary Assembly of the Council of Europe have, in non-binding resolutions, directly addressed sexual and reproductive rights issues, including some of the increasing barriers to abortion women in Europe face. They have, for example, supported bold pronouncements calling for the decriminalisation of abortion and liberalisation of abortion laws (PACE 2008). Support for ICPD and for relevant Millennium Development Goals and Sustainable Development Goals related to maternal and reproductive health, especially when it comes to support for developing countries, have also been consistently supported by these bodies.

In very recent years, however, due to the increasing influence of the Catholic Church hierarchy and stronger anti-abortion activism, as well as more conservative political parties gaining ground, the progressive pronouncements directly addressing abortion at the European level that earlier garnered overwhelming support have failed to do so.

European Parliament

While it is in the competency of member states of the European Union to formulate laws on sexual and reproductive health and rights, the EU can exercise policymaking competencies in the area of public health, gender equality and non-discrimination (ASTRA 2006). The EU, though, has generally failed to support better realisation of sexual and reproductive health and rights within its borders, especially when it comes to abortion. The European Parliament, however, has taken up the issue in non-legislative resolutions. The first passed in 2002 and the second attempt to pass a similar resolution in 2013 failed, with the Parliament voting to send the report back to the FEMM (Women's Rights and Gender Equality) Committee where it originated without any substantive discussion on its merits. The report was subsequently voted down. The outcome is due to the growing conservative composition of the European Parliament and the increasing influence of anti-abortion actors at the European regional level (Datta 2013: 22–27). It is noteworthy, however, that the European Union has consistently supported sexual and reproductive health issues in its aid programme to less developed countries and also at the United Nations.

The recent failed resolution was similar to the resolution that passed in 2002, recognising the disparities between European countries in their protection of sexual and reproductive health and rights, including differences in access to contraception, teenage pregnancy rates, abortion rates, as well as access to evidence-based sexuality education. The resolution identified barriers to exercising sexual and reproductive rights, including the practice of conscience-based refusal, and made recommendations to member states and those being considered for membership to the European Union on how to address this situation. Most importantly, it reinforced the importance of safeguarding women's reproductive health and rights; recommending making abortion legal, safe and accessible to all (European Parliament 2013).

Parliamentary Assembly of the Council of Europe

Reflecting some of the challenges European countries face in terms of access to abortion, in 2008 the Parliamentary Assembly of the Council of Europe (PACE) adopted groundbreaking recommendations regarding women's right to abortion that provide guidance to member states on abortion and abortion-related issues. The 'Access to Safe and Legal Abortion in Europe' report calls upon member states to decriminalise abortion, guarantee women's effective exercise of their right to safe and legal abortion, remove restrictions that hinder de jure and de facto provision of abortion, and adopt evidence-based sexual and reproductive health strategies and policies, such as access to contraception at a reasonable cost and of suitable nature, and compulsory age-appropriate and gender sensitive sex and relationship education for young people (PACE 2008).

Two years later, however, in 2010, due to growing anti-abortion activities at the European bodies, a resolution that recommended member states of the Council of Europe to regulate the practice of conscience-based refusal in healthcare settings, including in relation to abortion, was defeated by conservative parties and revised to partly support continuing its unregulated practice (PACE 2010; Zampas and Andión-Ibañez 2012: 232).

Discourses at the Regional Level

Discourses at the regional level generally reflect discourses at the national level, as stated above. The organisations and individuals opposing abortion are often those who also oppose recognising equal rights on grounds of sexual orientation and gender identity; the discourse is ideologically based and does not reflect needs, desires or rights of concerned groups or individuals.

One of the discourses centred on respecting 'human dignity' includes protecting all prenatal life. Argumentation in support of this position is often garnered from intentional misrepresentation of legal and medical information. For example, an anti-abortion campaign called 'One of Us' seeks to 'advance the protection of human life from conception in Europe, within the possibilities of the competency of the EU'. The campaign has misrepresented international and European law and jurisprudence as supporting embryonic life to the detriment of women in the context of termination of pregnancy (One of Us 2013). This, despite that no international or regional human rights body has ever found a liberal abortion law to be contrary to international human rights standards and has never recognised embryos or foetuses as independent subjects of protection under international human rights law (Brüstle v. Greenpeace 2011: 49; Zampas and Gher 2008: 262).

Anti-abortion advocates often claim that any support for sexual and reproductive rights is a guise for supporting abortion, which would include maternal health programmes that seek to reduce maternal mortality and morbidity. At the European Union level, the opposition also strongly relies on arguments regarding subsidiarity, arguing that the EU has no competence in addressing issues of abortion within EU member states, even in a non-binding resolution (Federation of Catholic Families Associations in Europe 2013).

Pro-choice organisations, on the other hand, have tried to steer discourses towards the health and human rights of women. While maternal mortality and morbidity rates, two indicators for safe abortion, are low in Europe compared to the rest of the world, disparities between EU member states generally on sexual and reproductive rights issues are being used to highlight the need to ensure respect for women's choices *across* the continent. For example, teenage birth rates and use of modern contraceptives vary significantly between member states (IPPF-EN 2013: 7)

While argumentation around non-discrimination, equality and bodily autonomy are critically important and have been used by defenders of sexual and reproductive rights in the European Parliament, the arguments are often marginalised and viewed as being presented by abortion rights extremists that do not care about children.

Legal Discourses under the European Convention on Human Rights

The Court has developed some groundbreaking standards in recent years on abortion, including for the first time addressing abortion-related violations as inhuman and degrading treatment, articulating state obligations to regulate the practice of conscience-based refusals, and acknowledging a minor's autonomy in decision-making around abortion. However, it has consistently failed to address the inherent discriminatory aspect such practices and laws have on women, and as such has not found human rights violations on grounds of non-discrimination.

Discourse on abortion under the European Convention on Human Rights has focused primarily on the right to private life, that abortion is tied to respect for bodily autonomy and decision-making, rights that are protected under Article 8 (the right to private life) of the Convention. Convention bodies, the European Court of Human Rights and the now defunct European Commission on Human Rights have interpreted the right to respect for private life as extending to the physical and moral integrity of a person and that legislation regulating the termination of pregnancy touches upon the sphere of private life (Zampas and Gher 2008: 276). However, these convention bodies have not stated the extent to which abortion is protected under the Convention, which would require abortion to be legally available under domestic law (N. Priaulx 2008: 370, and J. Erdman 2010: 377). Current Convention law states that while not every restriction on abortion is a violation of the Convention (Brüggemann and Scheuten v. Federal Republic of Germany 1977), member states have a positive obligation to ensure measures are in place to guarantee women's access to abortion where legal. The European Court of Human Rights has applied its longstanding standard that the 'Convention is intended to guarantee not rights that are theoretical or illusory, but rights that are practical and effective' to the abortion context (Tysiąc v. Poland 2007: 113).

The Court has consistently found violations against a member state for failing to implement its own abortion regulation due to the absence of laws or procedural safeguards within the healthcare and legal systems that ensure women and girls access to lawful abortions. For example, in Tysiąc v. Poland, R. R. v. Poland (2011), and P. and S. v. Poland (2012) the Court found Poland in violation of the European Convention on Human Rights for failing to ensure legal and other measures were in place for women to access lawful abortion, including an effective and timely appeals mechanism to challenge healthcare providers' and health systems' denials of abortion. In A. B. C. v. Ireland, the European Court of Human Rights (2010) found a violation of the state's obligation to respect private life because of its failure to legislate on its constitutional protection guaranteeing the right to life of pregnant women.

The R. R. v. Poland decision is an example of how the Court addressed issues of autonomy in decision-making around termination of pregnancy. The case involved a deliberate delay in providing legal genetic testing after a sonogram indicated a possible severe impairment in the foetus, which is a ground for legal termination of pregnancy in Poland. The Court articulated the importance of personal autonomy in decision-making, and primarily relied on the health implications of not ensuring access to such information to make informed decisions. In finding a violation of the right to private life, the Court noted the crucial importance of timely access to information on one's health condition by stating that, 'in the context of pregnancy, the effective access to relevant information on the mother's and foetus' health, where legislation allows for abortion in certain situations, is directly relevant for the exercise of personal autonomy' (R. R. v. Poland 2011: 197).

The case of P. and S. v. Poland involved a fourteen-year-old girl who became pregnant as a result of rape, a ground for legal termination of pregnancy in Poland, by a boy her own age. Her access to abortion was obstructed in numerous ways, including being given false information on the procedural requirements for obtaining an abortion; breaches of confidentiality by a hospital; harassment and pressure by doctors, priests and anti-abortion activists to change her mind; being denied abortion without receiving referrals by doctors; and by removing her from the custody of her mother, who supported her decision, and placing her in a detention centre for one week for the primary purpose of preventing the abortion. Precisely at the gestational limitation for abortion, the Ministry of Health intervened and she underwent an abortion in a hospital 500 kilometres from her home, in essentially a clandestine manner; she was not registered in the hospital nor was she given information on the procedure nor informed that she would be undergoing anaesthesia. In addition, she was released from the hospital immediately after the procedure and given no post-abortion care. The Court found violations of numerous rights including the right to liberty and the right to private life. And for the first time the Court addressed the specific vulnerability of a pregnant adolescent seeking an abortion and recognised a minor's autonomy when it comes to decision-making on reproductive health. The Court noted that during P's entire ordeal, there was no proper regard for her 'vulnerability and young age and her own views and feelings' (P. and S. v. Poland 2012: 166). While in this case there was no conflict between the teenager and her mother about undergoing an abortion, the Court stated that 'legal guardianship cannot be considered to automatically confer on the parents of a minor the right to take decisions concerning the minor's reproductive choices, because proper regard must be had to the minor's personal autonomy in this sphere' (ibid.: 109).

With both P. and S. v. Poland and R. R. v. Poland, the European Court of Human Rights also found, for the first time in abortion-related cases, violations of the right to be free from inhuman and degrading treatment. The Court, in neither of the cases, found a violation of non-discrimination, despite such claims being made by the complainants.

Conclusion

Recognition of the principles of non-discrimination and gender equality lie at the heart of women's autonomous decision-making, including on abortion. International and regional human rights laws have been slow to recognise this and there is a long way to go before it is fully recognised in law. Even more challenging is a recognition of these principles in political decision-making. This is evidenced in the rejection of a report on sexual and reproductive rights by the European Parliament that would have acknowledged these principles and the increasing restrictions on abortion in some countries in Europe. The growing activity of anti-abortion activists, supported by the increasing influence of religious institutional hierarchies, and fuelled by growing populism in Europe and weariness over European-wide institutions, makes the need for clear articulation of these principles ever more necessary. Gender equality will not be achieved until women are able to exercise full and autonomous control over their bodies. Until that time comes, women will continue to be relegated to second class status, deprived of their agency and forced to risk their physical, mental, and social well-being, without full human rights protection.

Acknowledgments

The author would like to thank Professor Rebecca Cook of the University of Toronto for her thoughtful review of an early draft of this chapter. The author would also like to thank Adriana Lamačková and Johanna Westeson from the Center for Reproductive Rights for their insightful reflections on European law and policy, and to Marina Davidashvili and Nadine Kryostan from the European Parliamentary Forum on Population and Development (EPF) for sharing their extensive knowledge on abortion politics in Europe. The author also attempted to speak with anti-abortion activists but was refused.

Christina Zampas is a human rights lawyer focusing on sexual and reproductive rights. She has conducted litigation, advocacy and law reform across the globe, with a particular focus on Europe. She has worked at the Center for Reproductive Rights and at Amnesty International. She is currently Reproductive and Sexual Health Law Fellow, International Reproductive and Sexual Health Law Program, Faculty of Law, University of Toronto.

References

Academy of Medical Royal Colleges. 2011. 'Induced Abortion and Mental Health'. Retrieved 11 August 2016 from http://www.aomrc.org.uk/wp-content/uploads/2016/05/Induced_Abortion_Mental_Health_1211.pdf

Amnesty International. 2015. 'She is Not a Criminal: The Impact of Ireland's Abortion Law'. London: Amnesty International.

ASTRA Network. 2006. 'Sexual and Reproductive Health and Rights in Europe: Report to the European Union'. Retrieved 20 January 2014 from http://www.astra.org.pl/pdf/publications/srhrEU.pdf

Center for Reproductive Rights. 2015a. 'World's Abortion Laws 2015'. Retrieved 18 November 2015 from http://worldabortionlaws.com

———. 2015b. 'Mandatory Waiting Periods and Biased Counselling Requirements in Central and Eastern Europe'. Retrieved 25 June 2016 from http://www.reproductiverights.org/document/mandatory-waiting-periods-and-biased-counseling-requirements-in-central-and-eastern-europe

Chavkin, W., et al. 2013. 'Conscientious Objection to the Provision of Reproductive Health Care', *International Journal of Gynecology and Obstetrics* 123 (Supplement 3).

Convention on the Elimination of All Forms of Discrimination Against Women. 1981. United Nations.

Cook, R.J. and S. Cusak. 2010. *Gender Stereotyping: Transnational Legal Perspective*. University of Pennsylvania Press.

Cook, R.J., B. Dickens and M. Fathalla. 2003. *Reproductive Health and Human Rights: Integrating Medicine, Ethics, and Law*. Oxford University Press.

Cook, R. J. and S. Howard. 2007. 'Accommodating Women's Differences under the Women's Anti-Discrimination Convention', *Emory Law Journal* 59: 1039–51.

Constitution of Hungary. 2011. Article II.

Datta, N. 2013. 'Keeping it All in the Family: Europe's Antichoice Movement', *Catholics for Choice Conscience Magazine* 34(2): 22–27.

Dickens, B. and R.J. Cook. 2006. 'The Growing Abuse of Conscientious Objection', *Ethics Journal of the American Medical Association* 8(5): 337–40.

Erdman, J. 2010. 'Procedural Turn in Transnational Abortion Law'. Family, Sex, and Reproduction: Emerging Issues in International Law. ASIL Proceedings. 377.

European Committee of Social Rights. 2014. International Planned Parenthood Federation-European Network (IPPF-EN) v. Italy. Strasbourg.

European Court of Human Rights. 1977. Brüggemann and Scheuten v. Federal Republic of Germany. Strasbourg.

———. 2007. Tysiąc v. Poland. Strasbourg.

———. 2009. Opuz v. Turkey. Strasbourg.

———. 2010. A. B. and C. v. Ireland. Strasbourg.

———. 2011. R. R. v. Poland. Strasbourg.

———. 2012. P. and S. v. Poland. Strasbourg.

European Court of Justice. 2011. Brüstle v. Greenpeace. Luxembourg.

European Parliament. 2013. 'Motion for a Resolution on Sexual and Reproductive Health and Rights'. Retrieved 26 January 2014 from http://www.europarl.europa.eu/sides/getDoc.do?type=REPORT&reference=A7-2013-0306&language=EN#title1

'Failure in the Basic Care of Savita Halappanavar'. *BBC News*, 9 October 2013. Retrieved 18 January 2014 from http://www.bbc.co.uk/news/world-europe-24463106

Federation of Catholic Families Associations in Europe. 2013. '12 Reasons to Vote Against the Estrela Report'. Federation of Catholic Families Associations in Europe. Retrieved 26 January 2014 from http://www.fafce.org/index.php?option=com_content&view=article&id=85:12-reasons-to-vote-against-the-estrela-resolution-on-sexual-and-reproductive-health-and-rights&catid=9:news&Itemid=104&lang=en

Forowicz, M. 2010. *The Reception of International Law in the European Court of Human Rights*. Oxford University Press.

Heinrich Böll Foundation (ed.). 2015. *Anti-Gender Movements on the Rise: Strategising for Gender Equality in Central and Eastern Europe*. Berlin: Heinrich Böll Foundation.

Hungary. 2002. 'Act LXXXVII on the Amendment of Act LXXIX on the Protection of Foetal Life'.

International Covenant on Civil and Political Rights (ICCPR). 1977. Article 4. United Nations.

International Planned Parenthood Federation-European Network (IPPF-EN). 2013. 'Barometer of Women's Access to Contraceptive Choice in 10 EU Countries'. International Planned Parenthood Federation-European Network. Retrieved 26 January 2014 from http://www.ippfen.org/sites/default/files/Barometer_17-06_webfin.pdf

Italy, Ministry of Health. 2008. 'Report on the Ministry of Health on the Performance of the Law Containing Rules for the Social Care of Maternity and Voluntary Interruption of Pregnancy: 2006–07'. Rome.

Kligman, G. 1995. 'Political Demography: The Banning of Abortion in Ceausecu's Romania', in F.D. Ginsburg and R. Rapp (eds), *Conceiving the New World Order: The Global Politics of Reproduction*. Berkeley, CA: University of California Press, pp. 234–55.

Lamačková, A. 2014. 'Women's Rights in the Abortion Decision of the Slovak Constitutional Court', in R.J. Cook, J.N. Erdman, and B.M. Dickens (eds), *Abortion Law in Transnational Perspective: Cases and Controversies*. University of Pennsylvania Press, pp. 56–76.

MacKinnon, C. 1991. 'Reflections on Sex Equality Under Law', *Yale Law Journal* 100: 1281.

Omang, J. 2013. 'Playing Hardball Against Women's Rights, the Holy See at the U.N', *Catholics for Choice Conscience Magazine* 34(2): 19–21.

One of Us. 2013. 'European Citizens' Initiative'. Retrieved 26 January 2014 from http://www.oneofus.eu/initiative-explanation/

Parliamentary Assembly of the Council of Europe (PACE). 2008. 'Resolution 1607 Access to Safe and Legal Abortion in Europe'. Retrieved 12 December 2013 from http://www.assembly.coe.int/Main.asp?link=/Documents/adoptedText/ta08/ERES 1607.htm

———. 2010. 'Report on Women's Access to Lawful Medical Care: The Problem of Unregulated Use of Conscientious Objection'.

Poland. 1993 (amended 23 December 1997). 'Law on Family Planning, Human Embryo Protection, and Conditions of Legal Pregnancy Termination'.

Polish Federation for Women and Family Planning. 2013. 'Twenty Years of Anti-Abortion Law in Poland'. Federation for Women and Family Planning. Warsaw.

Priaulx, N. 2008. 'Testing the Margin of Appreciation: Therapeutic Abortion, Reproductive "Rights" and the Intriguing Case of Tysiac v. Poland', *European Journal of Health Law* 15: 370.

Russian Federation. 2012. 'Law on Basics of Health Protection of the Citizens of the Russian Federation'.

Seigal, R.B. 2012. 'The Constitutionalisation of Abortion' in M. Rosenfeld and A. Sajó (eds), *The Oxford Handbook of Comparative Constitutional Law*. Oxford University Press, ch. 52.

United Nations Committee on Economic, Social and Cultural Rights (CESCR). 2009. 'General Comment 20: Non-Discrimination in Economic, Social and Cultural Rights'.

United Nations Committee on the Elimination of All Forms of Discrimination Against Women (CEDAW).1994. 'General Recommendation 21: Equality in Marriage and Family Relations'.

———. 2004. 'General Recommendation 25: Temporary Special Measures'.

———. 2011. L.C. v. Peru. Geneva.

United Nations Human Rights Committee. 2005. K.L. v Peru. Geneva.

———. 2007. L.M.R. v. Argentina. Geneva.

———. 2016. Mellet v. Ireland. Geneva.

United Nations Human Rights Council. 2011. 'Resolution 11/8: Preventable Maternal Mortality and Human Rights'. Geneva.

United Nations International Conference on Population and Development (ICPD). 1994. Programme of Action. Cairo.

————. 1999. 'Key Actions for the Further Implementation of the Programme of Action'. New York.

United Nations Population Fund (UNFPA) and Center for Reproductive Rights. 'ICPD and Human Rights: 20 Years of Advancing Reproductive Rights through UN Treaty Bodies and Legal Reform'. Retrieved 26 January 2014 from http://www.unfpa.org/webdav/site/global/shared/documents/publications/2013/icpd_and_human_rights_20_years.pdf

World Health Organization (WHO). 2012. 'Safe Abortion: Technical and Policy Guidance for Health Systems', 2nd ed. Geneva.

————. 2011. 'Unsafe Abortion: Global and Regional Estimates of the Incidence of Unsafe Abortion and Associated Mortality in 2008', 6th ed. Geneva.

————. 2014. 'Preventing Unsafe Abortion'. Retrieved 26 January 2014 from http://www.who.int/reproductivehealth/topics/unsafe_abortion/magnitude/en/

WHO, UNICEF, UNFPA and the World Bank. 2010. 'Trends in Maternal Mortality: 1990–2008'. Geneva.

Zampas, C. and X. Andión-Ibañez. 2012. 'Conscientious Objection to Sexual and Reproductive Health Services: International Human Rights Standards and European Law and Practice', *European Journal of Health Law* 19: 231–56.

Zampas, C. and J. Gher. 2008. 'Abortion as a Human Right: International and Regional Standards', *Human Rights Law Review* 8(2): 249–94.

Chapter 2

Freeing Abortion in Sweden

by Annulla Linders and Danielle Bessett

In 1962, American TV host Sherri Finkbine travelled to Sweden to have an abortion. Having taken the drug Thalidomide during her pregnancy, she feared that the foetus might be deformed. She had initially been scheduled to have a therapeutic abortion at a hospital in Arizona, but by publicising the dangers of Thalidomide she scared the hospital into cancelling the abortion. Arizona at the time was guided by a 1901 law that recognised only risks to the mother's life as a justifiable reason for abortion. Having researched her remaining options, Finkbine chose Sweden, where the abortion law was somewhat more liberal than in Arizona. The case became a media spectacle in both nations and prompted considerable debate and commentary (Solinger 2005: 180). In Sweden, moreover, the case prompted a modest expansion of the abortion law. Yet, just two years later, abortion was back on the front pages of the Swedish newspapers. This time the entire media establishment was protesting the announcement by the Attorney General that he would start prosecuting Swedish women who travelled to Poland to obtain legal abortions that were unavailable in Sweden (Bergman 2003). The juxtaposition of these two events, we show in this chapter, provides insights into the process that 'freed' abortion in Sweden, to use the language of activists, but also highlights an inherent contradiction in the Swedish governance of abortion.

Demands that the authority over abortion decisions be shifted towards the woman were infrequent and controversial prior to the 1960s, but the debates triggered by the Finkbine case and the abortion trips to Poland provided the fuel that simultaneously brought such demands to the forefront and made them increasingly difficult to ignore. And, in less than a decade after Finkbine's abortion, virtually all major Swedish institutional actors had come around to the position that only women themselves could determine if abortion was the right decision for them. Despite a rich literature on developments in Sweden and elsewhere (Burns 2005; Glendon 1987; Halfmann 2011; Liljeström 1974; Luker 1984; Reagan 1997; Staggenborg 1991; Svärd 1984), this remarkable turnaround in Sweden's system of abortion governance – the 'freeing' of abortion – has not yet been fully explored.

In what follows, we describe the context of Swedish reproductive governance prior to the 1960s and, through the discussion of Finkbine and the Poland affair, trace the process whereby abortion in Sweden was made free, both legally and financially, normalizing it within the national health system. We are not suggesting that the controversies over Sherri Finkbine and the abortion trips to Poland determined the subsequent development of the abortion controversy, only that they served as important opportunities to formulate a narrative foundation upon which the demand for free abortion could be built. That is, we focus the analysis on the 'meaning work' that gave shape to the Swedish abortion debate. What we mean by 'meaning work' resembles what other scholars have referred to as abortion rhetoric (Condit 1990) and abortion framing (Ferree 2003; Rohlinger 2002). More specifically, we focus on the overall discursive logic that simultaneously grounds the question of abortion in the past and provides interpretive and legislative paths for the future (D'Anjou and Van Male 1998; Ferree et al. 2002). We conclude the chapter with a consideration of the advantages and limitations of the logic that guides Swedish understandings and practices concerning abortion.

The Legacy of Abortion in Sweden

When Sherri Finkbine arrived in Sweden to have her abortion there was already a law in place, adopted in 1938, that made it possible for some women under some select and limited circumstances to have a legal abortion.[1] That law identified three justifiable reasons, or indications, for legal abortion. The humanitarian indication addressed pregnancies caused by rape or incest. The eugenic indication for parental 'deficiencies' was an outgrowth of more widespread eugenic concern in Sweden and elsewhere about the health and 'quality' of the population stock (Kälvemark 1980; Kline 2001). The medical-social indication, which targeted women who were already mothers and who battled poverty and poor health while trying to take care of their existing children, was viewed as a holdover measure until the social conditions that placed mothers in this situation could be addressed and alleviated (Linders 2004). In 1946 a fourth indication, social-medical, was added to the abortion law. According to this indication an abortion could be granted to women who were assumed to suffer future medical or social problems ('anticipated weakness') associated with the birth of a child, even if such problems were not present at the time of the abortion. Although these may appear to be broad justifications, in practice very few women were selected to have an abortion: in the first five years of the 1938 abortion law, only 795 abortions were granted. The vast majority of these were for eugenic indications.[2]

This system of indications was the result of a slow erosion of the harsh punitive approach, established in the eighteenth century, which deemed abortion, alongside infanticide, a capital crime (Davidson and Forsling 1982; Klintskog 1953).[3] Throughout the nineteenth century, this harsh punishment of infanticide and abortion gave way to a legal view that favoured leniency over harshness and sympathy over condemnation, and in 1861 the lingering death penalty for these crimes was formally removed. Women guilty of infanticide were still punished for their crimes, but they were increasingly seen as victims of unfortunate circumstances rather than sinners. When abortion surpassed infanticide as a social and criminal problem in the early twentieth century, the framing of women as victims came to guide abortion policy as well. Women who sought abortion, while still criminals in the eyes of the law, were viewed as acting out of desperation, driven by motives much stronger than either the penal threat or the health risks involved in illegal procedures. Faced with alarming reports of abortion-related fatalities, coupled with a rapidly decreasing birth rate, legislators in the 1920s and 1930s embarked on a serious effort to combat the abortion problem, the solution to which could no longer be sought in criminal law. The result became the abortion law of 1938, which provided abortion to a limited number of women, whose applications were granted by designated authorities.

This law, although adopted in part to reduce the number of illegal abortions, was never meant to make it easy for women to obtain an abortion, on the contrary. The law was primarily designed to make abortion an alternative for women who were deemed unsuitable as mothers. The lowering of the abortion rate, reformers anticipated, would follow primarily from a series of policy measures aimed at removing circumstances that otherwise led women to seek abortions; such policy measures included prohibiting employers from dismissing women due to engagement, marriage, or pregnancy (1939–1945); granting women pregnancy leave (1945); expanding sex education (1942–1956); providing financial support to parents in the form of child allowances (1947); and a whole host of other policy measures assumed to alleviate the stress that compelled women to seek abortions (e.g., contraceptive services, childcare options, housing opportunities, maternity care, free pregnancy tests, etc.) (Linnér 1967). In addition, many supporters anticipated, or hoped at least, that the encounters – in part counselling, in part persuasion – between the woman and the state would also temper the abortion urge in all but the most afflicted women (Lennerhed 2008).

These two pillars of the abortion law, material help and dissuasion, were both grounded in an assumption that women, because they were women, would never willingly choose an abortion if they had a real option to choose otherwise (Linders 1998). This assumption, furthermore, grew increasingly entangled in the social democratic logic of state-building, which held that individual misfortunes, like unemployment, poverty, and unwanted pregnancy, are best understood as failures of the state (Carlson 1990; Hatje 1974; Hirdman 1989). This reconceptualisation of personal troubles also affected the legislative view of abortion in such a way that women who committed the crimes of abortion and infanticide were no longer seen primarily as the victims of unfortunate circumstances but increasingly as testimonies to the need for the state to better manage social life.

During the decades following the partial legalisation of abortion in the 1930s and 40s, however, assumptions about the law's effectiveness were continuously challenged by the persistently high illegal abortion rate. There was no evidence that this rate [4] was significantly affected by the abortion law, and little persuasive evidence that the improvement of women's economic conditions removed their abortion desires. Simultaneously, dissatisfaction in professional circles (doctors, counsellors, social workers, educators) with the abortion law grew stronger and stronger as persistent problems with implementation (especially the cumbersome and time-consuming application process that scared women away from applying), and the difficulties in reaching and informing women about their options, became increasingly difficult to ignore. The persistence, if not increase, of illegal abortions served as evidence that the policy package of which the abortion law was a part was not meeting its objectives.

Prior to the 1960s, then, neither abortion specifically nor reproductive rights more generally were approached politically as independent issues of women's rights. Moreover, virtually no one expressed the opinion that the solution to the abortion problem was to give women the sole authority over the decision. Nonetheless, it was out of the dissatisfaction with the abortion law, fuelled by the Sherri Finkbine case in 1962 and then fully ignited by the controversy a few years later over abortion trips to Poland, that the call for 'free abortion' (that is, abortion available on demand for those who need it) that swept Sweden during the 1960s emerged. It is to these developments that we turn, following a brief methodological discussion.

Methods and Data

This chapter is part of a larger historical comparative project aimed at documenting the sociopolitical transformation of abortion in Sweden and the United States during the past two centuries. The Swedish data sources include a range of primary documents (government, organisations, and professional records). We also use available secondary sources examining the Swedish abortion movement (Liljeström 1974; Svärd 1984) and the state's historical involvement in reproductive practices (e.g., Carlson 1990; Davidson and Forsling 1982; Hatje 1974; Hirdman 1989; Kälvemark 1980). Data on the public debate in Sweden come primarily from newspapers. To identify abortion-related newspaper articles, we relied on a newspaper archive (*Skytteanska Klipparkivet*) comprised of a politically representative sample of thirty-three Swedish newspapers for the period 1955–1985. This archive is organised around major political issues, of which abortion is one. The full sample of abortion-related coverage for the thirty-year period is comprised of thousands of news items, but for the analysis in this chapter we focus on the 690 articles published from 1960 through 1966, a period that encompasses our two focal events (see Figure 2.1). A full 25–30 per cent of these items are reader-generated opinion pieces (op-ed contributions and letters), thus signalling widespread public interest in the issue. Analytically speaking, the newspaper data allow us, first, to reconstruct the conflict over abortion as it unfolded during this critical period and, second, to identify the range of meaning clusters that participants in the debate generated, elaborated, and transformed over time.

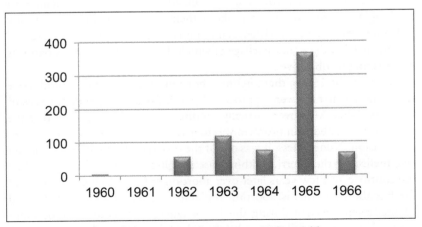

Figure 2.1 Number of abortion articles by year, 1960–1966

The Abortion Debate Explodes in the 1960s

The Sherri Finkbine Story

When Sherri Finkbine became pregnant with her fifth child in the spring of 1962, she had no idea she would end up at the centre of a major abortion controversy. She was happily married, wanted another child, and had a gratifying career as a host of a popular children's television programme in Phoenix, Arizona. By the time she was in her third month of pregnancy, however, she started to fear that there was something wrong with the foetus, because she learned that the sleeping pills she had taken contained thalidomide. After consultation with doctors, her request for an abortion at the Good Samaritan Hospital in Phoenix was initially granted and was scheduled for 26 July. Two psychiatrists had found that her 'mental health would be affected if she continued to carry the baby' (*New York Times* 26 July 1962) and a panel of staff physicians at the hospital 'had recommended that the abortion be performed' (*New York Times* 27 July 1962). Once Finkbine came forward with her story, however, the hospital decided to halt the abortion until they could get confirmation that such an abortion could be granted legally. The law guiding abortion in Arizona at the time was adopted in 1901 and held that abortion was illegal in all cases except to save the life of the mother. In order to get legal clarification, Finkbine, joined by the hospital, filed a suit in Maricopa County Superior Court on 25 July 'for a declaratory judgment against the legality of Arizona's law forbidding abortion' (*New York Times* 26 and 27 July 1962). After several weeks and a nationwide media furore, the judge dismissed the case on technical grounds, 'saying there was no legal controversy', that is, no legal contradiction to be resolved (*New York Times* 31 July 1962). Uncomfortable with the legal limbo of that non-decision, Finkbine and her husband announced they would 'seek help in a more favorable legal climate' (*The Times-News* 1 August 1962). They settled on Sweden where, according to a spokesman for the National Board of Health, seven pregnant Swedish women who had taken thalidomide had already been granted abortions (*Daytona Beach Morning Journal* 3 August 1962). Newspapers in both Sweden and the United States covered the case on a daily basis as Sherri Finkbine's request for a legal abortion in Sweden was considered and eventually granted by a unanimous committee of the State Medical Board. The abortion was performed successfully on 18 August; following the abortion, Finkbine's husband told reporters that 'the removed foetus was deformed' (*The Leader-Post* 18 August 1962).

Once the Finkbines had returned home, the American interest in the case waned considerably. In Sweden, however, the debate intensified and set in motion the protest movement that would lead to the liberalisation of the abortion law a decade later. Initially, the Finkbine case had reinforced the support for the Swedish approach to abortion, which, according to the prevailing consensus, amounted to an appreciation of the abortion-seeking woman's plight, a concern for the future well-being of her child, an agreement that it was part of the state's responsibility to prevent women from ending up in an abortion situation, and a sense that legal abortion under some circumstances was necessary and advisable but only as an emergency solution. In the aftermath of the case, however, the attention paid to the abortion law and its procedures slowly turned from the self-congratulatory attitude that had accompanied the Finkbine case to a more critical evaluation of how things really worked. Thus, while the most immediate consequence of the Finkbine spectacle for the Swedish approach to abortion was a formal expansion of the abortion law to recognise foetal damage as an indication for abortion (1964), the more significant and long-term consequence was an erosion of the logic that undergirded the system of indications. This is so because the Finkbine case so clearly demonstrated the real hardships to women of an overly restrictive abortion law; if the Swedish debate initially focused on the American abortion law, it quickly turned to an examination of the Swedish law as well.

Over the next few years, as support for a more liberal abortion law mounted, the debate over abortion continued unabated, and then exploded once again in 1965 when it was revealed not only that many Swedish women went to Poland, where the abortion law was liberalised in 1956 (see also Mishtal this volume), to have abortions, but also that those women were subject to prosecution in Sweden.

The Poland Affair

In the autumn of 1964, the Liberal Student Organisation in Stockholm organised a conference on Sex and Society in Stockholm. During this conference, an unidentified young Swedish woman told from a stage shrouded in darkness the story of how she had travelled to Poland to get an abortion after having been unable to secure one in Sweden (Bergman 2003). The word of this abortion option spread quickly, and one of the organisers of the conference, Hans Nestius, started getting inquiries from women about how to secure an abortion in Poland. A few months later, the Attorney General, Emanuel Walberg, announced he would seek indictments against both Nestius and the women he had helped secure abortions in Poland.

The story practically exploded on the pages of the nation's newspapers. Although the notion of 'free abortion' was still controversial, the critique directed at Walberg was almost unanimous. He started backtracking his statements about the women almost immediately, but he nonetheless organised a search of Hans Nestius' home for evidence related to his role in the affair. Regardless of position on abortion, this act was uniformly condemned as an overreach of power (e.g., *Expressen* 19 February 1965; *Gefle Dagblad* 19 February 1965; *Västerbottens-Kuriren* 19 February 1965), and most observers also chided the prosecutor for the hypocrisy involved in going after Swedish women who did exactly what Sherri Finkbine had done a few years earlier: seek a solution to their pregnancy troubles in a more hospitable climate than that of their home nation (e.g., *Expressen* 14 February 1965; *Upsala Nya Tidning* 15 February 1965). So strongly did the government feel the pressure that, within days, the minister of justice, Herman Kling, announced that a new commission would be appointed very shortly to once again examine the abortion law (*Arbetarbladet* 22 February 1965). A few days later the Attorney General announced that no further action would be taken against either the women in question or Hans Nestius (*Falu-Kuriren* 26 February 1965; *Dagens Nyheter* 26 February 1965).

The commission was formed in early March, and while one of the stated tasks was to examine the legal conundrum that the Poland affair had laid bare, the directives were wide enough to include a possible finding by the commission that abortion be made available on demand. The commission itself did not originally envision a law that would make abortion available on demand, but instead remained committed to the idea that it was possible to identify and specify situations in which a legal abortion would be an appropriate response. A few years into its work, however, the commission essentially abandoned the indication approach that for so long had guided Swedish abortion policy and instead concluded that:

> For a woman who is pregnant but does not want to take the responsibility to give birth, her pregnancy constitutes such a burden that she appropriately ought to be guaranteed a legal right to be operated on. (SOU 1971: 58: 20)

But the committee also emphasised …

> … that society, in abandoning the prohibition against abortion, does not liberate itself from its responsibility towards the women who are prepared to undergo an abortion operation. They are entitled to the same considerations that society extend to women who

give birth, to medical care without cost and to the same guarantees of the greatest possible mercy and the least possible risks. (SOU 1971: 58: 110)

During the six years that the commission worked on the abortion question, the delivery of legal abortion services was rapidly expanding, thus signalling that the logic that supported a more liberal law had already penetrated professional and bureaucratic ranks.[5]

In 1974, Parliament approved the new abortion law. According to this law the abortion decision rested with the woman up to eighteen weeks, although between twelve and eighteen weeks she was required to meet with a counsellor. After eighteen weeks, approval was required by the Medical Board. No abortions were permitted after twenty-four weeks unless the woman's life was in danger or other pressing circumstances made an abortion necessary. Free abortion was now the law in Sweden.[6]

Moving From Indications to Free Abortion

If it was during the debate around the Finkbine case that the Swedish path towards free abortion was first discernible, it was the scandal around the abortion trips to Poland a few years later that blazed the path wide open. This was so because, in the interim, there had been considerable mobilisation around the idea that abortion should be 'free' – that is, free, safe, and available to women on demand. Although the transformation of the Swedish abortion law was part of a liberalisation wave that swept Western Europe and the United States it still displays some unique features that helps explain the subsequent development of the approach to abortion.

In what follows we pay particular attention to the logics invoked by various participants in the efforts to free abortion. These efforts were less a coherent movement in the sense of the American pro-choice movement(s) (Staggenborg 1991) than multipronged constellations of interest (political parties, youth organisations, women's groups, media organisations, professionals) that converged in the mounting demands for free abortion. Hence, although no designated abortion-rights organisations formed in Sweden, there was significant mobilisation around the issue by a broad range of groups and organisations (Svärd 1984). Prior to the Finkbine case in 1962, the position that abortion should be free was practically unheard of, but after the conclusion of the Poland affair in 1965, support for a more liberal abortion law had grown exponentially. This transformation of Sweden's approach to abortion took shape in a way that was highly atypical for Sweden at the time. Under normal circumstances, the public debate would subside while the commission was at work; the commission system in Sweden is designed to produce consensus-based policy solutions that take into account the positions of major stakeholders (Heclo and Madsen 1987; Lewin 1992). In the case of abortion, however, it was primarily through an extraordinarily lively debate taking place in the newspapers that the demand for free abortion was generated. By the time the commission delivered its proposal in 1971, most major interest groups had already come around in favour of abortion on demand, as had most newspapers.

Generally speaking, the call for free abortion was initially formulated and spread by the various political youth organisations. Groups on the far left were also among the early proponents of liberalisation. The women's organisations of the major political parties generally arrived at a position favouring free abortion before the main party organisation did so, but typically after the youth groups (Eduards 1991). Some groups, especially the liberal (*Folkpartiet*) and centre (*Centerpartiet*) parties and the Swedish Church, were unable to achieve consensus among their members, whereas a few groups, especially sectarian religious organisations, remained consistently hostile to the idea of free abortion. The social democratic government essentially dodged the issue until the commission had delivered its proposal, while the Social Democratic Party itself made a cautious statement in favour of free abortion in 1972.

From the beginning it was clear that two broad and interrelated themes dominated the Swedish debate, one having to do with motherhood and the other with nationhood. The motherhood theme not only has deep roots in the past but is also part of the bedrock of the social democratic state-building project (see Orloff 2002). The nationhood theme has long served as a persistent backdrop against which participants in the Swedish abortion debate staked out their positions on abortion and, less directly, their definition of and commitment to the 'Swedish Way'. These two themes, as we discuss below, simultaneously grounded the problem in the past and provided a path for the future

Abortion and Motherhood

The logic underlying the demands for a more liberal abortion law remained lodged in a framework that linked women's actions and motivations to their actual or potential motherhood role. The notion of motherhood was inscribed into the social democratic state-building project from the beginning and, more or less directly, came to guide a wide range of policy initiatives aimed at facilitating and strengthening good motherhood (Hirdman 1989;

Kälvemark 1980; Palmblad 2000). This ambition is clearly evident in the system of abortion indications, which was designed to promote 'good' motherhood by making it possible for potentially 'bad' mothers (those too sick, poor, or deficient to deliver good mothering) to interrupt their pregnancies. In this sense, motherhood itself became a matter of the state (Bock and Thane 1991; Eduards 2007; Koven and Michel 1993; Yeo 1999).

It is for this reason that both reformers and activists throughout the 1960s emphasised that abortion signalled a 'defeat' on the part of society (*Göteborgsposten* 24 February 1965). It was the responsibility of the state to ensure that women had the resources they needed to both prevent the pregnancies they did not want and give birth to the children they did want (see above for policies adopted to make these dual goals possible). These kinds of policies, in other words, were necessary to prevent the need for abortion (*Eskilstuna Kuriren* 17 February 1965; *Upsala Nya Tidning* 17 February 1965). The underlying assumption here was that no woman would choose abortion unless her circumstances were dire, either socially, emotionally or financially (*Stockholm-Tidningen* 17 February 1965; *Västgöta-Demokraten* 17 February 1965). In short, because women were seen as naturally inclined towards motherhood, no woman would decide on an abortion without very compelling reasons.

And it was precisely those reasons that the public support system was supposed to address. The fact that so many women still had illegal abortions was hence evidence that, first, the level of support was insufficient and, second, that the legal abortion system was seriously wanting, marked as it was with 'scandalous delays' (*Stockholms-Tidningen* 18 February 1965); bureaucratic hassles (*Falu-Kuriren* 20 February 1965), and inequities (*Göteborgs Handels- och Sjöfartstidning* 19 February 1965). In other words, in calling the abortion law outmoded, newspapers in the 1960s called attention not only to the fate of the women who had been denied abortion but also to the 'inhumane' process that preceded the granting of a legal abortion, including 'interrogation, nervous tension, and uncertainty' (*Aftonbladet* 19 August 1962), and the 'worry and stress' that came with the cumbersome and seemingly arbitrary process (*Ny Tid* 21 August 1962).

In many ways, of course, the abortion law of 1974 constituted a major break with the view of abortion that had dominated policymaking for half a century. Previously viewed alternately as sinners, victims of socio-economic circumstances, and emotional wrecks, women had never before been seen as the appropriate authorities of their own abortion situations. And yet, at a fundamental level, the Swedish debate over abortion simultaneously reflected and reinforced the assumption that motherhood is a natural and, therefore, desirable goal for women. From this perspective, women would only override the dictates of nature and choose to interrupt their pregnancies if the circumstances prevented them from being good mothers (*Falu-Kuriren* 18 February 1965; *Vestmanlands Läns Tidning* 16 February 1965). For example, 'no woman should have to seek an abortion because she has no home or because there are not enough childcare facilities' (Nestius 1965). That is, women themselves know if they 'are strong enough to give birth to a child and develop an emotional connection with it' and are able to determine if they can manage motherhood even if 'the child's father doesn't want it' or if their parents 'distance themselves from it' (Gyllner 1964). Thus, commentators concluded, prohibiting abortion neither makes 'the mother stronger' nor 'improve[s] [her] life circumstances' (Gustafsson 1964).

Even as an increasing number of groups and organisations came around to the position that, in the end, women were the only ones who really could make the decision of whether or not to become mothers, many still balked at the idea of abortion 'on demand' if that meant that it would be possible for women to go to any clinic and 'just order' an abortion (*Upsala Nya Tidning* 22 February 1965). From a practical perspective, however, advocates of free abortion pointed out that it was tricky to give women the final authority over the abortion decision without also making abortion available to her 'on demand'. Hence the only way that 'women would be liberated from fear of pregnancy' (*Ny Tid* 21 August 1962) and the abortion problem could be solved was to grant women the right to make the final decision (*Dagens Nyheter* 20 August 1962).

This became the dominant position that undergirded the new abortion law. According to this position, abortion remained a social problem to be combated and was still linked with social policy shortcomings, but was also still viewed as an appropriate emergency measure to solve the problems of an unwanted pregnancy. Hence, despite the sharp increase in legal abortions towards the end of the 1960s the vision of abortion as a careless, irresponsible, frivolous, and essentially unnecessary undertaking of women never quite took root in the public debate. From a gender perspective, the more radical approach that women had a right to an abortion irrespective of their motives or the circumstances of their lives, emerged slowly and haltingly over the 1960s and was addressed in the public debate under the rubric 'right to abortion'. Throughout the period, 'free abortion' and 'right to abortion' were used interchangeably by participants in the debate, but from an analytic perspective they do point to somewhat different problems. And yet, in many ways the call for women's right to abortion meant, in effect, a call for a 'right to free abortion'; that is, the right was construed less as an absolute demand than as a realistic conclusion that as long as women need/seek abortions they have a right to have them safely and freely.

Nevertheless, the aspect of the new law that was truly revolutionary – granting women full authority over the abortion decision – did trigger a persistent force of opposition, although seldom framed in terms overtly or directly hostile to women. Conservative groups were concerned about the erosion of traditional morality and warned that women would become sexually more vulnerable to ruthless men without the protection of legal disapprobation of frivolous abortion. Moreover, they were concerned that, with a more liberal abortion law, women would lose 'their only protection against pressures' to have an abortion from parents and/or the men involved (Palmborg 1964). Religious groups raised concerns about foetal life, and pointed to the foetus as the most vulnerable and, in light of free abortion, completely unprotected stakeholder. These objections, however, did not lead to a wholesale rejection of the logical foundation concerning women's well-being that the law was built upon, and hence never gave rise to a politically effective countermovement like the pro-life movement in the United States.

In conclusion, although the right to abortion, both institutionally and politically speaking, is much better protected in Sweden than in many other places, it is still entangled in traditional notions of motherhood that, on balance, makes it less radical from a liberal-feminist perspective than in the United States, for example. In Sweden, the movement that freed abortion bridged rather than severed the connections to both the old abortion system, which linked women's abortion needs to hardship, and the traditional movement for women's rights, which linked women's plights to the class struggle. This heritage, as we have shown, had consequences not only for women's ability to secure an abortion but also for the larger narrative surrounding motherhood and women's position in social life more generally.

Abortion and Nationhood

Ever since the population crisis in the 1930s, when the birth rate declined rapidly, women's reproductive lives have loomed large in Swedish policy-making, inspiring a string of policies that combined carrots and sticks to make sure that enough children were born to the right kind of parents (SOU 1935: 15). In this sense, women's reproductive lives have always played a key role in the building of the nation (Palmblad 2000). By the time of the Finkbine case and the Poland affair, the primary nation-building concerns were no longer internal, but instead focused on Sweden in relation to other nations. This means that participants in the abortion debate used these cases to simultaneously reinforce their definition of Sweden and position Sweden in the world. The nationhood theme has remained at the forefront of abortion discussions in Sweden till this day, culminating in a 2008 change to the 1974 abortion law that eliminated the requirement that the woman be a Swedish citizen or a resident of Sweden (unless she had presented especially urgent circumstances, as Finkbine did).

By the 1960s, after almost thirty years of social democratic political dominance, what Heclo and Madsen (1987) term the 'Swedish Way' was already well established. The Swedish Way is a particular form of social democracy that holds the state responsible for the collective well-being of the people, whether the problem is maternity benefits or vacation, workplace safety or access to medical care (Esping-Andersen 1985). There is a continued expectation, among policymakers as well as the public at large, that the primary task of the government is to never rest in its efforts to move 'Swedish society in the "right" direction' (Heclo and Madsen 1987: 6). The development of the Swedish approach to abortion clearly fits this pattern. As Maud Eduards argues, the nation state is the frame through which the history of abortion is best understood (Eduards 2007). But here we also emphasise how the internal Swedish debate that sets the path for the future is always, more or less directly, formulated in terms of what the Swedish Way is not, that is, in relation to the ways of other nations. At a deeper level, such processes undergird the development of nations as 'imagined communities' (Anderson 1983); that is, they not only influence the development of an internal policy agenda but also play a role in how nations position themselves in relation to each other. It is in this light we analyse the Swedish abortion debate in the 1960s and beyond.

Few commentators failed to note the irony in the initial decision by the Attorney General to prosecute women who had received legal abortions in Poland only a few years after Finkbine came to Sweden to have her abortion. Most who weighed in on the Finkbine case were critical of the American laws that did not leave room for someone in Finkbine's position to have an abortion (*Dala-Demokraten* 4 August 1962), and practically no one argued against the decision by the Medical Board to grant Finkbine's request for an abortion. The consensus around Sherri Finkbine was facilitated by reports of foreign meddling in the case. Not only did the Swedish king receive telegrams from outraged Americans, but the Vatican officially denounced the whole Finkbine affair. These external forces provided a clear contrast to Swedish understandings. The position of the Catholic Church, according to several Swedish newspapers, 'constitutes an insensitive cruelty, and a belief in authority that we find both immoral and harmful' (*Aftonbladet* 22 August 1962). While acknowledging that 'the abortion question contains moral problems', one newspaper emphasised that 'it is not possible to escape the abortion problem simply by washing one's hands of it', as Catholics do by refusing to discuss any other position than prohibition (*Dagens Nyheter* 22 August 1962). Referring to the 'iron curtain of religious and moral prejudices' (*Dala-Demokraten* 4 August 1962) that prevented sound judgment from guiding abortion decisions in the United States, another newspaper took the opportunity to position Sweden well above the United States when it came to reasonable and rational governance, thus reinforcing one of the pillars of the Swedish Way.

The controversy over the Poland affair can only be understood in terms of an assault on how things are supposed to be done in Sweden. When the Attorney General announced he would seek charges against the women who had travelled to Poland, he explained that he viewed 'abortion of a *Swedish* foetus, as an affront to *Swedish* interests' (Eduards 2007: 95). Practically no observers were sympathetic to this position; instead, they argued, Swedish interests demanded not acting like a 'police state' (Östersunds *Posten* 19 February 1965), not subjecting citizens to 'man hunts' (*Dagens Nyheter* 18 February 1965), and certainly not prosecuting the poor women who in desperation had travelled to Poland to have their pregnancies terminated (*Aftonbladet* 2 February 1965).[7] Commentators observed that the reputation Sweden had gained after the Finkbine case as a nation with a humanitarian approach to abortion was severely undermined by the 'cat-and-mouse hunt' of possibly innocent people who had left Sweden to get an abortion elsewhere (*Dagens Nyheter* 19 February 1965). Rather than criticising the women who travelled to Poland, even opponents of a more liberal abortion law argued that a nation like Sweden ought to have enough resources to prevent the need for illegal abortions by providing enough assistance to mothers (*Skånska Dagbladet* 19 February 1965) and that the state had neglected its responsibility when it came to the work involved in preventing abortion (*Jönköpingsposten* 19 February 1965).

Once free abortion became the law of Sweden, the principles upon which it was based were incorporated into the Swedish Way and came to guide how Sweden acted not only domestically, but also internationally. Sweden has taken an active role in the international community to secure and protect reproductive rights for all women, and Swedish commentators still reaffirm the Swedish approach to abortion in depictions of other nations as hostile to women's needs. For example, an editorial in *Gotlands Tidningen* announced early in 2013 that 'In Sweden, the battle over the woman's right to control her own body has been won. [But] internationally speaking there is much work left to be done' (7 March 2013). Most recently, Swedish commentators have been very critical of the European Union for its spineless response to the abortion question and its failure to take a strong position in favour of women's rights (*Aftonbladet* 31 May 2013; *Expressen* 28 May 2013; *Göteborgs Posten* 7 April 2013).

The nationhood theme, then, allowed commentators to position access to abortion as a manifestation of the humanitarian Swedish Way, especially when compared to other international entities. Like the motherhood theme, the nationhood theme connected the abortion issues to both the past, when the primary questions concerned which kind of state to build, and to the future, when Sweden's standing as a nation among nations is of greater concern. The logic that produced a sustainable institutional space for women to secure abortions domestically has continued to undergird Sweden's subsequent involvement in transnational efforts at providing reproductive choices for women worldwide. Beginning with the Finkbine case, then, it is primarily in the debate over abortion politics elsewhere that Sweden keeps reaffirming both its self-appointed position as a world leader of women's reproductive rights and the particular narrative about women and parenthood that characterise the Swedish approach to abortion. In this sense, the story of abortion is also a story of nationhood.

Conclusion

Despite the widespread support behind the Swedish abortion law, few commentators think that the 1974 law itself constitutes a solution to the abortion problem. On the contrary, efforts to combat the need for abortion, especially through the prevention of unwanted pregnancies, are ongoing. These concerns suggest that Sweden has not so much abandoned the 'diagnostic' approach to policymaking around abortion (Liljeström 1974: 93) but shifted the focus from women in general to more specific vulnerable groups, such as the very young, the immigrants, and women around the world who have difficulties gaining control over their reproductive lives.

In this chapter we have examined the process whereby Sweden adopted a more liberal abortion law and the logics through which the political shifts were articulated and the legal expansion of abortion access justified. Although rapid once it was set in motion in the 1960s, the unravelling of a long history of 'disciplined reproduction' (Palmblad 2000) was bruising and never entirely completed. In a practical sense, abortion did indeed become free, at least during the first eighteen weeks of pregnancy, and it is a secure freedom, in the sense that it is currently unthinkable that it would be taken away from women. And yet, we conclude, the logic undergirding the abortion law and all other policy measures that remain implicated in the Swedish approach to abortion is still entangled, albeit much weaker than before, in traditional notions about the connections between womanhood, mother-hood and nationhood. The continued close monitoring of pregnancy and abortion patterns every so often give rise to new policy initiatives aimed at helping women and girls prevent unwanted pregnancies. Such initiatives are often grounded in assumptions about which kinds of pregnancies are, or ought to be, unwanted, such as those by the very young (Linders 2001). In this sense, women's reproductive practices are still subject to subtle norma-tive prodding, even though the direction of that prodding has taken a very different turn from when abortion was a crime.

Annulla Linders is an Associate Professor of Sociology at the University of Cincinnati. Her research sits at the intersection of history, culture, politics, and social protest, and deals with contentious sociopolitical issues such as abortion and capital punishment. She has done some comparative work on abortion politics, using Sweden and the United States as cases. She is cur-rently at work on a book about capital punishment in the United States, with a focus on historically grounded contentions around the audience of executions.

Danielle Bessett is an Associate Professor of Sociology at the University of Cincinnati, where she teaches courses on medicine, family, and reproduc-tion. Her research interests centre on the sociology of reproduction. She has published several peer-reviewed articles in this area. Her current projects include a book manuscript on women's experiences of pregnancy in the United States (forthcoming from New York University Press), and studies related to abortion access and care, disparities in infant mortality, and fac-tors that affect breastfeeding outcomes.

Notes

We thank the Kunz Center for Social Research for organizing the workshop where this work was first presented, and we thank the participants for valuable insights. The data collection for the study was made possible in part by a grant from the Council of European Studies, Columbia University.

1. Legal abortions approved by the Swedish Medical Board were always granted at no cost to the women. Subsequently, abortion services were covered under Sweden's universal healthcare system; this system was nationalised in 1955 (Heclo and Mad-sen 1987).
2. Of these 795 abortions, 7 per cent had been done under the medical-social indica-tion, 4.5 per cent under the humanitarian indication and 88 per cent under the eugenic indication (SOU 1944: 51).

3. Although there are few recorded cases of women actually being executed for abortion, executions for infanticide were numerous (Olivecrona 1891; Persson 1972).
4. The abortion commissions estimated between 10,000 and 20,000 illegal abortions per year, and also that more than 60 per cent of women whose application for legal abortion had been denied turned to an illegal abortionist (SOU 1944: 51; SOU 1953: 29).
5. Between 1950 and 1968, the number of legal abortions nearly doubled, from about 6,000 to almost 11,000 per year. By 1966, less than 9 per cent of abortion applications were rejected, down from almost 20 per cent two years earlier.
6. This is still the law in Sweden, albeit with a few subsequent modifications. The distinction between twelve and eighteen weeks has been removed; counselling is now a right for all abortion-seeking women (and men), but not a requirement for anyone; the twenty-four weeks outer limit has been replaced with a foetal viability determination (unless the mother's life is in danger, in which case there is no outer limit); and the law now applies to non-resident foreign women as well.
7. By the mid-sixties, prosecutions of individual women for illegal abortions in Sweden had practically ceased (SOU 1971: 58).

References

Anderson, B. 1983. *Imagined Communities: Reflections on the Origin and Spread of Nationalism*. London: Verso.

Bergman, Y. 2003. 'Polenaffären', in S. Andersson and S. Sjödahl (eds), *Sex: En Politisk Historia*. Stockholm: Alfabeta/RFSU, pp. 129–40.

Bock, G. and P. Thane (eds). 1991. *Maternity and Gender Politics: Women and the Rise of the European Welfare States, 1880–1950s*. New York: Routledge.

Burns, G. 2005. *The Moral Veto: Framing Contraception, Abortion, and Cultural Pluralism in the United States*. New York: Cambridge University Press.

Carlson, A. 1990. *The Swedish Experiment in Family Politics: The Myrdals and the Interwar Population Crisis*. New Brunswick, NJ: Transaction Publishers.

Condit, C.M. 1990. *Decoding Abortion Rhetoric: Communicating Social Change*. Urbana: University of Illinois Press.

D'Anjou, L. and J. Van Male. 1998. 'Between Old and New: Social Movements and Cultural Change', *Mobilization* 3(2): 2007–226.

Davidson, B. and C. Forsling. 1982. *Abort Förr och Nu: En Bok om Aborträtten och Synen på Kvinnan*. Stockholm: Bokförlaget Röda Rummet.

Eduards, M. 1991. 'Towards a Third Way: Women's Politics and Welfare Policies in Sweden', Social Research 58(3): 677–705.

———. 2007. *Kroppspolitik: Om Moder Svea och andra Kvinnor*. Stockholm: Atlas Akademi.

Esping-Andersen, G. 1985. *Politics against Markets: The Social Democratic Road to Power*. Princeton, NJ: Princeton University Press.

Ferree, M.M. 2003. 'Resonance and Radicalism: Feminist Framing in the Abortion Debates of the United States and Germany', *American Journal of Sociology* 109(2): 304–44.

Ferree, M.M., W.A. Gamson, J. Gerhards and D. Rucht. 2002. *Shaping Abortion Discourse: Democracy and the Public Sphere in Germany and the United States*. Cambridge University Press.

Glendon, M.A. 1987. *Abortion and Divorce in Western Law*. Cambridge, MA: Harvard University Press.

Gustafsson, B. 1964. 'Begreppet Barn', *Dagens Nyheter* 22 May 1964.

Gyllner, B. 1964. 'Ja till Fri Abort', *Dagens Nyheter* 1 August 1964.

Halfmann, D. 2011. *Doctors and Demonstrators: How Political Institutions Shape Abortion Law in the United States, Britain, and Canada*. Chicago, IL: University of Chicago Press.

Hatje, A-K. 1974. *Befolkningsfrågan och Välfärden*. Stockholm: Allmänna Förlaget.

Heclo, H. and H. Madsen. 1987. *Policy and Politics in Sweden: Principled Pragmatism*. Philadelphia, PA: Temple University.

Hirdman, Y. 1989. *Att Lägga Livet Till Rätta: Studier i Svensk Folkhemspolitik*. Stockholm: Carlssons.

Kälvemark, A-S. 1980. *More Children of Better Quality: Aspects on Swedish Population Policy in the 1930s*. Stockholm: Almqvist & Wicksell International.

Kline, W. 2001. *Building a Better Race: Gender, Sexuality, and Eugenics from the Turn of the Century to the Baby Boom*. Berkeley, CA: University of California Press.

Klintskog, E. 1953. 'Abortproblemets utveckling och rättsliga reglering i olika länder', in S. Ludvig (ed.), *De Legala Aborterna*. Stockholm: Hugo Gebers Förlag.

Koven, S. and S. Michel (eds). 1993. *Mothers of the New World: Maternalist Politics and the Origins of Welfare States*. New York: Routledge.

Lennerhed, L. 2005. 'Abortpolitiken i Sverige under 1900-talet', in *Statens Offentliga Utredningar, Vård i Sverige av Utlänningar*. SOU 2005: 90, pp. 181–84.

———. 2008. *Historier om ett Brott*. Stockholm: Atlas.

Lewin, L. 1992. *Ideologi och Strategi: Svensk Politik under 100 År*. Stockholm: Nordsteds Juridik.

Liljeström, R. 1974. *A Study of Abortion in Sweden. A Contribution to the United Nation's World Population Conference*. Sweden: Royal Ministry for Foreign Affairs.

Linders, A. 1998. 'Abortion as a Social Problem: The Construction of "Opposite" Solutions in Sweden and the United States', *Social Problems* 45(4): 488–509.

———. 2001. 'Teenage Pregnancy in Sweden', in A.L. Cherry, M.E. Dillon and D. Rugh (eds), *Teenage Pregnancy: A Global View*. Westport, CT: Greenwood Press.

———. 2004. 'Victory and Beyond: A Historical Comparative Analysis of the Outcomes of the Abortion Movements in Sweden and the United States', *Sociological Forum* 19(3): 371–404.

Linnér, B. 1967. *Sex and Society in Sweden*. New York: Pantheon Books.

Luker, K. 1984. *Abortion and the Politics of Motherhood*. Berkeley, CA: University of California Press.

Nestius, H. 1965. 'Vad Menar Dr. Westberg?', *Dagens Nyheter* 21 January 1965.

Olivecrona, K. 1891. *Om Dödsstraffet*, utvidgad upplaga. Stockholm.

Orloff, A. 2002. 'Explaining US Welfare Reform: Power, Gender, Race and the US Policy Legacy', *Critical Social Policy* 22(1): 96–118.

Palmblad, E. 2000. *Den Disciplinerade Reproduktionen: Abort- och Steriliseringspolitikens Dolda Dagordning*. Stockholm: Carlssons.

Palmborg, O. 1964. 'Abortdebattens Dubbelkommando', *Expressen* 6 August 1964.

Persson, B. 1972. 'Att vara ogift mor på 1700- och 1800-talet', in K. Westman Berg (ed.), *Könsdiskriminering Förr och Nu*. Stockholm: Prisma.

Reagan, L.J. 1997. *When Abortion Was a Crime: Women, Medicine, and Law in the United States, 1867–1973*. Berkeley, CA: University of California Press.

Rohlinger, D. 2002. 'Framing the Abortion Debate: Organizational Resources, Media Strategies, and Movement-Countermovement Dynamics', *Sociological Quarterly* 43(4): 479–507.

Solinger, R. 2005. *Pregnancy and Power: A Short History of Reproductive Politics in America*. New York: New York University Press.

Staggenborg, S. 1991. *The Pro-Choice Movement: Organization and Activism in the Abortion Conflict*. New York: Oxford University Press.

Statens Offentliga Utredningar [Government Commissions]
  SOU 1935: 15 Betänkande med förslag till lagstiftning om avbrytande av havandeskap
  SOU 1944: 51 Betänkande i abortfrågan
  SOU 1953: 29 Abortfrågan
  SOU 1971: 58 Rätten till abort

Svärd, S. 1984. *Varför Sverige fick Fri Abort: Ett Studium av en Policy Process*. Doctorsavhandling vid Statsvetenskapliga Institutionen. Stockholms Universitet.

Yeo, E.J. 1999. 'The Creation of "Motherhood" and Women's Responses in Britain and France, 1750–1914', *Women's History Review* 8(2): 201–18.

Chapter 3

Women's Liberation and the 'Right to Choose'

Struggling for Abortion in the United Kingdom and Switzerland

by Kristina Schulz and Leena Schmitter

In the early 1970s, Western women's liberation movements turned their attention to the subject of abortion. This thematisation is generally taken for granted; there were also other aspects of women's social, emotional and political situation that activists called into question, including wage inequality, the question of childcare and paid maternity leave. In the first half of the 1970s, however, none of these aspects became the focus of feminist agitation to the same degree as abortion. The reasons for addressing this issue cannot (as an essentialist viewpoint might suggest) be found in what is supposedly a 'natural' commonality among women, namely their role in the reproduction process. This view is supported, among other things, by the fact that many women – and some men – were committed to the struggle to liberalise abortion – activists who, because of their sexual orientation or their age, did not appear to personally have anything to gain from calling for the decriminalisation or liberalisation of abortion. We therefore assume that when it came to abortion, more was at stake than a legal regulation.

While it is undisputed that the struggle for abortion rights and the women's liberation movement were closely linked in many Western countries (Anton, Mitobe and Schulz 2012: 103–20; McBride 2001), discussions about legal reform began before the women's liberation movement emerged and outlasted it, in some countries by several decades. This was the case in Switzerland, where the relevant paragraphs 118–121 of the Swiss penal code of 1942 remained unchanged until 2002. Thus, the legalisation in terms of abortion on demand took place more than a decade after the Swiss women's liberation movement had lost its momentum and given way to a loose alliance of autonomous groups, partially publicly financed projects and institutionalised advocates of gender equality. In the United Kingdom on the other hand, the Parliament adopted a law providing for the de-criminalisation of abortion within certain limits as early as 1967, at a time when the women's liberation movement was only in the process of forming. Precisely because the chronology of legal reform only partially merged into the mobilisation dynamics of the women's liberation movement, the United Kingdom and Switzerland are useful case studies, on the one hand for inves-tigating the role of abortion in the mobilisation dynamics of the women's liberation movement and, on the other hand, for considering the meanings and connotations that abortion took over time and in different contexts. We especially trace the interpretation of abortion through innovations in feminist thinking and practice after 1968.

A Note on Methodology

This chapter offers a comparative perspective on the women's liberation movement in Switzerland and the United Kingdom. If, in the 1970s, Western women's liberation movements everywhere stressed the universal-ity of their claims and thought 'sisterhood' to be 'global' (Morgan 1984), they were still acting in national contexts, and their reference frames dif-fered – be it in terms of protest traditions, or of legal or political systems. The history of feminisms therefore is neither a purely national nor an exclu-sively international matter, but has always had to look at both dimensions. In order to identify both national specificities and common features in a cross-country comparison, a tertium comperationis is required (Welskopp 1995: 345). In our case, it is offered by the concept of 'social movement', developed by historically informed social sciences.[1] Analytically taken, the women's liberation movements can be seen as collective actors: groups and networks characterised by a collective identity, which challenge the political and/or societal order in order to produce, prevent or reverse social change by means of public protest.[2] More precisely we are interested in mobilisa-tion dynamics and the question of how some topics become central to col-lective mobilisation while others do not. We do not think that certain issues are intrinsically tied to special groups but that mobilisation around certain issues is – at least up to a certain point – contingent. A historical perspec-tive on the perception of abortion in the women's liberation movement might shed light on the question of how collective actors take possession of a topic, as well as on the processes of its appropriation and reinterpretation. In light of these questions, we examine, first, the campaigns for the legalisation of abortion in the United Kingdom and Switzerland in the 1970s, as well as preliminary events and initiatives that offered a 'window of opportunity' (Ferree 2012: 11) and made abortion likely to become an issue on the political agenda. We then outline some central aspects of New Left thinking concerning the link between power and sexuality, ideas that circulated widely in Western protest cultures at the end of the 1960s. We argue that those ideas offered an important discursive opportunity for the reframing of abortion as the linchpin of women's emancipation. Finally, based on textual analysis of written documents and oral testimony, we profile feminists' reframing of abortion by contrasting it to socialist and liberal interpretations of abortion.

Campaigning for the Right to Chose

In order to determine the relationship between state regulation of reproduction and the mobilisation strategies of the women's liberation movement, we shall first turn to the United Kingdom, then to Switzerland.

The United Kingdom

As indicated, the legal reform initiative in the United Kingdom did not arise from feminist activities. When Liberal MP David Steel, who was then somewhat marginal, submitted the proposal for a new abortion law to Parliament in 1966, about a hundred national women's organisations existed (*The Observer* 14 February 1971) that were affiliated with trade unions, parties, churches or charities. However, the women's liberation movement – a network of mobilised networks, according to Friedhelm Neidhardt's definition of social movements (1985: 197) – occurred only after the Abortion Act entered into force in October 1967. The law, which applied to England, Wales and Scotland but not Northern Ireland, provided for legalisation of abortion in the first twenty-eight weeks of gestation, if performed by 'a registered medical practitioner' on condition of medical, ethical, or social indications.[3]

David Steel's reform initiative was not entirely plucked out of thin air. As early as the 1930s, objections had been raised to the restrictive provisions of the 1861 Offences Against the Person Act, which declared abortion illegal under all circumstances.[4] In 1936, parts of the women's liberation movement and the Labour Party, together with progressive members of the medical profession, founded a lobbying group to legalise abortion, the Abortion Law Reform Association (ALRA). Yet it was not until the 1960s that a widespread campaign in favour of legal reform could be initiated, not least of all because there was no consensus on this question among the members of the Labour Party, and the party's support of ALRA was therefore limited (cf. Thane 1990). Yet, as Stephen Brooke has illustrated, the ALRA activists' pro-abortion arguments were closely linked to class-specific discrimination right up until the 1960s: 'Speaking about sexuality through the abortion issue inevitably meant talking about working-class sexuality' (Brooke 2009: 78). In the 1960s, the association started intensifying its public relations work and developing regional networks. At the same time, it changed its argumentative approach: in calling for legal abortion, it no longer referred to overworked, working-class mothers with children but construed abortion as a problem of modern liberal society. This shift allowed collaboration with the Liberal MP David Steel, whom ALRA supported with its expertise. In 1966–1967, he succeeded in pushing through the legislative amendment by way of a private member's bill. Research attributes this political success to several factors, including David Steel's particular political abilities, the government's favourable attitude, the thalidomide scandal (a toxic medication that caused birth defects) and the skilful negotiating style of ALRA (cf. Lovenduski and Outshoorn 1986).

While it is clear that members of the women's rights movement during the 1930s were involved in the initial efforts to establish ALRA, it is still an open question as to what extent the women's liberation movement was involved in the reform process. The first autonomous women's groups emerged in Britain in the course of 1968. By 1969, there were around seventy local groups in London alone (Meehan 1990: 193).[5] In 1975, *The Times* (16 June 1975) refers to 1,500 groups nationwide, while the feminist monthly *Spare Rib* reached a readership of up to 32,000 in the 1970s (Bouchier 1983: 101). The first national workshop of what became the women's liberation movement took place in 1970 at Ruskin College in Oxford, where 600 women attended. The event contributed significantly to the national networking of the decentralised and mostly informally organised groups (Coote and Campbell 1982: 21ff.)· It revealed that the movement had found supporters throughout the British Isles by that point. From then on, national women's meetings were held annually until 1978, when the movement – which was losing its cohesion in the late 1970s – was no longer able to overcome the divergences between different feminist camps (Rees 2010).

The Ruskin College workshop attendees listed four central demands, which included free contraception and a regulation on abortion on demand alongside equal career opportunities and 24-hour childcare. In the years that followed, the movement defended the 1967 law, which was repeatedly attacked by pro-life groups. In 1972, a group within the women's liberation movement started focusing on the abortion issue and founded the National Abortion Campaign (NAC) in 1975. The NAC became a member of the Coordinating Committee in Defence of the 1967 Act, which until 1983 coordinated over fifty organisations, including liberal and conservative, labour and medical organisations, and conducted campaigns on an ad hoc basis. One highlight was a 1979 demonstration in London supported by trade unions as well as leftist and liberal parties, attended by some 100,000 people. The demonstration aimed at defending the law against attempts of the Conservative Party to reinstall a more restrictive regime on abortion (cf. Hoggart 2003: 141ff.). We can thus conclude that even though abortion had already been liberalised before the formation of the women's liberation movement in a law that was progressive for its time, the abortion issue was considered an important aspect of the feminist struggle. How significant an issue did the activists consider abortion to be? Before focusing on this question, we will now turn to Switzerland by retracing, first, the political discussions around abortion in the first half of the 1970s and, second and more precisely, by analysing the engagement of the women's liberation movement.

Switzerland

The Swiss penal code came into force on 1 January 1942. Before that date, criminal law had been a matter of the cantons and therefore heterogeneous, also with regards to abortion. On the matter of abortion, the penal code, which had been discussed for decades before being put to the vote in 1937, distinguished between 'abortion' – punishable because it was clandestine – and an 'interruption of pregnancy'. The later was considered to be legal in certain limited cases ('in order to save the life of the pregnant woman') as long as it was approved by medical expertise and carried out by a certified doctor. This position was considered to be progressive, especially against the repressive regulations in force in Nazi Germany and other totalitarian regimes of that time.[6] Three decades later, however, the medicalisation and stigmatisation, and women's ongoing deprivation of the right of decision were widely criticised. Furthermore, the cantons interpreted the legislation very differently, fuelling 'abortion tourism' between liberal and restrictive cantons.

The fight for legalised abortion in Switzerland was long and tough. It took place within the limits and opportunities offered by a Swiss semi-direct political system where the popular initiative was, and is, a legitimate means of legal change. Concerned citizens – individuals, groups, organisations, and parties – have the possibility to launch a campaign in order to present political issues to the people. The popular initiative was (and still is) an instrument of Swiss direct democracy by which groups that are not represented in the parliamentary process can suggest a concrete draft bill in order to change the existing law. According to the Swiss political system of that time, a popular initiative on the federal level required 50,000 signatures before being put to the popular vote (100,000 from 1977 onwards). Also, Swiss women were not considered full citizens until 1971. Therefore the campaign for legalisation was one of the very first popular initiatives in which women could participate as equals to male citizens. Until that moment, Swiss male voters had, by the majority, refused to concede the vote rights to women. Scarcely three weeks after the vote of 7 February 1971 on women's right to vote, which opened the way to real universal suffrage on the federal level, a cross-party committee launched the 'Popular Initiative for the Decriminalisation of Abortion' on 19 June 1971 (cf. *Tages-Anzeiger* 22 July 1971). By the end of November 1971, 59,000 people had already signed the brief and succinct text, which stated that 'No punishment may be imposed on grounds of abortion'.[7] The initiative, which was one of the first that Swiss women were allowed to sign, was submitted on 1 December 1971 (cf. Linder and Rielle 2010: 684). When it became clear in the mid 1970s that it did not stand a chance of getting a majority, the initiative committee withdrew the submission and instead prepared a more moderate legislative proposal, the 'Popular Initiative for the Regulation on Abortion on Demand'. It was put to a vote in 1977, but rejected by the majority of voters. One of the reasons for the defeat was the emotionalisation of the campaign, which was further heightened by a 1972 petition submitted by Catholic groups, 'Yes to Life – No to Abortion'. The committee Helping Instead of Killing (Helfen statt Töten) also entered the fray. It united so called 'pro-life' religious groups from the conservative protestant and Free Church milieu. The abortion rights initiative thus had an influential and resourceful opponent, which organised quickly and conducted effective counter-propaganda.[8] Still, the popular initiative of 1985 against abortion rights, launched by circles around Helping Instead of Killing, failed. In the following decade, numerous attempts to change the law were made by both opponents and advocates of the liberalisation of abortion, but it was only in 2002 that the electorate agreed on a change in the Swiss penal code. On 2 June 2002 the voters agreed with a clear majority of 71.2 per cent of votes in favour of a liberal regulation on abortion on demand, which entered into force on 1 October 2002. During the same vote, the people also had to decide on the 'pro-life' popular initiative, 'For mother and child – for the protection of the unborn child and help for its mother in need', which was soundly rejected with 81.8 per cent of votes opposed (cf. inter alia: Linder and Rielle 2010: 676).

In Switzerland, the women's liberation movement participated in discussions about legalisation of abortion, as was the case in Britain. The women's liberation movement in Switzerland emerged in the course of the 1968 movement. At the end of 1968 a group of young women provoked unrest by disrupting the 75th anniversary celebrations of the Zurich Women's Suffrage Association. By proclaiming, 'The right to vote is not enough', young female intruders questioned the effectiveness of traditional political instruments. In February 1969, the group appeared for the first time under the name of women's liberation movement (Frauenbefreiungsbewegung FBB) and called for equal rights beyond the right to vote (cf. Bucher and Schmucki 1995: 21). This was followed by the formation of feminist groups in the French- and Italian-speaking areas of Switzerland. These groups were loosely connected with each other (Castelletti 2007) and used provocative types of collective action, such as interfering in the elections of 'Miss Switzerland', throwing wet nappies during a session in the House of Parliament, or occupying a location intended for abolition in order to organise an improvised women's centre. They called for 'emancipation instead of equality' (*'Emanzipation statt Gleichberechtigung'* (Bucher and Schmucki 1995: 8)) and, beyond gender equality in legal terms, strived for a fundamental change in the hierarchical structure of gender relations (Broda, Joris and Müller 1998: 201).

Abortion was an issue to this new generation of feminists from the very beginning onwards. When the first initiative for the legalisation of abortion was launched in 1971, the women's liberation groups helped to collect signatures by campaigning in the street, in front of supermarkets, or in women's groups. A federal council commission tasked with revising abortion legislation was convened as early as December of that year, but since its experts could not agree on a draft, they proposed three variants: firstly, an indication-based option (in case of a medical indication: impunity only if the mother's life is at risk; on legal/ethical grounds: in cases of sexual offences; on eugenic grounds: in the event of foetal physical/mental impairment); secondly, an extended indication-based option (social and socio-economic indication) and, thirdly, a regulation on abortion on demand within the first twelve weeks (EKF 2001: Mappe 3.8). Large parts of the women's liberation movement rejected all three variants and returned to their original demand, namely the complete deletion of paragraphs 118–121 of the Swiss penal code (StGB).[9] In what framework did the feminists construe their demands?

New Left Interpretations of the Relationship between Sexuality, Oppression and Liberation

In order to historically situate women's liberation movements' understanding of abortion, we need to consider ideas of the New Left, which had been discussed in dissident leftist intellectual groups since the late 1950s and had a major influence on the 1968 movement in all Western countries.[10] In both Switzerland and the United Kingdom, early women's groups formed in the context of the upheavals of 1968. They introduced, and not without critical revision, New Left thinking into the women's liberation movement.

Psychoanalysts and scholars in the social sciences, especially education, provided the key words for New Left thinking. Intellectuals like Wilhelm Reich, Vera Schmidt or representatives of the Frankfurt School had pondered the reasons for social oppression as early as the 1930s. They had expanded the classic Marxist analysis of capitalism with findings from psychoanalysis and crowd psychology.[11] As they were initially written in the language of the host country, it was particularly the texts of the Frankfurt School members exiled in the United States that found a wide audience in the English-speaking world, before they were published in German and later in French. This was true for the 'Authoritarian Personality' studies led by Max Horkheimer, Theodor Adorno and Erich Fromm (English in 1950, German in 1973) as well as for Herbert Marcuse's 'The One-Dimensional Man' (English in 1964, German in 1967). Such texts were circulated simultaneously in Britain and Switzerland, which influenced the student New Left, pupils' movements as well as the first women's groups.

With regards to the connection between New Left social analysis and the abortion struggle of the women's liberation movement two points are of importance. On the one hand, the New Left postulated that the working class could no longer be seen as an engine of social change, but, as Marcuse put it, 'outcasts and outsiders' (Marcuse 1967: 267) would now have to perform this function. By the New Left's breaking away from its fixation on the working class, its focus shifted to conditions of oppression that were based on social categorisations other than class affiliation, namely skin colour and gender. This shift in focus made it possible to think of women as the subject of change.

On the other hand, the New Left shifted the focus to the concept of alienation, thereby breaking away from contemplating exploitive relationships that had traditionally been the interest of the Left. Following Marx's early work,[12] the New Left criticised human alienation from one another, which, they maintained, manifested in increasing isolation. In view of a growing disintegration of work processes, they called for the abolition of any hierarchical division of labour, not only in the area of production but also, very importantly, of reproduction. They strived for an alternative model that involved collectivising the education of children – for example in alternative childcare facilities – and overcoming the traditional division of labour within the family through the formation of communes. How were these elements of the cognitive orientation of the 1968 movement seized on by the women's liberation movement?

Feminist Construals of Abortion

The women's liberation movement identified with the assumption that social conditions could be changed only by way of a 'revolution of everyday life'. 'The personal is political' was the motto of the Anglo-Saxon women's liberation movement, echoed as *'Das Private ist politisch!'* in Zurich, Bern and Basel. The conclusion drawn from this was that oppression in relationships was not a personal misfortune but rather a reflection of inequalities in society as a whole. The fight against this inequality, it was hoped, would also improve personal relationships between women and men. When the sociologist and psychoanalyst Juliet Mitchell held an open university course in London in 1969 on the 'role of women in society', one female attendee declared that 'there was that feeling of militancy that I'd never experienced before ... I was no longer alone, but part of a movement which was primarily political but could be personal to me' (Coote and Campbell 1982: 17)· Declaring the personal political did not mean dragging partnership conflicts into the public eye but rather recognising that women's subordination, hitherto seen as individual destiny, was a structural problem to be combated. The women's liberation movement was thus not concerned with publicising individual marital conflicts but rather with exposing 'the microstructures of dominance' (Studer 2011: 24), questioning the boundaries between private and public, and thereby expanding the understanding of politics. In answer to the question 'what is politics?' one activist from the Swiss FBB said, 'Being a woman and standing up for that is political to me; how I live, how I treat my body and deal with my relationships; how I am with other women' (*Fraue-Zitig* 18/1980: 15). From the activists' point of view, only by talking about the asymmetries of gender relations in ostensibly private spheres was it possible to create an awareness that other women were experiencing the same issues and organise themselves in collectives. As one *Spare Rib* reader wrote in a letter to the editor: 'Until I read "Spare Rib", I thought I was the only woman who felt like this' (Anderson and Zinsser 1995: 497).

The thematisation of abortion in the women's liberation movement subscribed to this strategy of declaring personal matters political. The movement considered the legal and safe termination of pregnancy to be one of its central objectives. In so doing, feminists were concerned with 'far more than a paragraph' (FBB 1974: 25f.). From a feminist point of view, women's autonomy and right to decide about their bodies and their lives were at stake in a very general and fundamental way. It was in this, finally, that the feminist construal of abortion differed from a liberal or socialist interpretation. Even though within the women's liberation movement arguments from a variety of movement strands were adopted and temporary coalitions formed on the basis of partial agreement, the core of the feminist construal differed from that of other interpretations. In order to distinguish the feminist position, we will, lastly, present the values to which the various groups in each case adhered in their campaign to liberalise abortion.

The liberal construal that was adopted in the United Kingdom by David Steel and parts of ALRA, and in Switzerland by middle-class women's organisations and the initiative committee, referred to the personal rights of individuals, thereby connecting with traditional liberal demands. In the 1930s, middle-class efforts to legalise abortion were considered philanthropic activity and were also shaped by professionalisation efforts of medical practitioners. Social selection arguments also came into play, namely that legalisation of abortion would counteract the increase in socially disadvantaged families. There was less focus on such lines of argument in the 1960s, even though they could still be encountered even then. The key issue now, though, was the protection and autonomy of the middle-class individual and the adoption of a restrictive regulation that no longer corresponded with actual opinions on and practices of abortion. From the point of view of the liberal pro-abortion camp, professionally performed abortion was preferable to countless clandestine and illegal abortions, as it was the only way that compliance with the law could be guaranteed. State prohibition of abortion was questioned because it constituted a violation of privacy and therefore a violation of an important pillar of middle socio-economic class order.

The socialist construal was traditionally espoused by leftist parties and groups such as the National Abortion Campaign in the United Kingdom and the LMR (Ligue Marxiste Révolutionnaire) in French-speaking Switzerland. This view did not, however, prevent the LMR from voting for the regulation on abortion on demand in 1977, as this would bring about at least a slight improvement.[13] In the name of equality, these groups put abortion in the context of the labour movement struggle. From that point of view, liberalised abortion was one step towards improving the living conditions of lower-class women. Prohibition of abortion was construed as a class privilege of the bourgeoisie, as middle-class women had ways and means available to get around the prohibition, whereas socially deprived women were victims of class injustice on the one hand and exposed to health risks on the other.

Parts of the women's liberation movement were quite supportive of these construals, for instance when they declared themselves in favour of the national health system covering the costs of abortion. Yet from a feminist point of view, it was not only a question of social equality. The principal imperative of the women's liberation movement in the fight over abortion was women's freedom to decide, independently of any authorities (husbands, doctors, lawyers or clergy), whether they wished to continue a pregnancy to term or terminate it. The slogans thus ran 'A woman's right to choose' and 'Children or no children, we alone decide!' (*Neue Zürcher Nachrichten* 17 March 1975).

Even though the FBB, which saw at least some slight progress in the regulation on abortion on demand, campaigned for corresponding legislation, it did so with substantial reservations. For its rallying cry was not legalisation of abortion subject to certain conditions, but rather the liberalisation of abortion. Construing the legal system in itself as androcentric and misogynist, they saw the abortion ban as a means of suppressing female self-determination and, thus, as an instrument of the patriarchy. To summarise, the women's liberation movement located the abortion issue within the context of a feminist critique of society. This is particularly apparent in the case of Switzerland, as the activists here wanted to use the initiative as a means for 'discussion (both within and outside the FBB) of the abortion issue in connection with the oppression of women as a whole'.[14] In expounding the problems of the abortion ban, they were concerned with 'recognizing the connections between personal experience and social situation'.[15] Thus, what was formerly assigned to the private sphere, namely female physical and life experiences, became politicised in the course of the discussions about liberalising abortion.

Conclusion

We have considered the relationship between the women's liberation movement and abortion with regards to two aspects, namely the importance of abortion legislation in the mobilisation process of the women's liberation movement in Switzerland and the United Kingdom, and the new perspective it brought to the debate about legalising abortion.

Concerning the British situation (where abortion legislation had already been liberalised in 1967), in terms of mobilisation dynamics, we have shown that the National Abortion Campaign assumed great importance in the women's liberation movement given its success in uniting proponents of different currents of feminism. Yet the strategic divergences between proponents of radical-autonomous and those of socialist positions within feminism also determined the discussions within the National Abortion Campaign, making for clearly visible and noticeable conflicts of objectives within feminism (Hoggart 2003: 165f.). A broader look, which is outside the scope of this chapter, would also have made clear that even though allies outside the women's liberation movement (such as parts of the trade unions and socialist parties) were prepared to back the feminist groups regarding this issue, they could not be counted upon in the same way for support in other matters. And lastly, even though the National Abortion Campaign in the United Kingdom was the only action committee besides the women's emergency call service Women's Aid to be organised at a national level, the women's liberation movement treated the abortion issue merely as one issue among many. In the first half of the 1970s, protests against initiatives by conservative politicians and pro-life lobbyists accompanied the emergence of women's groups, but those protests' contribution to the networking of these groups was patchy. The abortion question was thus an important but not a constitutive element of the women's liberation movement in the United Kingdom.

The same conclusion can be reached when it comes to Switzerland, albeit for different reasons. It is true that the cantonal groups of the women's liberation movement came in contact with each other (and with non-feminist groups) particularly in dealing with the abortion ban, thereby shaping the development of the liberalisation process. Here too, however, a broad mobilisation of the women's liberation movement such as could be discerned in Germany or France failed, not least because a national movement for the long term could not be established.

Particularly in the development of debates on the legalisation of abortion in Switzerland, the political system played an important role. Direct democracy was (and continues to be) an important part of the political culture of Switzerland (Linder and Rielle 2010: 675). Political science studies therefore assume that social movements in Switzerland would thus have a structurally conservative effect, because any member of the Swiss electorate can launch a popular initiative to demand an amendment to the Federal Constitution (Epple-Gass 1991). It can be argued, however, that Switzerland's women's liberation movement was in no way characterised by structural conservatism. Even though it participated in petitioning, it nevertheless criticised the medium of the popular initiative and sought other ways of pursuing its agenda, thereby rekindling the political realm in principle and influencing it in real terms. The approach of the women's liberation movement is thus characterised by its simultaneous treading on an institutionally provided path as well as one based on scandalising and on breaking taboos in the public sector.[16]

If we try to generalise from our case studies, it becomes apparent that the feminist construal of abortion went beyond liberal and socialist reasoning for decriminalisation. The women's liberation movements aimed at making the abortion ban a matter of general concern, namely the question of sexualised and gendered power relations, which revealed itself in the freedom of choice or the lack thereof. Whether in the slogan 'My body belongs to me' or in the title of the feminist health guide 'Our Bodies, Ourselves', the focus was on autonomy over one's own body, and thus the right to self-determination. With the slogan 'the personal is political', however, the position of the women's liberation movement departed from liberal pro-choice demands. Whereas the latter held to the stable, socially better-off family that had to be protected from state intervention, the feminists fundamentally questioned the family as the nucleus of society as well as the function assigned to women (as mothers) in it. The feminist argumentation in favour of abortion also differed from a socialist pro-choice position. Women's liberation activists were not concerned with preserving a sphere in which privacy had to be protected from prying eyes from outside but, on the contrary, with directing people's attention to the relationship between people, particularly between men and women, and declaring what went on there a social and political matter. As is illustrated by the thematisation of abortion in the British and Swiss Women's liberation movements, 'recognizing the connections between personal experience and social situation'[17] is part of the legacy of the new women's liberation movement even in places where the legislative process (in the course of which abortion was liberalised) preceded or outlasted the women's liberation movement.

Kristina Schulz is a Senior Lecturer in Contemporary and Migration History at the University of Berne, Switzerland. She received her PhD from the Universities of Paris 7 (France) and Bielefeld (Germany). She is a specialist of Western feminist history in comparative perspective and is the author of several articles and books, including (with Leena Schmitter and Sarah Kiani) *Frauenbewegung: Die Schweiz seit 1968* (Baden 2014), a guide to sources and archives concerning the Swiss Women's liberation movement. For the past few years she has also been looking at the history of migration and exile through a gendered lens.

Kristina Schulz, PhD, is Senior Lecturer for Contemporary History and Migration History at the University of Berne, Switzerland. She is a specialist of Western feminist history in comparative perspective and is the author of a book on the French and German women's liberation movement: *'Der lange Atem der Provokation.' Die Frauenbewegung in der Bundesrepublik und in Frankreich (1968–1976)*. She has also edited a special number on Swiss women's liberation (*Schweizerische Zeitschrift für Geschichte* 57 (2007). Together with Leena Schmitter and Sarah Kiani she published a source and archive guide about the Swiss Women's Liberation Movement fron the Sixties to the present (*Frauenbewegung: Die Schweiz seit 1968*, Baden 2014).

Leena Schmitter is adjunct researcher at the chair for Swiss History at the University of Bern, Switzerland and is currently media spokesperson at the largest Swiss trade union. She received her PhD from the University of Bern in 2014. For the past few years she has been working on the women's liberation movement in Europe and the history of feminisms in Switzerland. Her areas of expertise include new political history, history of sexuality and the body, as well as gender studies and feminist theory.

Notes

1. Social Movement Research has developed enormously since the 1980s. For an introduction see McAdam, McCarthy and Zald (1988) and on comparison: Klandermans (1993) and McAdam, McCarthy and Zald (1996). The historical dimension is at the centre of Charles Tilly's works, especially Tilly and Wood (2009).
2. For a conceptual framework see Raschke (1985); Dalton and Kuechler (1990) and recently Pettenkofer (2010).
3. The National Archives. Abortion Act 1967. Retrieved 4 May 2011 from http://www.legislation.gov.uk/ukpga/1967/87/contents/enacted
4. Cf. Brooke (2001). In 1929 the Act was supplemented with the addition that abortion was legal if it allowed the mother's life to be saved.
5. On the women's liberation movement in the United Kingdom, see also the summaries in Bouchier (1983) as well as the early reconstruction based on verbal reports by Coote and Campbell (1982) and Mitchell (1981).
6. We would like to thank Thierry Delessert, University of Lausanne, for the advice given on this paragraph.
7. Cf. wording of initiative text retrieved 17 May 2011 from Swiss Federal Chancellery website: http://www.admin.ch/ch/d/pore/vi/vis103t.html
8. Cf. inter alia: Lenzin (2000: 148).
9. FBB. Document without title or date [1971]. Schweizerisches Sozialarchiv Zürich, Ar 465.10.1, Mappe 2.
10. On the cognitive orientation of the New Left, cf. Gilcher-Holtey (1995: 44ff). On the New Left in the United Kingdom: Davis (2008: 45–55). The New Left in

Switzerland has not been systematically researched. Generally, however, the protests that flared up in many places throughout Switzerland around 1968 were oriented to the movements of their larger neighbouring countries. On 1968 in Switzerland, cf. inter alia Peter (2008); Schaufelbuehl and Pereira (2009); Schär et al. (2008); Hebeisen et al. (2008).

11. Cf. especially Schmidt (1969); Reich (1966, original in parts 1933, England 1945); Marcuse (1964, German 1967, French 1968); Horkheimer et al. (1936); Adorno (1969).

12. In particular: Karl Marx and Friedrich Engels. *Die deutsche Ideologie* (1845/46) (first published in 1932).

13. See LMR, 'Pour le droit à l'avortement! Pour une maternité désirée' September 1977, in Gosteli Stiftung – Archiv zur Geschichte der schweizerischen Frauenbewegung Worblaufen, ASDAC/SGRA, Schachtel 9: Campagne 1977–1979.

14. FBB, 'Zur Abtreibungskampagne' no date, in: Gosteli Stiftung – Archiv zur Geschichte der schweizerischen Frauenbewegung Worblaufen, 601, Aktivitäten, Frauenbefreiungsbewegung, 1978–1983, Dossier 24–01.

15. Handwritten note, 'Das Privat[e] ist politisch Thesen', no date, Schweizerisches Sozialarchiv Zürich, Ar 465.11.1, Mappe 1.

16. A dissertation project by Leena Schmitter (2014) was conducted as part of a study, led by Kristina Schulz, to analyse the women's liberation movement in Switzerland and is devoted to these issues, among others.

17. Handwritten note, 'Das Privat[e] ist politisch Thesen', no date, Schweizerisches Sozialarchiv Zürich, Ar 465.11.1, Mappe 1.

References

Adorno, T. 1969. *Der autoritäre Charakter. Studien über Autorität und Vorurteil.* Amsterdam: Verlag De Munter.

Anderson, B. and J. Zinsser. 1995. 'Die Frauenbefreiungsbewegung (Women's Lib)', in B. Anderson and J. Zinsser (eds), *Eine eigene Geschichte. Frauen in Europa, Volume 2: Aufbruch. Vom Absolutismus zur Gegenwart.* Frankfurt am Main: Fischer Taschenbuch Verlag, pp. 490–615.

Anton, L., Y. Mitobe and K. Schulz. 2012. 'Politics of Reproduction in a Divided Europe: Abortion, Protest Movements, and State Intervention after World War II', in K. Fahlenbach, et al. (eds), *The Establishment Responds. Power, Politics, and Protest since 1945.* New York: Palgrave Macmillan, pp. 103–20.

Bouchier, D. 1983. *The Feminist Challenge. The Movement for Women's Liberation in Britain and the USA.* London: Macmillan.

Broda, M., E. Joris and R. Müller. 1998. 'Die alte und die neue Frauenbewegung', in M. König (ed.), *Dynamisierung und Umbau. Die Schweiz in den 60er und 70er Jahren.* Zürich: Chronos, pp. 201–26.

Brooke, S. 2001. 'A New World for Women? Abortion Law Reform in Britain during the 1930s', *American Historical Review* 106: 431–59.

————. 2009. 'The Sphere of Sexual Politics: The Abortion Law Reform Association, 1930s to 1960s', in N. Crowson, M. Hilton and J. Mc Kay (eds), *NGOs in Contemporary Britain. Non-state Actors and Politics since 1945*. New York, Basingstoke: Palgrave Macmillan, pp. 77–94.

Bucher, J. and B. Schmucki. 1995. *FBB. Fotogeschichte der Frauenbefreiungsbewegung Zürich*. Zürich: Limmat Verlag.

Castelletti, S. 2007. 'Les mouvements féministes tessinois face aux mutations historiques', *Schweizerische Zeitschrift für Geschichte* 57: 296–309.

Coote, A. and B. Campbell. 1982. *Sweet Freedom. The Struggle for Women's Liberation*. London: Pan Books.

Dalton R.J. and M. Kuechler (eds). 1990. *Challenging the Political Order. New Social and Political Movements in Western Democracies*. Cambridge: Cambridge University Press.

Davis, M. 2008. 'The Origins of the British New Left', in M. Klimke and J. Scharloth (eds), *1968 in Europe. A History of Protest and Activism, 1956–1977*. New York, Basingstoke: Palgrave Macmillan, pp. 45–56.

Eidgenössische Kommission für Frauenfragen. 2001. 'Frauen – Macht – Geschichte. Zur Geschichte der Gleichstellung in der Schweiz (1848–2000)'. Retrieved 11 March 2013 from EKF database.

Epple-Gass, R. 1991. 'Neue Formen politischer Mobilisierung: (k)eine Herausforderung der Schweizer Demokratie?', *Annuaire Suisse de Science Politique. Schweizerisches Jahrbuch für politische Wissenschaft* 31: 151–71.

'FBB, Recht auf den eigenen Bauch'. 1974. *Focus* 50. Schweizerisches Sozialarchiv Zürich, Ar 65.11.1, Mappe 4.

Ferree, M.M. 2012. *Varieties of Feminism: German Gender Politics in Global Perspective*. Stanford: Stanford University Press.

Gilcher-Holtey, I. 1995. *'Die Phantasie an die Macht.' Mai 68 in Frankreich*. Frankfurt: Suhrkamp.

Hebeisen, E., et al. (eds). 2008. *Zürich 68. Kollektive Aufbrüche ins Ungewisse*. Baden: Hier + Jetzt.

Hoggart, L. 2003. *Feminist Campaigns for Birth Control and Abortion Rights in Britain*. New York: Thed Ewin Mellen Press.

Horkheimer, M., et al. 1936. *Studien über Autorität und Familie*. Paris: Librairie Félix Alcan.

Klandermans, B. 1993. 'A Theoretical Framework for Comparisons of Social Movement Participation', *Sociological Forum* 8(3): 383–402.

Lenzin, D. 2000. *Die Sache der Frauen. OFRA und die Frauenbewegung in der Schweiz*. Zürich: Rotpunktverlag.

Linder, W. and Y. Rielle (eds). 2010. *Handbuch der eidgenössischen Volksabstimmungen 1848–2007*. Bern: Haupt.

Lovenduski J. and J. Outshoorn (eds). 1986. *The New Politics of Abortion*. London: Sage.

Marcuse, H. 1964. *The One-Dimensional Man*. London: Routledge & Kegan Paul.

————. 1967. *Der eindimensionale Mensch. Studien zur Ideologie der fortgeschrittenen Industriegesellschaften*. Darmstadt/Neuwied: Luchterhand.

McAdam, D., J. McCarthy and M.N. Zald. 1988. 'Social movements', in N.J. Smelser (ed.), *Handbook of Sociology*. Beverly Hills: Sage Publications, pp. 695–737.

_____. (eds). 1996. *Comparative Perspectives on Social Movements. Political Opportunities, Mobilizing Structures, and Cultural Framings*. Cambridge: Cambridge University Press.

McBride, D. (ed.). 2001. *Abortion Politics, Women's Movements, and the Democratic State. A Comparative Study of State Feminism*. Oxford: Oxford University Press.

Meehan, E. 1990. 'British Feminism from the 1960s to the 1980s', in H.L. Smith (ed.), *British Feminism in the Twentieth Century*. Amherst, MA: University of Massachusetts Press, pp. 189–204.

Mitchell, J. 1981. *Frauenbewegung – Frauenbefreiung*. Frankfurt am Main: Ullstein.

Morgan, R. (ed.). 1984. *Sisterhood is Global. The International Women's Movement Anthology*. New York: Doubleday and Anchor Books.

Neidhardt, F. 1985. 'Einige Ideen zu einer allgemeinen Theorie sozialer Bewegungen', in S. Hradil (ed.), *Sozialstruktur im Umbruch*. Opladen: Leske + Budrich, pp. 193–204.

Peter, N. 2008. 'Switzerland', in M. Klimke and J. Scharloth (eds), *1968 in Europe. A History of Protest and Activism, 1956–1977*. New York, Basingstoke: Palgrave Macmillan, pp. 229–37.

Pettenkofer, A. 2010. *Radikaler Protest, Zur soziologischen Theorie sozialer Bewegungen*. Frankfurt am Main: Campus.

Raschke, J. 1985. *Soziale Bewegungen*. Frankfurt am Main: Campus.

Rees, J. 2010. 'A Look Back in Anger: The Women's Liberation Movement in 1978', *Women's History Review* 19: 337–56.

Reich, W. 1966. *Die sexuelle Revolution: zur charakterlichen Selbststeuerung des Menschen*. Frankfurt: Europäische Verlaganstalt.

Schär, B.C., et al. (eds). 2008. *Bern 68. Lokalgeschichte eines globalen Aufbruchs – Ereignisse und Erinnerungen*. Baden: Hier + Jetzt.

Schaufelbuehl, J.M. and N. Pereira. 2009. *1968–1978. Ein bewegtes Jahrzehnt in der Schweiz. Une décennie mouvementée en Suisse*. Zürich: Chronos Verlag.

Schmidt, V. 1969. *Antiautoritäre Erziehung und Kinderanalyse*. Hamburg/Berlin/Havanna: Zerschlagt das bürgerliche Copyright.

Schmitter, L. 2014. 'Die öffentliche Deklaration des Privaten. Die Neue Frauenbewegung und die Legalisierung des Schwangerschaftsabbruchs in der Schweiz (1971–2002)', Ph.D. dissertation. Bern: University of Bern.

Studer, B. 2011. *1968 und die Formung des feministischen Subjekts*. Wien: Picus Verlag.

Thane, P. 1990. 'The Women of the British Labour Party and Feminism 1906–1945', in H.L. Smith (ed.), *British Feminism in the Twentieth Century*. Amherst, MA: University of Massachusetts Press, pp. 124–43.

Tilly, C. and L. Wood. 2009. *Social Movements 1768–2008*. Boulder: Paradigm.

Welskopp, T. 1995. 'Stolpersteine auf dem Königsweg. Methodenkritische Anmerkungen zum internationalen Vergleich in der Gesellschaftsgeschichte', *Archiv für Sozialgeschichte* 35: 339–67.

Part II

Anti-abortion Rights Activism, Movements, Strategies, and Protest Logics

Chapter 4

Contesting Abortion Rights in Contemporary Italy
Discourses and Practices of Pro-life Activism

by Claudia Mattalucci

Elena is sixty-two and lives in a town in northern Italy. Her mother died when she was a teenager, leaving eight children orphans. While she was still at school, Elena started working; thanks to this job, she later enrolled at university. She then married and had three children. In the meantime, she graduated and got a job as a religious education teacher. For years, Elena told her students that she could have been aborted. Since childhood she has been through very hard times, but this, she says, is the reason why she gained great respect for life and a strong motivation to help others. Elena is now retired and works as a volunteer at the local pro-life help centre, a facility that helps women facing the difficulty of an unwanted pregnancy. She also volunteers for Defending Life with Mary, an association that takes care of burying 'babies who die before they are born'. 'At the pro-life help centre' she says, 'we take care of children who need to be born. At Defending Life with Mary we care for children who have died. Then there are groups that comfort mothers who have had abortions, like 'Rachel's Vineyard', an association that organ- ises psycho-spiritual retreats for 'healing the wounds of abortion'. One of Elena's daughters is finishing her degree in psychology, and Elena hopes that one day she will work in this field. Opposing abortion, from the point of view of this activist, requires multiple forms of action: from social and charitable interventions carried out by the pro-life help centres, to reparative interventions such as the ceremonies intended to honour the dead bodies of aborted 'babies', and paths of post-abortion healing, addressing and treating the psychological effects of abortion on women (and men) who have experienced it.

In Italy, while the activities of pro-life help centres have an established history, the burial of abortion remains and post-abortion healing are newly introduced practices. Defending Life with Mary was formed in the late 1990s, and although activists' sensitivity to the psychological consequences of abortion emerged in the first half of the 1990s (Garrone 1998), only in the 2000s were the first conferences organised and specific pathways of healing singled out.

In this chapter, I will analyse the strategies and discourses used in pro-life activism to challenge abortion, based on ethnographic research conducted in northern Italy between 2009 and 2013.[1] In the first part, I will reconstruct the emergence of the Italian pro-life movement in the years when abortion was legalised, and briefly describe its practices and protest logics. In the second part, I will focus on the two dominant discourses of contemporary pro-life activism: one that centres on the embryos/foetuses as 'unborn children' and another that centres on women (and men) as 'victims of abortion'. I therefore take into consideration the burial of abortion remains and post-abortion healing as practices based, respectively, on the first and the second discourse. Both are carried out by organisations that, despite being close to the pro-life movement, are not part of it. I will argue that such practices, which both stem from Catholicism, are based on specific cultural constructions of subjectivity, guilt and pain associated with abortion. The burial of embryo and foetal remains and the paths for healing are not only aimed at the 'salvation' of maternal and foetal subjects, but are also strategies to oppose the law. For pro-lifers, the funerals for 'unborn children' and the testimonies of women and men wounded by abortion serve as moral injunctions to influence social policies and individual behaviours, contesting the idea that abortion is a right.

The Legalisation of Abortion and the Rise of Pro-life Activism

In Italy, Law 194 regulates the voluntary termination of pregnancy. Prior to its approval in 1978, abortion was a crime. During the 1970s, the press began to emphasise the deaths caused by illegal abortions, and several demonstrations took place. In 1973, the Information Centre for Sterilisation and

Abortion was founded in Milan to assist women seeking terminations. Up to that time, safe terminations were only available to upper- and middle-class women, who could afford to go abroad or pay the expensive services of a complacent gynaecologist in their own country. Pro-choice activists started performing abortions in private centres at low prices as a form of civil disobedience (Sciré 2008). In 1976, an industrial accident that took place in Seveso (northern Milan) caused the leakage of a cloud of dioxin, a substance considered highly teratogenic. The Ministers of Health and Justice subsequently authorised the first voluntary terminations. Progressively, the decriminalisation of abortion gained public support, and diverse political subjects presented proposals for revising the fascist law, which was still in force. In catholic circles, the idea to create a national pro-life movement gradually gained ground to counteract the actions of the feminist movement, pro-choice political parties and the press. In 1975, the first pro-life help centre was opened in Florence, and in later years the first local movements were formed. Since its constitution, the Italian pro-life movement has proven to be very active: it prepared an alternative bill to the one in discussion in the House of Parliament, campaigned among politicians, and promoted initiatives to raise public awareness, etc. (Pirovano 1981). In 1978, however, Parliament passed Law 194: 'Norms for the social protection of motherhood and the voluntary termination of pregnancy'.[2]

The approval of the law displeased various components of civil society and politics. The Catholic Church expressed strong condemnation of the law, and invited all believers to actively engage in the defence of life. In 1981, a referendum was held. The Radical Party – secular and pro-choice – promoted a revision designed to make access to abortion easier. The pro-life movement, in contrast, proposed to narrow the limits of the Act's applicability. At the polls, however, the electorate confirmed its support for the existing law. Despite losing the referendum, the movement continued to be the main political subject on the Italian pro-life scene.[3] Abandoning legal pathways, it has concentrated its actions on two fronts: the cultural and political front of local movements, which are aimed at the dissemination of a 'culture of life' through cultural, educational and political initiatives;[4] and the socio-charitable front of the pro-life help centres that materially and emotionally support women who find themselves in difficulty coping with an unwanted pregnancy, endeavouring to 'save babies from abortion'.[5]

After the referendum, the pro-life movement kept a low profile. Between the 1990s and the early 2000s, however, the political weight of its position grew, and the protest logic against abortion gained visibility. Several factors contributed to this change: the renewed importance of Catholic ideology as a factor in political consensus, lower visibility of feminist activism in the public arena, debates related to medically assisted procreation, experimentation on embryo stem cells, abortion drugs, etc. (Calloni 2001; Hanafin 2007). Representatives of the government and institutions have repeatedly recognised the subjectivity and the right to life of the unborn. In 1996 the National Committee on Bioethics published an opinion on the 'Identity and status of the human embryo' which affirmed 'the moral duty to treat the human embryo, from fertilisation on, according to the criteria of respect and protection which must be adopted towards human individuals, the same which are commonly attributed to personhood'. In 2004, Parliament passed a law on medically assisted procreation (Law 40), which protects the embryo as a 'subject of the procreative process' (Mattalucci 2013). As was the case for the law on abortion, the medically assisted procreation law was followed by a referendum. The law is particularly restrictive,[6] and the four referendum questions proposed wanted to grant freer access to available techniques. With the support of the Catholic Church, the pro-life movement organised a campaign to promote abstention. The quorum was not reached, a result that represented a victory for pro-lifers and made up for the defeat in 1981.

Today, the pro-life movement occupies the centre of the Italian pro-life scene. Although it is non-denominational and apolitical by statute, it has the approval of the Episcopal Conference.[7] Compared to other pro-life subjects, it has a less aggressive communication style that tends to highlight 'the wonder of life' rather than 'the horror of abortion'. In the political debate over ethical issues, its members tend to mediate and assume moderate positions. In the Italian pro-life universe, there are other organisations that prefer stronger forms of antagonism, such as the renewed request to repeal Law 194, prayer marathons in front of the hospitals where terminations are practised, the use of powerful symbols such as bloody images of foetuses in pieces, etc. There are also groups and individuals that, while not in contrast to the pro-life movement, maintain a separate identity. Among these, there are the two associations that I will describe below.

Victims of Abortion

Before moving on to examine what activists call 'funerals for unborn children' and post-abortion healing as forms of protest to the right to abortion, I would like to focus on two dominant discourses in contemporary pro-life activism: one that centres on the embryo/foetus as a child, and another that centres on women (and increasingly, men) as 'victims of abortion'. In presenting these beliefs, I do not discuss their validity. My goal is to provide a better understanding of contemporary pro-life protest logic and their construction of foetal and female subjectivity.

The first discourse has a long history. Since its establishment, the pro-life movement has embraced the mission of protecting the 'conceived child that is not born yet'. For pro-lifers, the *concepito* (literally, 'conceptus') is a human being, with the same rights and the same value as a born child. Based on the cultural and political initiatives carried out by the movement during the period of time in which I conducted my fieldwork, essentially two versions of this discourse emerge. The first uses arguments drawn from embryology, to show the ontological continuity between the embryo, the child, and the adult it will become. The description of the development from conception to birth is always accompanied by images that isolate the embryo/foetus from the mother's body.[8] The movement favours the use of pictures that emphasise the 'beauty' of prenatal life, such as the well-known photographs by the Swedish medical photographer Lennart Nilsson. In the past the movement translated and distributed *The Silent Scream*, a documentary produced in the United States in the 1980s showing a voluntary termination of pregnancy by ultrasound (Petchesky 1987). Today, however, the use of violent images, such as photographs of late abortions, is rare and generally discouraged by the movement's leadership.

A further argument centred on the embryo/foetus as a child refers to human rights. For pro-life activists, the unborn is a 'person' with the dignity and rights of every other human being. It is 'one of us', a term used to name an initiative launched at EU level to request the suspension of financing all activities involving the destruction of human embryos.[9] The reference to the embryo/foetus as 'one of us' appeals to a sense of shared humanity that is the basis for recognising the unborn as a subject with rights, and identifying with it. From the point of view of the initiators of the campaign, identification is the raison d'être of physicians' conscientious objection, of the 'sacrifice' of mothers who decide to continue their pregnancy despite prenatal screening providing positive results, and of the pain of women affected by the experience of abortion.

For pro-lifers, embryos and foetuses are not the only victims of abortion. Even 'mothers' are victims. In addition to the discourse that is centred on the unborn as a child, in the 1990s and especially in the 2000s, a new discourse that was centred on women progressively gained ground. It stated that abortion is wrong because it affects mothers. Pregnancy, particularly if unexpected, produces a state of fragility, ambivalence and emotional instability in women that undermines their ability to choose. Often their partners, or in the case of minors their parents, do not support them. In clinics and hospitals, signals of ambivalence are deliberately ignored. Thus, according to activists, the very people and institutions that should guarantee women's right to choose, 'impose' unwanted abortions that women will end up regretting for the rest of their lives.

Compared to what happened in the United States, Canada, or in other European countries (among others, see Hopkins, Reicher and Saleem 1996; Lee 2003), the debate in Italy on the psychological consequences of abortion is recent in pro-life circles. The first round table devoted to this subject was held in Rome in 2007.[10] Since then several events on the negative effects of abortion on women's mental health (often described through the language of trauma) have been held all around the country.[11] News and articles written by psychologists, doctors or simple pro-life volunteers appear regularly in the newsletters of local movements. Due to extensive disclosure, in pro-life circles the conviction is now rooted that abortion is a traumatic event, a harbinger of serious psychological consequences that primarily affect women but also their partners and other relatives. From pro-lifers' point of view, the traumatic effects of the voluntary termination of pregnancy are strengthened by the political and cultural negation of post-abortion syndrome, made evident by the lack of epidemiological data regarding Italy. Moreover, the lack of recognition of the consequences that abortion has on women's mental health prevents public opinion from questioning, if not the law itself, at least its application. According to pro-life activists, as Law 194 grants the possibility for the voluntary termination of pregnancy to protect women's physical and mental health, if abortion itself is a health risk, the proper application of the law should require women to be made aware of the potential risks of the procedure (Pittino and Buongiovanni 2011).

The discourses on the unborn as a child and on women as victims of abortion are connected to the practices that I will describe below: the burial of abortion remains and post-abortion healing. In describing these practices, I will focus on two specific associations: Defending Life with Mary and Rachel's Vineyard. The first was established in 1999, and today it is present in sixteen out of twenty regions. The association signs agreements with hospitals that engage in the voluntary interruption of pregnancy in order to periodically collect the remains. It also signs agreements with municipalities to grant the use of reserved plots in cemeteries. Once it has signed the agreement and obtained a plot, the local committee of the association starts celebrating Catholic funerals, which usually take place once a month.

Rachel's Vineyard is an association that organises post-abortion healing retreats. It was founded in the United States in the mid 1990s.[12] In Italy, the first retreat was held in 2010. The retreats last for a weekend and take place twice a year. Through spiritual exercises and moments of re-elaboration in groups, the participants are invited to express grief and pain, entering into communication with 'their inner voice', other participants, team members and God.[13] Rachel's Vineyard is not the only association in Italy that deals with post-abortion recovery. There are other pro-life organisations and in-dependent professionals (psychologists, family counsellors, etc.) who offer individual or group healing.[14]

I have pointed out elsewhere that, although the pro-life movement has a deeply Catholic militant base, it publicly claims to have a non-denomi-national identity (Mattalucci 2012). In contrast, both Defending Life with Mary and Rachel's Vineyard have an explicit link with the Catholic religion. The first is an association of the faithful, and its president is a priest. The second carries an 'apostolate' with the imprimatur of the Catholic Church. During the retreats there is always a priest present.

Funerals for the Unborn

The appointment is at the hospital morgue at 8:30. The president, the vice president, the secretary and another volunteer have per-mission to go into the downstairs room where the 'small coffins' are prepared. A hearse waits at the entrance. They go inside carry-ing two white cardboard boxes decorated by the volunteers. The containers holding the abortion remains and the aborted foetuses wrapped in 'sheets' of cellophane will be placed in the 'small cof-fins' and carried upstairs. Today there are thirty-nine 'children': four miscarriages, twenty voluntary terminations of pregnancy and fifteen 'ovular abortions'.[15] Near the entrance gate, in a room used as a chapel, an altar is covered with white satin and bunches of white chrysanthemums. Volunteers come up from the morgue carrying the two boxes. In the meantime, a couple arrives. Follow-ing miscarriage, they have lost their baby. He will be buried today along with the other remains. The president of the local commit-tee begins to recite the rosary. In the meantime, another couple arrives. They remain at the door and join in with the prayer. Then the priest comes. He devotes a few words to the mystery of these lives ended before they had begun. Then, he recites the rite for the children who died without baptism. The celebration concludes with a song. The small boxes, closed with a white satin ribbon and decorated with flowers, are delivered to the operators of the funeral home. The hearse moves towards the cemetery, where about thirty people are reciting the rosary. Among them are members of the association, people supporting its work and two nuns; there is also a woman with a baby in a pram. She has had three miscarriages. At first she came for her own 'children', and then she continued to come. The hearse moves slowly along the path followed by the little crowd. The area granted by the municipality is covered with white gravel. Small marble plaques are aligned, each reporting the date of burial. In the centre on a pedestal there is a Madonna and child, beneath a small plaque bearing the name of the association. Although the local committee began to perform burials in 2000, the oldest tombstones are from 2008. The land granted by the city measures a few square meters, and after five years the 'bodies' are exhumed to make room for others. On some graves there are flowers, toys, framed pictures, or messages for the dead 'children'.

The people gather round. The priest offers a new speech and says words of sympathy for the parents. Then he proceeds with the celebration. Finally, he sprinkles the 'coffins' and signals the workers to proceed with the burial. The boxes are laid in the grave and covered with earth. With a final prayer the ceremony ends. Some of the volunteers pay their condolences and say a word of comfort to the two couples. Gradually the group disperses.

The ceremony I described took place in June 2013. The local hospital was one of the first to sign an agreement with Defending Life with Mary. Women who undergo voluntary termination of pregnancy or have spontaneous abortions are asked to fill out a form agreeing to burial by the association. The regional regulations concerning burial plans require that for pregnancy terminations, either voluntary, spontaneous or medical and regardless of gestational age, the hospital inform the parents about the opportunity to request the remains for private burial. In the event that such a request is not submitted, the remains, which prior to the approval of this regulation in 2007 were disposed of as special waste, are treated as recognisable anatomical parts, namely, cremated or buried in special areas within a cemetery.[16] If the hospital has an agreement with the association, the latter carries out the burial and bears all its costs. Defending Life with Mary buries the remains of abortion that are not requested by 'parents' for private burial. Most of them are from first trimester terminations, and usually those involved in the ceremony have no biogenetic ties with the remains being buried. Sometimes, however, as in the case described, 'parents' too participate in the function.

The remains are preserved in the morgue according to the gestational age and the techniques used for termination. Those from first trimester abortions are sealed in special biodegradable containers. The bodies of mis-carried or aborted foetuses, whose births were induced, are wrapped in bio-degradable cellophane. While the former are not visible, the latter are. The volunteers in charge of recovering the remains from the morgue describe the view of the little dead bodies as a shocking experience. The practice of burial, in fact, puts them in front of a reversal of the cultural norms that forbid the sight of dead foetuses. As Lynn Morgan (2009) argues, until the 1960s, seeing embryos and foetuses preserved in formaldehyde was com-mon: they were used for research, teaching, in museums, etc. The spread of visualisation technologies, however, has gradually led to their disappear-ance. Dead samples have been replaced by images of living embryos and foetuses, which have become the 'icons of life'. As mentioned above, pro-life imagery is populated with living embryos and foetuses. Burials also give visibility to embryos and foetuses that died without showing their bodies. Coffins, flowers and small graves counteract what the association calls the 'collective repression' surrounding abortion. 'Seeing the graves will make people understand and be ashamed', the vice president of the association said when giving a public speech. 'They will despair and finally mourn the death of their children'.

Defending Life with Mary asks volunteers to celebrate the ceremony with discretion. In some cases, the 'funeral' is announced in the parishes. Tombs are anonymous: the only distinctive sign is a plaque with the date of the burial. According to the association's members, objects and words sometimes found on the graves, such as those mentioned in the descrip-tion above, are the work of 'parents' and are usually left there privately, after the public ceremony. Funerals remove the individual histories that produced the remains. Regardless of the circumstances of conception and death, Defending Life with Mary honours all of the unborn equally.

On several occasions, the association has been accused of using funer-als to attack Law 194 and women's freedom of choice. Its representatives have replied that 'funerals' are not intended to denounce or hurt women, who, for the most part, deal with the experience of abortion with great pain and suffering. The lack of distinction and the equal treatment of voluntary terminations and miscarriages, as well as the occasional participation of par-ents at funerals celebrated by the association, fuels the idea that spontane-ous and voluntary abortion are equally tragic events where the victims are both the unborn and the women. During an interview, a volunteer told me:

In general, women who have voluntary terminations of pregnancy do not attend the funeral. But then we see flowers on the tombs, and maybe that month there had been no miscarriages. I shudder

… you know, since they signed the form and knew there was a ceremony, the mothers come, and then everything is at the mercy of God because anyone who has had an abortion sooner or later pays for it psychologically.

Post-abortion Suffering and Healing

The closing event of the retreat is the memorial service that takes place on Sunday afternoon. This time, in addition to the team members,[17] there are only six women. Their faces are marked by fatigue and by the strong emotions they faced during the weekend. Today, however, they seem more serene. For the occasion they have dressed up and put on make-up. At lunch, two guests arrive: someone's partner and another one's friend. The presence of partners was strongly encouraged, but most of the women's husbands or partners did not come. The ceremony takes place in the chapel. Before starting, the coordinator of Rachel's Vineyard speaks to guests about the hard work that the participants have undertaken. She then explains how the ceremony will take place: a symbol of the baby will be placed in a 'grave'. This act will help the 'mothers' to let go of their 'children'. The two guests barely contain their tears.

In turn, the women stand near the altar and read the letter that they wrote to their 'children' the previous night. They address them by name or call them 'my love', 'my soul', 'my angel'. They carry the small 'mourning dolls' received the night before and with whom they spent the night. These are the symbols from which they will have to separate. After reading their letters, just about holding back their tears, they reach the altar, and free the dolls from the swaddling bands in which they had wrapped them the night before. They rewrap them in new bands and place them in small decorative boxes that serve as coffins. Before closing the lids, they place a toy, a dummy or a cross chosen from a basket placed on the altar next to boxes of different sizes and paper tissues used for the wrappings. Once closed, the boxes are laid in a basket at the foot of the altar. Before returning to their seats, participants receive one (or more) 'life certificate(s)' reporting the name given to each 'child', and a white fabric angel as a memento. The symbolic burial concludes with a prayer in which the participants reaffirm their repentance, sorrow and love for their 'children', who are now in God's hands.

The ritual is followed by a mass officiated by the priest who accompanied participants during the retreat.

The above description refers to the second retreat organised by Rachel's Vineyard, which took place in November 2010. The memorial is the culmination of a three-day journey full of events and emotions. Through spiritual exercises,[18] ritual acts and moments of sharing, the participants are called to give voice to their pain and guilt associated with abortion and to correlate this event (or events, in the case of repeated terminations) with the experiences of rejection, loss, violence or abuse they have suffered. They are also invited to recognise their 'aborted children' by giving them a name and entering into communication with them, and to trust in God's mercy and power of salvation. The road to recovery has the tripartite structure of the Passion. Friday is dominated by the themes of suffering and death: that of the 'aborted baby' and that of the 'mother' who died with him. Saturday is the time when the death experience is deepened, but it is also the time when the 'child' is revived as a person: it is given a name and a body (the mourning doll) and visualised through imagining. Sunday is the day of resurrection: after a night of vigil where participants pray, write a letter to their 'child' (or 'children') and receive the sacrament of confession, 'children' are left to go through a memorial mass, and 'mothers' (and 'fathers'), who receive God's forgiveness, begin their new life.

The retreat is aimed at women (and men) who underwent voluntary termination of pregnancy. However, women who miscarried can also participate,[19] since, according to Rachel's Vineyard staff, they too, like women who have had terminations, have a grief to mourn and often a sense of guilt for their reproductive failure. Although the team recognises a difference between spontaneous and induced abortions, which affects participants' personal responsibility, from their point of view most induced abortions cannot be said to be truly voluntary. The weekend offers an opportunity to honour the memory of 'children' who were aborted (or miscarried) by participants, but also of those aborted by parents, siblings, or friends. These 'children' are also given a body, mourned and named. A 'life certificate' is drawn up for them too, in which the participant is listed as 'sister/brother' or 'aunt/uncle'.

During preliminary interviews leading up to the retreat, when the team assesses participants' motives, couple participation is strongly encouraged. The retreats, however, are predominantly attended by women: it is mainly 'mothers who suffer from abortion and feel responsible for mourning and expiating their guilt'. From the association's point of view, however, women should not be alone as mothers. Male participation is considered valuable because abortion concerns men too, and because their presence can offer women, who are there by themselves, models of masculinity and relationships different from those they have experienced in their daily lives.

Participants approach Rachel's Vineyard seeking spiritual reconciliation. To benefit from the retreat they must, as the team says, 'open their heart so that it can be touched by the grace of God'. At the basis of the healing path there is an understanding of abortion as a traumatic event that leaves deep wounds in the body and soul of parents. Abortion is never considered a conscious choice: it is assumed that women who have had abortions did so without realising what was really going on, that they were ill-advised, left alone or forced to have abortions. The same is assumed for men, who due to weakness were unable to assume their responsibilities as fathers, stay close to their companions, support them or oppose their decision to have an abortion. Abortion, moreover, is never solely attributed to the specific circumstances in which it occurred, but linked to personal histories, which are supposed to be marked by lack of affection, ill treatment and violence that have undermined the self-esteem of the parent-to-be and her/his ability to welcome a new life. During the retreat, the participants are invited to mourn the loss of their child, but also to express the pain and anger for the injuries they suffered. The fact that from the point of view of the association abortion is never a truly free, conscious choice does not eliminate the responsibility of those who did it. Thus, it is assumed that participants feel guilty. Women (and men) who participate in retreats never question this disposition. According to both the participants and the team, guilt is not only an emotional state, but rather an objective condition: from the point of view of the Catholic religion, in fact, people who have had abortions have committed a sin.

During the retreats I attended, most of the female participants, soon after their arrival, spontaneously declared that they had 'killed their babies', 'indelibly stained their existence', 'felt unworthy', etc. Healing does not erase participants' guilt; it involves an assumption of responsibility, the understanding of its roots and the acceptance of God's forgiveness. Rachel's Vineyard considers healing to be a long process that is not completed in a weekend. When they leave the retreat, participants are given tools to continue their path to recovery: readings, websites, contacts, suggestions for improving spiritual life, family relationships, etc. One of the forms of healing and renewal encouraged by team members is to make a commitment to defend life. People who have had abortions are invited to actively participate in initiatives aimed at 'increasing the cultural awareness of the negative effects of voluntary termination of pregnancy'.

Reading Pro-lifers' New Practices

As the testimony quoted at the beginning of this chapter suggests, burials of abortion remains and post-abortion healing have complementary functions. Apparently unlike other forms of action, such as those carried out by local movements and pro-life help centres, they do not address prevention, but rather what remains after an abortion. The material traces are buried following the ritual for children who have died without baptism. Wounds left in women's (and men's) flesh and souls are healed through ritual and sharing.

However, both 'funerals' and retreats are also meant to oppose abortion. Ceremonies, no matter how discreet, are public events, and the anonymous tombstones in cemeteries are visible. Through these signs, Defending Life with Mary aims to 'raise awareness'. Although its primary mission is to honour the flesh of the 'aborted babies', the association also, and perhaps more importantly, addresses the living: couples who miscarried a wanted child, for whom the ritual can provide a way to face the pain; women who terminated unwanted pregnancies and who, although they did not request or participate in the burial, may one day regret the choice they made, and more generally the entire society, 'so that', as the president of the association said during a ceremony, 'we can remember that we are still human'. Unlike funerals, post-abortion healing retreats are not public events. However, through participants' personal experience, they contribute, too, to anti-abortion protest logics. While expressions of individual pain and healing are confined to the retreats and protected by strict privacy policies, public testimony of post-abortion suffering by members of the team and participants takes on a political role. They denounce abortion as a form of violence, not only against embryos/foetuses, but also against women (and men).

Another common element in the burial of abortion remains and post-abortion healing is that they both establish a sort of equality between unwanted and desired pregnancies, voluntary terminations and miscarriages. This point is important in the economy of the contemporary abortion debate. In Italy, parents who have suffered a pregnancy loss have recently begun to claim the right to burial and specific psychological assistance. Pro-lifers have endorsed their requests, blurring the public debate on the subject. The equivalence established by pro-lifers between voluntary terminations and pregnancy loss challenges the idea that choice is the foundation of contemporary parenting (Boltanski 2004; Gauchet 2004). The associations celebrating 'funerals for unborn children' and offering post-abortion healing consider that personhood and parenthood originate at conception. Sometimes, however, parents' recognition of the new life may not develop in early pregnancy. In these cases, women may decide to have an abortion. But from the pro-lifers' point of view, this cannot be considered to be a conscious, free choice. As the description provided shows, activists present the traces left by the tombstones and women's experiences during post-abortion healing retreats as evidence that the acknowledgement of parental bonds sometimes needs time: it can also take place after, and notwithstanding, an abortion. Guilt, which mainly afflicts women, stems from their inner awareness, nurtured by the healing process itself, of being mothers of their aborted babies.

Conclusion

The discourses and practices described in this chapter show some of the current directions of the anti-abortion activism in Italy. As in other EU and non-EU countries, social groups and individual actors who fight against abortion make use of the language of rights and of the language of violence. The recognition of the embryo/foetus as a subject, which was a part of the debate on medically assisted procreation, reinforced the contrast between the embryo's/foetus' right to life and women's rights. The burial of abortion remains builds on the idea of embryos' and foetuses' rights. By adding the right to a funeral to the right to life, activists bestow human dignity on the embryos'/foetuses' remains. Their description of post-abortion suffering (and healing practices), on the other hand, reverses the terms of the feminist discourse, constructing abortion as a risk factor for women's health and choice as a mere illusion. According to this perspective, abortion is not a way of protecting women's physical and mental health, but it is an authorised violence against women. Besides, women who have an abortion are not free actors, but victims of structural conditions and/or dysfunctional relationships that force them to refuse motherhood.

Burials of abortion remains and post-abortion healing are both ways of challenging the idea that abortion should be a right, and that reproduction and parenthood are the products of a conscious choice. To a certain extent, these practices are new ways to convey old meanings. However, their occurrence, the reactions they provoke and the attraction they exert on some women are connected to a contemporary understanding of and sensitivity to reproduction. To overlook these practices as the work of a small minority, a fringe of the anti-abortion movement, is likely to obscure some of the themes of the current debate on abortion and women's health, letting the anti-abortion activism monopolise them. As I mentioned before, in Italy the association between the burial of embryos/foetuses and anti-abortion activism has led to a substantial misunderstanding of the claims advanced by couples who have suffered a pregnancy loss. Similarly in public debates, grief, which may follow terminations, is often silenced, because it could eventually confirm the anti-abortion stance that terminations are harmful to all women. Understanding arguments and practices of anti-abortion activism, no matter how marginal or seemingly strange, may help us to go beyond the logic of confrontation, to look carefully at the complexity of individual and collective claims, and to question the ways in which different actors involved in reproductive and abortion governance respond to them.

Claudia Mattalucci is an Assistant Professor at the University of Milan-Bicocca, where she teaches Anthropology of Kinship and Gender. After completing the Scuola di Alti Studi in Sciences of Culture at the Fondazione Collegio San Carlo in Modena, she obtained a scholarship from the Fyssen Foundation in Paris. She has worked on missions and missionary ethnography and on the anthropology of the body. Over the last seven years she has been working on abortion and pregnancy loss in Italy.

Notes

1. The research was conducted in Piedmont and Lombardy for a total of twelve months, with the financial support of the University of Milano-Bicocca. During this time, I participated in cultural events and awareness days organised by local pro-life movements; I interviewed the members of local movements, volunteers who work in life help-centers, and pro-lifers who are not part of the Pro-life Movement. I also attended the activities organised by the two associations that I describe in this chapter, participating in several funerals and two post-abortion retreats.
2. The law establishes that during the first trimester, termination is allowed for a woman for whom 'the continuation of the pregnancy, childbirth or maternity would result in a serious threat to her physical or mental health'. After the first trimester the law authorises the interruption: 'a) when pregnancy or childbirth poses severe danger to the woman's life, [and] b) when there are ascertained pathological processes, including those related to major foetal malformations, which create severe danger to the physical or mental health of the woman' (Article 6).
3. The Italian pro-life movement is a federation of local movements and life help centres. There are several publications on its history by activists who have held or hold important roles within it; among others, see Pirovano (1981) and Agasso (2011).
4. Local movements organise conferences, debates and exhibitions; in schools, they offer training courses for students and teachers; at local and political elections they support candidates who share their beliefs, etc.
5. Life help centres offer economic aid, necessities (nappies, second-hand clothing, food, etc.), emotional support and in some cases psychological aid and medical examinations. Although their purpose is to prevent abortions by helping women in

their first trimester of pregnancy who have a certificate attesting their request for an abortion, they often also help women whose pregnancy is past the time limit within which termination can be performed.

6. The law prohibits heterologous fertilisation (Article 4) and only allows heterosexual infertile couples to use medically assisted procreation techniques (Article 4 and 5). It prohibits pre-implantation diagnosis, cryopreservation, and allows for the production of a number of embryos used for a single transfer (Article 14). A ruling of the Constitutional Court of 2009 lifted the last two restrictions. In 2014, the Constitutional Court also abolished the ban on heterologous fertilisation.

7. In the Roman Catholic Church, the Episcopal Conference is the assembly of the bishops of a certain territory. Each conference exercises pastoral functions for the people of faith of the country or countries within its jurisdiction. The support of the Episcopal Conference presently confers prestige and authority on the movement. According to activists, for years the defence of life has not been the core of Catholic pastoral activities. Although popes have always advocated the defence of the unborn, until the 1990s most of the bishops and priests had not openly addressed the abortion issue, nor supported the pro-life movement.

8. The effect of this type of representation has been the subject of numerous critical analyses. Among others, see Duden (1993); Newman (1996); Michaels (1999).

9. http://www.oneofus.eu/

10. Rome, 25 November 2007, 'Sindrome post-aborto e riconciliazione', round table at the XXVII National Conference of the life help centres.

11. Among these, it is important to note a training course that was held in Brescia 8–9 May 2009 entitled 'Donne e libertà. Le conseguenze psichiche dell'aborto'. See the acts: Cantelemi, Cacace and Pittino (2011).

12. The founder is an American psychologist who developed a method for conducting retreats. Together with her husband, she directs Rachel's Vineyard internationally.

13. www.vignadirachele.org

14. To my knowledge there is at least one other association that organises retreats for post-abortion healing and self-help groups. During this study, on the initiatives organised by the pro-life movement, I met some professionals who work individually; I also closely followed the work of a psychologist and family counsellor.

15. Abortions taking place within the eight weeks of pregnancy are called 'ovular'. They are often due to alterations of the egg or failures in ova implantation.

16. The national law related to the burial of the products of conception (DPR n. 285, 10 September 1990) states that the burial of a stillborn follows the provisions in force for all deceased human beings. For the burial of abortion remains with a gestational age from twenty to twenty-eight weeks and foetuses with an intrauterine age of twenty-eight weeks, who have not been declared stillbirths, permits for transport and burial are issued from the local health authority. This law also states that 'upon the request of parents, the gestational products of less than twenty weeks can be laid to rest in the same way in the cemetery' (Article 7, § 3). In these cases, parents are required to submit an application for burial at the local health department within twenty-four hours of the expulsion or extraction of the foetus.

17. On this occasion, the team was composed of the coordinator of the association, her husband, a psychologist and a priest. On subsequent retreats with a greater number of participants, some former participants were also involved as team members.

18. The exercises called 'living scriptures' are inspired by Ignatius spiritual exercises. Listening to a passage from the gospel is followed by a meditation session in which the participants relive the same episode, identifying with one or more characters. Afterwards, the central message of the reading is symbolically acted out. At the end of the ritual, participants are asked to verbalise feelings and emotions. Overall, the method of Rachel's Vineyard echoes the Catholic charismatic rites for post-abortion healing analysed by Thomas Csordas (1996). A comparison of the two deserves further investigation.

19. My participation in the retreats was possible because I agreed to share a personal experience of miscarriage with other participants.

References

Agasso, R. 2011. *Sì alla vita Storia e prospettive del Movimento per la Vita. Intervista a Carlo Casini*. Cinisello Balsamo: San Paolo.

Boltanski, L. 2004. *La condition fœtale: Une sociologie de l'avortement et de l'engendrement*. Paris: Gallimard.

Calloni, M. 2001. 'Debates and Controversies on Abortion in Italy', in D. McBride Stetson (ed.), *Abortion Politics, Women Movements, and the Democratic State: A Comparative Study of State Feminism*. Oxford: Oxford University Press, pp. 181–203.

Cantelemi, T., C. Cacace and E. Pittino (eds). 2011. *Maternità interrotte. Le conseguenze psichiche dell'IVG*. Cinisello Balsamo: San Paolo.

Csordas, T. 1996. 'A Handmaid's Tale: The Rhetoric of Personhood in American and Japanese Healing of Abortions', in C.F. Sargent and C. Brettell (eds), *Gender and Health: An International Perspective*. Englewood Cliffs: Prentice-Hall, pp. 227–41.

Duden, B. 1993. *Disembodying Women. Perspectives on Pregnancy and the Unborn*. Cambridge, MA: Harvard University Press.

Garrone, G. 1998. *Ma questo è un figlio*. Milano: Gribaudi.

Gauchet, M. 2004. 'L'enfant du désir', *Le Débat* 132: 9–22.

Hanafin, P. 2007. *Conceiving Life. Reproductive Politics and Law in Contemporary Italy*. Adershot-Burlington: Ashgate.

Hopkins, N., S. Reicher and J. Saleem. 1996. 'Constructing Women's Psychological Health in Anti-abortion Rhetoric', *The Sociological Review* 44: 539–64.

Lee, E.E. 2003. *Abortion, Motherhood, and Mental Health: Medicalizing Reproduction in the United States and Great Britain*. New York: Aldin de Gruyter.

Mattalucci, C. 2012. 'Pro-Life Activism, Abortion and Subjectivity before Birth: Discursive Practices and Anthropological Perspectives', *Mediterranean Journal of Social Sciences* 3(10): 109–18.

———. 2013. 'Between the Law and Bioethics: Placing the Unborn in Contemporary Italy', *Academic Journal of Interdisciplinary Studies* 3: 284–90.

Michaels, M. 1999. 'Fetal Galaxies: Some Questions About What We See', in Morgan, L. and Michaels, M. (eds), *Fetal Subjects, Feminist Positions*. Philadelphia: University of Pennsylvania Press, pp. 113–32.

Morgan, L. 2009. *Icons of Life: A Cultural History of Human Embryos*. Berkeley: University of California Press.

Newman, K. 1996. *Fetal Positions, Individualism, Science, Visuality*. Stanford: Stanford University Press.

Petchesky, R. 1987. 'Foetal Images: The Power of Visual Culture in the Politics of Reproduction', in M. Stanworth 1987 (ed.), *Reproductive Technologies: Gender, Motherhood and Medicine*. Cambridge: Polity Press, pp. 57–80.

Pirovano, P. 1981. *Per la vita oltre il referendum – Nascita e storia di un movimento*. Milano: Amici per la vita Edizioni.

Pittino, E. and A. Buongiovanni. 2011. 'Legge 194/78, consenso informato, libertà di scelta', in T. Cantelemi, C. Cacace and E. Pittino, *Maternità interrotte. Le conseguenze psichiche dell'IVG*. Cinisello Balsamo: San Paolo.

Sciré, G. 2008. *L'aborto in Italia. Storia di una legge*. Milano: Bruno Mondadori.

Chapter 5

Innocence and Demographic Crisis
Transposing Post-abortion Syndrome into a Russian Orthodox Key

by Sonja Luehrmann

'Our whole society has post-abortion syndrome'.
—Elena, pro-life activist in her early twenties, Kazan, 2012

'It could be said that we engage in anti-state activity. Because the state permits abortions, and we fight against them'. With these words, Galina Semionovna, the director of a crisis pregnancy centre in Saint Petersburg, Russia, characterised the sensibility that guided her group's work.[1] When talking about her own motivation for engaging in such anti-state activity, the retired university instructor in her seventies recalled how she reinterpreted her own reproductive decisions during the religious revival of the 1990s. A mother of three children born between 1962 and 1977, she had had three abortions between these births, a spacing mechanism common for Soviet women of her generation. When she turned to Russian Orthodox Christianity in the wake of the collapse of the Soviet Union, she came to see her abortions as sins and confessed them to a priest, who had her complete a series of penitential prayers. Upon granting her absolution, he said, 'And now, get to work!' This launched her on a path of anti-abortion activism that culminated in the opening of the crisis pregnancy centre in 2003.

While conducting ethnographic research among anti-abortion activists in several Russian cities, I often heard middle-aged and elderly women explain their involvement by citing feelings of regret and repentance for their own abortions. In narrating the urge to turn personal regrets into political activism, they supplemented Eastern Orthodox theologies of confession and forgiveness with references to post-abortion syndrome (PAS), a controversial psychological disorder described in Western pro-life literature.

For younger activists, by contrast, abortion was not a common personal experience but a historical burden carried forward from the previous generation. They used the language of psychological affliction in a collective and metaphorical sense, to explain obstacles to spreading their message.

PAS is a travelling term that spreads along with particular forms of activism such as the crisis pregnancy centre, but is taken up differently by activists according to their national and religious contexts. By 'following the metaphor' or concept (Marcus 1995: 108) of PAS in Russian society, I show how localised histories of abortion's use as a reproductive technology give different inflections to struggles about its legal and moral permissibility. In addition to showing the complex relationship of the Russian movement to transnational pro-life discourse, references to PAS in Russia exemplify the larger stakes of reproductive debates for different generations of women. Living in what they perceived to be a politically passive society, early twenty-first century activists used psychological terminology to explain their own unusual propensity for activism. Galina Semionovna brought up PAS when I asked her to describe the support base of her centre. 'There is this so-called post-abortion syndrome, when the heart cannot calm down *(serdtse ne us-pokaivaetsia)*. You repented, went to confession, completed your penance, were admitted to communion, but the heart still hurts.' Those who help the centre financially or by participating in outreach activities are people with a personal experience of the issue 'whose conscience has woken up'. These could be women who have undergone abortions, men who advised their partners to terminate a pregnancy, or young people who were shocked to learn about the magnitude of the phenomenon in Russia. For activists of different generations, abortion memories epitomise the problems of the Soviet gender order and the post-Soviet inability to mourn. In a context where critical reflection on the past is seldom publically encouraged but demographic developments raise anxiety over the future, 'procreation stories' (Ginsburg 1998) become one of the unlikely places where questions of historical memory and national identity can be addressed.

Abortion in Russia

Anti-abortion activists in Russia can simultaneously see themselves as anti-state activists and patriots because of the specific history of abortion and reproductive legislation in the Soviet Union. In 1920, the Bolshevik government legalised abortion, making revolutionary Russia the first modern state that made the procedure available to women on demand at medical institutions. Stalin restricted access in 1936, requiring women to prove to a board of medical experts that they were unable to carry a pregnancy to term. Reasons recognised by these boards included risks to maternal health, indications of foetal abnormalities, and the presence of nursing infants or children with disabilities in the household.[2] Stalin's successor Nikita Khrushchev reinstated abortion-on-demand, acknowledging that the restrictions had failed to reach the goal of raising the birth rate and led to increased maternal mortality through illegal abortions. The 1955 law 'On lifting the ban against abortion' acknowledged that the goal was 'to enable women to decide the question of maternity for themselves', but also noted that 'lowering the number of abortions can henceforth be accomplished by extending measures to reward maternity, and also by measures of educational character' (quoted in Nakachi 2008: 560). Abortion was still presented as a less than ideal choice, but in line with Khrushchev's general appeal to popular morality and voluntarism, the struggle was now to be conducted through educating women about the health risks posed by abortion and promoting other methods of fertility control, such as condoms and vaginal caps. Officially, abortion remained an evil to be combatted, even as numbers of abortions skyrocketed (Field 2007).

Given that the rubber products required for barrier contraception were always in short supply, abortion represented an accessible and socially accepted, though painful, way to regulate family size and space births. It was often performed without any form of anaesthesia, and many older women remembered the derogatory attitude of medical personnel towards patients who had not managed to avoid an unwanted pregnancy. In 1965 the abortion ratio for the Soviet Union peaked at 2745 abortions per 1000 live births – a ratio of almost three to one (Sakevich 2009: 137). Hormonal contraceptives were briefly introduced in the early 1970s, then taken off production and import because of the side effects of this first generation of the pill, while condoms remained hard to find, unreliable, and unpopular with men. The IUD received some measure of state support, but there never was a widespread campaign to promote its use comparable to some developing countries. What emerges from Soviet-era surveys and oral history interviews is that couples practised various versions of the rhythm method, and when that failed, the woman 'took care of the problem' through an abortion (Larivaara 2009; Popov, Visser and Ketting 1993; Zdravomyslova 2009). Although sexual health education at schools was minimal, efforts to promote other methods of fertility control through displays at women's health clinics and physician advice did show some success – the abortion ratio fell to 1754 per 1000 live births in 1987. Even so, during the two final decades of the Soviet Union's existence, the average Soviet woman had five abortions over her reproductive lifespan (Hutter 2003).

Abortion rates peaked again in the early 1990s, a time now widely remembered for social and economic chaos and uncertainty. Throughout the post-Soviet era, abortion has remained legal and available on demand during the first trimester, and for medical and a limited number of social indications at any stage in pregnancy. It is free when performed at a state-run health clinic and available for a fee at many private facilities. Abortion rates have been slowly falling, mainly in response to increased use of oral contraceptives, but also because of a slight rise in the birth rate (Vishnevskii 2011: 86–87). Russia remains one of the countries with the highest abortion rates in the world. In 2008, the number of abortions fell below that of live births for the first time since 1955, but remained almost three times as high as analogous figures for the United States (Denisov, Sakevich and Jasilioniene 2012). With a few exceptions, even the activists I interviewed did not see the prohibition of abortion as a realistic mid-range goal, but rather worked towards introducing restrictions such as mandatory psychological counselling and the right of obstetricians to conscientious objection against abortion.[3]

This history of abortion in Soviet and post-Soviet Russia shows that its changing legal status never was the result of popular political mobilisation, but responded to the priorities of the state. Moreover, abortion policy was repeatedly pinpointed as key to solving population problems. Stalin-era efforts to combat abortion peaked towards the final years and in the immediate aftermath of the Second World War, as if reducing abortions and improving care of premature and weak infants could do the work of 'replacing the dead' of the war and the Gulag (Nakachi 2008). The decision to restore on-demand access to abortion in 1955 was again justified by the need to safeguard women's health and capacity to work in the labour force, fulfilling the ideal gender role of 'working mother' (Zdravomyslova 2009).

Perhaps because granting or restricting access was a matter of raison d'état, abortion was rarely regarded as a 'right', but emerges in interviews more as an unpleasant duty and necessity. Regardless of whether or not they supported their continued legality, women often used the expression *prishlos*', it was necessary, when speaking about their past abortions. This reflexive phrase without a subject is an impersonal way of acknowledging that circumstances forced one to do something. The passive voice removed the topic of abortion from the sphere of human choice and moral judgement, and also presented the experience of undergoing the procedure as one of the inevitable hardships of women's lives rather than a marker of gender equality. This is the background on which post-Soviet anti-abortion activists see themselves as engaging in countercultural work, even as they participate in wider pronatalist tendencies that enjoy increasing government support.

The Spectre of Demographic Decline

In Soviet medical literature, the high rates of abortion were treated as a health concern for women, with possible consequences including secondary infertility, increased risks of complications during subsequent births, and psychological problems. The unborn foetus as a rights-bearing person did not enter Soviet discourse (Morgan and Michaels 2002). But there was a growing concern, starting in the 1970s, about declining birth rates in the European parts of the Soviet Union (Leykin 2011). Still, efforts to encourage women to give birth emphasised quality over quantity and the unborn child's potential contributions to society over his or her inherent rights as a person. In a poem that I first saw on a sticker distributed by the crisis pregnancy centre in Saint Petersburg, but later found in a Soviet women's health guide, author Irina Bychenkova (1965) asked the pregnant woman considering an abortion to 'stop to think!' Perhaps, the poem suggests, the one 'whose life now hangs on a thin thread,/will turn out to be a scholar or a poet,/and the whole world will speak of him'.

Different from the foetuses of Western pro-life activism, the imagined value of the unborn child lay not so much in its ability to personify the sanctity of life itself (Morgan 2009), but in its status as a potential member of society with beneficial contributions to make. Since coming into power in 2000, President Vladimir Putin has introduced a series of measures to reverse the catastrophic post-Soviet decline of the birth rate, including the provision of roughly 10,000 U.S. dollars of 'maternity capital' to a woman who gives birth to her second child (Rivkin-Fish 2010). When I began research on church-based reproductive activism in 2008, activists in Moscow who had been working on the issue since the early 1990s were excited to feel growing government support. They had received permission to place free advertising on municipally owned billboards in the Moscow underground. Although abortion remained legal, the idea of unborn children as potential reinforcements for a numerically shrinking nation moved anti-abortion activism closer to the mainstream.

In this context of increased media attention and heightened social stakes of reproductive decisions, older women who regretted past abortions could derive a certain moral authority from this virtuous hindsight. A poster hanging in the psychologist's office at the Saint Petersburg crisis pregnancy centre urges younger women to listen to experience and anticipate the regrets they might have in old age. The poster is titled 'The life of a woman who has a child and one who has an abortion'. It pictures a young woman in peasant garb whose head is tilted to one side as if listening or thinking intensely, while her hands embrace her abdomen. 'What Choice to Make?' is written under her portrait. Around this central image a frame made up of smaller squares tells two possible stories of the woman's life, in the style of an icon with scenes from the saint's life. In the version going clockwise from the left side across the top to the right, she gives birth, has a large and prosperous family, and is surrounded by her descendants in old

Figure 5.1 'What Choice to Make?' Poster from the offices of a crisis pregnancy centre in Saint Petersburg. Artist unknown. Photograph courtesy of Tsentr Zhizn.

age as a respected matron. The alternative, shown counter clockwise across the bottom half of the frame, shows the woman who had an abortion, is abandoned by her husband, and left to face poverty and a lonely and destitute old age. In one of the images, the aborted child appears to the sleeping woman in a dream.

With its stark alternatives – either give birth to every conceived child and live as a large peasant family, or terminate and die alone – the poster failed to reflect the reality of most of the women who worked and volunteered at the centre. They tended to be mothers and grandmothers who had also used abortion when they felt that the demands of their job and the size of their apartment placed limits on their family size. But the idea of past decisions returning to haunt a woman in the shape of her aborted foetus formed part of the wider imaginary of the centre. Images and narratives of foetal ghosts gave tangible shape to the state of a 'heart refusing to calm down' as described by Galina Semionovna. The label 'post-abortion syndrome' lifted this feeling out of its post-Soviet context, endowing it with the aura of scientific universality. At the same time, their particular understanding of PAS as refracted through Orthodox Christian teachings about sin and repentance directed the women's attention back to the details of Soviet and post-Soviet life, turning reproductive decisions into an interpretive key through which they criticised the gender ideal of the working mother.

Trauma as a Motivation for Social Action

'Every other sin one should confess and forget. But abortion is the sin that must not and cannot be forgotten'. This statement, made by a priest whom I interviewed at an anti-abortion rally on International Children's Day (1 June 2010) in Saint Petersburg, frames abortion as a case of exception in Orthodox Christian dealings with sin. Usually the Church advised people to avoid dwelling on their sins, but confess them and then focus on cultivating a counteracting virtue. For example, if someone repented of the sin of stinginess or greed, a priest might advise them to deliberately give money to the poor.

Within this economy of vices and virtues, abortion is framed as a counter-natural act that leaves deeper traces in the human psyche than others. To explain the resistance of abortion memories to the normal workings of confession, activists like Galina Semionovna used the psychologising language of PAS, which they took as a fact discovered by Western scientists. But compared to Protestant and Catholic-inspired organisations, Russian activists were less familiar with psychological discourses and imagined the workings of the human psyche somewhat differently. As a result, the recommended responses to post-abortion syndrome also differ from North American approaches to religiously based trauma therapy. Instead of attempting to singularise a woman's memory and personalise the aborted foetus, there is a focus on transforming oneself through deeds that directly draws some women into activism.

In English-language psychological literature, the term post-abortion syndrome (PAS) or post-abortion trauma appeared in the early 1980s, with diagnostic criteria modelled after those of post-traumatic stress disorder (PTSD). PTSD itself was a newly recognised affliction at the time, first included in the 1980 edition of the American Psychiatric Association's *Diagnostic and Statistical Manual of Mental Disorders* (Lee 2003: 25–26, 62). Literature on PAS treated abortion as the 'stressor', analogous to exposure to war or abuse in PTSD, and diagnosed a syndrome in cases where women suffered from unwanted memories of the abortion, dreams of the unborn foetus, a sense of decreased self-worth, changed feelings towards their living children, aversion or exaggerated attachment to the father of the child, or feelings of envy or aggression towards babies and their parents. Different from PTSD, PAS was never recognised as a disorder by the American Psychiatric Association or analogous professional bodies, and arguments over whether or not it exists tend to reproduce political divisions in pro-life/pro-choice debates (Dadlez and Andrews 2010; Ney 1993). Psychologists who argue that PAS exists emphasise that signs of distress can appear quite late, often many years after the procedure was performed. The abortion becomes a key event by reference to which any later occurrences of stress, sadness, or changes in personality can be explained (Burke and Reardon 2002).

The term *postabortnyi sindrom* was introduced to post-Soviet Russia through the writings of anti-abortion activists. Its use as an organising concept incorporated older, more diffuse discourses about the long-term personal and collective effects of reproductive decisions, and gave these discourses a new level of scientific authority and mobilising power. The adoption of the term points to a paradox of Russian Orthodox pro-life activism: although many activists are deeply suspicious of Western influences and ecumenical endeavours, they accept psychological expertise that is largely mediated by Catholic and Protestant sources. In 2003, the Life Centre in Moscow published a translation of John and Barbara Willke's book *Why Can't We Love them Both*, with the imprinted blessing of Patriarch Aleksii II (Uillke and Uillke 2003). The book describes PAS as a delayed psychological reaction that eventually comes through despite cultural denial. The Life Centre's founder, Orthodox priest Maksim Obukhov, endorses the book by American Catholics as 'a wonderful source of information for doctors, teachers, and priests who are responsible for the spiritual and physical health of the Russian nation' (Obukhov 2003: 3).

When discussing PAS, Russian pro-life print and online publications frequently cite a paper by another Catholic author, Wanda Połtawska (b. 1921), a Polish psychiatrist, survivor of Nazi concentration camps and personal friend of Pope John Paul II (Połtawska 1962). Russianised as Pultavskaia, the Polish origin of the author's name is not immediately apparent. Neither do many readers know that her paper on 'The influence of abortion on a woman's psyche', originally delivered at Warsaw's 1994 International Congress of the Family, was published in Russian under the auspices of 'Renovabis', the Catholic organisation of outreach to the former Soviet Union. Though cited in Russian cyberspace as a foundational text on PAS, Połtawska herself does not use the term, since the psychological and theological literature she cites dates from the 1960s and 1970s. She describes long-term effects of irritability, self-hate, aversion to the opposite sex or overprotective motherhood, which she herself likens to those of menopause, with the difference that they can occur at any time after the abortion, independent of a woman's biological age. The Willkes deliberately try to separate such psychological reactions from any religious framework, arguing that they occur among women who are not church members and are thus not simply feelings of guilt induced by pro-life clergy (Uillke and Uillke 2003: 33). Połtawska, by contrast, interprets symptoms described in psychological literature through an unapologetically Catholic lens.

Instead of recommending a therapy process that is modelled on that for trauma victims as do later Anglophone authors (Burke and Reardon 2002), Połtawska says that there is no psychiatric therapy for the consequences of abortion, because 'the murder of one's own child damages the deep structure of the personality and directly affects the human soul' (Połtawska 1996: 279). Even confession to a priest cannot completely give a woman peace. Instead, she needs to 'find her place as a "child of God" through penance (*iskuplenie*)' (ibid.: 280). Abortion here is not a stressor that is dealt with through memory work, but a special kind of sin that causes lasting distortions in the person who commits it and can only be countered through sacramental action. When Russian Orthodox activists speak of *postabortnyi sindrom*, they borrow a term from the Willkes and other English-language writers, but what they describe is closer to Połtawska's understanding.

At the Russian Orthodox pregnancy consultation centres in Moscow, Saint Petersburg, and Nizhnii Novgorod that I visited between 2008 and 2012, the existence of PAS was taken for granted. Activists used the term as a scientific explanation as to why women who had abortions needed to participate in the struggle to prevent them. Galina Semionovna recalled that one of the reasons that brought her to practise Orthodox Christianity, starting in 1993, was a growing feeling of irritability *(razdrazhitel'nost')* and a tendency to use a 'dictatorial tone' with her children and husband that she did not know how to deal with. In the course of catechiser classes at the Saint Petersburg Spiritual Academy, Galina came to interpret these feelings as a consequence of her unexpiated abortions. She wrote a final paper on PAS, confessed her abortions as sins, completed penitential prayers for them and received absolution and admittance to communion. 'This urge to destroy, to cause harm stays with you as post-abortion syndrome', she concluded. Her greatest pride in running the centre was the elderly women who gave part of their pension each month to support it. During a tea break shared by the staff, Galina mentioned that she had received a phone call from an elderly woman who said that her conscience was torturing her after her abortion. 'She has *postabortnyi sindrom*', Galina explained, 'we need to find something for her to do. I told her to come volunteer at our next public rally.'

For other staff members as well, the process of entering the church's worldview was intertwined with the developing need to address their past abortions through action. 'In 2006 I came to faith and started to rethink my life. The greatest sin that cannot be corrected is abortion', was how the staff psychologist of the Saint Petersburg centre, a mother of two who had terminated her first pregnancy, started her narrative of how she heard about the centre and became involved in its work. She began to counsel pregnant women, with little initial experience, but found that 'a psychologist is always strong in those areas where he [sic] has lived through something himself emotionally; he can give another person advice, guide them so they can become aware of their mistakes'.

In their effort to keep younger women from repeating the same mistakes they had made, the volunteers in various cities handed out flyers and information at legal pickets in public spaces, occasionally in front of gynaecological clinics. They also committed mildly illegal acts, such as putting up stickers in underground trains or on the lamp posts in the city. I remember one animated discussion over tea in which several respectable matrons in their sixties exchanged advice on the best times and places for putting up unauthorised stickers in the Saint Petersburg metro. Like conservative women activists elsewhere in the world (Blee and Deutsch 2012; Ginsburg 1998), these women's convictions sometimes set them against the prevailing social order even as they see themselves as working to uphold its ideals.

Transformative Actions

When reading the North American literature on trauma and PAS, Russian activists interpret it through the lens of teachings about the consequences of sinful and virtuous actions that they learn through their involvement with the Church. Different from evangelical Protestant understandings of a one-time voluntary act of handing one's sins over to Jesus, but also from the Catholic emphasis on the priest's power to bestow forgiveness, Orthodox practices of penance emphasise the ongoing need to work on changing habits and inclinations. These changes happen through outward actions more than through inward self-examination, shifting the work of dealing with PAS away from seeking to make peace with a dead child towards healing the gaps in kin groups and national collectives that were caused by abortion.

The priest's counsel to confess and forget and the psychologist's idea of counselling as warning others against repeating one's own mistakes both express a theory of the human psyche that coincides not only with Orthodox theology, but also with Soviet Marxist reservations against the Freudian psychology of subconscious drives (Kharkhordin 1999; Oushakine 2004). Instead of dwelling on one's sins through introspection, the imperative is to confess them and put them out of one's mind, and cultivate opposing virtues in oneself and the world. This is why abortion is problematic as a 'sin that cannot be corrected', because there is no easily identifiable balancing virtue. The child, as the priest in Saint Petersburg went on to say, cannot be brought back. What priests do advise is to support life as it is embodied in other children and their families. For many activists this means persuading pregnant women not to have abortions and supporting them materially and morally while their children are young, either quietly through giving money to individuals or publicly through handing out flyers and protesting abortion clinics.

During my research I sometimes became the object of such penitential exercises. In Saint Petersburg in 2010, I attended several events and prayer services sponsored by the crisis pregnancy centre with my infant daughter, who was less than six months old at the time. On two occasions, an elderly woman slipped money into my hand, each of them almost begging me to take it 'in aid'. By appearing at a church service with an infant, I marked myself as a deserving recipient. Not wanting to hurt the donor, I accepted the money and placed it in the centre's donation box, assuming that in this way it would serve its intended purpose.

Some of these theologically motivated psychologies recall those of the Western pro-life movement, where public avowals of past abortions are part of evangelical narrative conventions of 'witnessing' to the sinfulness one has overcome (Harding 2000). One difference lies in the near-universality of the experience of abortion among women who came of age in the Soviet Union. The sheer number of abortions makes it more difficult to commemorate aborted foetuses as individuals. There are simply too many of them, and general expectations of human life chances are perhaps too realistic (Ransel 2000) to treat foetuses as the special individuals with an inherent right to live as they appear, for example, in North American pro-life activism.

Abortion politics in North America often involve memory practices that retroactively endow aborted foetuses with personhood. The 2004 documentary *Jesus Camp* shows children in an evangelical youth camp in North Dakota handling plastic dolls that represent foetuses at various stages of gestation, while adult counsellors tell them that these would have been their friends and siblings had it not been for the Roe v. Wade decision (Ewing and Grady 2006). The Japanese custom of putting up small statues *(mizuko)* in commemoration of aborted foetuses (Hardacre 1998) is recommended by English-language websites of pro-choice as well as pro-life orientation.[4]

Such personification of foetuses occurs only to a limited degree in the Russian Orthodox Church. The plastic dolls of 'preborn' children came to Russia as gifts from Western pro-lifers, and are now locally made. I saw them used in psychologists' offices for consultations with pregnant women, but never to symbolise or commemorate past abortions. Namings, funerals, or posthumous baptisms were also categorically rejected by priests, who emphasised that baptism can only be bestowed on a living person. Since only baptism provides a person with the name of a saint by which he or she can be referred to in prayer, the impossibility of posthumous baptism also meant that believers could not include aborted foetuses among the deceased relatives for whom they prayed or commissioned prayers.

To commemorate abortions, official Church publications recommend only a very general prayer that asks God's mercy for all 'the souls of your departed servants the infants who died in the wombs of Orthodox mothers, either unintentionally ... or consciously killed and therefore not having received baptism'. Only at the end is the woman supposed to mention her own abortions, again in the plural and without a name: 'Lord, have mercy on my children, who died in my womb. By my faith and my tears and for the sake of Your mercy, Lord, do not deprive them of Your divine light' (Anonymous 2005: 55).

Not having received social personhood through baptism (Hirschon 2010), aborted foetuses are merely potential members of their families and the Russian nation. Collective commemorations sponsored by the anti-abortion movement use a symbol that points away from individualised acts of abortion to state-sponsored mass killing: the icon of the 14,000 Holy

Innocent Infants of Bethlehem in Judah, killed by Herod. Catholic tradition calls this subject the Slaughter of the Innocents, and it refers to the gospel narrative of King Herod ordering the killing of all children under two in the attempt to kill the new-born Jesus.

The icon's association with abortion is a post-Soviet invention stemming from the Life Centre in Moscow, again with precedents in international Catholicism (Stycos 1965). Different from the Japanese mizuko statues, icons of the Infants of Bethlehem represent a crowd of '14,000' slain children, and thus do not lend themselves to becoming the focus of mourning an individual. By depicting a large group of child victims and likening abortion to an act of state violence, the icon speaks to the shared experience of women whose reproductive lives fell into the Soviet period. 'What, you haven't had any abortions?' a retired train conductor and grandmother who regularly attended her parish church in Nizhnii Novgorod asked me when I told her about my research. The icon reframes this common experience as a condition of complicity or victimhood in a programme of government-sanctioned murder. Most of the blame appears to shift to the Soviet state, the most obvious analogy of King Herod. But activists also explained the icon as showing that the root cause of abortion is the search for personal glory and gain, linking Herod's quest to keep his throne to the concern with material comfort and security that they see as a cause of low birth rates and continuing high abortion rates in post-Soviet Russia.

In Saint Petersburg and Nizhnii Novgorod, regular prayer services in front of icons of the Infants of Bethlehem ask collective forgiveness for past abortions and divine mercy for aborted souls, but mainly focus on litanies of names of living people: pregnant women, newly born children, childless couples, and donors of the centre. Participating in these prayers and donating to pro-life causes gives women an opportunity to do the kind of 'work' that is supposed to put their hearts at ease. But for some, these officially sanctioned venerations are not enough. I met at least three women who mentioned having engaged in the so-called 'Rule of the Schemanun Antonia', a prayer litany in the course of which a mother picks a name for the aborted foetus and asks John the Baptist to baptise the child by that name. After reciting the litany, the prescription is to donate a baptismal robe and baptismal cross to a church to sponsor the baptism of a poor or orphaned child. 'Over there in the other world it all comes true right away, and your children are no longer bloody demons, but beautiful babies waiting for their mama', as a woman in her twenties explained to a fellow pilgrim during a walking pilgrimage in Kirov region in 2013. The ritual resolved the double bind created by Orthodox doctrine. By official church teachings, abortion was murder because it killed a real person, but that person could never be equal to ordinary dead relatives. Posthumous baptism or dreams in which the Virgin Mary or a saint revealed the child's name made it possible to imagine the aborted foetus as a full-fledged family member rather than an angry ghost.

While the women who used it found it comforting, many priests denounced posthumous baptism as 'paganism'. Besides dogmatic objections to the idea of baptising a dead person, one reason clergy were opposed to these practices was that they distracted from the kind of public outreach that should be the sign of true repentance. 'I don't encourage women to think about it as "I need to pray for the child because he is suffering over there"', explained a priest in Moscow. 'Better persuade a young woman not to have an abortion, or help a family with many children'.

This insistence on public and collective commemoration and outreach rather than personification of individual foetuses as the correct way to deal with memories of abortion sometimes becomes part of a larger diagnosis in which society as a whole is afflicted with PAS, rather than individuals. For younger activists in particular, the psychological discourse of abortion trauma becomes a way of claiming their place in national history.

PAS as a Collective Affliction

Anthropological work on discourses of trauma understands them as a way of imbuing historical suffering with moral significance and identifying key past events for explaining present problems (Antze and Lambek 1996; Fassin and Rechtman 2009). In post-Soviet Russia, survivors of Stalin's GULag and later persecutions mobilise in various organisations, but they have not achieved the iconic status of moral spokespersons of, for example, holocaust survivors in North America.[5] Recent work on memory in Putin-era Russia has pointed to the way in which public criticism of Soviet history has become muted, and often relegated to the 'magical historicism' of fiction (Etkind 2009). Among the many 'undead in the land of the unburied', foetuses are perhaps easiest to mourn as innocent victims because they pose no threat to present political elites. Instead, anxieties about demographic development turn unborn children into symbols of a desired future.

Elena, a university student in Kazan, led a local chapter of the 'Warriors of Life', a more militant pro-life organisation that organised pickets in front of gynaecological clinics and consciously emulated the tactics of North American 'hard pro-life'. In an interview with a journalist at a picket in 2012, the young activist diagnosed all of Russian society with PAS. When I asked her later what she meant by that, she described a collective psyche that was damaged by the repeated actions of many. The high numbers of abortions made the whole society 'evil, irritable, with an inclination toward violence'. On the positive side, Elena said that getting involved in anti-abortion activism had made her feel more connected to children, who had meant little to her before as a non-parent. Now she thought of all children as 'our future'.

This collectivised notion of PAS was sometimes referred to by younger activists to explain why not all of the older women who had had abortions became involved in the movement. 'Perhaps it is postabortion syndrome that is keeping them from recognising this sin', speculated the organiser of a yearly pro-life festival that brought together groups from across the former Soviet Union in Moscow. A retired obstetrician from Perm' also referred to a collective state of trauma and denial to explain why it was hard to change doctors' attitudes to abortion: 'I really think postabortion syndrome exists; they all performed abortions for so many years, and it affects a person, I remember it from myself'.

When referring to a group of people rather than an individual, talk about PAS is a way of evaluating the past and the present, and diagnosing contemporary Russia with a collective amnesia akin to the 'inability to mourn' of postwar Germany (Mitscherlich and Mitscherlich 1967). The focus of criticism is the compromises Soviet generations of women made in the name of the 'gendered citizenship of the working mother' (Zdravomyslova 2009: 113), but also the enduring effects of Soviet policy on post-Soviet expectations of family size and gender roles. Trying to promote patriotism at the same time as denouncing legal abortions and picketing state-funded clinics, Russian Orthodox pro-lifers hold a complex position in relation to their country and its history. The psychological metaphor of trauma naturalises opposition to abortion, allowing activists to denounce social ills without appearing unpatriotic. If abortion is the root cause of problems with unstable families, divorce, poor infant health, and substance abuse, this means that its critics align themselves with government efforts to raise the birth rate (Rivkin-Fish 2010). By claiming to free their society of a debilitating trauma while attacking physicians and clinics who work according to legal mandate, activists carve out a difficult role in the polarised political climate of Putin's Russia: that of a loyal critic of the status quo.

Conclusion: Key Events and Intergenerational Activism

Susan Gal and Gail Kligman (2000) suggest that reproductive policy was an attractive area of engagement for post-socialist governments because it allowed them to win popular trust by constructing a sense of harmonious conjuncture between citizens' personal concerns and political initiatives. Although Russia has not seen the same sharp reversals of abortion legislation as post-socialist Poland and Romania (Kligman 1998; Zielinska 2000), the idea of individual and collective trauma caused by past abortions serves as such a harmonising discourse. Blaming the Soviet gender order helps erase current differences between a pronatalist government that upholds the legality of abortion and activists who claim that the moral and physical survival of the nation depends on abolishing the procedure.

At the level of national history, activists point to the legalisation of abortion first in 1920 and then again in 1955 as successive turning points towards destroying natural orders of gender and reproductive life. But Orthodox activists and clergy go further than most secular politicians by tracing all mistakes of the Soviet gender order back to the foundational crime of regicide: the execution of Tsar Nicholas II with his wife and children by the Bolsheviks in 1918. Anti-abortion activists tend to be sympathetic to monarchist wings of the Russian Orthodox Church, who argue that repentance of the murder of the tsar is the key to solving Russia's social and economic problems (Papkova 2011). Icons of the imperial couple with their five children, all canonised in 2000, grace many offices of church organisations concerned with children, education, or childbirth. They offer a window back to a point in time at which history might have taken a different turn. Like individual abortions, the royal deaths serve as an explanatory device for any misfortune that followed.

At the individual level, activists and penitents often had more specific regrets that did not directly correspond to such a national narrative. Even interviewees who endorsed the view that abortion was a sin often turned out to regret a specific abortion because they wondered how it had changed their life course. A teacher in Kazan who attended devotions to the Holy Innocent Infants mentioned that she had undergone 'more than one' abortion, but kept talking about her last pregnancy in 1991. She had toyed with the idea of having a third child, but her husband counselled against it, given the unstable economic situation. Two elderly women I met were mothers of sons and remembered a particular abortion as one where they speculated the foetus might have been a girl. They imagined what old age might be like with the support of a daughter, rather than having to depend on tenuous membership in their married sons' households. 'A daughter-in-law is not a daughter', as a woman in her eighties who had moved from Central Asia to live with her son in Saint Petersburg said wistfully.

For these women, rethinking past reproductive decisions was a way of imagining alternative life courses and locating points where things might have gone differently. At such moments of concreteness, rarely did women mention demographic development or the size of the Russian nation as a whole; nor did they necessarily reject the notion of working outside the home while raising a family. Rather, they linked a general negative attitude to abortion to regrets over not having attained a preferred family size or gender composition, and affirmed themselves as moral individuals who would have acted differently if given more information or support. The gap left by abortion was one of nostalgic possibility rather than a traumatic destruction of the natural order of things.

Remembered as a necessity rather than a right, widespread abortions are perhaps a predictable starting point for critical views of Soviet society. While numerically small and limited in their influence, anti-abortion activists connect to wider ambiguities about decisions people made during decades of changing gender and family roles. As remembered and commemorated events, the Bolshevik regicide and Soviet-era abortions serve as sites of imagined possibility by virtue of their irreversibility: since it is impossible to go back to the point of decision, it is safe to dream about alternative outcomes. By labelling these turning points traumatic, and proposing social outreach or charity as a cure, the diagnosis of PAS endows speculative hindsight with practical consequences. Abortion in Russia is not just a matter of abstract moral principle, but also of living memory, and this combination makes for a distinctive activist scene.

Sonja Luehrmann is Associate Professor of Anthropology at Simon Fraser University in Vancouver, Canada. Her research focuses on religious and secular ideologies and popular mobilisation in Soviet and post-Soviet Russia. Her publications include *Secularism Soviet Style: Teaching Atheism and Religion in a Volga Republic* (Indiana University Press, 2011) and *Religion in Secular Archives: Soviet Atheism and Historical Knowledge* (Oxford University Press, 2015). She is currently working on a book on anti-abortion activism in the Russian Orthodox Church.

Notes

1. Materials in this chapter are drawn from ethnographic field research conducted in European Russia between 2008 and 2014, in the cities of Moscow, Saint Petersburg, Kazan and Nizhnii Novgorod and in Kirov region. In the first four locations, I regularly attended meetings and events in church-based pregnancy consultation centres over periods ranging between two weeks and four months. I conducted interviews with staff members and volunteers, as well as with gynaecologists, clergy, and activists in the field of reproductive and family policy affiliated with other religious and secular organisations. In Kirov region, I participated in a three-day

walking pilgrimage in August 2013 and interviewed clergy in the regional centre. To protect the privacy of interviewees, names have been changed. I am indebted to Anastasia Rogova for assistance with transcription and library research, and gratefully acknowledge financial support from the UBC Killam Trust, IREX (with funds provided through the Title VIII Program of the U.S. State Department), and the Social Science Research Council. An earlier version of this chapter benefited from discussions at the Symposium 'Post-Socialist Psy-ences: From the New Socialist Person to Global Mental Health', held at the University of Chicago in April 2013.

2. Central Archives of Nizhnii Novgorod Region (TsANO), f. 3118, op. 1, d. 224a, l. 81, Regional Health Authority, Yearly report for 1954.

3. These restrictions include a mandatory waiting period of up to seven days between a woman's first presenting for an abortion and the date of the procedure, mandatory counselling by an in-house psychologist during this period, and the right to conscientious objection for obstetricians. They were introduced in 2011 through changes to the health code of the Russian Federation. Little research has been done on the implementation of the new legislation. For the text of the law, see http://www.rg.ru/2011/11/23/zdorovie-dok.html. Retrieved 28 February 2014.

4. Jennifer Ramsay, Mizuko. http://mizuko.com.au/order-a-jizo.html. Retrieved 15 April 2013.

5. For a genealogy of the use of holocaust analogies in North American abortion debates, see Mensch and Freeman 1993.

References

Anonymous. 2005. *Pravo na zhizn': O smertnom grekhe aborta.* Pochaev: Izdatel'stvo Pochaevskoi lavry.

Antze, P. and M. Lambek. 1996. *Tense Past: Cultural Essays in Trauma and Memory.* New York: Routledge.

Blee, K. and S.M. Deutsch (eds). 2012. *Women of the Right: Comparisons and Interplay Across Borders.* University Park: Penn State University Press.

Burke, T. with D. Reardon. 2002. *Forbidden Grief: The Unspoken Pain of Abortion.* Springfield, IL: Acorn Books.

Bychenkova, I. 1965. 'Pust' on uvidit solntse', in O. V. Makeeva, *Zdorov'e zhenshchiny.* Moscow: Meditsina, p. 129.

Dadlez, E.M. and W.L. Andrews. 2010. 'Post-abortion Syndrome: Creating an Affliction', *Bioethics* 24(9): 445–52.

Denisov, B.P., V.I. Sakevich and A. Jasilioniene. 2012. 'Divergent Trends in Abortion and Birth Control Practices in Belarus, Russia and Ukraine', *PLoS ONE* 7 (11): e49986. doi:10.1371/journal.pone.0049986

Etkind, A. 2009. 'Stories of the Undead in the Land of the Unburied: Magical Historicism in Contemporary Russian Fiction', *Slavic Review* 68(3): 631–58.

Ewing, H. and R. Grady. 2006. *Jesus Camp.* Documentary film. Los Angeles: A & E Indiefilms and Magnolia Pictures.

Fassin, D. and R. Rechtman. 2009. *The Empire of Trauma: An Inquiry into the Condition of Victimhood.* Princeton: Princeton University Press.

Field, D. 2007. *Private Life and Communist Morality in Khrushchev's Russia.* New York: Peter Lang.

Gal, S. and G. Kligman. 2000. *The Politics of Gender after Socialism: A Comparative-Historical Essay.* Princeton: Princeton University Press.

Ginsburg, F. 1998. *Contested Lives: The Abortion Debate in an American Community.* Berkeley/Los Angeles: University of California Press.

Hardacre, H. 1997. *Marketing the Menacing Foetus in Japan.* Berkeley/Los Angeles: University of California Press.

Harding, S. 2000. *The Book of Jerry Falwell: Fundamentalist Language and Politics.* Princeton: Princeton University Press.

Hirschon, R. 2010. 'Indigenous Persons and Imported Individuals: Changing Paradigms of Personal Identity in Contemporary Greece', in C. Hann and H. Goltz (eds), *Eastern Christians in Anthropological Perspective.* Berkeley: University of California Press, pp. 289–310.

Hutter, I. 2003. 'Determinants of Abortion and Contraceptive Behavior in Russia,' in A.M. Basu (ed.), *The Sociocultural and Political Aspects of Abortion: Global Perspectives.* Westport: Praeger, pp. 185–202.

Kharkhordin, O. 1999. *The Collective and the Individual in Russia: A Study of Practices.* Berkeley/L.A.: University of California Press.

Kligman, G. 1998. *The Politics of Duplicity: Controlling Reproduction in Ceausescu's Romania.* Berkeley/Los Angeles: University of California Press.

Larivaara, M. 2009. 'Moral'naia otvetstvennost' zhenshchin i avtoritet vrachei: Vzaimodeistvie ginekologov i patsientok', in E. Zdravomyslova, A. Rotkirch and A. Temkina (eds), *Novyi byt v sovremennoi Rossii: Gendernye issledovaniia povsednevnosti.* Saint Petersburg: Izdatel'stvo Evropeiskogo universiteta, pp. 313–45.

Lee, E. 2003. *Abortion, Motherhood, and Mental Health.* New York: Aldine de Gruyter.

Leykin, I. 2011. 'Population Prescriptions: (Sanitary) Culture and Biomedical Authority in Contemporary Russia,' *Anthropology of East Europe Review* 29(1): 60–81.

Marcus, G. 1995. 'Ethnography in/of the World System: The Emergence of Multi-sited Ethnography', *Annual Review of Anthropology* 24: 95–117.

Mensch, E. and A. Freeman. 1993. *The Politics of Virtue: Is Abortion Debatable?* Durham and London: Duke University Press.

Mitscherlich, A. and M. 1967. *Die Unfähigkeit zu trauern: Grundlagen kollektiven Verhaltens.* Munich: Piper.

Morgan, L.M. 2009. *Icons of Life: A Cultural History of Human Embryos.* Berkeley/Los Angeles: University of California Press.

Morgan, L.M. and M. Michaels (eds). 2002. *Foetal Subjects, Feminist Positions.* Philadelphia: University of Pennsylvania Press.

Nakachi, M. 2008. 'Replacing the Dead: The Politics of Reproduction in the Post-war Soviet Union, 1944–1955', Ph.D. dissertation. Chicago: University of Chicago.

Ney, P.G. 1993. 'Post-abortion Survivors Syndrome', *The Canadian Journal of Psychiatry / La Revue Canadienne de Psychiatrie* 38(8): 577–78.

Obukhov, M. 2003. 'K tret'emu izdaniiu knigi Dzhona i Barbary Uillke', in D. Uillke and B. Uillke, *My mozhem liubit' ikh oboikh. Abort: Voprosy i otvety*. Moscow: Tsentr Zhizn', p. 3.

Oushakine, S.A. 2004. 'The Flexible and the Pliant: Disturbed Organisms of Soviet Modernity', *Cultural Anthropology* 19(3): 392–429.

Papkova, I. 2011. *The Orthodox Church and Russian Politics*. New York: Oxford University Press.

Połtawska, W. [V. Pultavskaia]. 1962. *I boję się snow*. Warsaw: Czytelnik.

———. 1996. 'Vliianie preryvaniia beremennosti na psikhiku zhenshchiny', in Famille de Demain, Bruxelles (ed.), *XVIII Mezhdunarodnyi Kongress Sem'i*. Moscow: Rudomino, pp. 256–83.

Popov, A., A. Visser and E. Ketting. 1993. 'Contraceptive Knowledge, Attitudes, and Practice in Russia during the 1980s', *Studies in Family Planning* 24(4): 227–35.

Ransel, D. 2000. *Village Mothers: Three Generations of Change in Russia and Tataria*. Bloomington: Indiana University Press.

Rivkin-Fish, M. 2010. 'Pronatalism, Gender Politics, and the Renewal of Family Support in Russia: Toward a Feminist Anthropology of Maternity Capital', *Slavic Review* 69(3): 701–24.

Sakevich, V. 2009. 'Problema aborta v sovremennoi Rossii', in E. Zdravomyslova and A. Temkina (eds), *Zdorov'e i doverie: gendernyi podkhod k reproduktivnoi meditsine*. Saint Petersburg: Izdatel'stvo Evropeiskogo universiteta, pp. 136–52.

Stycos, J.M. 1965. 'Opinions of Latin-American Intellectuals on Population Problems and Birth Control', *Annals of the American Academy of Political and Social Science* 360: 11–26.

Uillke, D. and B. Uillke. 2003. *My mozhem liubit' ikh oboikh. Abort: Voprosy i otvety*. Moscow: Tsentr Zhizn'.

Vishnevskii, A.G (ed.). 2011. *Naselenie Rossii 2009: Semnadtsatyi ezhegodnyi demograficheskii doklad*. Moscow: Izdatel'skii dom Vysshei shkoly ekonomiki.

Zdravomyslova, E. 2009. 'Gendernoe grazhdanstvo i abortnaia kul'tura', in E. Zdravomyslova and A. Temkina (eds), *Zdorov'e i doverie: gendernyi podkhod k reproduktivnoi meditsine*. Saint Petersburg: Izdatel'stvo Evropeiskogo universiteta, pp. 108–35.

Zielinska. 2000. 'Between Ideology, Politics, and Common Sense: The Discourse of Reproductive Rights in Poland,' in S. Gal and G. Kligman (eds), *Reproducing Gender: Politics, Publics, and Everyday Life after Socialism*. Princeton: Princeton University Press, pp. 23–57.

Chapter 6

Still a Woman's Right?
Feminist and Other Discourses in Belgium's
Abortion Struggles

by Karen Celis and Gily Coene

Introduction

In 1990, after a long and salient political struggle, Belgium adopted a law
that partially legalised abortion. Since 1867, abortion, performed for whatever reason, had legally been a 'crime against the order of the family and
public morality'.[1] Compared to other European countries, Belgium was
particularly late to legalise abortion, and it cannot claim to have established
the most generous legalisation of abortion. Once enacted, though, the 1990
abortion law seemed to have installed a solid status quo, which in light of
the evolution of abortion debates and legislation in other European countries seems to have foremost prevented any conservative reform restricting
the right to abortion in Belgium. The flipside, however, is that proponents
of a broader legalisation of abortion have also been unsuccessful.

This chapter will first discuss the history and content of the 1990 law,
shedding light on its key proponents and opponents, and on the exception-
ally long and difficult decision-making process. The subsequent section will
describe the very few political and societal debates about abortion that have
taken place in Belgium since 1990, when the abortion legislation seems to
have almost silenced all debate on the issue. The final section will explore
several explanations for this absence of political debate and activist struggle
in Belgium. The chapter is based on an extensive literature review and on
analysis of written press and online sources for the post 1990 period.

The History of the 1990 Abortion Law

The Women's Movement: Driving Force behind the Legalisation of Abortion

Though the socialist women's movement has strived for reproductive rights for women, including the decriminalisation of abortion, since the first half of the twentieth century, their demands were not heard for several decades – neither in nor outside the ranks of the socialist movement (Celis 1993). It was only in the 1970s that the 'Second Wave' women's movement managed to politicise the demand for a right to abortion. With the iconic slogan 'Master over one's own belly' they combatively campaigned for access to contraception – only in 1973 was the 1923 law forbidding distribution and information on contraception abolished – and for the decriminalisation of abortion throughout the 1970s.

Notwithstanding internal differences and disputes, feminist organisations managed to join forces on the abortion issue. In 1978, International Women's Day events were entirely devoted to the abortion question. It was decided that an abortion demonstration would be held in March every following year (Vander Stichele 1983: 18; Van Mechelen 1996 [1979]; Vanmeenen 1991: 30). With such initiatives, the women's movement kept the abortion issue on the streets and on the political agenda. Their efforts to influence the political decision-making process were successful: in 1988 a memorandum putting forth the National Women's Council's position was included in the appendix of the official parliamentary report of the commission dealing with the abortion bills. The appeals and petitions of women's organisations and lobbies in favour of liberalisation were referred to in the 1989–1990 parliamentary debates, amongst others by the president of the National Women's Council, who was at the same time a Member of Parliament.

The women's movement did not stand alone in this debate, however. The liberal-secular humanist movement strongly supported the women's movement's claims concerning women's rights to reproductive autonomy. The legalisation of abortion debates was part of a broader emancipatory struggle to free Belgian society, legislation, and politics from the dominance of the Catholic Church. Like later ethical struggles about euthanasia and same-sex marriages, the right to abortion was also a paradigmatic test for the secularity of the state, the respect for moral pluralism, and freedom of conscience of non-believers (Witte 1993). In addition, medical doctors who publicly testified that they were performing abortions played a key role in the public and political debate. Although it remained legally forbidden, abortions were performed from the seventies onwards by well-trained medical doctors, under safe medical conditions in hospitals and – inspired by the example of the Netherlands – in specialised polyclinic abortion care centres.[2] Although the costs of an abortion as such were not reimbursed by health insurance, women who could not afford it were regularly helped through solidarity funds and free medical help.

The Anti-abortion Movement

Before the abortion debate arrived on the political agenda there was no active countermovement. Pro Vita – a Roman Catholic[3] anti-abortion organisation – was only formed as a result of the first bill proposal in 1971. It opposed all forms of abortion, but remained in the background during the 1970s (Marques-Pereira 1989; Witte 1990). In the 1980s, Pro Vita's campaign became stronger and more clear-cut, as their militants also personally approached members of Parliament. At the same time though, tolerance for abortion was growing in Catholic circles (Marques-Pereira 1989: 65; Witte 1990: 454), which undermined the recruitment basis for the pro-life movement. A survey conducted in the 1990s by the women's section of the Christian Democratic Party (CVP) (*Vrouw en Maatschappij* –Woman and Society) showed that even a significant number of its own members were in favour of liberalising abortion legislation (Witte 1990: 454). Furthermore, the Christian Democratic women increasingly showed their dissatisfaction with the obstructionist politics of their party, which we will discuss in the next section (Celis 2001).

The countermovement, with Pro Vita at its forefront, nevertheless campaigned heavily during the final phase of the abortion debate. It tried to get its message across using phone calls, threatening and slanderous letters, pamphlets, and films. Their campaign was so shocking in its brutality that it actually alienated many opponents of abortion reform (Witte 1990: 477–78).

The Political Decision-Making Process Leading to the 1990 Abortion Law

Notwithstanding the strong societal pressures to legalise abortion and the rather weak countermovement, it would take nearly twenty years to reach a political agreement on the liberalisation of abortion. The two decades between the first bill proposal in 1971 and the passing of the 1990 law were to be marked by diligent activity in Parliament. In time, even if legally forbidden, abortion also became more accessible for women, with a more open execution of abortions in Belgium and the possibility for Belgian women to legally terminate their pregnancies in neighbouring countries, like England, France and the Netherlands. The loud protests of the advocates of liberalisation and the silent but growing gap between abortion law and practice made the situation untenable.

The main political obstacle to abortion legislation was the CVP, which had been in government non-stop since World War II. The liberalisation of abortion was simply not negotiable for this party that closely adhered to its Catholic values. Aside from submitting bill proposals, the other government and opposition parties applied a variety of political strategies. The pro-legalisation front tried to depoliticise the issue by calling in medical and legal experts to advise on the issue. Each and every time though, the CVP used its power to block abortion legislation.

After twenty years of political debate, the only remaining option was to form a majority in favour of abortion legalisation without the governing CVP. This was a highly unusual and politically risky scenario, because it could mean the end of the coalition and the fall of the government. On 29 March 1990, the Chamber passed the Lallemand-Herman-Michielsens bill to decriminalise abortion in the first twelve weeks, by a majority and without the support of the governing CVP. This shook the foundations of the Belgian state. Though the government did not fall, it did result in a small royalty crisis. Whereas royal assent is always required for a bill to become a formal law, this process is usually a formality. In this case, however, King Baudoin refused to assent on 'moral grounds' and was thus 'temporarily considered incapable to reign'. The ministers in the Cabinet had to step in to ratify and enact the bill (Witte 1990: 480–1).

The 1990 Abortion Law

The 1990 abortion law[4] permits abortions within the first twelve weeks of the pregnancy when it causes a 'state of distress' for the pregnant woman, for instance due to a pregnancy as a result of rape or incest. The law, however, does not define this state of distress and leaves the appreciation of this condition up to the woman who is considering ending her pregnancy. The law furthermore stipulates compulsory counselling on alternatives to abortion, a six-day waiting period ('period of reflection'), and a 'unity of place' of the first counselling and the operation. After twelve weeks, abortion is only allowed in cases where the pregnancy poses a serious health risk to the woman or in cases where the foetus suffers from a serious and incurable disease. In such situations the attending doctor – after seeking a second opinion from a colleague – decides whether at least one of these conditions is fulfilled and whether the termination of a pregnancy is legal.

The law also established a National Evaluation Commission to supervise and evaluate the implementation of the law. The Commission gathers data on the number of abortions and reports to Parliament. A recurrent finding of the Commission is that the number of abortions in Belgium is consistently low. In 2009, 18.870 Belgian women underwent an abortion, from a total population of approximately eleven million inhabitants. With 9.28 abortions for 1,000 pregnancies in 2009 (Temmerman 2013: 110), Belgium has one of the lowest abortion rates in Europe. This appears to be due to its open and efficient prevention campaigns and contraceptive policies. Abortions are performed in specialised centres and are generally considered to be accessible and of high medical quality (Temmerman 2013; Vrancken 2013). Except when performed abroad, the costs of abortions are largely covered by the national health insurance.

Abortion Protests and Activism since 1990

The controversy concerning the right to abortion almost disappeared from public and political life after the introduction of the 1990 abortion law. Though the right to have an abortion in a case of an unwanted pregnancy has become more commonly accepted, anti-abortion activism nevertheless still exists in Belgian society. The following section maps both the pro-choice and the anti-abortion debates and movements that have occurred since 1990.

Unsuccessful Political Attempts to Modify the 1990 Abortion Law

During the 1990s, the extreme-right party Vlaams Belang was the main political actor fighting the abortion law. The party published an anti-abortion pamphlet (Meeus and Annemans 1996), and introduced law proposals and parliamentary questions aiming to restrict abortion rights.[5] The youth section of the party was often involved in anti-abortion demonstrations at care centres performing abortions. In 2009, for instance, they protested against the establishment of an abortion care centre with the slogan 'An abortion clinic is a murder clinic' (De Vlaams Belang Jongeren 2009).

Although the 1990 law came as a big victory for the feminist movement and the final bill met the women's movement request for legal abortion (Celis 2001, 2013), pro-choice activists kept on criticising the law for its paternalistic character (Cosyns 2013; Van Crombrugge 2013). According to these critics, four elements still prevent women from making full use of their right to abortion: first, the time limit of twelve weeks is very restrictive, thus encouraging abortion tourism (especially to the Netherlands, where abortion is legal until twenty-four weeks). Second and third, it installs a six-day reflection period and requires a unity of place of abortion counselling and implementation. The fourth criticism concerns the reimbursement of the costs only for interventions in Belgium, thus not covering abortions performed abroad (Commissie voor Welzijn 1997).

For these reasons, the Minister of Social Affairs and Public Health, Laurette Onkelinx (Parti Socialiste – Francophone Socialist Party) called for a debate about the twelve-week stipulation, in a 2010 newspaper interview on the occasion of the twentieth anniversary of the abortion law. According to her, this period was too short for certain groups of women – that is, women who do not live in major cities, who have no access to the necessary information, or who for other reasons find out too late they are pregnant (*Abortustermijn* 2010). Shortly thereafter, the VLD (Flemish Liberal Democratic Party) also called for an extension of the legal term (Open VLD 2010).

This initiative evoked strong negative reactions, not only from the extreme-right party (Vlaams Belang 2010), but also from CVP. The president of their youth section called an abortion after twelve weeks 'unthinkable', because 'the first trimester has passed and the unborn child is almost 'completed', and any abortion after twenty-two weeks a 'horrible idea', as the child 'has a chance to survive outside of the mother or is not very far from the moment of having that' (Maréchal 2010). However, the youth section of CVP did not question the existing legitimacy of an abortion until twelve weeks, a fact that could point to a possible shift towards the acceptance of legal abortion.

This shift was clearly exemplified the same year in the position of the Katholieke Arbeidersvrouwen (Flemish Catholic Women's Movement), which called for an improvement of the law, based on the ethical position that when a pregnant woman considers having an abortion, priority should be given to her autonomous right to decide, even when she is a minor. Although they were not very specific about it, they showed openness towards an extension of the legal term. However, they did not support extending the legal term to twenty-two/twenty-four weeks,[6] for this would come close to the viability limit as well as the twenty-four week term in which a dead born child is legally recognised (Katholieke Arbeidersvrouwen 2010).

A year later, the *Nederlandstalige Vrouwenraad* (Flemish Women's Council) – a network of the major women's organisations in Flanders, including the Flemish Catholic Women's Movement – called for an extension of the legal term to sixteen/eighteen weeks and a reduction of the reflection period from six days to forty-eight hours (Abortus is een recht 2011). They also proposed that medical doctors who refuse to perform an abortion should automatically refer the patient to another colleague, and they recommended that a pregnancy due to failing contraceptives should be included in the list of emergency situations that is provided by the National Evaluation Commission. This position was adopted by almost all members of the Women's Council in the board of directors meeting of 3 February 2011, with the exception of the members of the abstaining Nieuw-Vlaamse Alliantie-Vrouwenwerking (the nationalist New-Flemish Alliance Party's women's organisation). Though the New-Flemish Alliance[7] does not oppose the abortion law, it emphasises the need for more effective prevention and a more detailed registration of abortion requests (Sleurs 2012).

At the time that the potential reforms to the 1990 abortion law were launched and debated, the first anti-abortion 'March for Life' was organised in Brussels. Out of fear that a revision of the law would open the door for conservative reforms, further attempts to liberalise existing legislation were considered politically inopportune (Detiège 2013: 59; Temmerman 2013: 128). Until 2016, no political initiative has been taken to broaden the law.

March for Life and Recent Abortion Activism

Since 2010, a March for Life has been organised in Brussels annually. According to the newspaper *Le Soir*, Brussels police counted 2,840 participants in 2011 (Mgr. Léonard 2011).[8] The first was organised by a group of young students, who, while some acknowledged that they were religious believers,[9] stressed in media interviews that they were not politically or religiously affiliated with a particular party or organisation.[10] Their charter explains that the organisation is not only concerned with abortion but that it 'seeks to promote respect for human life from conception to natural death' and that they strive to 'to rescind or amend all laws and judicial decisions contrary to full respect for human life'.[11] On their website (www.marche-pourlaviebruxelles.org), the organisation presents itself as a four-member team (a group of students and young professionals) demanding that 'the right to life – at every stage –receives public attention'.[12] The website also includes a petition and a list of persons (academics and religious leaders) and organisations (anti-abortion and Christian organisations) that support March for Life.[13]

The participation of the archbishop of Belgium Mgr. André Léonard in the 2010 March attracted a lot of attention (André Léonard 2010). In contrast to his predecessor, Cardinal Danneels, who had a more progressive attitude towards ethical issues, Léonard is notorious for his ethical conservatism with regards to issues such as abortion or homosexuality. With the Catholic Church already in a deep crisis because of the child abuse scandals, the archbishop was strongly criticised when he called AIDS 'a kind of immanent justice' and homosexuality 'a wrong form of sexuality' while almost simultaneously calling for a more humane approach of paedophile senior clergymen (Aartsbisschop 2010). Activists, including Belgian (former) Femen members, attracted the attention of the media in demonstrations against the archbishop's positions on abortion and/or his offensive statements against homosexuality.

Today, Pro Vita continues to propagate traditional sexual morality and its anti-abortion position in schools and youth organisations (Gallasz 2013), while campaigning publicly against contraception, abortion, sex outside marriage, homosexuality, and euthanasia. Since the 1990s it has occasionally demonstrated outside abortion healthcare centres, showing graphic images to the centres' clients in an attempt to change their minds. Pro Vita has also initiated several lawsuits claiming that a foetus' biological father should have a right to decide whether it is aborted. Other organisations, such as 'Helpers of God's Precious Infants' hold prayer sessions and 'sidewalk counselling' in front of abortion centres on a monthly basis.

Whereas Catholic organisations such as Pro Vita had in the past a monopoly on anti-abortion positions and actions, recently they have been joined by a number of organisations that often present themselves as 'youth organisations' and operate through the Internet, such as Jongeren Info Life (Youth Info Life) or Levensadem/Souffle de Vie (Breath of Life). Apart from the aforementioned organisations, there are Jongeren voor het leven/ Jeunes pour la vie (Youngster for Life), Generation pour la vie (Generations for Life), Youth4Life, and Alternatives. Some of these organisations signed March for Life's petition, but what their precise (inter)connections are, or whether and to which extent they are involved in the organisation of the marches remains unclear. Whereas the anti-abortion lobby in the past was clearly associated with established organisations such as Pro Vita, abortion activism today seems to be more diffuse and to be comprised of different groups campaigning online.[14] A striking difference with pre-1990 anti-abortion activism is that a lot of effort is made to give anti-abortion activism a young, soft, and acceptable face (already apparent in the names of the aforementioned organisations). In documentaries about anti-abortion demonstrations, young activists are for instance especially put front and centre, and a March for Life is often represented as an independent student initiative.

Another shift within anti-abortion activism concerns the more traditional religiously condemnatory rhetoric having been replaced with an emphasis on the 'respect for persons' and 'the need to protect vulnerable beings'. As traditional religious doctrines and notions such as 'sin' have lost influence, particularly amongst young people, this rhetoric is perhaps thought to be closer to their ethical sensitivities. The charter of the March for Life (Mars voor het Leven 2013), for instance, affirms that 'the participants dissociate themselves from any offensive stance towards women who have had abortions. Participants do not judge but instead seek to help such women to make a new start'. The charter also emphasises that flags are forbidden during the demonstration and it also bans other visible symbols of support to a particular political regime, as well as clothing and symbols that are provocative or offensive.

In response to March for Life, the pro-choice side has organised counterdemonstrations, such as the 'March for the Right to Abortion in Europe' in 2012, and has established the 'Platform for the Right to Abortion in Europe'. This platform is a feminist and pluralist initiative that includes over twenty Belgian organisations. Its scope is, as the titles already indicate, not Belgium, but Europe. The Platform was established as a response to March for Life and similar movements around the world in order to defend the right to abortion in European countries that do not recognise this right today (Ireland, Malta, Cyprus, Poland). Its goal is to enhance access to abortion and improve the conditions under which they are performed (Memorandum 2014). The platform comprises different and powerful civil society organisations, including women's and secular humanist organisations, the socialist labour union, the socialist health insurance and federations of family planning centres. As such, the platform is able to mobilise among different groups in society and thus offers a broad-based response to recent anti-abortions discourses and actions. It organises petitions, counterdemonstrations to March for Life, and publishes memoranda in the run to elections.

A Distinct Debate: The Case of Disabled Foetuses

In general, pro-choice statements and activism have in the past stressed the right to abortion in cases of an unwanted pregnancy, implying that terminating a pregnancy for other reasons, for example if Down's syndrome is diagnosed, is a different and more complex issue. Although the abortion law includes the legal possibility for a termination of a pregnancy in the case of a severely disabled foetus, this has not been a major issue in the previous abortion debates. However, due to ongoing developments in prenatal diagnostics, the increasing pressure on women to perform such tests, and the lowering of the age of viability of a foetus, the termination of a pregnancy in cases where the foetus is handicapped has also become subject to societal debate.[15]

According to the Law on Medically Assisted Reproduction (2007), genetic pre-implementation diagnosis may not be used to select non-pathological genetic properties. Sex selection is thus also forbidden, though the Law's Article 67 allows for an exception to prevent sex-based diseases, thus recognising that preventing diseases and disabilities is legally permitted.

In the absence of clear legislation on this matter, medical abortion on the basis of a prenatal diagnosis is granted depending on the views of the attending doctor and the policies of the hospital. In the case of a refusal, the demand can be further submitted to the hospital's ethical committee, which extends the waiting period and may not necessarily end in a positive response. In order to avoid this, the woman/couple can only individually seek help elsewhere, as the doctor who refuses the demand is not required to refer the patient to another colleague or institution. The absence of clear-cut legislation also generates insecurity and a risk of doctors being prosecuted. In December 2011 for example, in a so-called 'wrongful life decision' a gynaecologist was condemned to pay compensation to the parents of a severely disabled child. While the gynaecologist should have seen after fifteen weeks that the child had a severe handicap (spina bifida), he informed the parents only after thirty weeks into the pregnancy. The case highlighted the law's lack of clarity, particularly with regards to the point in time at which a termination of the pregnancy is legally allowed. According to some legal experts (de Hert and Colette 2013: 89), the situation was ambiguous because, even if the law's explanatory memorandum mentions the 'viability of the foetus' as a limit, it does not provide further specifics. Thus, the absence of clear time specifications leaves room for interpretations, including the one that abortions can legally be performed until the time of birth.

In 2008, Caritas, the Catholic organisation of health institutions, advised its hospitals (which comprise 65 per cent of Flanders' hospitals) not to perform abortions in cases where a prenatal diagnosis indicates that the foetus is disabled (Verbond der Verzorgingsinstellingen 2008: 14). This led to critical political responses that stressed the right of the mother to decide (Abortus bij handicap 2008) [16] or criticised the lack of clarity and the puritanical character of the advice (Marleen Temmerman 2008).[17] For the Flemish humanist liberal/secular organisation Humanistisch-Vrijzinnige Vereniging (HVV), it was unacceptable that subsidised hospitals would not respect the pluralism in society, and abuse their monopoly position to enforce ethical views that are not shared by the majority (Siffer 2008).

A 2012 television documentary[18] in which parents testified that they had opted for an abortion because their baby would have otherwise suffered

from a severe disability again evoked critical responses. One of the key organisations in Belgium for persons with disabilities, GRIP (Equal Rights
for Every Person with a Disability), expressed some reservations, though
it has so far not taken a position on the issue,[19] while the Francophone
Association socialiste de la personne handicapée (Socialist Association
for Disabled People) (2012) explicitly distanced itself from anti-abortion
claims.[20] Terminations of pregnancies in cases where it is diagnosed that the
foetus is disabled will most probably become more salient in the future, as
the law is not very specific on the required conditions and because practices
evolve in a rather arbitrary way, depending on the ideological view of the
involved doctors and hospitals. The anti-abortion front uses these cases to
stress the dangers of abortion legislation, in terms of leading to an elimination policy of so-called non-perfect people. Putting this issue on the political agenda thus entails a risk of a backlash against abortion legislation.

Explaining the Status Quo

The previous section discussed both the few unsuccessful attempts to
broaden the 1990 abortion law and the anti-abortion activism that overall has so far been rather marginal and small-scale. None of these actions
has seriously threatened the status quo established by the 1990 abortion
law. A specification of the abortion law might be underway for cases where
disabled foetuses are concerned, but this will most certainly be a technical
matter, not a fundamental reform of the abortion law.

Although explaining the absence of social phenomena and events is often harder than explaining their manifestation, especially when the research
design is not a comparative one, this section will cautiously suggest several
explanations for both the overall small number of attempts to broaden the
1990 abortion law and the limited size and momentum of the anti-abortion
mobilisations.

The first set of reasons can be found in the history of the 1990 abortion law described earlier in the chapter. The legalisation of abortion had
been the result of a fierce struggle that had dominated politics for over
twenty years and, in the end phase of the decision-making process, risked
destabilising the entire Belgian political system. This seems to have taught
the political parties that sustaining the status quo with regards to abortion
legislation was by far the better option, and can be seen as the main reason
why the initial attempts to extend the legal term for abortion beyond the
first term of pregnancy were not followed up on. The history of the 1990
abortion law also shows that the anti-abortion movement never had the

same amount of political power and support in society as the feminist and humanist pro-choice movement. In conclusion, the power imbalance in favour of the pro-choice movement has always been solid.

The second set of explanations point to the more prominent position in the public sphere of other ethical debates during the 2000s. After a historic electoral defeat in 1999, the CVP was no longer part of the national government and this resulted in an ethically progressive climate in Belgian politics leading to liberal laws regarding patients' rights (2002), euthanasia (2002), same-sex marriages (2003), adoption by same-sex couples (2006), and medically assisted reproduction (2007). In contrast to the legalisation of abortion in which Belgium was a laggard compared to other European countries, it was to be ahead of many other countries in ethical issues from the new millennium onwards. It even became known as one of the most progressive countries in the world. Belgium was, for instance, the second country in the world to legalise voluntary assisted euthanasia and adapted in the same year a very progressive bill on Patient Rights that also implements the right to autonomy and individual freedom of choice in ethical matters. This series of ethically progressive laws indirectly protected the 1990 abortion law. First, it reoriented anti-abortion activists as well as ethically conservative politicians and organisations to focus on other salient ethical debates. Second, each ethically progressive pro-choice law further isolated the extreme-right party with their claims to recriminalise abortion and restrict women's rights to abortion. The latter position increasingly came to be at odds with the overall ethical climate and the broader legislative framework concerning ethical issues that stress individual autonomy.

The third set of explanations can be found in the structural power position of feminism and the women's movement since the enactment of the 1990 abortion law, discouraging pro-life mobilisation. Belgium is a consensus democracy with strong state-civil society interaction. The interest group structure is highly neo-corporatist; with the 'social partners' at its apex, corporatist networks are also customary in other sectors where the state meets society. Traditionally, political culture is characterised by consultation with the involved interests, compromise between conflicting demands, and the quest for consensus. Oppositional movements are invited to 'join the table' by the political elites to reach a settlement with regards to their demands; this strategy of co-optation also aims to downplay conflict. This political culture of consultation and consensus-seeking also extends to civil society-state interactions in general and civil society groups striving for the equality of, for instance, women, ethnic minorities, LGBT people, different age groups, and disabled people. These groups are consulted on a structural basis by the government, for instance through membership of official advisory bodies, and hence are considered to be representatives of these societal groups and/or experts on a specific inequality strand. In return, these civil society groups have been receiving government funding, enabling them to set up an organisation with a certain degree of autonomy and leadership.

The women's movement, supporting the pro-choice side of the abortion debates, is one of the civil society organisations that, through the women's policy agencies, has a (relatively) privileged relationship with the state. Women's policy agencies are those state departments or institutions that have the explicit task to foster gender equality. In the Belgian federal state these women's policy agencies are established at the various (national and sub-state) policy levels. At Belgium's state level, the women's policy agencies consist of a member of the executive (at first a state secretary and since early 1990 a minister of equal opportunities in charge of gender equality policies) and an Institute for the Equality between Women and Men (Celis and Meier 2006, 2007). There is also an official advisory body for gender equality (Council of Equal Opportunities for Men and Women), which includes representatives of a broad spectrum of women's organisations. Between the mid 1990s and 2004 all the Belgian regions and communities – with the exception of the German-speaking community – established women's policy agencies composed of a member of the executive in charge of equal opportunities and an administrative unit for equality policies.

The women's policy agencies at all levels of the Belgian federal state provide the women's movement with various access points to the state and to decision-making that could (and surely would) be used to block any undesired conservative abortion law reform. The presence of the women's policy agencies supports the status quo with regards to abortion legislation and is thus highly discouraging for the anti-abortion movement.

A fourth explanation can be found in the specificities of the Belgian political party landscape. None of the governing parties, not even the ones on the right of the political spectrum, have an anti-feminist and an anti-abortion agenda that weighs on the political decision-making. The CVP may be socially conservative and morally traditionalist; their claims often concern the appreciation of the specific role of women in the family and society, and the party does not adopt a progressive position on moral-ethical issues (Celis 2006). Having said that, the party has nevertheless implemented gender quotas since the 1970s, earning a rather feminist profile and a strong track record in women's rights bills in socio-economic and welfare issues (Celis 2006; Erzeel 2012). The main reason for its feminist profile is the party's strong women's ancillary organisation, which would not allow the CVP to make an anti-feminist turn by, for instance, officially supporting anti-abortion claims. To avoid dividing the party, it is safer for CVP to take morally and ethically conservative stances concerning different, more topically salient issues such as euthanasia and same-sex marriage.

The two other main right-wing parties adopting conservative standpoints on moral-ethical issues are the regionalist party Nieuw-Vlaamse Alliantie (New-Flemish Alliance, N-VA) and the extreme-right party Vlaams Belang. As discussed above, the latter party in the 1990s had more outspoken traditional (and even anti-feminist) views, both on the public and private role of women and on issues such as abortion (Van Molle and Gubin 1998). Today, these explicitly anti-feminist standpoints are no longer in play (Erzeel 2012). Furthermore, because of its racist party programme – the party was even convicted for violating anti-racism laws – all the other parties have agreed never to govern with the Vlaams Belang at any policy level. All parties also distance themselves as explicitly as possible from the extreme-right party's agenda. The Vlaams Belang's anti-abortion standpoint thus actually supported the status quo, by making the other parties even more inclined to defend the existing abortion law.

The other conservative party, N-VA, has so far not taken an explicit stance on the topic. While it does not oppose the right to abortion, it does, for instance, emphasise the need for more prevention. As discussed above, however, the women's section of the party did abstain from voting on the Flemish Women's Council's memorandum on the right to abortion in 2011. This also speaks to the party's ambivalent position concerning abortion. If the party moved in a more ethically conservative direction, though, this could be a threat to the existing abortion legislation. Since its establishment in 2001, the party has seen a sharp growth in votes and seats, and today it is a powerful party that could have the political capacity to put the abortion issue back on the table and actually instigate conservative reform.

Conclusion

The two decades before the 1990 abortion law were marked by societal mobilisation – of which the feminist movement was the key driver – and fierce political debates and struggles. The two decades after 1990 were foremost marked by a low degree of societal and political activity and controversy. Although the abortion controversy was occasionally revitalised and several debates took place post 1990, especially with regards to the legal time limit and the case of medical abortion of disabled foetuses, the status quo was never seriously challenged.

This chapter described these two highly distinct periods and explored some of the potential explanations for the lack of strong activism after 1990. The history of the 1990 Belgian abortion bill was responsible for two lessons: one teaching political parties that it is better to refrain from reforming abortion legislation; and the second teaching the anti-abortion front that the feminist pro-choice front was cohesive and powerful in the sense of having access to political elites.

Since 1990, the Belgian political system has evolved in such a way that it further closed down opportunities for the anti-abortion movement: a series of ethically progressive legislation was enacted, women's policy agencies were established at all policy levels providing the women's movement access to the state and decision-making, and powerful anti-feminist discourses remain absent from the Belgian political party landscape. Nevertheless, together with a recent rise of anti-abortion protests and Internet activism, pro-choice and feminist activism has also been revitalised. As such, the struggle for abortion is not a closed chapter. At a time when individual autonomy over one's body is widely accepted and protected in different laws, anti-abortion discourses are also being reframed. In youth and Internet activism, religious and explicit anti-feminist rhetoric is being replaced by claims to assist vulnerable pregnant women and unborn children.

Karen Celis is Research Professor at the Department of Political Science, Vrije Universiteit Brussel, and co-director Research of RHEA (Centre of Expertise Gender Diversity and Intersectionality). She conducts theoretical and empirical research (qualitative, comparative) on political representation of groups (women, ethnic minorities, class, age groups, LGBT), equality policies and state feminism. She is co-editor of *The Oxford Handbook on Gender and Politics* (Oxford University Press, 2013; with G. Waylen, L. Weldon and J. Kantola), *Gender, Conservatism and Representation* (ECPRPress, 2015; with S. Childs), and of the book series *Gender and Comparative Politics* (Routledge; with I. Engeli).

Gily Coene (Ph.D. in Moral Sciences, Ghent University, 2004) is Assistant Professor at the Department of Philosophy and Ethics and the Department of Political Science, Vrije Universiteit Brussel (Brussels University). She is Director of RHEA, the Centre of Expertise on Gender, Diversity and Intersectionality. Her research concentrates on normative issues related to gender equality and multiculturalism, harmful cultural practices, and reproductive rights.

Notes

1. All English translations are the authors'.
2. In the early seventies, Dr Amy and Dr Hubinont had started with an abortion practice at the Dutch-speaking and French-speaking University of Brussels (Vrije Universiteit Brussel and Université Libre de Bruxelles) where they also trained new medical students in abortion techniques. These students later extended the medical help in Belgium. Although forbidden, medical doctors performed abortions and were initially not persecuted. This changed with the 1973 arrestment of Dr Willy Peers, who had always been very open about performing abortions. The arrestment had an enormous impact and broke the taboo: petitions demanding his release were signed by a large portion of the population; manifestations were held; other medical doctors testified that they also performed abortions; women and medical doctors that had been involved in an abortion declared themselves by name. After a period of political agreement not to persecute medical doctors, persecutions started again from the early eighties. In the meantime, inspired by similar initiatives in the Netherlands, smaller polyclinic abortion centres had been established in the country, working clandestinely. In 1983, the abortion centre in Ghent was searched. Sixty people were persecuted under the charge of performing, undergoing or collaborating with an abortion. The legal process took years; the persecutions were finally cancelled when the abortion law in 1990 was enacted (Trommelmans 2006).
3. Although radical anti-abortion stances are voiced by certain protestant organisations, their impact is relatively low for Belgium, historically a predominantly Catholic country.
4. Wet betreffende de zwangerschapsafbreking, tot wijziging van de artikelen 348, 350, 351 en 352 van het Strafwetboek en tot opheffing van artikel 353 van hetzelfde wetboek, *Belgisch Staatsblad*, 5 April 1990, 6379–6381. (Law concerning the termination of a pregnancy, in order to change the articles 348, 350, 351 and 352 of the Criminal Law and to delete article 353 of the same law, 5 April 1990.)
5. For example, a law project proposed to grant legal personhood to the unborn child from the date of conception (Belgische Kamer van Volksvertegenwoordigers 2003).
6. Twenty-two weeks after conception or twenty-four weeks after the last menstruation.
7. After the elections of 2009, the nationalist Nieuw-Vlaamse Alliantie (New-Flemish Alliance, N-VA) became part of the Flemish Government and had overwhelming electoral success in the federal elections of 2010. In contrast to the extreme right-wing party, Vlaams Belang, NV-A does not defend a radical 'pro-life' stance. For instance, in their note on euthanasia they support some extensions of the law (for instance to minors and assisted suicide). Retrieved 5 December 2013 from https://www.n-va.be/sites/default/files/generated/files/dossier/nota_euthanasie.pdf
8. The newspaper refers to 3–4,000 protesters participating in 2012, but their number had in 2013 declined to 500 (Gutiérrez 2013).
9. Some explicitly declared that they were not Catholic or even not religious at all (Gutiérrez 2011).
10. Their website Charter states that March for Life is 'a citizens' initiative and is independent of any political party'. The website does not note any particular persons

or organisations from which one could deduce a particular political or religious affiliation, but it does contain a video featuring interviews with demonstrators of previous marches made by the organisation Schreeuw om Leven (Cry for Life), a Dutch Christian anti-abortion organisation that also organises marches in the Netherlands and is also mentioned as an organisation supporting the marches on the Francophone website 'marchepourlaviebruxelles'. Retrieved 5 December 2013 from http://www.youtube.com/watch?v=-085CoYpkPs; http://www.schreeuwom-leven.nl/index.php?paginaID=16

11. They share the opinion that abortion increases the risk of breast cancer, infertility and – as a consequence of the so-called 'Post-Abortion Syndrome'– depression and suicide (Mars voor het Leven 2010).

12. Retrieved 5 December 2013 from http://www.marchepourlaviebruxelles.org/eacutequipe.html. Information no longer available on 19 July 2016.

13. The religious leaders who support the March for Life are predominantly Catholic. Nevertheless, one Imam and an Islamic teacher also openly supported the marches. Retrieved 5 December 2013 from http://www.marchepourlaviebruxelles.org/qui-nous-soutient.html Information no longer available on 19 July 2016.

14. The above-mentioned organisations all have extensive websites in different languages. Jongeren Info Life was established in 2004 with 'the aim to provide information and education in schools on the origin of life, to assist mother and child who are in need or in an emergency during pregnancy, to assist in coping with an abortion experience, to help partners and educators with relational and sexual education and to educate the youth' (summary of the website text, in our translation). The organisation offers workshops and training. Retrieved 5 December 2013 from http://www.jongereninfolife.be/site/. Levensadem (souffledevie – antenne francophone), a Christian-inspired organisation, offers information and assistance to pregnant women and couples. Retrieved 5 December 2013 from http://www.levensadem.be/

15. The debate remains societal; no political initiatives have been taken so far.

16. Patrick Vankrunkelsven was senator for the Flemish Liberal Democrats (VLD) at that time.

17. Marleen Temmerman was at that time senator for the Flemish Social Democrats (sp.a).

18. The documentary *Als het geen leven wordt* (*If it does not become a life*), directed by Ludo Penninckx, was broadcast on public television on 12 January 2012. It featured interviews with people who decided to terminate a pregnancy after they had been informed that the child would suffer from a severe disability. Retrieved 2 April 2014 from http://www.deredactie.be/cm/vrtnieuws/videozone/archief/programmas/panorama/1.1194400

19. The organisation emphasises that it is not against euthanasia or abortion, but instead asserts that they want to bring different perspectives to the foreground and that they are especially concerned with negative stereotypes and harmful representations of disabled persons (GRIP 2013).

20. Though they emphasise that they support the struggle against negative stereotypes linked to having a disability and that the quality of life of a disabled person is a

subjective matter that cannot be judged by another person, they also refuse to accept that this struggle would become 'a Trojan horse for people who oppose the voluntary termination of a pregnancy'.

References

'Aartsbisschop Léonard: "Aids soort van rechtvaardigheid"'. 2010, *De Morgen*, 14 October. Retrieved 5 December 2013 from http://www.demorgen.be/dm/nl/989/Binnenland/article/detail/1169682/2010/10/14/Aartsbisschop-Leonard-Aids-soort-van-rechtv

'Abortus bij handicap: Caritas gaat te ver'. 2008, *De Morgen*, 5 May. Retrieved 5 December 2013 from http://www.demorgen.be/dm/nl/2461/Opinie/article/detail/301676/2008/06/05/Abortus-bij-handicap-Caritas-gaat-te-ver.dhtml

'Abortus is een recht'. 2011, *Nederlandstalige Vrouwenraad*, 25 March. Retrieved 5 December 2013 from http://vrouwenraad.axoclub.be/file?fle=17050&ssn=

'Abortustermijn van 12 weken is misschien wat kort'. 2010, *De Morgen*, 26 March. Retrieved 5 December 2013 from http://www.demorgen.be/dm/nl/5036/Wetstraat/article/detail/1085180/2010/03/26/Abortustermijn-van-12-weken-is-misschien-wat-kort.dhtml

'André Léonard stapt mee in betoging tegen abortus'. 2010, *Belang Van Limburg*, 28 March. Retrieved 5 December 2013 from http://www.hbvl.be/nieuws/binnenland/aid914565/andre-leonard-stapt-mee-in-mars-voor-het-leven.aspx

Association socialiste de la personne handicapée. 2012. 'Avortement, Manifestation du 24 mars', *ASPH*. Retrieved 5 December 2013 from www.asph.be/NotreAssociation/NotrePositionnement/Pages/Avortement.aspx

Belgische Kamer van Volksvertegenwoordigers. 2003. 'Wetsvoorstel tot het verlenen van rechtspersoonlijkheid aan het ongeboren kind, ingediend door de heer Gerolf Annemans en mevrouw Alexandra Colen, 20 November 2003' (DOC 51 0461/001). Retrieved 10 December 2013 from http://www.dekamer.be/FLWB/pdf/51/0461/51K0461001.pdf

Celis, K. 1993. 'Socialisme en seksuele fraude. De houding van de Belgische socialisten tegenover abortus en anticonceptie (1880–1990)', in *Begeerte heeft ons aangeraakt. Socialisten, sekse en seksualiteit*. Gent: AMSAB, pp. 161–84.

———. 2001. 'The Abortion Debates in Belgium (1974–1990)', in D. Stetson (ed.) *Abortion Politics, Women's Movements and the Democratic State. A Comparative Study of State Feminism*. New York: Oxford University Press, pp. 39–61.

———. 2006. 'Substantive Representation of Women and the Impact of Descriptive Representation. Case: The Belgian Lower House 1900–1979', *Journal of Women, Politics and Policy* 28(2): 85–114.

———. 2013. 'De legalisering van abortus in België: een vertegenwoordigingsvraagstuk', in G. Coene and S. Bollen (eds), *Tweespraak Vrouwenstudies. 20 jaar abortuswet en – praktijk*. Brussels: VUBPRESS, pp. 23–63.

Celis, K. and P. Meier. 2006. *De macht van het Geslacht. Gender, politiek en beleid in België*. Louvain: Acco.

———. 2007. 'Gelijke kansen in België: een verkenning van de invloed van de federale beleidsstructuur', *Burger, Bestuur en Beleid* 2007: 89–100.

'Commissie voor Welzijn, Gezondheid en Gezin Vergadering van 30/09/1997. Mondelinge vraag van de heer Felic Strackx tot de heer Luc Martens, Vlaams minister van Cultuur, Gezin en Welzijn, over het terugbetalen van de kosten van abortussen door het OCMW'. 1997, *Vlaams Parlement*. Retrieved 10 December 2013 from http://www.vlaamsparlement.be/Proteus5/showVIVerslag.action?id=257473

Cosyns, M. 2013. 'Commentaren bij: Een nationaal- en internationaalrechtelijk perspectief op abortus en het zelfsbeschikkingsrecht van de vrouw', in G. Coene and S. Bollen (eds), *Tweespraak Vrouwenstudies. 20 jaar abortuswet en –praktijk*. Brussels: VUBPRESS, pp. 83–85.

De Hert, P. and M. Colette. 2013. 'Een nationaal- en internationaalrechtelijk perspectief op abortus en het zelfsbeschikkingsrecht van de vrouw', in G. Coene and S. Bollen (eds), *Tweespraak Vrouwenstudies. 20 jaar abortuswet en –praktijk*. Brussels: VUBPRESS, pp. 65–108.

Detiège, L. 2013. 'Persoonlijke commentaar op de wet en het besluit', in G. Coene and S. Bollen (eds), *Tweespraak Vrouwenstudies. 20 jaar abortuswet en –praktijk*. Brussels: VUBPRESS, pp. 59–60.

'De Vlaams Belang Jongeren voeren actie "Abortuskliniek is Moordfabriek"'. 2009, *Vlaams Belang Jongeren*, 20 December. Retrieved 5 December 2013 from http://vbj.org/blog/de-vlaams-belang-jongeren-voeren-actie-abortuskliniek-is-moordfabriek/

'Sleurs, E. 2012. 'Abortuscijfers: N-VA vraagt meer doelgerichte preventieve acties', *N-VA*, 24 September 2012. Retrieved 5 December 2013 from https://www.n-va.be/persbericht/abortuscijfers-n-va-vraagt-meer-doelgerichte-preventieve-acties

Erzeel, S. 2012. 'Women's Substantive Representation in the Belgian Chamber of Representatives: Testing the Added Value of a Claims-Making Approach', *World Political Science Review* 8(1): 28–47.

Gallasz, P. 2013. 'Antiabortusgroep aan het schoolbord. Pro Vita leert tienjarige leerlingen dat seks alleen voor het huwelijk kan'. *De Morgen*, 6 July 2013, 5. Retrieved 5 December 2013 from http://www.demorgen.be/binnenland/antiabortusgroep-predikt-in-vlaamse-scholen-tegen-voorbehoedmiddelen-bf211c2b/

GRIP. 2013. 'Abortus, Euthanasie en handicap'. *GRIP – Gelijke Rechten voor Iedere Persoon met een Handicap*, 23 January 2013. Retrieved 5 December 2013 from http://www.gripvzw.be/beeldvorming/789-abortus-euthanasie-en-handicap.html

Gutiérrez, R. 2011. 'Le nouveau visage de la lutte contre l'IVG'. *Le Soir*, 26 March 2011. Retrieved 5 December 2013 from http://archives.lesoir.be/le-nouveau-visage-de-la-lutte-contre-l-8217-ivg_t-20110326-01APKA.html

———. 2013. '"La Marche pour la vie" fait un flop'. *Le Soir*, 24 March 2013. Retrieved 5 December 2013 from http://www.lesoir.be/213680/article/actualite/belgique/2013-03-24/%C2%ABmarche-pour-vie%C2%BB-fait-un-flop

Katholieke Arbeidersvrouwen. 2010. 'Abortus en KAV anno 2010. Nota voor de raad van bestuur van 18 September'. Retrieved 9 August 2016 from https://www.yumpu.com/nl/document/view/20302001/abortus-en-kav-anno-2010-femma

Maréchal, P. 2010. 'Abortus niet uitbreiden'. *De Standaard*, 2 April 2010. Retrieved 5 December 2013 from http://pietermarechal.typepad.com/DS.020410.p26.pdf

'Marleen Temmerman: "Puriteinse oproep"'. 2008, *De Morgen*, 4 June. Retrieved 5 December 2013 from http://www.demorgen.be/dm/nl/993/Gezondheid/article/detail/300153/2008/06/04/Marleen-Temmerman-Puriteinse-oproep.dhtml

Marques-Pereira B. 1989. *L'avortement en Belgique. De la clandestinité au débat politique*. Brussels: Editions de l'Université de Bruxelles.

'Mars voor het leven handvest'. 2013, *March for life*. Retrieved 9 August 2016 from http://marchforlife.be/nl/het-handvest/

'Mars voor het leven' tegen abortus in Brussel'. 2010, *De Morgen*, 28 March. Retrieved 5 December 2013 from http://www.demorgen.be/dm/nl/989/Binnenland/article/detail/1085958/2010/03/28/Mars-voor-het-leven-tegen-abortus-in-Brussel.dhtml

Meeus P. and G. Annemans. 1996. *De moord op Beethoven: het Vlaams Blok zes jaar na de abortuswet: een onverminderd pleidooi voor het leven*. Brussels: Vlaams Blok.

'Memorandum 2014: Platform voor abortusrecht'. 2014, *Abortion Right*. Retrieved 5 December 2013 from http://www.abortionright.eu/spip.php?article752

'Mgr. Léonard défile contre l'avortement'. 2011, *Le Soir*, 27 March 2011. Retrieved 5 December 2013 from http://www.lesoir.be/archives?url=/actualite/belgique/2011-03-27/mgr-leonard-defile-contre-l-avortement-830757.php

'Open Vld wil meer abortuscentra en beter preventiebeleid'. 2010, *De Morgen*, 1 April. Retrieved 5 December 2013 from www.demorgen.be/dm/nl/5036/Wetstraat/article/detail/1087756/2010/04/01/Open-Vld-wil-meer-abortuscentra-en-beter-preventiebeleid.dhtml

Siffer, B. 2008. 'Standpunt HVV over abortusrichtlijn christelijke ziekenhuiskoepel'. *Humanistisch-Vrijzinnige Vereniging*. Retrieved 5 December 2013 from http://www.hvv.be/dmdocuments/Standpunt%20Abortus.pdf

Temmerman, M. 2013. 'Recht op abortus: reflecties op de Belgische wetgeving en praktijk', in G. Coene and S. Bollen (eds), *Tweespraak Vrouwenstudies. 20 jaar abortuswet en –praktijk*. Brussels: VUBPRESS, pp. 109–32.

Trommelmans, W. 2006 'Abortus. Baas in eigen buik', in *Vlaanderen vrijt! 50 jaar seks in Vlaanderen*. Antwerp: Van Halewijck, pp. 60–71.

Van Crombrugge, L. 2013. 'Commentaren bij 'Een nationaal- en internationaalrechtelijk perspectief op abortus en het zelfsbeschikkingsrecht van de vrouw' in G. Coene and S. Bollen (eds), *Tweespraak Vrouwenstudies. 20 jaar abortuswet en –praktijk*. Brussels: VUBPRESS, pp. 101–4.

Vander Stichele, C. 1983. 'Het abortusprobleem in de feministische pers: confrontatie met de moraaltheologische reflectie', unpublished licentiate paper. Brussels: Catholic University of Leuven.

Van Mechelen, R. 1996 [1979]. *Uit eigen beweging. Balans van de vrouwenbeweging in Vlaanderen, 1970–1978*. Leuven: Kritak.

Vanmeenen, E. 1991. 'De betekenis van de Feministisch-socialistische koördinatie in de vrouwenbeweging en in de strijd om abortus uit het strtafrecht te halen (1976–1982)', unpublished licentiate paper. Vrije Universiteit Brussel.

Van Molle, L. and E. Gubin. 1998. *Vrouw en Politiek in België*. Tielt: Lannoo.

Verbond der Verzorgingsinstellingen. 2008. 'Advies 13. Het zorgproces inzake zwanger-schapsafbreking na prenatale diagnostiek, Brussel, 24 April 2008'. Retrieved 5 December 2013 from http://www.standaard.be/extra/pdf/advies13.pdf

Vlaams Belang, 2010. 'Twintig jaar abortuswet'. Retrieved 5 December 2013 from http://www.vlaamsbelang.org/nieuws/7122

Vrancken, C. 2013. 'Commentaren bij "recht op abortus: reflecties op de Belgische wetgeving en praktijk"', in G. Coene and S. Bollen (eds), *Tweespraak Vrouwenstudies. 20 jaar abortuswet en –praktijk*. Brussels: VUBPRESS, pp. 125–26.

Witte, E. 1990. 'Twintig jaar strijd rond de abortuswetgeving in België (1970–1990)', *Res Publica* XXXII(4): 427–87.

———. 1993. 'De liberalisering van de Abortus-wetgeving in België (1970–1990)', in M. Scheys (ed.), *Abortus. Rapporten en perspectieven omtrent vrouwenstudies, 4*. Brussels: VUBPRESS, pp. 21–102.

Health Professionals'/Providers' Involvement in the Pro- or Anti-abortion Rights Debate and Access to Services

Part III

Health Professionals'/Providers' Involvement in the Pro- or Anti-abortion Rights Debate and Access to Services

Chapter 7

'Good Doctors Do Not Object'

Obstetricians-Gynaecologists' Perspectives on
Conscientious Objection to Abortion Care and
their Engagement with Pro-abortion Rights
Protests in Italy

by Silvia De Zordo

In this chapter I analyse how 'abortion governance' (Morgan 2014 [2012])
is changing in Italy and how new actors and political rationalities are emerging from the abortion debate, particularly since the increase of conscientious
objection to abortion care, which became the main focus in the years right
after I concluded research on this topic in Rome and Milan in 2011.[1] These
cities are the capitals of two key regions in the Italian economic and political life – Lombardia and Lazio – where the public debate on abortion has
always been very intense. In the first part of the chapter I discuss the Italian
law on abortion and the debate around it, showing how its focus has progressively shifted, over the last decade, from women's to 'foetal rights'. Is the
increase in conscientious objection rates among physicians and other health
professionals a result of this shift? Can we consider conscientious objection
as civil disobedience, and, therefore, as a form of active protest against the
abortion law and women's rights?[2] I will answer these questions by examining obstetricians-gynaecologists' experiences and attitudes to abortion, its
stigmatisation, and conscientious objection, based on a study carried out
at four public maternity hospitals providing abortion care, two of which
were located in Milan and two Rome,[3] as well as on my participation in
the debate on abortion and conscientious objection during my fieldwork
in Italy. This chapter aims at advancing the debate on abortion stigma,[4]
by exploring the social and cultural constructions of the stigma associated

with abortion in clinical contexts, and by focusing on the potential role of abortion providers in reproducing and perpetuating it, which is an under-researched topic, especially in Europe. In fact, the few existing qualitative studies on abortion providers' experiences and perspectives on abortion and its stigmatisation, carried out mainly in the United States, Latin America and Africa, have focused on the way in which providers feel stigmatised, particularly by peers and patients (Harris et al. 2011; O'Donnell and Weitz and Freedman 2011). Most of these studies have shown how a range of structural issues, including legal restrictions, can negatively affect training as well as abortion provision, often perceived as a 'dirty work' (De Zordo and Mishtal J. 2011; Freedman et al. 2010; Payne and Debbink and Steele 2013). Some researchers have also highlighted how the stigmatisation of abortion provision can be and actually is resisted and challenged by some abortion providers (Joffe 2014; Martin et al. 2014; O'Donnell and Weitz and Freedman 2011). However, with a few exceptions (Beynon-Jones 2013) these studies have not examined how abortion providers also contribute to reproducing abortion stigma.

Furthermore, this chapter aims to expand the existing, limited literature on conscientious objection to abortion care (see Global Doctors for Choice 2013) by examining the main factors leading obstetricians-gynaecologists to refuse to provide abortion; why conscientious objection rates are higher in some contexts than in others; and how the increasing participation of abortion providers in the abortion debate may influence physicians' choices and change the nature of pro-abortion rights protests in Italy in the future.

The Abortion Law and Conscientious Objection in Italy

Conscientious objection has recently emerged as a hot, contentious issue in the Italian public debate, because the rate of obstetricians-gynaecologists at the national level who refuse to perform terminations has dramatically increased from 59.1 per cent in 1983 (which was already relatively high) to 70 per cent in the 2000s, and over to 80 per cent in the south and in key regions of the north – Veneto – and of the centre – Lazio (Italia, Ministero della Salute 2013-2014-2015).[5] Lazio has very high rates of conscientious objection among gynaecologists – 80.7 per cent in 2011 and in 2013 – while Lombardia reports lower rates – 63.6 per cent in the same years (Italia, Ministero della Salute 2013-2014-2015). Not only obstetricians-gynaecologists, but also anaesthesiologists, midwives and nurses object. As a result, many hospitals, particularly in the south, do not provide abortion care, so women must travel to other cities and regions to seek abortion care, which is a violation of their sexual and reproductive rights (Zampas 2012). This is exactly what the Italian feminist movement feared when abortion was legalised in 1978, a few years after the legalisation of divorce (1975), as a result of a decade of protests for women's self-determination led by feminist groups[6] and by some leftist political parties, particularly by the Radical Party. Abortion was allowed only under certain circumstances and within specific time limits and it remained in the penal code. Women had to get a certification signed by a doctor to have their termination at a public state hospital or at private clinics subsidised by the state. However, many private clinics providing family and reproductive healthcare are Catholic; therefore, they do not actually provide such a service. As a result, the public sector is the main abortion provider in Italy, with the exception of a few southern regions, where conscientious objection rates are very high.

The Italian abortion law was the result of a very difficult negotiation between Catholic and non-Catholic political forces. It was called, in fact, 'Norms for the social protection of motherhood and for the voluntary interruption of pregnancy', and established in its first article that:

> the state grants the right to conscientious and responsible procreation, it recognises the *social value of motherhood* and *the protection of human life since its beginning* ...The state, the regions and local institutions ... promote and develop social-health services ... to prevent abortion being used to limit births.[7] (Parlamento Italiano, Legge 194-1978, art. 1, emphasis added)

As Luisa Passerini (1994) and other Italian feminist scholars point out, this law was offered to Italian women as a paternalistic concession of a patriarchal benevolent state concerned with the use of abortion and contraceptives as a means of birth control and willing to reassert the crucial importance of motherhood at a social and symbolic level.

Most of the abortion providers I interviewed for my study agreed that 'this law was a compromise'. However, they always added: 'but it's a good law', or 'but it is a beautiful/a fantastic law'. Some of the more senior abortion providers, aged fifty-five to sixty-five, had participated in the abortion debate in the 1970s, with some as active feminist or radical militants, and others as young medical students or recently graduated physicians willing to put an end to the tragedy of unsafe abortion. In their perspective, Law 194 was good because it established that the welfare of the embryo or foetus did not override the woman's right to health and allowed women to have safe, legal, free abortions, even if only under certain circumstances. The law asserts, in fact, that abortion is legal up to ninety days 'if carrying the pregnancy ahead and motherhood would put the woman's physical/psychological health in danger, because of her health, economic, social or family conditions', while in the second trimester it is allowed only 'if the woman's life is at risk or in case of verified pathologies, including foetal anomalies or malformations that represent a serious danger for the woman's physical or psychological health' (Parlamento Italiano, Legge 194-1978, art. 4–6).

In many regards, the Italian abortion law is more restrictive than other European abortion laws (IPPF 2012), such as the British law that states that abortion is legal on broad grounds up to twenty-four weeks of pregnancy and also beyond in specific cases (maternal life risk, risk of grave physical and mental injury to the woman and severe foetal abnormality). Likewise the French law in similar cases does not establish a specific time limit for terminations. On the contrary, in Italy abortion is legal only up to foetal viability, which means until the foetus is able to survive outside the uterus (under intensive medical care in case of extremely premature newborns). Therefore, it is impossible to have a termination at twenty-three weeks of pregnancy or above, because the foetus' chances of survival at this gestational age have dramatically increased, due to new neonatal intensive care techniques. The vast majority of terminations are performed under twelve weeks in Italy (only 4.2 per cent were performed beyond twelve weeks of gestation in 2013; Italia, 2015). Nonetheless, a small proportion of women still need abortions at later gestational stages, mainly due to late or uncertain diagnosis of severe foetal malformations. Moreover, some procedures are not routinely taught nor performed, particularly surgical termination via D&E (dilatation and evacuation) after fourteen or fifteen weeks and foeticide[8] above twenty weeks of gestation. As a result, in case of late diagnosis of severe foetal malformations, and particularly if women wish to have a surgical abortion under general anaesthesia instead of undergoing a long and painful labour, they have no alternative but to travel to other countries, if they can afford the cost. The same occurs to those women who exceed the time limits for legal abortion because they find out late that they are pregnant or have difficulties in making a decision and/or in accessing abortion services. Many abortion providers interviewed for this study said they usually suggest to these women to seek abortion care in France, Spain or in the United Kingdom. As recent data show, Italian women represent the second largest national group of non-resident women (after Irish women) travelling to England to seek abortion services (UK, Department of Health 2015).

Abortion providers I interviewed in Rome highlighted that not only access, but also the quality of abortion care is currently at risk because of the high number of objectors, which obliges women to travel to the capital from other cities/regions, increasing the workload of doctors in Rome and creating long waiting lists for first trimester procedures. As a result, the quality of abortion services has worsened and the working conditions of the few Roman consultants in obstetrics-gynaecology who still provide abortion care have become very difficult. They cannot always grant a good quality abortion service, particularly in the case of second trimester abortion, which requires hospitalisation and is a more time-intensive procedure. In fact, they cannot always assist women during the entire duration of labour induction, because they have to manage all gynaecological-obstetrics procedures, including first trimester abortions, deliveries and emergencies. Furthermore, if they are the only consultants providing second trimester abortion, nobody can replace them when they get sick. Finally, they have less time to dedicate to other aspects of their clinical practice because they have to focus on abortion care.

All these daily problems create tensions between abortion providers and objectors,[9] and sometimes lead to denunciations. Laiga, the 'Free Association of Italian gynaecologists for the defense of Law 194' (the abortion law) was founded in 2010 by a female consultant in gynaecology-obstetrics who worked at a hospital in Rome that was denounced by a female patient because she had not been properly assisted during a second trimester abortion via labour induction. Laiga has been protesting since then over the lack of serious monitoring of conscientious objection and has lodged a collective complaint with the International Planned Parenthood Federation European Network (IPPF EN) against Italy, stating that the weak regulation of health personnel's conscientious objection violates the right to health protection. The claim was successful. In fact, the Council of Europe's Committee of Social Rights declared on 8 March 2014 that the Italian state must organise abortion services in a way that ensures that patients' needs are met (Council of Europe 2014). On April 11 2016, the same Committee answered to a similar complaint issued in 2013 by CGIL (Confederazione Generale Italiana del Lavoro, the Italian leftist trade union). It declared once again that in Italy women's right to health is violated because of the high rates of conscientious objection and added that abortion providers are and should not be discriminated for providing abortion care (Council of Europe, 2016).

As Laiga has stated on numerous occasions, the state should verify that all the Italian regions, which are in charge of the administration of public health services, comply with the current abortion law. The law establishes that: 'Health professionals shall not take part in the procedures at art. 5–7 [pre-abortion counselling and signing abortion certificates] and in terminations when they express their conscientious objection, which must be preventively declared ... They are exempted from all procedures and activities aimed at provoking the termination, but not from assistance before and after them' (Parlamento Italiano, Legge 194-1978, art. 9). Moreover, regions/hospitals must comply with the law: if they need abortion providers, hospitals can hire physicians working elsewhere or must find other ways to provide abortion care.

Why are those regions and hospitals that do not comply with the abortion law not sanctioned? This is what Laiga has asked the government along with a number of other associations, such as the Consulta di Bioetica (Council of Bioethics), the Association Luca Coscioni for freedom of scientific research, Usciamo dal silenzio (Let's break silence), a network of feminist groups, and AIED (Italian Association for Demographic Education). During Laiga's first national conference, held in Rome in October 2011, its founder, Dr Agatone, explained that the main objectives of the association were: equal working opportunities and legal support for 'non-objectors' (the term usually used for abortion providers), who are often discriminated against for choosing to provide abortion care; monitoring the application of Law 194 in each region/hospital; and, finally, training young residents in abortion care. 'We must transmit the pride of an ethical choice to young physicians', she said. An old, famous abortion provider from Milan, Dr Buscaglia, added that young medical students should be taught that 'good doctors do not object' because they take good care of their patients, women, and respect their decisions even if they do not always understand or agree with them. Not all participants agreed with his opinion – many said that objectors may also be good doctors and should not be discriminated against for refusing to provide abortion. 'Good doctors do not object', however, was the slogan chosen by the Consulta di Bioetica for its national one-day campaign against conscientious objection to abortion care, which managed to mobilise a large number of associations. On 6 June 2012, public debates on this topic addressed a large heterogeneous public, including health professionals, and were organised in different cities, from the north to the south. At the public debates in which I participated in Florence and Rome, several abortion providers pointed out that it was difficult to teach the importance and dignity of their profession to medical students and residents, because abortion care is marginalised in hospitals and the increase in conscientious objection rates means an increasing workload for a minority of abortion providers that often suffer from burnout. Some also highlighted that in many regions (like Lombardia and Lazio) Catholic parties and groups had been administering public health services for decades, leading to the discrimination of abortion providers in hospitals and to advantages for objectors in terms of career. During my fieldwork, a female Roman gynaecologist aged forty-nine who had been an objector for most of her professional life[10] told me: 'You have to consider that we are much closer to the Vatican and to the Pope here ... Romans' choices are always and above all conditioned by that'. Is that true? What has the Vatican said on abortion over the last decade?

From Women's Rights to the 'Rights of the Conceived'

Pope Benedict XVI and his predecessor have been strongly critical of abortion, and over the past decades the Vatican has become increasingly engaged in the debate over the status of the embryo and conscientious objection, which was mentioned on numerous occasions by Papa Francesco in 2014, including in a meeting with the U.S. President Barack Obama.[11] In Italy the pressure of the Vatican has manifested in the long delay in the approval of the abortion-inducing drug RU-486 that was introduced only in 2010 – twenty-two years after France and nineteen years after the United Kingdom. Its introduction came along with guidelines requiring women's hospitalisation for first trimester abortion until the expulsion of the foetus, which is not medically justified, according to the international medical literature (WHO 2012). This unnecessary obligation for hospitals and women has prevented the diffusion of this method, which was used to perform only 9.7 percent of terminations in Italy in 2013 (Italia, Ministero della Salute 2015). Another clear example of the Vatican's influence on reproductive rights restrictions is the controversial law on Assisted Reproductive Technologies (ARTs) of 2004. This law prohibited a number of procedures, including gamete donation, and excluded same sex couples from accessing ARTs. Vatican's pressure on politicians to vote 'according to conscience' contributed to the failure of a referendum aimed at changing it. However, numerous articles of the law were modified, as a result of the protests of ARTs users' associations, LGBT and feminist groups, as well as leftist physicians and politicians, but not the first article, which 'ensures the rights of all subjects involved, including the "*concepito*" [literally "the conceived"]' (Parlamento Italiano, Legge 40-2004, art. 1), equalising the woman's rights and the 'rights of the "conceived"'.

After this ART law passed, conservative Catholic members of Berlusconi's government and party started to attack the abortion law, seeing a potential opportunity to restrict abortion further. The response was a massive demonstration of more than 100,000 people in favour of abortion rights, organised in Milan in January 2006 by Usciamo dal silenzio. One year later, a smaller demonstration in support of abortion rights was organised in the same city to protest against a new regional regulation, which imposed the obligation on abortion providers to ask their patients if they wished to bury their embryo or foetus, and placed the duty to conduct the 'burial' on the hospital in the event that a woman declined (Consiglio Regionale della Lombardia 2007). Since then, these burials are sometimes celebrated by Catholic groups that have special agreements with some public hospitals, even without a woman's authorisation (see Mattalucci in this volume). The underlying idea of this new regulation was that the embryo and the foetus were 'persons'. Therefore, their 'rights', including the right to be buried, had to be respected, as Roberto Formigoni, president of the region, a member of Berlusconi's party and representative of a Catholic right-wing movement (Communion and Liberation), explained. To better convey this message during the anti-abortion campaigns at that time, the foetus was often represented as a newborn. The response of local feminist groups was an ironic march and a funeral 'for all non- fertilised eggs' in front of the regional government. An open coffin containing a giant sanitary pad coloured in red was left outside the building, and smaller sanitary pads also coloured in red were hung on the walls. In 2008 the same regional government passed another internal regulation fixing the limit for second trimester terminations at twenty-two weeks and three days. This regulation was considered not valid and rejected after a number of abortion providers denounced it as incompatible with the national abortion law, which does not establish a specific time limit, but 'viability'. More recently, a regional decree dated June 2010 instituted a public fund of five million euros to be directed at low-income women who choose to carry the pregnancy to term, instead of a termination. Public family planning clinics were required to coordinate with Catholic pro-life centres, which are present at a number of public hospitals providing abortion care and were charged with the responsibility of disbursing the funds and monitoring their use.

All these interventions highlight the status of the 'conceived' embryos and foetuses 'as biopolitical subjects' (Kaufman and Morgan 2005: 328) and 'citizens ...worthy of state protection' (Casper and Morgan 2004: 17). Yet, as Lynn Morgan points out, 'embryos as we know them today are a relatively recent invention' (Morgan 2009: 4). They are historical and scientific constructions that, as a result of new developments in biology, embryology and prenatal screening techniques, have recently become 'recognizable human beings' (Morgan 1999: 57) and 'icons for Life' (Duden 1999: 15). As Sarah Franklin argues, the embryo has become a 'fetish' (Franklin 1999: 70), the 'sacred image of life itself ... able to represent the human, the nation, the species and the future' (ibid.: 64). In the Italian case, the embryo/foetus, often represented as a white male baby in anti-abortion rights protests, seems to stand for a nation/state that rejects everything that threatens its supposedly monolithic Christian-Catholic roots and values such as women's and the LGBT community's sexual and reproductive rights. But how do obstetricians-gynaecologists working in state hospitals speak of the embryo/foetus and of women's reproductive rights? Does the public debate on abortion and the embryo's/foetus' rights affect their attitudes towards it?

Who is the Patient? Physicians' Difficult Choice between the Woman and the Foetus

Most objectors interviewed in Rome and Milan[12] defined themselves as religious, but only a minority as practicing Catholics, and in a hospital in Rome (HA) four out of eleven objectors said they were 'non religious', 'not practising' or of a different religion, like Buddhism. Moreover, only a strict minority defined abortion as a 'sin' or a 'crime' in the questionnaire, mostly older, female physicians. Why, then, did most of these physicians decide to object to abortion provision? Many objectors said that terminating a pregnancy did not feel right to them because the embryo/foetus was a 'life', or a 'potential life' they should take care of, regardless of their religiosity. Abortion was perceived, in this sense, as something 'against the medical profession' or 'unethical', as some objectors said. However, many objectors pointed out that there are different 'forms of life' and the life of a woman and of an adult in general is not the same as the life of an embryo/foetus. In fact, the latter 'is not autonomous', 'has no free will'; therefore, it cannot be considered as a person entitled to rights. Actually, most objectors agreed with the definition of abortion as a fundamental woman's right: abortion should be legal within certain time limits[13] to avoid the dramatic consequences of illegal, unsafe abortion. However, many were unclear or ambivalent when asked whose health and rights were paramount, whether the woman's or the embryo's/foetus'. In particular, when asked what would happen if most physicians were objectors in Italy, the majority tended either to avoid the question ('well, we are not at this point, are we?') or minimise the problem ('there will always be someone providing this service at another hospital or in another city'). Many suspected that in Italy most physicians were objectors, but only a few knew how high the rate of conscientious objection actually is.

Similar to objectors, most abortion providers also defined the embryo/foetus as 'life' or 'potential life'. However, they gave to these terms a more neutral, scientific sense – 'it is an assemblage of cells', many said, or 'it is life as an ant or a plant is life'. Moreover, many distinguished 'life' from 'quality of life', and the majority asserted that taking care of a woman's and the future baby's quality of life (in case of foetal anomalies) was their primary duty. In their perspective, the woman was a 'person entitled to rights', while the embryo and the foetus were not. Some abortion providers defined the foetus as a 'potential person' but for the majority personhood started with the first breathing act. Only a few abortion providers and objectors affirmed that the foetus could be considered as a person at viability.

The foetus and the embryo were not a person, but they were not the same thing, in both objectors and abortion providers' views. In fact, at twelve weeks of gestation or more, many said it 'looks/behaves like a baby'. This may explain why most physicians agreed that after a second trimester abortion women and couples should be given the possibility of burying the aborted foetus or 'their baby', as many defined it, while they considered 'absurd' the mandatory burial of aborted embryos after first trimester terminations in Lombardia.

Some female abortion providers from Rome mentioned the emotional distress and moral conflicts raised by 'seeing' and 'showing' the foetus via sophisticated antenatal screening techniques and then terminating it, particularly in cases of foetal anomalies in which it can be difficult to predict the impact on the health outcomes of the future baby (Down's syndrome and rare brain malformations were often mentioned). However, most abortion providers said that they continued to perform terminations despite their moral dilemmas because they had to take care of their 'main' patient, the woman. Other motivations they mentioned were social justice (unsafe abortion mainly kills poor women) and their strong beliefs in women's autonomy and rights, mentioned particularly by female physicians.[14]

Particularly important to abortion providers from Rome was providing good abortion care to women undergoing second trimester 'therapeutic' abortions, as terminations for foetal malformations were usually defined by physicians. These procedures are performed at obstetrics-gynaecology wards, where other women give birth, and often in 'inhuman conditions', as a physician from Rome said. In fact, in hospitals where there are high rates of conscientious objection, women are sometimes abandoned during their long and painful labour or at the moment of expulsion.[15] Some hospitals in Rome have actually been denounced by women patients for this reason. After witnessing how badly these women were treated, two Roman female objectors told me that they had decided to provide terminations at least in the second trimester.[16] Many objectors, particularly those from Rome, said they did not badly judge their colleagues providing abortion care and would eventually 'help' those providing second trimester abortion by assisting their patients, to avoid these women's 'suffering', and their 'discrimination'. However, several Roman abortion providers said they sometimes had conflicts with objectors because they were not always available, particularly during night shifts, and also, eventually, with neonatologists. A female abortion provider who had been working for many years in abortion services explained:

What happens if somebody calls the neonatologist? If there isn't a chief gynaecologist who says: "if this is a therapeutic abortion below 23 weeks, the foetus must not be resuscitated full stop"... I mean, of course above 23 weeks it is different ... but some midwives do it in a fit of pique: "What's that? Infanticide! Now I call the neonatologist!", and he comes and resuscitates the foetus without even asking the parents ... It's clear that involving the parents in this decision is dramatic ... your child is breathing, you know that he will have an unhappy life ... If a woman has decided to terminate that pregnancy ... it is the woman who decides.

The induction of foetal demise prior to termination is not usually performed, so the expelled foetus can sometimes show some signs of life, even if only for a very short time. As abortion providers explained, this procedure is not usually taught or performed, mainly to avoid potential sources of tension with objectors and with Catholic groups that are present in a number of public hospitals with their pro-life centres.[17]

The majority of abortion providers did not define themselves as religious, but between a quarter and a third of abortion providers in Milan and Rome did. However, they stated that they did not always agree with the Catholic doctrine and dogmas, particularly when it came to contraception and abortion. This was true also for most objectors. Some objectors had actually been abortion providers. A female physician from Milan in her mid fifties had decided to object while she was pregnant, after terminating a second trimester pregnancy that required the surgical extraction of 'bodily parts'. That experience, described as 'bloody', had troubled her so much that she had asked the chief gynaecologist if she could provide only first trimester abortion. As he said no, she decided to object. At the same hospital a young female resident had decided to object because, she explained, 'at twelve weeks one works on a form of life that is already formed, it has legs and everything. I don't feel like doing that ... I see it moving ... for me it is abominable to terminate a pregnancy. It is not for my religiosity ... it is something that really disgusts me'. Another female resident from Rome had objected on her first working day for similar reasons: 'I would not like inducing the abortion, even if it is a woman's right. I don't want to be the "maker" (*artefice*, in Italian) ... it is not for my religious convictions, it's because it would involve me emotionally'.

Dr Aurora, an old female objector from Milan who defined herself as religious and was an expert of prenatal screening, pointed out that thanks to sophisticated antenatal screening techniques the embryo/foetus has become obstetricians-gynaecologists' main 'patient':

I think that it's this concept that the foetus has become the patient. There isn't only the mother anymore. The mother is only, in some way, the receptacle ... for the obstetrician the patient is, in reality, the foetus ... and then the woman too, but ... one sees how it grows, how it develops, what kind of illnesses it can have, what infections ...

She suggested that the increasing focus on the foetus as patient could be one of the reasons why conscientious objection rates have dramatically increased. In fact, the development of new prenatal screening techniques, which may lead to termination, as well as foetal surgery (Casper 1998), have transformed the embryo/foetus into physicians' 'main' patient, and this may have increased the stigmatisation of abortion in case of 'minor' malformations or unwanted pregnancy, when the embryo/foetus is (potentially) 'healthy'. This shift in the biomedical domain, from the woman to the foetus, has transformed not only pregnant women, as the U.S. anthropologist Rayna Rapp has stated (Rapp 2000), but also physicians into 'moral pioneers' facing sometimes difficult decisions.

'Fake Objectors': The Impact of Abortion Stigma on Physicians' Training and Choices

Female physicians, including abortion providers, tended to talk more openly of their emotions towards the embryo-foetus, or 'the baby', as many defined the foetus. Most of them, however, including objectors, were strongly in favour of women's right to choose. On the contrary, male objectors rarely talked about their feelings and mentioned different reasons to explain why they had opted out of abortion care,[18] particularly those working in Rome. Some said they did not want to be the only physician who performed terminations at their hospital; this would mean, in fact, being obliged to do most of the time an 'unpleasant', 'not gratifying' and, ultimately, 'not interesting' job (from a technical perspective), as most physicians (including many abortion providers) defined it. A male resident in Rome said he had decided to declare himself an objector, despite not having moral or religious convictions against abortion, 'to play it safe'. In fact, some objectors told him that if he chose to provide abortions he would only do that and would therefore put his future career at risk, as he would not have time to specialise in other domains. He pointed out, as many other residents in both cities, that an open discussion on abortion and conscientious objection is not promoted in medical schools, where only an optional seminar is provided to discuss the legislation on abortion and assisted reproduction and no specific training in abortion care is offered to residents. Other objectors said they had opted out because abortion care was an 'optional', or an 'extra' job (*un lavoro in più*, in Italian) that presented potential medical and legal risks, such as uterine perforation or denunciations for misdiagnosis in case of terminations for foetal anomalies. Many objectors and young physicians perceived as risky very simple procedures such as aspiration in the first trimester, and abortion providers did not know very well and considered unsafe some procedures, such as D&E, which is performed in other countries in case of second trimester terminations, and do not present a higher risk than pharmacological abortion (Grimes 2008; Lohr and Hayes and Gemzell-Daniellsson 2008).

Interestingly, both objectors and abortion providers asserted that in Italy there are many 'fake objectors', meaning physicians that opt out of abortion provision to avoid a heavier workload and discrimination. Many physicians also cited well-known cases of objectors denounced over the last decade for providing terminations at private clinics that were not registered as abortion providers, in exchange for money. A few abortion providers said that the provision of terminations should also be allowed privately at public hospitals, as it happens with other procedures, to disincentive objection. The majority, however, did not agree. They thought that women should never pay for an abortion. Many abortion providers highlighted that the main problem in Italy is that abortion care is considered the 'Cinderella of gynaecology', a 'dirty job' that 'nobody wants to do'. Some of them, particularly those from Rome, said they had been discriminated for choosing to provide abortion care and had been obliged to renounce a potentially brilliant career by their chief gynaecologists who were objectors.

In Rome most chief gynaecologists were male and objectors, while in Milan most were abortion providers, two of which were women. This is not surprising. In fact, obstetrics-gynaecology has undergone an accelerated feminisation process over the last few decades at the national level. However, in Milan, unlike in Rome, there is a long tradition of famous, progressive, male (and more recently female) abortion providers who have been teaching and working as renowned researchers and chief gynaecologists at local universities and hospitals. This may partially explain the lower rates of conscientious objection in Milan's hospitals.

As my study shows, most obstetricians-gynaecologists did not object because they were against legal abortion, but for other reasons. Their 'objection' to abortion care cannot be considered, therefore, as an act of civil disobedience. On the contrary, many physicians highlighted that the Law 194 was a good law, even if some aspects of it had been neglected, particularly the prevention of unwanted pregnancies and the support to pregnant women with serious family or economic problems. Interestingly, not only objectors but also many abortion providers defined abortion in case of unwanted pregnancy as a 'failure' or an event that should be prevented via the effective use of contraceptives, and not as a 'normal' event in women's reproductive lives. 'There are a lot of contraceptives', many physicians pointed out; therefore, abortion should not be used as a contraceptive, 'as many immigrant women do'.[19] Two male physicians, a young resident in Milan, and an older physician in Rome, who had been an abortion provider in the past, said they had objected to abortion care after realising that abortion had been 'trivialised': many women, particularly young and foreign, 'abuse it', the young resident said.

Most physicians, including abortion providers, defined abortion as a social and public health problem, despite the fact that the abortion rate has gradually decreased in Italy since abortion was legalised (1978) and is currently among the lowest rates in Europe.[20] Women having repeated abortions (19 per cent of all women having an abortion had already had one in 2013; see Italia, Ministero della Salute 2015) were described both by abortion providers and objectors as 'ignorant' (of their own bodies as well as of contraception) and/or as 'irresponsible' towards themselves and their own health, because repeated terminations can negatively affect their reproductive health, which is not actually accurate in the case of safe abortions.[21] Many physicians, including abortion providers, contended that repeated abortions are quite common among foreign women, particularly among women from Eastern Europe and, more specifically, among Romanian women. These women were often described not only as 'ignorant', but also as 'victims' of their own 'culture', which was defined as *'machista'* (male chauvinist, sexist), because it leads them to avoid using contraception or to use it ineffectively. Only a few physicians, particularly abortion providers who had worked at public family planning centres, mentioned male participation in contraception and the limited use of condoms in Italy, or the fact that contraceptives are not freely provided at public family planning centres,[22] which have suffered dramatic cuts over the last decade. Moreover, only a small minority of physicians, mainly abortion providers, knew how easily accessible contraception and safe abortion were in the past and are nowadays in Eastern Europe.[23] Women having abortions because of foetal anomalies were the object of much more empathy. They were often described as 'victims' because they 'want' to be mothers and therefore 'suffer' more than women terminating unwanted pregnancies.

Conclusion

Kumar, Hessini and Mitchell (2009) argued in their well-known article on abortion stigma that despite its legalisation abortion still is highly stigmatised, including in Western, Christian countries, not only because it is envisaged as the termination of a (sacred) 'Life', the murder of a 'baby', but also because it is conceived as a transgression of traditional gender norms and values concerning sexuality, femininity and motherhood. Most objectors interviewed for this study did not affirm that all women should be mothers: on the contrary, they agreed with their patients using medical contraceptives, and said they did and would prescribe the morning after pill as a way of preventing abortion.[24] However, objectors and also many abortion providers considered women who terminate an unintended pregnancy, and particularly those who have repeated terminations, 'irresponsible' because they do not embody the 'contraceptive norm' by assuming the (entire) responsibility of (effective) contraception, which is considered primarily and exclusively the woman's responsibility. As Nathalie Bajos and other French researchers have argued (Bajos and Ferrand 2002), this is partly the result of the medicalisation of contraception. The widespread use of hormonal contraception has introduced the idea that women's bodies are easily programmable and controllable, which is not always possible, as sexuality and desire are complex phenomena that involve affective/power relations. Moreover, most contraceptives are directed at women, but they are not always easily accessible, can have collateral effects and are not always 100 per cent effective. Therefore, it is not always possible to avoid unintended pregnancies.

This study partly confirms what Kumar et al. have argued, by showing that conservative views of gender norms and values influence many Italian physicians, including abortion providers, in their relationships with their female patients seeking abortion care. It also shows that physicians' ignorance and prejudice against foreign patients' 'culture' affects their attitudes towards them as well. Abortion is stigmatised, however, also because the embryo/foetus is envisaged as 'a potential life' and, more importantly, a 'patient' that physicians should take care of. This study shows that sophisticated antenatal screening techniques can contribute to increased abortion stigma and strongly impact on physicians' experiences with pregnancy and abortion, influencing their choices concerning conscientious objection. It also confirms what Norris et al. (2011) have argued: the stigmatisation of abortion negatively impacts on medical training in abortion care and on physicians' experiences and choices concerning abortion on the ground. In fact, as it happens in other countries and parts of the world (Global Doctors for Choice 2013) Italian physicians claim conscientious objection not only because of the reasons mentioned above, but also due to their fear/experience with abortion stigma and discrimination, and to the lack of training in abortion care. It is a vicious circle. In fact, the opposite is also true: high rates of conscientious objection increase the marginalisation and stigmatisation of abortion provision by negatively impacting on abortion providers' medical training and working life and on the quality of abortion care. In this context, conscientious objection seems to be more than an individual choice: it emerges as a 'systemic' practice, as anthropologist Joanna Mishtal has argued in the case of Poland (Mishtal 2009, 2015).

However, where well-known physicians and university professors are abortion providers and chief gynaecologists, abortion care is 'normalised' as part of physicians' daily routine (as it happens in Milan) and obstetricians-gynaecologists do not feel as significantly discriminated against and stigmatised as in other contexts, where the opposite occurs. This is the case with some of Rome's hospitals, where conscientious objection rates are higher and abortion stigma is stronger, which shows that the two phenomena are strictly related to each other. Thanks to Laiga, however, abortion providers are increasingly participating in pro-abortion rights protests and striving for better quality medical training and abortion services. This may have an important impact on abortion providers' working conditions and on physicians' professional choices in regards to conscientious objection as well as on access to abortion care. Their protests are already changing the nature of the public debate on abortion, by introducing new themes, such as medical ethics and doctors' duties towards their female patients as well as towards the state, and the necessity of fighting against the stigmatisation and discrimination of abortion providers. By doing so, abortion providers are progressively shifting the focus of the debate away from the foetus and are successfully enlarging the scope of pro-abortion rights protests, by including the defence of abortion providers' rights along with women's health and rights.

Silvia De Zordo (Ph.D. in Social Anthropology at EHESS, Paris, 2008) is a Senior Researcher at the Universitat de Barcelona, Department of Anthropology. Her research interests encompass contraception, abortion and conscientious objection in Latin America and Europe. She has published several peer-reviewed articles and co-edited three books, including *Reproduction and Biopolitics: Ethnographies of Governance, 'Irrationality' and Resistance* (Routledge, 2014). She has recently been awarded an ERC Starting Grant to study the impact on women of barriers to legal abortion in Europe.

Notes

The author would like to thank the Marie Curie Fellowship, the physicians and health professionals who agreed to participate in her research, the chief gynaecologists who facilitated this fieldwork, and her research assistants (R. Lombardi and A. Martino).

1. From 2011 to 2012, as a Postdoctoral Research Fellow at Goldsmiths University of London, I carried out a study on health professionals' experiences and attitudes to abortion and conscientious objection in Italy and the United Kingdom. This study was funded by a Marie Curie International Incoming Fellowship and was approved by the Ethics Committee of Goldsmiths University of London, as well as by the Ethics Committees of all the hospitals involved in the project. Participants had to read and sign an informed consent form prior to the questionnaire/interview. Pseudonyms for participants and fictitious names for the hospitals involved in the study were used throughout data collection, analysis and dissemination, in order to grant participants anonymity and confidentiality.

2. See Lalli (2011) for a discussion of conscientious objection versus civil disobedience and a comparison between conscientious objection to military service and to abortion care in Italy.

3. The duration of the study was two months in each city (total: four months in 2011). Questionnaires and in-depth interviews were conducted with obstetricians-gynaecologists, residents and other health professionals – mainly midwives and nurses – working at each hospital. In this chapter I focus on obstetricians-gynaecologists. All physicians working at the hospitals were invited to participate. In Milan 50 per cent of consultants in obstetrics-gynaecology were recruited at each hospital (HP, HF), while in Rome respectively 43 per cent and 12 per cent of consultants were recruited at each hospital (HA, HB). In each city a total of 27 obstetricians-gynaecologists working at the hospitals participated in the study, as well as a number of abortion providers working at other health facilities.

4. I also explore this topic in other publications (De Zordo 2015, 2016).

5. This section and the following one were the result of my study, my occasional participation in the political debate on abortion in Italy, and a paper that I co-wrote in 2010 for the American Anthropological Association Conference with Milena Marchesi, an Italian anthropologist based in the United States who has done extensive work on artificial reproductive technologies in Italy (De Zordo and Marchesi 2010; Marchesi, 2014 [2012]).

6. For an historical, critical account of the feminist debate on women's rights and abortion in the 1970s see Libreria della donne di Milano (1987).

7. All translations from Italian into English are mine.

8. This procedure is usually performed before medical and surgical abortion in the second and third trimesters 'to avoid signs of life at induction or in the belief that it makes the procedure easier and safer'. The most common methods are intra-cardiac injection of potassium chloride, intra-amniotic injection of digoxin, and transection of the umbilical cord. See http://www.reproductivereview.org/index.php/site/article/1093/ [Retrieved 30 July 2016].

9. This was the case at HB in Rome, where I had serious difficulties with recruiting participants for my study at the obstetrics-gynaecology ward because of the tensions between this service, with high rates of conscientious objection, and the abortion service.

10. She had recently decided to provide second trimester abortions, but not first trimester terminations. See note 16 for further details.

11. See http://en.radiovaticana.va/news/2014/03/27/vatican_statement_on_meeting_of_pope_francis_and_president_obama/en1-785409 [Retrieved 30 July 2016].

12. In Milan 50 per cent of consultants were objectors at HP and 60 per cent at HF and respectively 30 per cent and 50 per cent of them were recruited for this study. In Rome objectors' rates were 90 per cent at HA and 88 per cent at HB and respectively 32 per cent and 9 per cent of them participated in the study. In Rome all abortion providers participated in the study at HA and 70 per cent of abortion providers at HB, while in Milan 72 per cent of them participated at HP and 43 per cent at HF.

13. Those established by the abortion law were considered satisfactory by the majority. However, many objectors and also some abortion providers said they would prefer a precise legal time limit in the second trimester, instead of viability.

14. In Milan's hospitals the large majority of consultants and residents in obstetrics-gynaecology, both abortion providers and objectors, were female. Most male consultants were abortion providers at one hospital (HP), while at the other one (HF) they were objectors. At one hospital (HF) most (female) residents were abortion providers. In Rome's hospitals most consultants were male physicians, most female and male consultants were objectors and the large majority of abortion providers were female physicians especially hired to work at the abortion service. Some of them had been or were feminist activists, others had worked in public family planning centres and a few of them had chosen to work at the abortion service because they could not reconcile their long working hours at the obstetrics ward with their family duties.

15. News of women abandoned during their labour by objectors recently came out in the media, nationally and internationally. See http://the-view-from-rome.blogautore.repubblica.it/2014/03/11/woman-aborts-alone-because-of-staffs-conscience/ and http://tempsreel.nouvelobs.com/monde/20150625.OBS1509/italie-tu-avorteras-dans-la-douleur.html [Retrieved 30 July 2016].

16. 'Selective' conscientious objection is not allowed by the abortion law, but it seems to be tolerated in some hospitals.

17. Some abortion providers from Milan had been denounced by pro-life centres more than once for supposed illegal abortions, but they had always been found innocent.

18. Unfortunately, the Ministry of Health does not provide data on conscientious objection by gender and the sample of physicians and residents interviewed for this study is too limited to get to any conclusions regarding the influence of gender on conscientious objection.

19. Seven per cent of all terminations were performed on non-Italian women in 1995, 34 percent in 2013. Over the last two decades the highest abortion rate and re-

peated abortion rate have been registered among immigrant women. However, since 2003 these rates have started to decrease (see Italia, Ministero della Salute 2015).

20. The number of terminations has decreased by 58.5 per cent since 1982, when the abortion rate reached its highest levels after the legalisation of abortion. In 2014 the abortion rate was 7.2/1000 women in reproductive age (see Italia, Ministero della Salute 2015).

21. If terminations are performed by trained abortion providers with safe techniques and unnecessary curettages are avoided (which is not always the case in Italy) there is a very low risk of complication and negative consequences for women's reproductive health (see WHO 2012).

22. Hormonal contraceptives must be prescribed by physicians and women have to buy them at pharmacies, where condoms are also sold. The IUD is the only contraceptive freely provided at public family planning centres, where women have to pay a small amount of money for its insertion.

23. For a discussion of reproductive politics in Eastern, former socialist countries see Anton and Mishtal in this volume.

24. Until 2015, in Italy the morning after pills (Levonorgestrel, effective for 72 hours, and Ellaone, effective for 5 days) had to be prescribed by a physician and the prescription could be used only once. Moreover, they were not always easily accessible because many physicians inappropriately used conscientious objection, which should be limited to abortion procedures, to refuse prescribing them. Since March 2015 only minors must have a medical prescription to buy the morning after pill. However, these pills are not reimbursed or freely provided to adolescents, as it happens in other European countries.

References

Bajos, N. and M. Ferrand. 2002. *De la contraception à l'avortement. Sociologie des grossesses non prévues*. Paris: Inserm.

Beynon-Jones, S.M. 2013. 'Expecting Motherhood? Stratifying Reproduction in 21st-Century Scottish Abortion Practice', *Sociology* 47(3): 509–25.

Casper, M.J. 1998. *The Making of the Unborn Patient. A Social Anatomy of Fetal Surgery*. New Brunswick, New Jersey, and London: Rutgers University Press.

Casper, M.J. and L.M. Morgan. 2004. 'Constructing Fetal Citizens', *Anthropology Newsletter* 45(9): 17–18.

Consiglio Regionale della Lombardia. January 30, 2007. 'Modifiche al Regolamento regionale del 9 novembre 2004, n. 6- Regolamento in materia di attività funebri e cimiteriali'. Milano.

Council of Europe, Committee of Social Rights. 2014. 'Decision on the Merits of: International Planned Parenthood Federation – European Network (IPPF EN) v. Italy, Complaint No. 87/2012'. Brussels: Council of Europe.

———. 2016. Decision on Admissibility and the Merits of: Confederazione Nazionale del Lavoro v. Italy, Complaint No. 91/2013. Brussels: Council of Europe.

De Zordo, S. 2015. 'Interruption volontaire de grossesse et clause de conscience en Italie et en Espagne, entre droits des femmes et "droits" du fœtus/patient', *Sociologie, Santé* (Sup.) 38: 107–29.

———. 2016. 'Lo stigma dell'aborto e l'obiezione di coscienza: l'esperienza e le opinioni dei ginecologi in Italia e in Catalogna (Spagna)' in C. Lalli (ed.), 'Aborto: stigma, senso di colpa, silenzio. Si può parlare di aborto?', *Medicina nei Secoli* (Sup.) 28(1): 195–248.

De Zordo, S. and M. Marchesi. 2010. 'Disciplining the Family, Governing Society in the Age of Subsidiarity: The Politics of Life in Contemporary Italy', *AAA (American Anthropological Association) annual Conference. Panel: 'Circulation of Political and Religious Discourses on Reproductive Health and Rights in Europe: Generating New Divides, Strengthening Old Inequalities?' 20 November 2010.* New Orleans.

De Zordo, S. and J. Mishtal. 2011. 'Physicians and Abortion: Provision, Political Participation and Conflicts on the Ground. The Cases of Brazil and Poland', *Women's Health Issues* (Sup.) 21 (35): S 32–S36.

Duden, B. 1999. 'The Fetus on the "Farther Shore": Towards a History of the Unborn', in L.M. Morgan and M. W. Michaels (eds), *Fetal Subjects, Feminist Positions*. Philadelphia: University of Pennsylvania Press, pp. 13–25.

Franklin, S. 1999. 'Dead Embryos: Feminism in Suspension', in L.M. Morgan and M.W. Michaels (eds), *Fetal Subjects, Feminist Positions*. Philadelphia: University of Pennsylvania Press, pp. 61–82.

Freedman, L. et al. 2010. 'Obstacles to the Integration of Abortion into Obstetrics and Gynecology Practice', *Perspectives on Sexual and Reproductive Health* 42(3): 146–51.

Global Doctors for Choice and collaborators. 2013. 'Conscientious Refusal of Reproductive Health Care. A White Paper Examining Prevalence, Health Consequences and Policy Responses', *International Journal of Gynecology and Obstetrics* 123(Sup. 3): 41–56.

Grimes, D.A. 2008. 'The Choice of Second Trimester Abortion Method: Evolution, Evidence and Ethics', *Reproductive Health Matters* 16(Sup. 31):183–88.

Harris, L.H. et al. 2011. 'Dynamics of Stigma in Abortion Work: Findings from a Pilot Study of the Providers Share Workshop', *Social Science & Medicine* 73: 1062–70.

IPPF (International Planned Parenthood Federation). 2012. Abortion Legislation in Europe. Brussels: IPPF.

Italia, Ministero della Salute. 2013-2014-2015. 'Relazione del Ministero della Salute sull'attuazione della Legge contenente norme per la tutela della tutela sociale della maternità e per l'interruzione volontaria della gravidanza. Dati preliminari 2012-2013-2014. Dati definitivi 2011-2012-2013'. Roma.

Joffe, C. 2014. 'Commentary: Abortion Provider Stigma and Mainstream Medicine', *Women Health* 54(7): 666–71.

Kaufman, S.R. and L.M. Morgan. 2005. 'The Anthropology of the Beginnings and Ends of Life', *Annual Review of Anthropology* 34: 317–41.

Kumar, A. and L. Hessini and M.N.H. Mitchell. 2009. 'Conceptualizing Abortion Stigma', *Culture, Health and Society* 11(6): 625–39.

Lalli, C. 2011. *C'è chi dice no. Dalla leva all'aborto. Come cambia l'obiezione di coscienza.* Milano: Il Saggiatore.

Libreria della donne di Milano. 1987. *Non credere di avere dei diritti.* Milano: Rosenberg & Sellier.

Lohr P.A., J.L. Hayes and K. Gemzell-Daniellsson. 2008. 'Surgical versus Medical Methods for Second Trimester Induced Abortion', *The Cochrane Library*, 3: 1–26.

Marchesi, M. 2014. 'Reproducing Italians: Contested Biopolitics in the Age of "Replacement Anxiety"', in S. De Zordo and M. Marchesi (eds), *Reproduction and Biopolitics: Ethnographies of Governance, "Irrationality" and Resistance.* London and New York: Routledge, pp. 35–52. Reprint from: 2012. *Anthropology and Medicine* 19(2-Special Issue): 171–88.

Martin, L.A. et al. 2014. 'Abortion Providers, Stigma and Professional Quality of Life', *Contraception* 90(6): 581–87.

Mishtal, J. 2009. 'Matters of Conscience: The Politics of Reproductive Healthcare in Poland', *Medical Anthropology Quarterly* 23(2): 161–83.

———. 2015. *Politics of Morality: The Church, the State, and Reproductive Rights in Postsocialist Poland.* Athens: Ohio University Press.

Morgan, L.M. 1999. 'Materializing the Fetal Body, Or, What Are Those Corpses Doing in Biology's Basement?' in L.M. Morgan and M.W. Michaels (eds), *Fetal Subjects, Feminist Positions.* Philadelphia: University of Pennsylvania Press, pp. 43–60.

———. 2009. *Icons of Life. A Cultural History of Human Embryos.* Berkeley-Los Angeles: University of California Press.

———. 2014. 'Reproductive Governance in Latin America', in De Zordo, S. and M. Marchesi (eds). *Reproduction and Biopolitics: Ethnographies of Governance, "Irrationality" and Resistance.* London and New York: Routledge, pp. 105–18. Reprint from: 2012. *Anthropology & Medicine* 19(2 Special Issue): 241–54.

Norris, A. et al. 2011. 'Abortion Stigma: A Reconceptualization of Constituents, Causes and Consequences', *Women's Health Issues* 21(35 Supplement): S49–S54.

O'Donnell, J., T.A. Weitz and L.R. Freedman. 2011. 'Resistance and Vulnerability to Stigmatization in Abortion Work', *Social Science & Medicine* 73: 1357–364.

Parlamento italiano, Legge 40-2004. Roma.

Parlamento italiano, Legge 194-1978. Roma.

Passerini, L. 1994. 'The Interpretation of Democracy in the Italian Women's Movement of the 1970s and 1980s', *Women's Studies International Forum* 17: 235–40.

Payne, C.M., M.P. Debbink and E.A. Steele. 2013. 'Why Women are Dying from Unsafe Abortion: Narratives of Ghanaian Abortion Providers', *African Journal of Reproductive Health* 17(2): 118–28.

Rapp, R. 2000. *Testing Women, Testing the Fetus: The Social Impact of Amniocentesis in America.* New York-London: Routledge.

UK, Department of Health. 2015. 'Abortion Statistics England and Wales: 2014'. Retrieved 31 July 2016 from: https://www.gov.uk/government/statistical-data-sets/abortion-statistics-england-and-wales-2014

World Health Organization, Department of Reproductive Health and Research. 2012. 'Safe Abortion: Technical and Policy Guidance for Health Systems'. Retrieved 1 August 2016 from http://www.who.int/reproductivehealth/publications/unsafe_abortion/9789241548434/en/

Zampas, C. and X. Andión-Ibañez. 2012. 'Conscientious Objection to Sexual and Reproductive Health Services: International Human Rights Standards and European Law and Practice', *European Journal of Health Law* 19: 231–56.

Chapter 8

Women Rights or 'Unborn' Rights?

Laws and Loopholes in Madrid's Public Healthcare Services' Abortion Provision to Migrant Women

by Beatriz Aragón Martín

Introduction

Abortion legislation and its provision by the public health services has been a recurrent topic both in public and political debates since Spain's transition to democracy. After the Francoist dictatorship government, which lasted from 1939 to 1975, abortion was regulated twice: first in 1985 with the decriminalisation of abortion under specific circumstances and second in 2010 when abortion on demand during the first fourteen weeks was granted. The 1985 Act was the first regulation of abortion in Spain, with the only exception being a decree law in Catalonia, which permitted abortion on the grounds of women's health, during the years of the civil war (1936–39).

While the 1985 act maintained abortion under the penal code regulation, the 2010 Spanish sexual and reproductive health law echoes the rights-based approach to reproductive health fostered by international agencies such as the WHO (World Health Organization). Since the Cairo International Conference on Population and Development in 1994, there has been an international trend to frame reproductive and sexual health issues in terms of individual rights (Goldberg 2009). Morgan and Roberts argue that 'This discursive formulation has created an opening for competition between the "right-to-life" of the "unborn" and the "reproductive rights" of women' (Morgan and Roberts 2012: 245). The shift to a rights-based rhetoric was previously present in the legal and political arenas, but since the law was passed it has been reinvigorated. It pertains not only to women's versus foetus' rights, but also to public health workers' rights to religious freedom, granted by the Spanish Constitution Act, and their right to refuse the provision of lawful care.

Despite the fact that abortion provision has been included as another service provided by the public health system since 1985,[1] to this day it is not integrated in public hospitals on a regular basis. Public hospitals performing abortions are scarce and their geographical distribution shows the inequity between regions for accessing abortion. For example, in Navarra – a northern region with an important presence of conservative Catholic groups such as Opus Dei – no private or public hospitals performed abortions until 2011 and women seeking abortions had to travel to neighbouring cities without any of their expenses being covered by the public health system (O'Kelly and Zumarán 2008). Hence, depending on geographical location, the opportunity to access free lawful care varies hugely.

Why do professionals in the public health system seem so reticent to perform abortions? This is an under-researched topic in which different factors are implicated. The initial failure of the public health system to begin providing abortions or training for providers back in 1985 fostered the creation of an alternative network of private clinics that perform abortions. In Spain, and specifically in my research fieldwork area, Madrid, information about abortion in the public health system is difficult to access: the techniques are not systematically included in medical schools or gynaecology training, it is difficult to know which public hospitals provide this service, and it is even more difficult for patients to know which professionals are conscientious objectors. The majority of women go directly to the private clinics advertised in different media and a mere third of them claim public health insurance coverage.[2] It seems that there is neither a political nor professional willingness to integrate abortion into the public health system. During my fieldwork, most of the public healthcare workers I worked with had an indifferent attitude towards the multiple obstacles women had to get round to access abortion.

Research studies in the United States have shown that inadequate funding for abortion disproportionately affects poor women (Boonstra 2007; Leviné, Trainor and Zimmerman 1996). In 2012, in the context of economic recession, Spain implemented neoliberal economic policies that reduced universal healthcare coverage.[3] Until 2012, undocumented migrants were entitled to access healthcare on equal grounds to nationals, but it was hardly possible for migrants to fulfil all of the administrative requirements and access healthcare (Chauvin et al. 2010). Still, after the law was passed in April 2012, undocumented migrants were left outside of public healthcare entitlement. Before the law, obtaining a healthcare card was difficult because of the administrative process, but after the law was passed, it became impossible. Interestingly, pregnant women – regardless of their nationality and their insurance status – are eligible for public healthcare, as are children under eighteen years old. Pregnant women's entitlement is grounded on the state protection of the foetus as an unborn child, not on women's reproductive health rights. Indeed, access to healthcare for pregnant women in Spain was granted in 1990, when Spain ratified the UN Convention on the Rights of the Child (BOE 1990). Article 24, section D included the government's duty 'To ensure appropriate pre-natal and post-natal healthcare for mothers' (BOE 1990; UN 1990).

In this chapter I explore how abortion legislation is implemented in public healthcare facilities in Madrid. The chapter reflects on how the translation of the law in everyday practice generates a specific constellation of opportunities and constraints, which accounts for the great heterogeneity in the provision of reproductive services in this local scenario. The data I present in this chapter are drawn from my own experience working as a general practitioner in a programme for undocumented migrants over five years (2007–2011), which was part of the public healthcare system. From a medical anthropological perspective, I analyse how the duel of claiming rights (from pro-choice and pro-life groups) shapes the provision of abortion in Madrid and the strategies to make abortion accessible for migrant women.

In the first part, I look at the changes in the abortion laws and the shift from the penal code to a rights discourse. I then assess the policies regarding access to healthcare and their inclusion and exclusion logic. Finally, I examine the implementation of both the sexual and reproductive health law and the healthcare entitlement law to explain the possibilities within the public health system of contesting the politics of exclusion by exploiting legal loopholes.

Abortion Law: From Penal Code to Rights' Discourse

Before 1985, legislation ensuring access to safe, legal abortion was inexistent in Spain. Similarly to other European countries, the Spanish feminist movement had worked for the decriminalisation of abortion since the 1970s, but it was not until the first years of democracy, in the early eighties, that their voices were heard. Abortion was a vexed issue during the democratic transition, causing deep division between left-wing and right-wing political parties that were preparing the Spanish Democratic Constitutional Act. Finally, to avoid potential conflict, they agreed not to make explicit mention of abortion in the Act at all (Cambronero-Saiz et al. 2007). After forty years of the Franco dictatorship, with the strong influence of the Catholic Church, it was difficult to find a consensus between the different political parties. The way to reach that consensus was to modify the penal code to ensure legal abortion in certain circumstances. Therefore, in 1985, the Socialist Party presented a bill in Parliament to amend the penal code and decriminalise abortion under three circumstances: when pregnancy constitutes a danger to the pregnant woman's physical or psychological health; when the foetus has severe malformations; and finally, when the pregnancy is the result of rape (BOE 1985).

This first abortion regulation, which lasted twenty-five years, was an intermediate solution that appeased the Catholic Church and right-wing parties by maintaining abortion under criminal legislation, while pro-choice activists considered it a starting point to abortion decriminalisation. Even though the Act was a necessary starting point, after some years it was not popular, either with those activists who were against abortion regulation under the penal code and who had advocated for the recognition of women's sexual and reproductive rights, or with pro-life and conservative groups, who claimed that the law was implemented in a very permissive way (Rodríguez-Armas 2012). What was clear was that the bill was not issued to grant women body autonomy or gender equality. Indeed, the process of accessing abortion required a woman to have the permission of at least two different doctors who had evaluated her case.

Socio-economic circumstances were not considered a legitimate reason to obtain a legal abortion, although this was the most common reason for abortion in Spain during that period [4] (Lete and Martínez-Etayo 2004). Therefore, 98 per cent of the abortions officially registered from 1992 to 2004 were performed because the pregnancy represented a serious risk to the woman's mental health, and a psychiatrist had to sign clinical records certifying that this was so.

The process of 'medicalisation' of socio-economic factors is obvious in the Spanish abortion governance up until 2010, and it reflects the way abortion was problematised in the public sphere during that period. As Susan Gal (1994) suggests, the nature of the abortion discourse tells a great deal, not only about reproductive rights and women but also about the nature and concerns of democracy as a whole. Only on the authoritative knowledge of a doctor, in this case a psychiatrist, could an abortion be certified as legal on the grounds that there was a serious health risk to the woman, even though that risk may have derived from other factors that may have been indirectly related to health. Psychiatrists were therefore placed in a very uncomfortable position. On the one hand, they were the key specialists who could ensure access to safe abortion for women; on the other hand, to do so, they had to certify that there was a mental health risk to the mother, even though such a risk was not the main reason for the abortion. Even though there were only a few cases, some psychiatrists were prosecuted and faced the risk of being professionally disqualified for certifying a mental health risk. It is understandable that, in this context, certifying abortions was not a very appealing task for psychiatrists, as it entailed certain professional risks. Psychiatrist Dr Rendueles, reflecting on two different trials that he participated in as an expert, reminds us of the need to change an Act that, in his view, 'is a perverse norm for psychiatry, in the sense that it is one of those norms that is never followed and therefore, being transgressed by everybody, it generates a demoralizing environment. Few transgressors are prosecuted hazardously, while the rest continue in the same ambiguity that is transmitted to the whole system' (Rendueles 1998:240). The ambiguity of the law could threaten psychiatrists' professional career with legal prosecution. Moreover, the career projections of those professionals who participated in abortion provision could be affected, as it was not a normalised service in public hospitals (O'Kelly and Zumarán 2008).

During the 1990s and the first years of the 2000s, abortion seemed to be off the political agenda and it was not considered as a social problem. There was a lack of debate on abortion as a women's health issue, as the justice commission in charge of regulating abortion considered only legal or juridical points and health professionals had no voice. In 2008, the Socialist Party reintroduced abortion into the political agenda, starting with the development of a reproductive and sexual health law, which was finally passed in March 2010. This law was framed in terms of reproductive and sexual rights for women, following recommendations from international institutions such as the UN and the European Council, and the agreements reached at the 1995 Beijing Women Conference. The law finally took abortion in the first trimester of pregnancy out of the penal regulation and ensured abortion on demand during the first fourteen weeks. The law acknowledged the regional inequalities in the provision of abortion and it emphasised the importance of progressively including reproductive health and abortion services in the public health system.

Highly contested by anti-choice and conservative groups,[5] the law is currently under revision by the conservative government. Actually, abortion has erupted again as a vexed issue in the public sphere, since the Minister for Justice, Ruiz-Gallardón, announced new plans to prohibit abortion on demand in the first fourteen weeks, and in cases of malformation up until twenty-five weeks. There have also been criticisms of the 2010 law within the medical sector. In 2011, the Royal College of Physicians of Madrid made public a report made by their Deontological Committee showing their outright rejection of the law. Claiming representative power,[6] they affirmed that all doctors should be against the law because it threatens their ethical duty to protect life, in this case the life of the embryo or the foetus (ICOMEN 2011). There was a similar reaction from the Spanish Association of Pro-Life Gynaecologists (Ginecologos DAV), which issued a report emphasising the rights of the 'unborn', the rights of the gynaecologist to express their conscientious objection and the potential harm for women, who can suffer post-abortion syndrome (DAV 2010). Both reports were contested by the Association of Accredited Clinics for Voluntary Termination of Pregnancy (Asociación de Clínicas Acreditadas para la Interrupción Voluntaria del Embarazo, ACAI), because, despite the fact that some of their professionals belong to the Royal College of Physicians of Madrid, they are neither represented in the report nor had they been consulted for its elaboration. ACAI claims to have clinical experience on providing abortion that has been excluded from the report.[7]

The moral discourses on the embryo as a bearer of rights and on abortion as a 'social evil' to be avoided were central to the debate over the new regulation of reproductive health. In these reports, abortion is treated as a social problem, a failure in contraception and something undesirable for everybody. The DAV gynaecologist representative even compared abortion with traffic accidents and called on the government to implement measures to reduce the number of abortions by facilitating access to contraceptives instead of ensuring safe abortion on demand. During my fieldwork, most of the physicians I worked with tended to perceive abortion as a contraceptive failure, rather than as another technique of fertility control. This finding is similar to those of Seoane (2006), regarding healthcare workers' attitudes to migrant patients in Madrid. In his study, Seoane found that most of the clinicians perceived the higher rates of abortion in migrant women as a striking indicator of their misuse of contraceptive methods and of the healthcare system in general. In clinical arenas, contraceptive control is perceived as a natural female task, which is not carried out correctly in cases of undesired pregnancy, and because of this health professionals have to intervene to correct it by performing an abortion (Beynon-Jones 2013).

The erroneous claim that abortion rates would increase with a pro-choice law appears repeatedly in conservative and pro-life discourses. This claim has been proven wrong not only in international research (see for example Reicher and Hopkins 1996) but also in the local data recorded on abortion during the first two years following the implementation of the law.[8] Madrid's register shows a steady increase in the number abortions from 1986 to 2008, and from 2008 onwards the rate remains stable. The implementation of a less restrictive law did not trigger an exponential in-crease in the number of abortions as the anti-choice activists maintained.[9]

Madrid's epidemiological bulletins offer information about abortion provision over the last two decades. As previously mentioned, from 1990 to 2011, almost all abortions in Madrid were performed in private clinics (as in most Spanish cities) and more than half of the women found their infor-mation about the procedure outside of the public healthcare centres.[10] Less than one third of abortions were funded by the public healthcare system up until 2010,[11] a figure that increased to 54.4 per cent after the implementa-tion of the new Act. It seems that there is an increasing tendency to seek information about abortion from public facilities. Interestingly, the number of women from other regions seeking abortions in Madrid is not negligible (around 20 per cent) and signals the inequalities in the provision of abor-tions between Spanish regions.

Since 2003 the country of origin has been included in the annual reports on the application of the abortion law, showing that more than half of the women who have had abortions were migrant women living in Spain. As abortion rates are higher among migrant women than among the autochthonous, they are presented as a group in need of specific preven-tion programmes. Cultural differences are acknowledged, mainly for mi-grant women from Eastern Europe. As one of the reports states, '10% of Romanian women *confess* that contraceptives are not necessary because you can always have an abortion' (*Boletín Epidemiológico de la Comunidad de Madrid* 2008: 53, emphasis added). This discourse is consistent with the idea of abortion being an undesirable fertility control technique and a solu-tion to contraceptive failure. Therefore, those women who confess that they consider abortion to be a legitimate fertility control technique should be re-educated through specific healthcare programmes, which target migrants as a population with reproductive health problems.

There has been increasing alarm in the media and among healthcare professionals about pharmacological clandestine abortions linked to Latin American communities in Madrid. The use of misoprostol, an accessible drug used for abortion in the first trimester, is common in some Latin American countries (Zamberlin et al. 2012). In Spain it was not approved for gynaecological purposes until 2008 and is seldom used in healthcare facilities.[12] The use of misoprostol without medical supervision by migrant women may help us to reflect on the numerous obstacles they face to ac-cess medical abortion. Some of these obstacles are due to administrative procedures, delays in the provision of care and, in some cases, language barriers. Rosana Triviño argues that the debate about the use of misoprostol not only highlights the dysfunction of the public healthcare system, but it also reveals discourses about identity and citizenship (2012: 31). Migrant women may find it difficult to be recognised as legitimate citizens in healthcare settings because they are stereotypically represented as illegitimate in the public sphere. Those subtle difficulties, which arise from the moral judgements of local healthcare staff about who deserves and who does not deserve care, show migrants' precarious form of citizenship.

Healthcare Coverage: Inclusion and Exclusion Logics

The Spanish Public Health Service (SNS) was funded during the transitional democratic period in the eighties and is based on the principles of universalism and equity following the 1978 Constitution Act, in which the right to protection of health for all Spaniards is recognised. The General Health Care Act approved in 1986 was passed to consolidate the national public health system, mainly financed through general taxation, and aimed at universal coverage and providing healthcare free of charge at the point of delivery. The Act introduced the necessary changes to ensure the development of a primary healthcare-based system and political devolution to regional-based health services, organised into health areas and basic health zones (García-Armesto et al. 2010). The coverage was extended gradually to those without economic resources, and by the year 2000 the law guaranteed the right to access healthcare to irregular migrants. Meanwhile, the decentralisation process was accomplished and from 2002 every region was in charge of its own healthcare services and the Ministry of Health coordinated and guaranteed the cohesion of this quasi-federal system.

Although the SNS faces serious challenges such as the control of its pharmaceutical expenditure – hospital drug expenditure grew by 55 per cent from 2006 to 2010 (García 2011) – and the regional differences in accessibility to and quality of the care provided, the SNS ranks fairly high when it is evaluated according to international healthcare standards. In 2000, the WHO listed the SNS as the seventh best healthcare system in the world and it is remarkable that these achievements have been attained with relatively low public expenditure – a mere 6.5 per cent of the GDP.[13] Nevertheless, the sustainability of the SNS has been an incessant topic in the Spanish media over recent years, and before the 2011 national elections there was much scaremongering about healthcare costs in the media (García 2011).

In April 2012, the new conservative government passed a Decree Law excluding undocumented migrants and others[14] from healthcare coverage (BOE 2012). This measure was pushed forward to guarantee the economic sustainability and technological development of the public healthcare system. Despite the fact that the public discourse often emphasises the drain on national resources (whether in the medical sector or other social services) generated by immigrants, the Decree was not popular either in public healthcare arenas or in wider society. According to a survey carried out by Madrid GPs' association, 69.6 per cent of the doctors who answered the questionnaire perceived the measure as ineffective for containing public healthcare expenditure and most of the doctors believed that excluding undocumented migrants from the public system entailed important Public Health risks (Grupo de trabajo en inmigración, Sociedad Española de Medicina Familiar y Comunitaria, Semfyc forthcoming). Even though it was not a mainstream contestation, healthcare workers claimed their right to conscientiously object to the Decree Law. Grounded on the same legal principle as those who refuse to help with or provide abortion – the religious and beliefs freedom granted at the Spanish Constitution Act – physicians – taking the Hippocratic oath as their deontological code – claimed their duty to attend to anyone who needs medical care, regardless of their religious beliefs, socio-economic conditions or legal status. Again, the discourse of rights is mobilised to contest what is perceived as an unfair law.

It is crucial to bear in mind that, beyond restrictive policies and questions of legal status, obstacles to accessing care are significantly associated with low socio-economic status and overlap with constraints affecting not only migrants but also other low-income populations (Sargent and Larchanché 2011). Policies of entitlement and exclusion determine health vulnerabilities and access to healthcare, which is ultimately entangled with the local ways of reckoning health-related deservingness (Willen 2012). Migration has often elicited discourses of illegitimacy (Fassin 2004) or anxieties about the 'exotic' diseases that migrants may transmit (Chavez 2008). Migrant reproductive behaviour has frequently elicited public concern and hostility in different European countries (see the Italian example described by Marchesi 2012). In the local context where this research takes place, most of the public health studies on migrant health have focused on reproductive issues. In Madrid, the Public Health Institute commissioned a report on healthcare professionals' attitudes towards migrants. The researchers found that healthcare workers perceived migrants as problematic patients who do not know how the healthcare system functions and who demand more attention than the locals. Migrants are perceived as consuming more resources, not accepting the norms, and challenging medical authority (Seoane 2006). Their reproductive behaviour and the use of abortion as an emergency contraceptive technique is also criticised and migrant women are seen as scroungers of the public healthcare system (ibid.: 127).

The report shows how the social construction of immigrant groups in receiving societies is translated into the healthcare realm and impacts the care provided. Migrants are perceived as people who have adopted wrongly the medical relationship with the body, health and illness; what Charles L. Briggs and Clara Mantini-Briggs (2005) call the 'unsanitary citizen'. Thus, migrants are problematised as a population in need of specific programmes to assimilate them to the dominant groups. Access to healthcare is also influenced by the construction of migrants as 'illegitimate' (Larchanché 2011). Before 2012, and despite universal healthcare coverage, a non-negligible number of migrants did not have access to public services due in part to the complicated administrative procedure to obtain a healthcare card. The healthcare card is an indispensable requisite and is issued in primary healthcare centres. The documentation required was proof of identity, a social security number and a recent proof of registration at the local civil registry. These requirements frequently left a number of undocumented migrants who were not able to register in the local civil registry outside of the system. De facto, universal health coverage was limited.

To address these access limitations, the Madrid healthcare institution created a parallel system of documents, which could be substituted for the healthcare card in cases that did not comply with the administrative requisites to grant access to care in special situations. Instead of simplifying the administrative process to ensure universal coverage, new forms of entitlement were created based on medical criteria. A new hierarchy of deservingness was put in place, founded on a patient's age, pregnancy, and chronic diseases. Children were granted a regular healthcare card through the certification of social problems. Pregnant women, once they could prove they were pregnant, received a paper document that granted them healthcare during their pregnancy and for forty days after giving birth. This entitlement document was grounded on the principle that every child had the right to healthcare, and pregnant women were considered as carrying a child-to-be, who is a rights-bearer. The document did not aim to protect women during pregnancy but the product of the pregnancy. The third document was called DAS (Documento de Atención Sanitaria, healthcare document) and was mainly purposed to provide healthcare to people with chronic conditions. Ironically, to claim this document, a certificate from a physician of the public healthcare system was required, even though the patient did not have access to these doctors before obtaining the document. The DAS was valid only for six months and was renewable for another six months, and patients could be forced to interrupt their treatments.

Laws and Loopholes in Clinical Practice

Not only were specific administrative exceptions made, but also healthcare programmes targeting migrant and undeserving populations were implemented. In 2007, five months before the regional elections, Madrid's regional healthcare office announced a new Primary Healthcare unit that aimed to provide healthcare to people living in informal settlements on the outskirts of Madrid. It was called 'Equipo de Intervención con Población Excluida' (Intervention team with socially excluded population) and was created to bridge the gap between the formal healthcare network and the population living in the settlements, where no public services are available. In creating this kind of programme, the regional healthcare office acknowledged that a significant number of people were excluded from the system and that this ultimately posed a public health risk to the rest of the population. Indeed, the creation of this programme was triggered by the claims of social workers and NGO (non-governmental organisation) workers in the settlement, who had previously had to deal with a number of cases of tuberculosis for which they required medical support.

The initial objectives of the programme were to diagnose infectious diseases, drug use and dependence, sexually transmitted diseases and mental health problems, as well as to undertake coordinated work with other institutional programmes targeting the same marginal populations. These objectives enable us to reflect on the moral dimension of public health interventions. The rationale behind these objectives is grounded on moral images and stereotypes of migrants and marginal populations that obviously, in this case, set the public agenda (Morone 1997). Interestingly, when I accepted a position working on this programme as a general practitioner, I was asked if I would mind appearing in the media to explain the programme to a wider audience. It seemed that one of the implicit objectives of the programme was to show wider society the efforts of the public healthcare system in dealing with the public health threat posed by marginal populations.

As Pussetti and Barros argue, 'The analysis of the health and social care practices responsible for promoting immigrants' integration in the western modern way of life illustrates that health and social professionals interventions are a mix of good intentions, developmental ambitions, paternalistic attitudes and desire to control deviant populations' (2012: 47). The programme I present here is a clear example of this mixture of good intentions and control of populations. It also sheds lights on the politics of humanitarianism and the logic that underpins it. In this case, a medical unit was considered more important that providing clean water infrastructure or sanitation in the area, even though these measures have been proven to improve health outcomes more than access to healthcare. Again, we can perceive the medicalisation of socio-economic conditions instead of addressing those conditions directly. The priority is to control the possible health threat posed by marginal populations, not to improve the health status of the people living in social exclusion.

After some months working at the settlement, all of the initial objectives proved to be rarely applicable in that context: the population we found had the same healthcare problems as non-marginal populations, but the conditions they lived in affected the course of the diseases and constrained the possibilities for treatment. Working mainly with young people, most of their healthcare needs were related to reproductive and maternal and child health. Due to the unhealthy living conditions, a good number of consultations were accidents and injuries. Nevertheless, a vast number of consultations were related to administrative advice related to obtaining healthcare cards or other documents. In this context, the healthcare card is perceived not only as a document, but as symbolic of inclusion and access to citizenship. This is similar to what Liliana Suárez-Navaz has called the 'fetishization of papers', referring to the special value ascribed to the stay and work permit for immigrants (1999). In the clinical practice we found some cases of women demanding abortion. These demands were difficult to address because multiple obstacles had to be overcome in order to access secure abortion. First of all, the clinics performing abortions were located far from the settlement and the women usually needed some economic or logistic support to get there. Secondly, in cases where they already had children, they needed to find someone to take care of them while they were away. If they were working, either in regular or irregular jobs, this implied taking a day off, which generated an indirect cost. Thirdly, the price of the intervention made abortion inaccessible for a great number of women if it was not subsidised by the public healthcare system. However, in order to be eligible for abortion funding, it is essential to have a healthcare card.

As exposed previously, every pregnant woman is entitled to healthcare during pregnancy. Prenatal care and any other health issue during pregnancy are covered by the public healthcare system. Taking into account that there was nothing explicitly referring to pregnancy interruption, healthcare workers exploited this ambiguity to claim abortion funding without the healthcare card but with the pregnancy health document. Surprisingly, the claims for funding were accepted and women were able to have an abortion without having to pay for it directly. Women without a healthcare card could access abortion free of charge through this path, even though the purpose of the pregnancy health document was to protect the rights of the 'unborn'. Albeit just a small example, this shows that there are some opportunities to circumvent exclusionary policies by exploiting law loopholes. This path to obtaining abortion funding from public healthcare is not exclusively used in the unit I worked in; most of the abortion clinics in Madrid inform their patients about the possibility of obtaining the funding in this way. Moreover, abortion clinics lobby to compel the healthcare office to maintain this method of funding, as there is no legal reason not to consider interrupting pregnancy as another health issue during pregnancy (Ortiz, personal communication). Nevertheless, using this legal loophole requires a willingness and knowledge of it among the different actors: the administrative staff who issue the pregnancy document; the doctors, nurses and social workers, both in the public facilities and in private clinics, who give the information; and the regional health office staff who finally approve the procedure and funding.

It is difficult to know how extensive this practice is, as there is no research on it and the regional healthcare office does not keep records of the number of abortions funded with the pregnancy health document. One of the obstacles found was the unfamiliarity of the administrative staff with the pregnancy document and therefore it was found that they do not issue it. This evidences the gap between the legal norm and how it is put into practice. This gap accounts for the heterogeneity in the provision of general health services for migrant populations and specifically in the case of seeking abortion, which is a more complicated pathway because it is not integrated in the public network.

Conclusion

Abortion is still a contested issue in democratic Spain. The debates about restricting access to abortion have gained relevance in the public sphere again due to the rise of pro-life groups, which find the current legislation too permissive. Following the global trend, both pro-choice and pro-life groups mobilise discourses of rights: the former defends the 'right to life' of the foetus and the latter claims women's 'right to decide'. Immigrants are also a frequent topic in the media, and since the economic recession they are frequently portrayed as a drain on resources from the state. In this context, where the rights discourse is prevailing, immigrants are perceived in the public arena as rights-bearers if they have legal status or as people whose rights can be withheld if they are irregular migrants.

Some physicians working with migrant women successfully exploit legal loopholes to make the public healthcare service cover the costs of the intervention and therefore make it possible for these women to exercise their right to abortion. The instrumental use of a document primarily conceived to protect the rights of the 'unborn' paradoxically enables women to exercise their rights. This example reveals one of the mechanisms by which doctors and women bypass the non-evident obstacles to exercise the right to abort.

Even though the data presented here are drawn from limited clinical experience, they highlight the heterogeneous attitudes towards abortion in clinical settings, which are far from the frequent portrayal of public healthcare workers refusing to provide abortions. Multiple actors are implicated in the process of granting funding for abortion to migrant women, and different strategies are followed to bypass the obstacles.

The rights framework, under which laws and their contestations exist, permits the use of similar principles to defend opposing moral regimes. As previously exposed, the religious and belief freedom granted at the Spanish Constitution Act is mobilised both by pro-life groups and activists of universal health coverage. The former mobilise belief freedom to support the right of healthcare professionals to contentiously object to providing abortions, whereas the latter use it to enable doctors to object to the law that excludes migrants and uninsured people from public healthcare. Both healthcare staff and migrant women contest health entitlement law by using the pregnancy healthcare document as a means to access abortion funded by the public system. Paradoxically, the pregnancy document is granted to protect the foetus, understood to be a child and therefore under the protection of the state. But as it is not specified in the law that it only covers prenatal care, women seeking an abortion are entitled as much as any other women to a regular healthcare card.

Beatriz Aragón Martín is a former doctoral fellow at the Max Planck Institute for the study of Religious and Ethnic diversity and a Ph.D. candidate in Anthropology at University College London. She has been working as a medical doctor with ethnic minorities in Spain. Her current research deals with issues of cultural difference in healthcare facilities, specifically with Roma people in Madrid.

Notes

I would like to thank the La Caixa scholarship programme and the Max Planck Institute for the Study of Religious and Ethnic Diversity for their financial support. I am also very grateful to Dr Julia Cecilia Navazo for her inestimable help in making this research possible.

1. Even though the 1985 abortion law stated that legal abortion should be provided in public healthcare facilities, to this day most of the abortions are performed in private healthcare facilities. The 2010 law acknowledges the lack of public healthcare hospitals performing abortions and suggests some measures to facilitate the inclusion of abortion provision in public healthcare facilities.
2. See *Boletín Epidemiológico de la Comunidad de Madrid* 2007–2009.
3. Spain has a tax-based National Health System with a remarkable decentralisation of competencies to the autonomous communities. There are also special public and private insurance schemes for certain professions, and private health insurance. As a general principle, healthcare is provided free of charge in health centres and hospitals within the National Health System to 'all Spaniards and foreign nationals residing in the national territory'. The only requirement needed is to be registered in the local civil registry.
4. In 1995 a new bill was voted and passed in the congress of deputies to extend the grounds for abortion to include socioeconomic circumstances. Still, the bill never reached the senate for approval due to the arrival of the conservative party to government.
5. The Sexual and Reproductive bill gained a lot of media attention before it was passed in March 2010. The most controversial aspect of the bill in the media revolved around a woman's age and whether she should be considered adult enough not to need her parents' permission to interrupt her pregnancy.
6. This claim is made on the basis that all the medical doctors are registered by the Royal College of Physicians. The registration is compulsory for clinical practice, but physicians seldom participate in Royal College activities and elections.
7. ACAI public stance is available on line at http://nosotrasdecidimos.org/wp-content/uploads/ACAI-COLEGIO-M%C3%89DICOS-MADRID-21-03-121.pdf (retrieved 15 December 2013).
8. Accredited clinics and public hospitals performing abortions have to report data about their activity to the Ministry of Health. These data are published yearly in the Boletines Epidemiológicos by regions and they include demographic information such as age, country of origin, place of residency, number of children, and other data concerning the reasons for abortion, previous abortions and contraceptive use. Data about referrals and funding from the public health system are also recorded.
9. To see how the 1986 Law affected the abortion rates in Spain, see Peiró et al. (2001). They found that abortion decriminalisation did not have an effect on the trends in abortion, which remained stable, but it reduced access inequalities, as abortion became available locally.
10. See *Boletín Epidemiológico de la Comunidad de Madrid* 2007–2009.
11. Before the implementation of the 2010 reproductive health law, accessing publicly funded abortion was a long and complicated process. Women needed to be referred to a healthcare social worker, who provided information about the funding process and referred women to the private clinics. Sometimes the itinerary to get public funding required six or more appointments with different healthcare professionals,

in different places. Llácer Gil de Ramales et al. (2006) identified delays in treatment and over-bureaucracy as the main barriers to get a state-funded abortion.

12. Spain has one of the lowest rates of pharmacological abortions in Europe – just a mere 5 per cent, a fact that was echoed by the mainstream media. See, for example http://elpais.com/diario/2010/11/23/salud/1290466801_850215.html (retrieved15 December 2013).

13. Organisation for economic cooperation and development. Available online at: http://www.oecd-ilibrary.org/docserver/download/8111101ec061.pdf?expires=14 70948615&id=id&accname=guest&checksum=A457CC6476495B2AE254B040 5D7AFB4D

14. Not only undocumented migrants are excluded, but also those who do not comply with all the requirements to get public health coverage: unemployed people without job-seeking benefits are left outside the system too.

References

Beynon-Jones, S.M. 2013. '"We View That as Contraceptive Failure": Containing the "Multiplicity" of Contraception and Abortion within Scottish Reproductive Healthcare', *Social Sciences & Medicine* 80: 105–12.

BOE. 1990. 'Instrumento de Ratificación de la Convención sobre los Derechos del Niño, adoptada por la Asamblea General de las Naciones Unidas el 20 de noviembre de 1989'. Retrieved 15 December 2013 from https://www.boe.es/buscar/doc. php?id=BOE-A-1990-31312

Boonstra, H.D. 2007. 'The Heart of the Matter: Public Funding of Abortion for Poor Women in the United States', *Guttmacher Policy Review* 10(2007): 1.

Briggs, C.L. 2005. 'Communicability, Racial Discourse and Disease', *Annual Review of Anthropology* 34: 269–91.

Cambronero-Saiz, B., M.T. Ruiz Cantero, C. Vives-Cases, and M. Carrasco Portiño. 2007. 'Abortion in Democratic Spain: The Parliamentary Political Agenda 1979–2004', *Reproductive Health Matters* 15(29): 85–96.

Chauvin, P., I. Parizot and I. Simonnot. 2010. 'HUMA Report: Access To Healthcare for Undocumented Migrants in Eleven European Countries'.

Chavez, L.R. 2008. *The Latino Threat. Constructing Immigrants, Citizens, and the Nation.* Stanford, CA: Stanford University Press.

Fassin, D. 2004. 'Social Illegitimacy as a Foundation of Health Inequality: How the Political Treatment of Immigrants Illuminates a French Paradox', In A. Castro and M. Singer, *Unhealthy Health Policies.* Walnut Creek, CA: Alta Mira. pp. 203–14.

Gal, S. 1994. 'Gender in the Post-socialist Transition: The Abortion Debate in Hungary', *East European Politics and Societies* 8: 256.

García-Armesto, S., M.B. Abadía-Taira, A. Durán, C. Hernández-Quevedo and E. Bernal-Delgado. 2010. 'Spain: Health System Review', *Health Systems in Transition* 12(4): 1–295.

García Rada, A. 2011. 'Is Spanish Public Health Sinking?' *BMJ* 343: d7445.

Ginecólogos DAV, Comisión deontológica. 2010. 'Informe Sobre La Declaración De La SEGO (Sociedad Española De Ginecología Y Obstetricia) Ante La Ley De

Aborto'. Retrieved 15 December 2013 from http://www.icomem.es/verDocumento. ashx?Id=303

Goldberg, M. 2009. *The Means of Reproduction: Sex, Power, and the Future of the World.* New York: Penguin Press.

HUMA Network. 2009. 'Access to Healthcare for Undocumented Migrants and Asylum Seekers in 10 EU Countries. Law and Practice'. Retrieved 15 December 2013 from http://www.episouth.org/doc/r_documents/Rapport_huma-network.pdf

ICOMEN. 2011. 'Reflexiones Sobre la Ley del Aborto y la Implicación Deontológica de los Médicos. Comisión Deontológica del Colegio Oficial de Médicos de Madrid'. Retrieved 15 December 2013 from http://www.abortoinformacionmedica.es/wp-content/uploads/2012/03/aborto-informe-icomem1.pdf

'Interrupciones voluntarias del embarazo notificadas en la Comunidad de Madrid en 2007'. *Boletín Epidemiológico de la comunidad de Madrid.* Número 4, Volumen 14, Abril 2008.

'Interrupciones voluntarias del embarazo notificadas en la Comunidad de Madrid en 2008'. *Boletín Epidemiológico de la comunidad de Madrid.* Número 4, Volumen 15, Abril 2009.

'Interrupciones voluntarias del embarazo notificadas en la Comunidad de Madrid en 2009'. *Boletín Epidemiológico de la comunidad de Madrid.* Número 5, Volumen 16, Abril 2010.

'Interrupciones voluntarias del embarazo notificadas en la Comunidad de Madrid en 2010'. *Boletín Epidemiológico de la comunidad de Madrid.* Número 2, Volumen 17, Febrero 2011.

'Interrupciones voluntarias del embarazo notificadas en la Comunidad de Madrid en 2011'. *Boletín Epidemiológico de la comunidad de Madrid.* Número 18, Volumen 5, Junio 2012.

Lancharchè, S. 2012. 'Intangible Obstacles: Health Implications of Stigmatization, Structural Violence, and Fear among Undocumented Immigrants in France', *Social Sciences & Medicine* 74(6): 858–63.

Lete, I., and M. Martinez-Etayo. 2004. 'Reproductive Health: Some Data and Reflections', *Gaceta Sanitaria* 18:170–74.

Leviné, P., A. Trainor and D. Zimmerman.1996. 'The Effect of Medicaid Abortion Funding Restrictions on Abortions, Pregnancies and Births', *Journal of Health Economics* 15: 555–78.

Ley Orgánica 9/1985 de Reforma del Artículo 417 bis del Código Penal. L. No.166 (Jul. 12, 1985). Boletín Oficial Del Estado (BOE) online access. Retrieved 15 December 2013 from http://www.boe.es/buscar/doc.php?id=BOE-A-1985-14138

Llácer Gil de Ramales, A., C. Morales Martín, S. Castillo Rodríguez, L. Mazarrasa Alvear and M.L. Martínez Blanco. 2006. 'El aborto en las mujeres inmigrantes. Una perspectiva desde los profesionales sociosanitarios que atienden la demanda en Madrid', *Index Enfermeria* 15(55).

Marchesi, M. 2012. 'Reproducing Italians: Contested Biopolitics in the Age of 'Replacement Anxiety''. *Anthropology & Medicine* 19 (2): 171–188.

Morgan, L.M. and E.F.S. Roberts. 2012. 'Reproductive Governance in Latin America', *Anthropology & Medicine* 19(2): 241–54.

Morone, J. 1997. 'Enemies of the People: The Moral Dimension to Public Health', *Journal of Health, Politics, Policy and Law* 22(4): 993–1020.

O'Kelly, M. and A. Zumarán. 2008. 'Acceso al aborto en el estado Español: un mapa de inequidad'. Informe del Grupo de Interés Español en Población, Desarrollo y Salud Sexual y Reproductiva. Retrieved 15 December 2013 from http://www.redxlasalud. org/index.php/mod.documentos/mem.descargar/fichero.DOC-315%232E%23pdf

Peiró, R., C. Colomer, C. Alvarez-Dardet and J.R Ashton. 2001. 'Does the Liberalisation of Abortion Laws Increase the Number of Abortions?' *European Journal of Public Health* 11(2): 190–94.

Pussetti, C. and V. Barros. 2012. 'The Care of the Immigrant Self: Technologies of Citizenship and the Healthcare Sector', *International Journal of Migration, Health and Social Care* 8(1): 42–50.

Real Decreto Ley 16/2012 de medidas urgentes para garantizar la sostenibilidad del Sistema nacional de Salud y mejorar la calidad y seguridad de sus prestaciones. Boletín Oficial del Estado (BOE). Retrieved 15 December 2013 from http://www.boe.es/ boe/dias/2012/04/24/pdfs/BOE-A-2012-5403.pdf

Reicher, S. and N. Hopkins.1996. 'Seeking Influence through Characterizing Self Categories: An Analysis of Anti-abortionist Rhetoric', *British Journal of Social Psychology* 35: 297–311.

Rendueles, G. 1998. 'Denuncia de una Sentencia', *Psiquiatría Pública* 10(5): 239–41.

Rodríguez-Armas, M.L. 2012. 'Del aborto a la interrupción voluntaria del embarazo: reflexiones jurídico-constitucionales en torno a la nueva Ley ante el anuncio de su reforma', *El Cronista del estado social democrático y de derecho* 31: 30–37.

Sargent, C. and S. Larchanché. 2011. 'Transnational Migration and Global Health: The Production and Management of Risk, Illness, and Access to Care', *Annual Review of Anthropology* 40: 345–61.

Seoane, L. 2006. *Actitudes y demandas de los profesionales de la salud hacia la atención sanitaria de los inmigrantes.* Documentos Técnicos de Salud Pública. Instituto de Salud Pública, Comunidad de Madrid.

Suárez-Navaz, L. 1999. 'La Construcción Social del "Fetichismo de los Papeles"'. Ley e identidad en la frontera sur de Europa. VIII congreso de Antropología Social.

Triviño, C.R. 2012. 'Mujeres migrantes y misoprostol: aborto privado, escándalo público', *Dilemata, revista internacional de* éticas *aplicadas* 4(10): 31–34.

UNHR. 1990. 'Convention on the Rights of the Child'. Retrieved 15 December 2013 from http://www.ohchr.org/en/professionalinterest/pages/crc.aspx

Willen, S.S. 2012. 'How is health-related "deservingness" reckoned?: Perspectives from Unauthorized Im/migrants in Tel Aviv'. *Social Science and Medicine* 74 (6): 812–821.

Zamberlin N., Romero M. and Ramos S. 2012. 'Latin American Women's Experiences with Medical Abortion in Settings where Abortion is legally restricted *Reproductive Health* 9(1): 34

Chapter 9

One Step Forward and Two Steps Back

Accessing Abortion in Norway

by Mette Løkeland

Like in many European countries, Norwegian women gained their right to abortion on demand as a result of systematic work from a coalition of feminist groups, political parties and others, including health personnel. A law on abortion was passed in 1975, but it was not until 1978 that the right to abortion on demand was passed in Parliament. This came about not as a victory with an overwhelming majority, but due to the double vote of the chairman of Odelstinget, one of the chambers in the Parliament (Austveg 2006: 124). Ever since then, women have had abortion on demand completely free of charge, up to twelve weeks gestation. The majority (76 per cent) of the population supports the law (NTB 2010), and there are few attacks on the right to first trimester abortions. The abortion rate has been stable since 1978 – around 13–14 per 1,000 women – and 95 per cent of all abortions are performed before twelve weeks (Registry of Pregnancy Termination 2013). Still, there are ongoing debates in Norway on different topics: claims about the mental hardship abortion inflicts on women who have the procedure (as mentioned by Løkeland (2013: 606)), medical doctors claiming conscientious objection, concerns about second trimester abortions, abortion on the grounds of malformation, and a delay in the process of simplifying access to medical abortion. No changes to the actual law have been attempted but there are continuing battles concerning interpretation and regulation of the law.

When the focus on women's reproductive and moral rights diminishes, a stronger moral defence for the foetus can arise (Saugstad 2008). Janet Hadley says that when you distance yourself from debating the morality of abortion and only concentrate on countering the 'awfulisation' of abortion, the members of the anti-abortion movement can present themselves as the only ones concerned about the foetus and claim a 'moral high ground' (1996: 60). We have seen this kind of effect in the debate about foetal malformations. Second trimester abortions on the grounds of malformations are called selective abortions in official reports like 'Evaluation of the biotechnology law' from the Norwegian Directorate of Health (2011). Women who request them are more or less perceived as selfish and unethical in the public debate, mainly by the right- wing; for instance, the medical doctor and Ph.D. candidate in medical ethics Magelssen on the website of the right-wing think tank Minerva (Magelssen 2011). But it is not always following the right-/left-wing axis. The debate has been highly dominated by parents of children with malformations or people with Down's syndrome, who feel unwelcome in a society that will allow abortion on these grounds. They have for instance made their own blog 'No to sorting' (http://neitilsortering.no/). Many critics of abortion based on malformations claim that we would develop a less tolerant society if we classify humans into wanted or unwanted varieties (Drabløs and Ridola 2013). Technology and modern medicine goes through constant development, which makes us able to find smaller irregularities in the foetus at an earlier age. At the same time we are able to save children born very prematurely and treat newborn babies with disabilities. These medical developments influence our view on human life and our belief in what modern technology could help us with. It also gives added argument to those who defend the rights of the foetus as a possible newborn child. In the Norwegian abortion law (Abortion law 1975), women's right to an abortion is weighed against the right to life of the foetus. Women's autonomy decreases with increasing gestational age and almost culminates with the viability of the foetus. The law states that termination of pregnancy in the third trimester is only accepted to save a woman's life or health; for example in cases of cancer and pre-eclampsia. With technology and modern medicine being able to save prematurely born babies at twenty-four weeks of gestation, late second trimester abortions will always be the battlefield for women's rights versus foetus' rights to life.

In the abortion debate health personnel can have both personal interests and hold ethical judgements that either make them sceptical to abortion or active participants in the fight for women's rights to abortion. An ethical judgement can be based on both political and religious background, as well as experiences in confrontations with the actual group of patients or problems. To illustrate the Norwegian abortion situation, I have chosen to present the three concrete, ongoing changes to abortion access and regulations that are happening at this present time in history. In the first case the access to abortion has been broadened by making medical abortion available outside of hospital, while in the latter two cases, regarding second trimester abortions and conscientious objection, the government has suggested changes to the abortion regulations that will limit and restrict women's access. Not all questions reach public interest or debate, while other questions flare-up and are strongly voiced through the news and social media. This is also the situation for these three cases, where the first two gained almost no public interest, with the question of conscientious objection having been one of the most important topics of public debate in 2013.

Medical Abortion Outside of Hospital

Medical abortion as an option for termination of pregnancy was first introduced in Norway in 1998. Up until then, vacuum aspiration under regional or general anaesthesia was the only option. Initially it was a procedure available for women with a gestational age of up to nine weeks and women were admitted as day patients while the abortion was conducted. Over the years, availability of medical abortion has increased to include medical abortion between nine and twelve weeks gestation (Løkeland et al. 2010: 962–68), and women can stay at home while the pregnancy is expulsed if they are less than nine weeks pregnant (Løkeland et al. 2014). Medical abortion has become the method of choice in most hospitals but women can still have a surgical abortion if they ask. Representatives from the Christian Democrats and the Conservative Party tried to ban the option of having a medical abortion at home in Parliament, but their proposal was refused (Parliament 2008). In 2013, 82.1 per cent of all abortions in Norway were done medically, as stated by the Registry of Pregnancy Termination (2015: 7). According to the Norwegian abortion law (1975), abortion is to be performed in hospitals but the County Governor can approve the use of a different institution. Making abortion available outside of hospitals would be in line with WHO recommendations to make abortion available at the lowest treatment level possible (WHO 2012: 8), and would highly increase the number of institutions where women can access abortion. The goal for most advocates and researchers of medical abortion worldwide has been to increase women's choice, improve confidentiality and facilitate a more intimate follow-up, with less people involved in the process.

In 2009, the Norwegian Association of Gynaecologists started working on the possibility of making medical abortion available up to nine weeks gestation through gynaecologists outside of hospital. As early as 2010, funds were allocated in the national budget, but in spite of this political proposal it has been a long and winding road to try and convince health authorities and break new ground. Along the way, there have been some concerns as to the Ministry of Health's real intentions, but gradually though slowly things have progressed. Money has been found, most of the necessary regulations have been put in place and the project kicked off in three cities in January 2015.[1]

Implementation of new procedures and medical advancement can either be a politically intended and controlled process, where a country's health authorities facilitate the implementation through different incentives or imposed regulations or it can be a process where individuals or academic groups introduce new techniques and spread the information through different channels available. The implementation of medical abortion in Norway has been the latter, where some individuals have led the way with the support of the Norwegian gynaecological academic environment.

Increased Limitation to Second Trimester Abortion

In May 2011 the head of staff at Oslo University Hospital's (OUS) Delivery ward, Rikshospitalet, sent a letter to the Hospital Ethical Committee and to the Norwegian Directorate of Health [2] about second trimester abortions being granted by the National Appeal Commission (NAC) and performed after the gestational age of twenty-two weeks (Norwegian Directorate of Health 2012). In the letter she raised a concern that this practice might be violating the law. This found the media's attention and led to a public debate that focused on an increased limitation of second trimester abortions. The debate was highly dominated by journalists, politicians and some feminists, like, for instance, Kaluza, who have been one of the main defenders of women's rights in the question of conscientious objection for general practitioners. Kaluza found it problematic to allow abortion almost at the same time as saving prematurely born, wanted children (Kaluza 2012).

After twelve weeks gestation, women, according to the law, have to pass through a commission of two doctors to obtain an abortion. In cases where the initial commission denies the abortion an appeal can be made to the NAC. The NAC was established in 2010 due to major regional differences in the number of second trimester abortions that were approved. The aim was to secure equal access for all women regardless of where they live. A report made by the Norwegian Board of Health Supervision found that national regulations were followed in each case, but that regional commissions exercised their discretional judgement differently (Helsetilsynet 2005: 4). The NAC has five members: two medical doctors (one a specialist in obstetrics and gynaecology), one lawyer, one social worker and a psychologist. They all support the abortion law.

Second trimester abortions constitute 4 per cent of all abortions in Norway. The commissions grant approximately 92 per cent of all second trimester abortions, and approximately 90 per cent of those that are denied are referred to the NAC. In 2012, fifty requests were sent to the NAC, thirty-six were considered (fourteen were withdrawn) and nineteen were denied. In 2012, 218 abortions were performed after eighteen weeks (Registry of Pregnancy Termination 2013). There are no official statistics on how many of these go to term or if women travel to, for instance, England for an abortion. In total the NAC approved nine abortions between twenty-two and twenty-three weeks gestation and one between twenty-three and twenty-four weeks gestation over a period of twenty-one months (Norwegian Directorate of Health 2012). Since its establishment, a higher number of second trimester abortions have been approved by the NAC, instead of the previous regional appeal commissions. In this way one can say that the NAC has shown a more liberal practice.

After twelve weeks gestation abortion can only be granted if there are particularly weighty reasons. These reasons are stated in §2 of the law and are; a) unreasonable physical or mental burden; b) could lead to a difficult life situation; c) foetal malformations or serious foetal illness; d) certain conditions mentioned in the penal code; for example, rape, incest and other forms of non-consensual sex; e) mental illness or disability (Abortion law 1975). After eighteen weeks gestation, women should, according to the law, only be granted an abortion if there are specifically aggravating reasons. The law does not specify which situations are more aggravating. In exercising their discretional judgement the commissions require gradually aggravated reasons for granting an abortion. One can say that the woman's right to have an abortion decreases with gestational age, and the foetus gains a right to life at the expense of the woman's bodily autonomy. The direct phrasing in the abortion law is that abortion cannot be granted if there is reason to believe that the foetus is viable (Abortion law 1975). Termination of pregnancy to save a woman's life is always accepted and foetuses with severe malformations incompatible with life can be aborted. In the Abortion Regulation[3] of 2001 viability is specified as the possibility of the foetus surviving outside the womb at the time of termination and with medical support available at the time (Abortion Regulation 2001). A further circular from the National Directorate of Health in 2001 (I-40/2001) refers to the guidelines following the Abortion Regulation, which states that a foetus normally will be viable at twenty-two weeks, defined as 154 days or twenty-one weeks and seven days from last menstrual period (LMP) (Norwegian Directorate of

Health 2012). Neither in the guidelines to the Abortion Regulation nor in the letters concerning this particular case is there any information on how this viability limit was established.

The NAC was asked to defend their decision to grant abortion after the limit of twenty-two weeks, and in their answer said that [4] the question of viability is up against the definition in the law, Abortion Regulation and current research. The Abortion Regulation states that one cannot grant an abortion if the actual foetus would be viable outside the womb with medical support at the time of termination. It does not define how probable a survival of the foetus should be. Is a probability of one per cent sufficient, or should the probability exceed fifty per cent? No relevant studies have found a case of survival before twenty-three weeks gestation, and only very limited survival between twenty-three and twenty-four weeks.[5] In the aftermath of this debate, an independent expert panel revised the guidelines to the commissions for second trimester abortion. Their mandate was to revise the medical development concerning viability of premature children, and evaluate the possible need for limiting the abortion to an even earlier gestational age (Norwegian Directorate of Health 2013a: 1–43). The expert panel[6] found the same probabilities for survival as the NAC, and referred to the National Birth Registry, which in line with WHO recommendations does not include births before twenty-two weeks in their perinatal mortality figures. They conclude that there are no medical reasons to further reduce the gestational age limit for abortion. Nowhere in the mandate from the National Directorate of Health were they asked to evaluate if the viability limit should be set at a later gestational age. Except for the NAC, nobody discusses or mentions this possibility. The NAC finds that the law is open for an evaluation of the probability of viability for each foetus in question. In light of current research they find that a pragmatic conclusion would be that in case of pregnancies earlier than twenty-three weeks abortion can be granted, but when 44 per cent survive at twenty-four weeks, the possibility of survival is so high that abortion cannot be granted. For foetuses between twenty-three and twenty-four weeks individual concerns have to be taken into account when the commissions make their judgement. They conclude that with particularly aggravating reasons, like conditions mentioned in the penal code (e.g., rape and incest), the law favours the woman in cases where the probability that the foetus is viable is very low.[7]

The legal text says, 'If the foetus is viable abortion cannot be granted'. It does not say viability using every medical treatment possible, and one can question if there are legal grounds as to make this definition. With no medical treatment the viability limit would probably be more or less stable over the years. Making use of every new medical development improves survival and hence could gradually eat away at the upper gestational age limit for abortion. In recent years, though, there have been almost no changes to the survival rate for prematurely born children under the age of twenty-four weeks. Many prematurely born children have severe medical problems. This was not discussed by either the NAC or the expert panel. The reason for this might be that the law only addresses viability, and that these pregnancies are prevented from being terminated prematurely.

Early pregnancy termination in Norway is handled by nursing staff at the Department of Gynaecology, while midwives handle second trimester abortions after a certain age limit. All second trimester abortions in Norway are done medically, and that is an old custom from long before mifepristone and misoprostol were made available. Very often the midwives who treat women having a second trimester abortion will also treat women with a wanted pregnancy who have a premature delivery. The commission grants the abortion and prescribes the necessary treatment and doses of medication. Midwives start the actual termination and are not formally informed about the reasons for granting an abortion, because this is confidential information given to the commission by the women. The NAC is affiliated with OUS, Rikshospitalet, and all abortions granted by the NAC were performed there. This was also the main national referral hospital for premature deliveries, and midwives felt it was a very difficult ethical situation having to deal with terminations of unwanted pregnancies and premature deliveries of wanted pregnancies at the same gestational age (Norwegian Directorate of Health 2012). It is impossible to know if a different organisation where women in their late second trimester have their terminations would have influenced the abortion guidelines. It is clear, though, that this actual case and limitation of women's access to second trimester abortion is the direct consequence of a letter from the midwives at OUS Rikshospitalet. The result was a thoroughly manifested demarcation line of at least a week between termination of pregnancy and the lower limit of IUC treatment for prematurely born children. Any possibility of discretionary judgement after the gestational age of twenty-one weeks and six days in favour of the woman by the NAC has completely been abandoned. In September 2013 the NAC was transferred from Rikshospitalet to Ullevål Hospital to avoid the link between prematurely born children and late term abortion (Norwegian Directorate of Health 2013b).

As a backdrop to the question on viability and an upper limit for second trimester abortion, it is important to remember that the abortion debate in Norway over the last ten years has been dominated by the discussion about so-called selective abortion. Selective abortion is defined as an abortion on the grounds of foetal malformations, a right that is granted by §2c) of the abortion law. This debate has also been mixed with a debate on the right to a routine, early ultrasound to look for foetal malformations, multiple pregnancies etc., making the access to ultrasound a debate on ethics rather than a discussion on medical usefulness. Participants in the debate have mainly been politicians, families of people with Down's syndrome and families who have undertaken abortions due to malformations. In general, those who argue for the right to early routine ultrasound do so on the grounds of equal rights for all women and the right to self-determination. In general, political parties to the left defend the right to early ultrasound, while parties on the centre-right axis do not (Gitlesen 2013). The Norwegian Association of Gynaecologists does not support routine early ultrasound, because it has not proved to be medically useful, and because there are other DNA blood tests available that should rather be used if one is looking for chromosomal anomalies. Families who have chosen to go to term when foetal malformations have been detected say they feel slightly pressured by health personnel to have an abortion (Randsborg 2012). The Conservative Party wanted to order a removal of §2c) in the abortion law, calling it the eugenic paragraph, but the internal opposition led by the Conservative Women's Committee managed to convince their general assembly to turn it down (Nykvist 2013). Though the National Directorate of Health states that the recommendations still permit termination at any time in the pregnancy in cases where there are severe foetal malformations incompatible with life, it is still unclear what types of malformations could be included. The only concrete suggestions that have been presented are anencephalic foetuses (no brain) and acrania (no cranium) and that in conditions where life expectancy does not exceed minutes, hours, days or a few weeks it would be defined as incompatible with life. Quite a number of severe chromosomal syndromes have an overall short life expectancy, but for most conditions it is possible to find examples of individual survival lengths up to a year or more. In light of how the National Directorate of Health has looked at probable viability, it is unclear how they will interpret the question of a foetus being incompatible with life. How much intensive care and operations should be included in the probability evaluation for each case? With these new limitations it is still unclear how many women could be forced to go to term with a foetus with a very limited life expectancy if these are detected after twenty-two weeks gestation.

In any case, the abortion debate will always be a discussion about women's rights as opposed to the right of the 'unborn'. The rights of other family members are not mentioned in the Norwegian debate on abortion. Laws can and will always be subject to interpretation. When dealing with legal issues there is also always the question of doubt, which in the end makes this ultimate restriction a political choice. In this Norwegian case the doubt is completely in favour of the 'unborn'. The government defines the law in a way that if by any minuscular chance an 'unborn' foetus could survive, the foetus' right to life is more important than the woman's right to decide over her own life. They have even included an extra week of possible doubt of viability beyond any available research. Not in any of the available documents, except for the letter from the NAC, have the woman's rights been raised. It is questionable if any of these limitations are legally durable. The right to have an abortion in case of rape has high moral support among the public; this goes for many of the conditions mentioned in the penal code. The Norwegian Association of Gynaecologists sent a letter[8] to the Health Minister and Parliament in December 2013 where they criticised these suggested limitations, and raised doubt about the legality in making such limitations. The Norwegian Press Bureau picked up on it, and the question flared up in the media in January 2014. The Secretary of State has now made it clear that these limitations in the abortion guidelines will be referred for public consideration.

Conscientious Objection: A Constant Debate

The right of health workers to consciously object to perform abortions is highly debated in many places, because such a right very often limits women's access to abortion. In the Norwegian abortion law the question of conscientious objection is handled in § 14 where it is written that; 'Regional Health institutions have to organise their hospital services in such a way that women at any time can access an abortion. In organising the hospital services one shall take into consideration health personnel who due to conscientious objection do not want to perform or assist under an abortion procedure' (Abortion law 1975). The law does not open up for conscientious objection in the case of handling a woman during her stay in hospital for any other situation than the actual abortion procedure; for example, performing or assisting with surgery, and prescribing abortion medication. In case of complications, which require post-abortion care, conscientious objection does not come into consideration because it is an emergency situation. Each health institution that performs abortions can also refuse to employ health workers that want to opt out from handling abortion (Abortion Regulation 2001).

Up until recently the health authorities have been indulgent towards a custom where some general practitioners due to conscientious objection have referred women to other colleagues for consultations concerning abortion. Some general practitioners have even entered into a contract with local authorities that grants them the right to opt out from certain topics like abortion and assisted reproduction, even though the law does not authorise this. The Ministry of Health felt the need to clarify regulations concerning conscientious objection in a circular (1–4/2011) dated 31 October 2011, and makes it clear that no general practitioner who receives funding from the government (which would be close to all) has the right to conscientious objection in the case of prescribing contraceptives, referring women for an abortion or referring lesbian couples for assisted reproduction. Neither do local authorities have the power to enter into contracts granting general practitioners conscientious objection. A governmental report (NOU[9]) from the Ministry of Culture analyses and evaluates the question of right to conscientious objection in the workplace, particularly in this specific case (NOU 2013). In the aftermath of the circular there was a massive public debate among medical doctors, politicians and others on the right to conscientious objection for general practitioners. Seven medical doctors sent a letter to the Minster of Health calling themselves 'The Committee for the right to conscientious objection for health personnel', defending the right to continue to refer these women to other colleagues instead of referring them for abortion themselves. In the letter they referred to a circular (IK-24/95) from the National Board of Health Supervision, which says that it is legitimate for health personnel to perform conscientious objection and not prescribe contraception that might harm an embryo (Felde et al. 2012: 1), and a resolution from the European Council called (Resolution 1763/2010) 'The right to conscientious objection in lawful medical care' (ibid.: 3). One of their views, among many, is that conscientious objection is necessary not only to safeguard the right to freedom of conscience for each doctor, but also to protect the integrity of the whole medical profession (Felde et al. 2012:3). They argue that it is a society's duty to protect the moral integrity of their health personnel, because strong professional ethics are necessary, and that it is a democratic right not to have to violate one's personal moral, ethical or religious values (ibid.: 4). On a more pragmatic level, they find it unreasonable to ban somebody from working when abortion patients only constitute about 0.5–3 per cent of all consultations during a year (Felde et al. 2012: 5). Magelssen and Fredheim (2011: 2518–19) tried to address and map out on which grounds health personnel should be given the right to conscientious objection and found that if certain criteria[10] were all present they should be respected. The right to conscientious objection is strengthened if the reason is grounded in certain medical principles (you shall not harm/kill) or if the actual medical procedure is new and controversial (ibid.). The NOU from the Ministry of Culture addressed conscientious objection and evaluated these different criteria put forward by Magelssen and Fredheim and the demands from the previously mentioned Committee (NOU 2013). The

NOU states that it is not a human right to have a particular job and as long as a person can quit and find a new job their human rights are not violated. The committee behind the NOU recognises individual conscience, and accepts the right to reserve oneself from actually performing an abortion. But they do not find a plausible difference between referring a woman to a colleague who then refers the woman for an abortion and formally referring the woman themselves (NOU 2013). At the general assembly of the Norwegian Medical Association (NMA) in 2013, the discussion ran high and culminated with a statement in favour of the right to conscientious objection both in referring a patient to a certain treatment and performing it.

> The Medical Association found reason to give the right to conscientious objection in case of performing and referring patients for treatment linked to questions related to life and death. The individual right for doctors to follow their conscience should not be of hindrance to the population in reaching their lawful rights. The right to conscientious objection should thus be evaluated at a local level in the health service to make the necessary considerations. Patients shall always be treated with understanding and respect. Predictability for the patients should be secured through good information.

The declaration had no immediate influence as the Minister of Health confirmed the previous conclusion that conscientious objection for general practitioners was not grounded in the law (Bjåen 2013).

Elisabeth Swensen, a general practitioner herself, has in the public media and in the Norwegian Medical Association been the clearest defender of patient's rights, and an opponent of the right to conscientious objection. She calls the custom of referring a patient to a colleague that in his/her place will refer the patient to, for instance, abortion 'the clean hands ethics'.

> It is important to have the right to conscientious objection in the case where the government imposes certain duties on their population, like for instance the Military Service. To become a general practitioner or gynaecologist in Norway is not an imposed duty; it is a well-informed choice on the top shelf in a privileged corner of the world. There is no reason to feel sorry for people who find they cannot undertake that job. (Swensen 2013)

She says that medical doctors need conscience and morals, but have to understand that every patient has their own moral compass for their decisions, and that integrity is opposed to professional elitism and anti-democratic thoughts. 'Believing that the doctor is better than the patient is out-dated and obviously unethical' (Swensen 2013). A study on Norwegian medical students' views on conscientious objection was published in 2013. The study found that only 10 per cent of students think it should be possible for GPs to refuse to refer a woman for an abortion and 4.9 per cent would refuse to refer a woman for an abortion themselves (Nordstrand 2013: 1–4).

In September 2013 Norway held its national election, and a constellation of the Conservative Party and the Progress Party formed government. Being a minority constellation, they have made certain agreements with the Christian Democrats and the Liberal Party to gain majority votes in most cases. This horse-trading led to an agreement with the Christian Democrats to grant the right to conscientious objection in case of abortion for general practitioners. This again led to a major public debate that had a daily presence in the news, debate programmes and columns over several weeks. Very early on, the current Minister of Health made it clear that the right to conscientious objection in the case of prescribing contraceptives, insertions of IUDs or the right to abstain from referring patients in cases of assisted reproduction would not be included in the current proposal. Regardless of this, conscientious objection, particularly to the latter case, had been made, especially in cases of lesbian couples (Buan et al. 2013).

In the first rounds of debate in 2011, it was interesting to see former central figures in the anti-abortion lobby being completely on the defensive side begging for their right to not take part in an abortion referral due to their conscience. They focused on the right to conscientious objection, and stressed that under no circumstances should this affect women's right to have an abortion. Even after the elections they kept a low profile, and every party defending conscientious objection repeated that women's right to have an abortion is not in question. It is only in a few cases, like in the newspaper *Bergens Tidende* where an editorial defending conscientious objection was illustrated by a foetus being strangled by a rope, that abortion itself has been questioned. The editorial, and in particular the illustration, led to massive critique. This caused the editor to remove the illustration and write an excuse saying the illustration was unintentional and should never have been published (Steiro 2013). After a week of criticism and debate they moderated their view and claimed they would always put women's right to an abortion before the right to conscientious objection, but thought it was possible to have both.

As mentioned, the Conservative Party won the national elections in 2013 and formed a coalition with the Progress Party to assure majority votes in Parliament. They also made an agreement with the Christian Democrats.

The Socialist Left Party demanded that the question of conscientious objection be debated in Parliament. They hoped to appeal to members of the Conservative Party, who in 2011 were strong opponents to general practitioners' right to refuse referral and to vote according to their conscience and not in loyalty to the political agreement made to the Christian Democrats (Johnsen 2013). After a few rounds, the Minister of Health came forward with a suggestion to change the law. When a proposal is ready, it is sent for political referral according to custom, and then tried in Parliament. His new proposal was a highly moderated version of the original proposal. General practitioners who want to abstain from referring abortions have to ask permission from their local health authorities. If it is impossible to find an arrangement where the woman can see a different doctor within twenty-four hours without having to travel far, the doctor will not get the permit to abstain. At the same time, general practitioners who want to object to referring women for abortion have to send a letter to each patient informing them of their moral view, and the information will also be available online where patients choose and register with a general practitioner (Høie 2013).[11] The Conservative Party has said that they will not let their members vote according to conscience.

During the development of the discussion, many members and subgroups of the Norwegian Medical Association made it clear that they had a different view from the statement made at the general assembly. The Norwegian Association of Gynaecologists stated on their web page (NAG 2013) that they were afraid the right to opt out of referring women for an abortion would deprive women of their rights. They invited women to come directly to them instead, and saw the right to conscientious objection as a violation of women's rights and morality. The Association for young doctors and trainees (Viseth 2013) and the head of the Nurses Ethics Committee (Flem 2013) also made clear statements defending women's rights over the right to conscientious objection. Except for the midwives associations, neither of which has made a clear statement in this case, these associations organise all the health personnel that would normally treat women for an unwanted pregnancy.

Conclusion

Though the right to an early abortion is widely accepted in Norway, there is still a lack of interest towards making abortion more easily available. In addition, the foetus has gained rights, including when it has a very limited life expectancy, and moral claims and attacks have shifted to second trimester abortions.

The later debates have shown us that the right to abortion is fragile. Very few people have shown an interest in defending women's rights in late second trimester. Instead, there is a growing defence of the foetus' right to life. Technology and modern medicine has made us able to save prematurely born babies at twenty-four weeks, and there is strong intent to push that to an even lower gestational age. Except from a few solitary cases, results have still not been very promising. If society wants to defend the foetus' right to life over the woman's right to decide over her own body, late second trimester abortions will always be the battlefield for women's rights versus the foetus' right to life. To secure women's rights in the era of modern medicine, one would have to shift some of the focus from the foetus back to women and stress the right of women to control their own body as a human right. There is a reason why very few women request an abortion late in pregnancy, and that is that most women would prefer to have an early one if possible. In the end, it is the woman who not only has to take responsibility for the pregnancy she is going through, but also for the child if it is born.

It might be that the growing defence for the foetus' right to life and accusations of selective abortion over the years, in addition to the relatively small number of women who are affected by these changes, have contributed to women's rights slipping under the radar, or just the lack of public interest. Janet Hadley describes very well how, after a constant battle, it seems like the defenders of safe abortion and the anti-abortion lobby have reached some kind of unanimity where they agree that abortion should never be a woman's most appropriate method of controlling her fertility (1996: 158). The same seems to be the case with late term abortion; where very few seem to be able to defend women's rights to an abortion up against the foetus' right to life.

What the debate on conscientious objection has shown us is that the majority of the Norwegian public's loyalty, sympathy and sense of justice lies with women and their right to blame free abortion, and not with the general practitioners who want to follow their conscience and demonstrate their resistance towards abortion. Norwegian health personnel play an active role in making new abortion methods more easily available and in defending women's right to have an abortion. Even though that is the case, recent events have shown that it is all too easy to sacrifice women's rights. This is evident when powerful parties, for instance the Medical Association, say they want no harm to come to their female patients, but in the end choose to stand by a small fraction of medical doctors claiming the right to conscientious objection for all doctors. In the end, even though the public and the majority of the political parties and politicians are against conscientious objection for general practitioners, they put women's rights and their own conscience on the line to make a political bargain.

Judging by the difference in public interest, one gets the impression that, at the moment, most of the public's loyalty and support goes towards women who have first trimester abortions. To enhance women's rights to abortion as a principle at any time in the pregnancy and for any reason, the right to control one's own body both as a legal and ethical right has to be reclaimed.

Mette Løkeland, MD, Ph.D., is currently working as a medical adviser at the Norwegian Abortion Registry, Department of Health Registries, Norwegian Institute of Public Health, and as a Gynaecologist at Betanien Hospital, Bergen, Norway. Over the last decade she has been working on abortion rights nationally and internationally.

Notes

1. Mette Løkeland is part of the Norwegian Directorate of Health's project group for medical abortion as a treatment option outside of hospital.
2. The Norwegian Directorate of Health is an executive agency and competent authority subordinate to the Norwegian Ministry of Health and Care Services. The political frameworks to which the Directorate is subject are the political platform of the government in office at any time and the resolutions of the government and of Parliament.
3. The Abortion Regulation specifies, interprets and explains the law. It is determined by the Ministry of Health or the National Directorate of Health.
4. Personal information from the head of the NAC, Britt Ingjerd Nesheim.
5. The NAC refers to two studies relevant to the Norwegian setting. The first, a Norwegian study, found 0 per cent survival among children born before twenty-three weeks, 16 per cent survival among those born between twenty-three and twenty-four weeks (39 per cent for those transferred to an intensive care unit (ICU)) and 40 per cent (60 per cent if transferred to ICU) for those born between twenty-four and twenty-five weeks gestation (Markestad et al. 2005:1289–98). The second, an English study, followed a cohort of children born prematurely in 1995 and found that among children born at twenty-three and twenty-four weeks 11 per cent survived to be discharged from hospital. Among children born at twenty-four and twenty-five weeks 26 per cent survived (EPICure 1995). EPICure 2 looks at children born in 2006. Survival at twenty-three weeks in this cohort is more or less unchanged at 16 per cent (EPICure 2006).
6. The expert panel consisted of sixteen people; nurses, midwives, gynaecologists, paediatricians, social workers, lawyers, etc.

7. The law has got a higher legal status than the guidelines to the Abortion Regulation and that is why they ended up with this conclusion.

8. Written by Mette Løkeland.

9. NOU is a Public National Report published by committees appointed by the government. They are very often the preparatory documents from the government to the parliament and are also referred to as legal papers by lawyers.

10. The criteria were: 1) that providing a particular service would harm or violate his/her moral or religious conviction; 2) the reasons for claiming conscientious objection have a plausible religious or moral conviction also to others; 3) a medical issue, which does not constitute a key element in that doctor's medical field of work; 4) the burden on the side of the patient is at an acceptable level and not a life-threatening condition and the doctor has tried to minimise the burden so that conscientious objection does not lead to extra cost or unreasonable delay for the patient to find medical help; 5) the burden for other colleagues and employers is at a reasonable level.

11. The Minister of Health withdrew his proposition to change the abortion law and include the right to conscientious objection for general practitioners on April 25 2014 (see http://www.nrk.no/norge/innforer-ikke-reservasjonsmulighet-1.11683314 [retrieved 15 May 2014]). This was initiated by the leader of the Christian Democrats Arild Hareide, who the previous day announced that they were willing to withdraw the proposition if doctors' right to protect their conscience was secured in other ways (see http://nrk.no/nyheter/1.11682930 [retrieved 15 May 2014]). Conscientious objection for general practitioners has mobilised women all over Norway in protection of women's rights. On International Women's Day the streets were flooded with people protesting the government's proposition. Not since the seventies had so many people marched in the streets for women's rights. In Bergen, where the author of this chapter was the main speaker, the record number of people marching was raised from 2,200 in the seventies to 4,000 (see http://www.nrk.no/hordaland/knuste-den-gamle-8.-mars-rekorden-1.11592341 [retrieved 15 May 2014]).

References

Abortion law. 1975. Retrieved 20 October 2013 from http://www.lovdata.no/all/hl-19750613-050.html

Abortion Regulation. 2001. Retrieved 20 October 2013 from http://www.lovdata.no/for/sf/ho/ho-20010615-0635.html

Austveg, B. 2006. *Kvinners helse på spill: Et historisk og globalt perspektiv på fødsel og abort.* Oslo: Universitetsforlaget (Women's Health at Stake: A Historical and Global Perspective on Birth and Abortion).

Bjåen, B.K. 2013. 'Støre avviser reservasjonsrett' ('Minister Rejects Right to Conscientious Objection'), *Vårtland.* Retrieved 21 October 2013 from http://www.vl.no/2.615/store-avviser-reservasjonsrett-1.46876

Buan, V. et al. 2013. 'Høie(H): Uaktuelt at man kan nekte å henvise lesbiske til assistert befruktning' ('Høie: It is Out of the Question to Deny Referral for Assisted

Reproduction for Lesbians'), *Aftenposten*. Retrieved 30 October 2013 from http://www.aftenposten.no/nyheter/Hoie-H-Uaktuelt-at-man-kan-nekte-a-henvise-lesbiske-til-assistert-befruktning-7329321.html

Drabløs, M.B and Ridola H.N. 2013. 'Prisvinner advarer mot sorteringssamfunnet' ('Prize Winner Warns against Sorting'), *NRK*. Retrieved 8 January 2014 from http://www.nrk.no/ostlandssendingen/advarer-mot-sorteringssamfunnet-1.10897402

EPICure. 1995. 'The First Study; Population Based Studies of Survival and Later Health Status in Extremely Premature Infants'. Retrieved 18 October 2013 from http://www.epicure.ac.uk/epicure-1995/

————. 2006. 'Why Was Another EPICure Study Needed?; Population Based Studies of Survival and Later Health Status in Extremely Premature Infants'. Retrieved 18 October 2013 from http://www.epicure.ac.uk/epicure-2/

Felde, G. et al. 2012. 'Vedrørende: Helsepersonells reservasjonsrett i etisk omstridte saker' ('Concerning: The Right to Conscientious Objection for Health Personnel in Ethically Controversial Cases'), Letter to the Minister of Health 28 January 2012. Retrieved 15 October 2013 from http://www.samvittighetsfrihet.org/brev-hod.pdf

Flem S.S. 2013. 'Reservasjonsretten: sykepleiere sier nei' ('Conscientious Objection: Nurses Say No'), *Bergens Tidende*, 29 October. Retrieved 31 October 2013 from http://www.bt.no/nyheter/innenriks/Reservasjonsretten-ASykepleiere-sier-nei-2994753.html

Gitlesen, J.P. 2013. 'Partienes syn på fosterdiagnostikk' ('The Political Parties View on Foetal Diagnostics'), *Norsk Forbund for Utviklingshemmede*. Retrieved 8 January 2014 from http://www.nfunorge.org/no/Dette-gjor-vi/Kurs-og-opplysning-for-mennesker-med-utviklingshemning/Stortingsvalg/Partienes-syn-pa-fosterdiagnostikk/

Hadley, J. 1996. *Abortion – Between Freedom and Necessity*. Philadelphia: Temple University Press.

Helsetilsynet. 2005. 'Oppsummeringsrapport fra tilsyn med abortnemnder I 2004' ('Summary Report on Supervision of Abortion Comissions'). Retrieved 5 January 2014 from https://www.helsetilsynet.no/upload/Publikasjoner/rapporter2005/helsetilsynetrapport1_2005.pdf

Høie, B. 2013. 'Hensynet til kvinnen viktigst' ('The Concern for the Woman is Most Important'), *Norsk rikskringkasting Ytring*, 31 October. Retrieved 31 October 2013 from http://www.nrk.no/ytring/hensynet-til-kvinnen-viktigst-1.11328432

Johnsen, A.B. 2013. 'SV vil stoppe abortlovendring' ('Socialist Left Party Will Stop Changes to the Abortion Law'), *Verdens gang*, 18 October. Retrieved 18 October 2013 from http://www.vg.no/nyheter/innenriks/norsk-politikk/artikkel.php?artid=10152569

Kaluza, S. 2012. 'Senabort eller tidlig fødsel? Hva er rett når et barn overlever en abort?' ('Late Term Abortion or Premature Birth? What is Right When a Child Survives an Abortion?'), *Side2*. Retrieved 8 January 2014 from http://www.susannekaluza.com/?p=1609

Løkeland, M. 2013. 'Gir abort seinverknader?' ('Does Abortion Lead to Adverse Effects?'), *Tidsskrift for den norske legeforening* 133: 606.

Løkeland, M. 2014. 'Medical Abortion with Home Administration of Misoprostol up to 63 Days Gestation', *Acta Obstet Gynecol Scand* 93(7): 647–53.

Løkeland, M. et al. 2010. 'Medical Abortion at 63 to 90 Days of Gestation', *Obstetrics and Gynecology* 115(5): 962–68.

Magelssen, M. 2011. 'Selektiv abort og menneskeverdet' ('Selective Abortion and Humanity'), Minerva nett. Retrieved 1 January 2014 from http://www.minervanett.no/selektiv-abort-og-menneskeverdet/

Magelssen, M. and O.M.S. Fredheim. 2011. 'Når bør leger ha reservasjonsrett?' ('When Should Doctors Have the Right to Conscientious Objection?'), *Tidsskrift for den norske legeforening* 131: 2518–19.

Markestad, T. et al. 2005. 'Early Death, Morbidity, and Need of Treatment among Extremely Premature Infants', *Pediatrics* 115: 1289–98.

Nordstrand, S.J. et al. 2013. 'Medical Students' Attitudes towards Conscientious Objection: A Survey', *Journal of Medical Ethics*. Retrieved 22 October 2013 from http://jme.bmj.com/content/early/2013/08/14/medethics-2013-101482.full

Norwegian Association of Gynaecologists. 2013. 'Reservasjonsrett' ('Conscientious Objection') Retrieved 31 October 2013 from http://legeforeningen.no/Fagmed/Norsk-gynekologisk-forening/Nyheter/2013/Reservasjonsrett/

Norwegian Directorate of Health. 2012. 'Ad levedyktighetsbegrepet og svangerskapets lengde i lov om svangerskapsavbrudd – momenter til vurdering ref 11/3902' ('Concerning the Concept of Viability Limit and Gestational Age in the Abortion Law – Elements to be Considered Ref 11/3902'), Letter to the Ministry of Health.

———. 2013a. 'Rapport: Uavhengig ekspertgruppe for vurdering av svangerskapsavbrudd' ('Report: Independent Expert Group for Evaluation of Termination of Pregnancy'). Retrieved 15 October 2013 from http://docplayer.me/4475998-Rapport-uavhengig-ekspertgruppe-for-vurdering-av-svangerskapsavbrudd.html

———. 2013b. 'Sentral klagenemnd for abortsaker flyttet til Ullevål' ('NAC Moved to Ullevål'). Retrieved 3 January 2014 from https://helsedirektoratet.no/Documents/Seksuell%20helse/Brev-Sentral%20klagenemnd%20for%20abortsaker%20flytter%20til%20Oslo%20universitetssykehus-Ullevaal.pdf

Norwegian Government Report (NOU). 2013. 'Det livssynsåpne samfunn' ('A Diverse Society's Tolerant Outlook on Life'), Ministry of Culture. Retrieved 15 October 2013 from https://www.regjeringen.no/no/aktuelt/nou-2013-1-det-livssynsapne-samfunn-en-h/id711620/

Norwegian Medical Association. 2013. 'Bred debatt om reservasjonsadgang' ('Broad Debate on the Right to Conscientious Objection'). Retrieved 30 October 2013 from http://legeforeningen.no/Nyheter/2013/Bred-debatt-om-reservasjonsadgang/

NTB. 2010. 'Befolkningen støtter eggdonasjon' ('The Population Supports Eggdonation'), *Norsk rikskringasting*, 8 September.

Nykvist, K. 2013. 'Seier til Høyres feminister' ('Victory for the Conservative Party's Feminists'), *Nationen*, 4 May.

Parliament 2008. 'Stortinget - Møte fredag den 7. mars 2008 kl. 10. Sak 6', Oslo. Retrieved 13 October 2013 from http://www.stortinget.no/no/Saker-og-publikasjoner/Publikasjoner/Referater/Stortinget/2007-2008/080307/6/

Randsborg, E. 2012 'Livredderen' ('The Lifesaver'), *Aftenposten*. Retrieved 8 January 2014 from http://www.aftenposten.no/nyheter/iriks/Livredderen-6952505.html#.Us6Sqo1H1O0

Registry of Pregnancy Termination. 2013. 'Rapport om svangerskapsavbrudd for 2012' ('Report on Termination of Pregnancy 2012'). Bergen: Folkehelseinstituttet.

Registry of Pregnancy Termination. 2015. 'Rapport om svangerskapsavbrudd for 2014' ('Report on Termination of Pregnancy 2014'). Bergen: Folkehelseinstituttet.

Saugstad, O.D. 2008. 'Ensidig abortdebatt' ('Unilateral Debate'), *Aftenposten*, 23 July.

Steiro, G. 2013. 'BT's leder om reservasjonsrett' ('BT's Editorial on Right to Conscientious Objection'), *Bergens Tidende*, 29 October. Retrieved 9 January 2014 from http://www.bt.no/steiro/BTs-leder-om-reservasjonsretten-2994868.html#.UtM8jY1H1O0

Swensen, E. 2013. 'Tilsynet for høy moral' ('Supervision of High Moral'), *Klassekampen*, 17 June.

Viseth, E. 2013. 'Yngre leger sier nei til reservasjonsrett' ('Young Doctors Say No to Conscientious Objection'), *Norsk rikskringkasting Ytring*, 28 October. Retrieved 29 October 2013 from http://www.nrk.no/norge/yngre-leger-ut-mot-reservasjonsrett-1.11323274

World Health Organization. 2012. 'Safe Abortion: Technical and Policy Guidance for Health Systems, Second Edition'. Geneva.

Pronatalism, Nationalism, and Resistance in Abortion Politics and Access to Abortion Services

Chapter 10

For the Good of the Nation

Pronatalism and Abortion Ban during Ceauşescu's Romania

by Lorena Anton

Reproduction control in Ceauşescu's Romania is considered to have been among the most repressive demographic politics of twentieth-century Europe. Draconian pronatalist policies were developed from 1966 to 1989 in the name of the socialist nation and its needs. Besides the lack of modern contraception, voluntary pregnancy interruptions (previously legalised in 1957) were forbidden and severely punished under the penal code. Subsequently, on the first day after Ceauşescu's trial and execution on 25 December 1989, the new Romanian government legalised again abortion on request (in the first trimester of pregnancy and under medical supervision). Currently, Romania's abortion rate is still among the highest in the European Union (according to the National Institute of Statistics, 21.3 for 1,000 women in 2009, versus 44.6 in 1999 and 177.6 in 1990), and maternal mortality due to unsafe, illegal abortion is still reported.[1] Legalising abortion on request at the end of December 1989 has thus represented a major shift in the country's biopolitics.

This change, along with intensive emigration, is considered by local demographers to be the cause of the demographic drop of 1.1 million people recorded in the first two post-communist decades – a significant demographic decline never experienced before in Romania (Gheţău 2004, 2007; Mureşan 2008). If emigration was silently encouraged by the post-communist state due to the importance of the remittances to the state budget, the constant decrease of the birth rate started to be perceived as a major national problem and possible solutions have been investigated. In the spring of 2012, a highly controversial legislative project proposed the creation of significant barriers for women seeking an abortion, including compulsory biased counselling at 'pregnancy crisis counselling offices' and a so-called 'reflection period' of five days before a woman seeking an abortion can obtain the procedure. For the very first time since the end of Ceaușescu's political demography project, the abortion issue was 'back in the limelight'. Civil society, as well as the medical profession, immediately protested against such control over women's bodies and decisions, and more than once former pronatalist biopolitics were recalled. But such a public protest never developed during the communist years.

In order to understand the lack of public protest concerning pronatalist policies and the development of underground abortion practices, this chapter examines the official construction of a pregnancy interruption as 'a social sin' during Ceaușescu's Romania, along with women's memories about that period of time. The analysis is based on long-term oral history and archival research (2005–2009), which addressed the issue of different forms of the memory of pronatalism in communist Romania.[2]

The first part of the chapter presents the 'birth' of the anti-abortion decree (Decree 770/196) at the highest levels of decision-making in the Communist Party and the pronatalist policies that were developed in parallel with the abortion ban. In order to understand why public protest was lacking during the twenty-three years of abortion ban, the second part analyses women's memories about this period and situates them within the official discourse of pronatalism. The conclusion underlines the chapter's main argument, namely that in a totalitarian regime that placed the 'good of the nation' before any individual rights, underground illegal abortions could be seen as the only possible form of resistance against the state's pronatalist policies.

The Life of a Pronatalist Decree: 770/1966

On 2 October 1966, Scînteia – the official journal of PCR (*Partidul Comunist Român*, the Romanian Communist Party[3]) – published a short article about a new decree of the communist regime. Constructed around 'the problems of fertility in socialist Romania',[4] the article announced the solution found by the regime to the low fertility 'problems', namely the banning of abortion 'on request' (*avortul la cerere*). The Decree 770/1966 – known since that day as the Anti-abortion Decree – had just been published in the country's Official Gazette. According to Romanian law, this legislative act would have automatically acquired operative power thirty days after its official publication. In fact, with this short article in Scînteia, the communist regime ruled by its newly elected leader, Nicolae Ceaușescu, simply announced to its subjects that the country's 'problems of fertility' had to be solved.

Abortion on request, or the interruption of pregnancy's course (întreruperea cursului sarcinii), previously legalised in 1957 following the model of the Soviet Union,[5] was not entirely forbidden by this new decree. Instead, Decree no.770/1966 limited abortion on request to any of the following circumstances: (1) for a woman whose life, in the judgement of a special commission, was endangered by the pregnancy; (2) when the foetus suffered from genetic diseases, or showed the risk of congenital deformity; (3) for women with physical, cognitive or sensory disabilities; (4) for women over forty-five years of age, (5) for women already supporting four or more children; and (6) in cases in which the pregnancy resulted from rape or incest. Until the end of the communist regime in December 1989, the medical body was intensely supervised by state police in the correct implementation of the new legislation. Pronatalism – the official ideology encouraging large families and the bearing of children for the greater good of the nation – became a daily reality, sustained by public policies as well as by powerful propaganda.

Nevertheless, the anti-abortion decree had never been announced or expected in the socialist society of 1960s Romania. Speaking about the existence of 'events' in recent history, historian Pierre Nora underlined the importance of their media coverage: 'The written press, the radio, the images themselves act not only as means from which the events are independent, but as the condition of their own existence' (1972: 162). Thus, even if the media coverage of a political turn in abortion politics does not equal its production, the media silence that surrounded the birth of Decree 770/1966 could be considered a paradox. The possible motives for such media silence may be many, starting with the fact that the anti-abortion decree had been enforced in a communist regime, soon to become totalitarian, in which individual rights were respected only as they served the society as a whole. In short, why orchestrate such a major social change for the good of the nation but without its expressed consent?

To answer such a complicated question, I have examined the internal archives of the Central Committee of the PCR one year prior to the implementation of the anti-abortion decree and the official written media, in parallel with literature readings in demography and social sciences in the Romanian scholarship.[6] My archival research took place in the summer of 2007, following the publication of the final report on the communist dictatorship in Romania (the Tismăneanu Report) and its presidential endorsement in December 2006. Documents I have consulted at the National Archives[7] can be classified into two categories: minutes of the official discussions of the Central Committee of PCR before the voting of the anti-abortion decree, as well as different text versions of this legislative act; and reports and classified studies written on the situation of reproductive health in socialist Romania, as well as internal documents for the Ministry of Health to implement the new abortion politics. In parallel, I have conducted oral-history research between 2004 and 2009 in Bucharest and Prahova County. Starting with women from my own family and home community, and following the method of snowball sampling, I have managed to conduct in-depth interviews (following the life history approach) with approximately forty persons (mostly women) who experienced communist pronatalism, ranging in age from mid thirties to mid eighties. Some of the interviews with my key informants were repeated over time, in order to identify possible relations between trauma and narration, as well as to understand the numerous silences that dominated their individual memory about abortion politics during the former communist regime.

From the minutes of the internal discussions of the Central Committee of the PCR concerning the problems of fertility in the Socialist Republic of Romania (RSR – *Republica Socialistă România*) one can observe that the Party started to consider this issue one year before the appearance of the anti-abortion decree. In 1965, the Ministry of Health were asked for a detailed report on the state of the population's health and, simultaneously, a report about fertility in Romania. In July 1966, the Commission of Education and Health of the Central Committee presented to the high officials of Ceauşescu's regime two summaries of these reports. The one to fuel the text of the anti-abortion decree, entitled 'Study on Fertility, and Proposals Concerning the Measures for Improving Fertility in our Country', was subsequently intensely debated during the summer of 1966.

This study analysed the dynamics of natural population growth, as well as the factors that had contributed to Romania's decline in fertility. According to official data, in 1965 RSR had a total fertility rate (TFR) of 1.9 (meaning that each woman had 1.9 children per lifetime), being the second country in Europe (after Hungary) to experience such a negative population change (significantly, a TFR of 2.1 is necessary for population replacement). Also, the study presented different pronatalist measures adopted by European countries, east or west of the Berlin Wall, to redress the postwar population imbalance. Included in the Appendix was a legislative proposal, centred on the creation of socio-economic measures meant to stimulate fertility. These measures would have been introduced in parallel with appropriate reproductive health education (with special attention to modern contraception), all over the country. Nevertheless, abortion on request would have continued to be available in special conditions: for women who already had two children, for women over forty or minors under sixteen, if medical problems were associated with the pregnancy or in special social circumstances (if the pregnancy was the result of rape, for example). Any request was to be closely analysed by a special commission, formed by a gynaecologist, an internal medicine physician and a social worker.

But these modern proposals were intensely criticised by the Party's officials, reunited for an official meeting at the beginning of August 1966, as being 'too indulgent'. The large majority of participants – all men, occupying high positions in the Party's hierarchy – believed that the cause of socialist Romania's low fertility was deficient legislation:

> In my opinion, the first cause is the legislation; it is that decree of 1957, that encouraged – along with a decrease in fertility – a low morality among the youth ... Before, there had been a restraint in the youth, because they were aware that there would be children and complications. Now there is this libertinism, encouraged by the deficiencies of this decree ...We have to finish with this sinful decree once and for all! (Comrade A.D., deputy prime minister, 2 August 1966)

Almost all Party men present agreed that a major and urgent change was needed to increase population growth. At the end of the meeting, Ceauşescu proposed the creation of a new legislative text, in which pregnancy interruptions were to be 'completely stopped', underlying that '... the problem of population is not a problem of a certain individual, of wishing or not wishing children, but it is a social problem – each individual has obligations to society'. Following the decisions taken during this meeting, another text was drawn up, in which abortion on request was strictly forbidden. Also, severe punishments associated to illegal interruption of the course of pregnancy were defined in order to be added to the penal code: women who self-performed or received illegal abortions were given prison sentences lasting from six months to two years, and persons supporting or helping with the procedure received similar or even harsher punishments (which could be as much as ten years' imprisonment if the procedure had resulted in the woman's death).

After mid September, this new proposal was debated with medical specialists. Even if some of them expressed their reservations, because they considered the legislative text too restrictive, many followed the Party line and enthusiastically expressed their support for the new legislation. Signed on 29 September 1966, the new decree was simply 'presented' to the people in the first days of October, on the front page of Scînteia. Thus, even though the measures to be adopted for solving Romania's 'problems of fertility' should have been publicly debated, that debate never occurred. Instead, the change had been decided and imposed from the top down, as the Party and its leader had to construct a bigger socialist nation. Six years later, Decree 53/1972 altered the anti-abortion law. The most significant change was the modification of the age at which a woman could request an abortion, lowered to forty.[8] In 1985, however, the required age threshold was once more raised to forty-five (Decree no.441/1985), as at the beginning of the 1980s Romania registered, again, very low fertility rates.

In order to support such a major political turn in Romania's abortion politics, Ceauşescu's regime needed an important change in the public discourse about maternity and the role of woman in socialist society. Thus, in parallel to the change in abortion legislation, two complementary modifications occurred: on the one hand, sustained pronatalist propaganda was implemented; on the other hand, a generalised 'carrot and stick' pronatalist policy was developed, in which pro-family measures were mixed with coercive measures. The pronatalist propaganda was constant and omnipresent all through the following twenty-three years of abortion ban. Nevertheless, it was constructed differently from one period to another, in direct relation with the women's indirect response to the Party's demographic plans. In the 1960s, for example, the propaganda was centred on the 'historical' role of the Romanian woman as mother, devoted to the bearing and education of children for the nation's vigour:

> One of the most important duties of women, mothers and educators, is to devote themselves to the raising of new generations in the spirit of ardent patriotism, of respect and esteem for the glorious past of the people, of the desire to sacrifice their entire life to the flourishing of the socialist Homeland and the ideals of communism. (Ceauşescu 1969: 477)

In contrast, pregnancy terminations – previously the main method of fertility control – were presented everywhere as a serious danger for the nation's well-being, with negative consequences for women's physical and psychological health. In the 1970s, the socialist woman was presented as 'the woman-creator', equal in all domains to socialist men, and even superior by her natural capacity of giving life and consequently of assuring the future of the nation. In the 1980s the propaganda evolved in order to include the children and their crucial role in the 'construction of communism'. Giving birth, raising and educating as many children as possible, was presented as a 'patriotic duty' of the Romanian woman, especially in light of the fact that the birth rates were again extremely low (in 1983, for example, the birth rate had fallen almost back to that of 1966, the year the anti-abortion decree was adopted). Family values were politically praised, in accordance with the metaphorical view of the Party-State as 'the people's family':

> The Executive Political Committee of the Central Committee of PCR appeals, at this time, to the entire population and to the working people of the towns and villages, to understand that the task of ensuring normal demographic growth in the population is a high honour and a patriotic duty for every family and for all people, who have always taken pride in strong families, with many children, whom they have raised with love, with ensuring the vitality, youth, and vigour of the entire nation. (Romanian Population Policy 1984: 573)

In 1986, Ceaușescu even proclaimed – in an interview given for the German magazine Das Spiegel – that 'the foetus is the socialist property of the whole society ... Those who refuse to have children are deserters, escaping the law of natural continuity' (cited in David and Băban 1996: 237). This importance given to possible future citizens in the 1980s – metaphorically called 'the Golden Era' of the Romanian socialist regime – was not attributing rights to the 'unborn', as later happened in many European countries at the beginning of the new millennium (as the result of an unprecedented development of assisted reproductive technologies and the visualisation of the foetus). Instead, it was another way of underlining the crucial role of children as 'the future of the nation'.

In parallel to this omnipresent propaganda, the communist regime also developed numerous pronatalist public policies.[9] The strategies consisted both of coercive and pro-family measures. For example, beginning the same year as the anti-abortion decree (1966), divorce became very difficult to obtain, especially for couples with children under sixteen years old. Family allowances were liberalised and increased, and income tax was reduced for families with three or more children. At the same time, a 'celibacy tax' (approximately two per cent of the individual's income) was introduced and levied on childless men and women over twenty-five, regardless of their marital status. Moreover, the official production and import of modern contraceptives, including birth control pills and condoms, gradually ceased (although the law did not prohibit their sale). In the 1980s, the last decade of communism, the regime tried to initiate even more direct control over women's bodies by introducing compulsory gynaecological examinations at the workplace to be generally conducted every three months. This measure,[10] presented as a public health policy claiming to maintain women's reproductive health, was in fact a strict manifestation of the Party's omnipresent power in the private sphere. Symbolically, the borders between the public and the private sphere were systematically violated.

Looking Back to the Past: Remembering Ceauşescu's Pronatalism as a 'Woman's Problem'

At the same time the regime's propaganda favouring the growth of the nation was unremitting and constant (Anton 2008), citizens developed thousands of strategies and counter-strategies to thwart the communist regime's absurd policies. This led to the formation of complex relations of solidarity in which trust was the main bond. Although the regime had some success initially in terms of stimulating demographic growth,[11] it never managed to foster any willing adherence to its pronatalist projects. The survival methods developed in the silent struggle against pronatalism became increasingly efficient as time passed. They consisted in both the development of illegal practices of abortion, as well as 'traditional methods' of contraception (identified as such in the memory-narratives collected, as opposed to 'modern' contraception [12]), that ranged from 'natural' (coitus interruptus or calendar-based methods) to 'potion' methods (home-preparation of various perceived contraceptive unguents, liquids or pills).

The official strategies for imposing pronatalism, ostensibly for the nation's good, had many indirect consequences on Romanians' daily life. In particular, over time, the self-proclaimed right of the state to keep watch over its subjects' sexual conduct brought about the violation of the privacy of each family involved, in a system that much resembled voyeurism (Keil and Andreescu 1999). By adopting a hypocritical morality, communist ideology totally eliminated any open discourse on sexuality not associated with the promotion of reproduction from the public sphere. As abortion was constructed by the daily propaganda as a 'woman's problem', it soon began to be perceived as such.

Perhaps because of this, it is mostly women who are the guardians of the socially shared memory of abortion during the communist period. When they have nothing to say about their own experience, they always have something to recount about a sister, a family member, a neighbour, a friend or a colleague from work. The men whom I have interviewed over the years prefer not to remember, but when they do, their accounts are lacking in detail, as most of them are reluctant to relate aspects about abortion under the communist regime. Typical statements ranged from 'Abortion was a woman's problem!' and 'I can't remember very well … But in any case, it was difficult, we were young and we didn't know anything!' to 'You certainly couldn't have four children as Ceaușescu wanted – what would we have brought them up with?' Men who are, or were, part of the medical profession said more, in more detail, but their stories reflect the experience of the medical professionals of the times, who were obliged to learn a pro-natalist discourse dictated from above and to apply it. The internal topography of the socially shared memory of pronatalism is therefore deeply related to gender; the female memory is one rich in details, emotions, characters and dialogues, while the male memory is often arid (when it is not completely supressed). By concentrating on the development of oral history and feminism, much research on social memory and recollection has revealed the connection between memory and gender (see, for example, Leydesdorff, Passerini and Thompson 2005 or Radstone and Hodgkin 2007). Ely and McCabe's observation (cited in Leydesdorff, Passerini and Thompson 2005) that men, in the memory discourse context, 'seem more willing to fill their stories with people whose voices are muted' is validated by my findings on the socially shared memory of abortion during communism.

When recalling abortion during communism, most of the women interviewed revealed in their autobiographical narratives how the regime organised their personal lives. The majority acknowledged their lack of sexual education before marriage, for their sexual life began with family life, 'not like today'. Ana, for example, started her narrative by remembering a horrific story about terminating a pregnancy illegally, immediately explaining that 'back then, we did not have contraception …We had vinegar, salt, lemon or aspirin instead. We had to prepare things with what we had; we prepared them at home, asking around'. Ana was born in 1952, and started her family (and her sexual life) during the time when pronatalism dominated the public sphere. Married at the end of the 1960s to a man from her home village, she also started working in the nearby salt mine. They had two children in the 1970s, then another one in the 1980s, but she did not have a lot of time for their education, as she was working three-team shifts at the mine, and was also responsible for all the housework, as well as the family's little farm. Her husband perceived himself as having an 'important job' and was away most of the time. Therefore, when she became pregnant, despite all precautions, she decided that she could not bear more children, and started to ask around about how to self-induce an abortion. Finally she used the 'probe':[13] she introduced one small tube into the uterus in order to perforate the placenta and induce a major haemorrhage. After using this method early one morning, she went to work where a massive second haemorrhage occurred:

Great, it was finally leaking away, I was cheerful! Later, on my way back from work, I realised that I was not seeing very well. I had to go home, to calm myself down! Home, with work, work, work like crazy, and then I lay in bed, with a big washbasin near me, and I stayed on it every time I felt the haemorrhage was too heavy. And once, when I was lying again in bed, I realised I could not see anymore. So ... I fetched some slippers, and slowly, very slowly, I left my house and my yard, and went to the middle of the road, with some money in my hand. And I tried to stop the first car, then a second one; they didn't stop. Then one driver stopped ... It was already five o'clock in the evening, and I was in my slippers – this is how I arrived at the hospital. I said "Drive!", and on the road I was saying "Keep driving ... just drive me there, to the hospital, I'll pay you whatever you want, I have two children already and I cannot die! If you drive me there, it will be alright, I will not die!" Poor man he was looking at the crazy me and just drove, speeding. (Ana, born 1952, mother of three children)

Then Ana remembered, in detail, how she finally arrived at the hospital and how one doctor saved her life that night, even before she was questioned by Securitatea's men. Then she remembered other women who self-induced abortions and with which she 'had to arrive at the hospital', and how the same doctor – who knew her by now – accused her of 'doing something': 'What do you mean, did I do something? I did everything, everything that I heard about I did, but now the bleeding will not stop, please make it stop!' Finally, she found herself summoned for an official interrogation, an episode that she recalled with a very comical tone. At the end of the interrogation, when she realised that they had nothing against her, just a big pronatalist discourse and a lot of threats, she announced to the Party's men that her file should 'remain at the top of the pile', as she might be back in the near future. 'Comrade, he said, do you think this is a joke? It is not a joke!' Ana finished her story with another recollection about the scarcity of contraception, and how she always felt that she was not with her husband in their bed, but 'in a kitchen, with all these potions ... What more should I say about that time, what else? There is nothing else to tell you. It was a nightmare – I'm telling you – it was a continuous nightmare. We had a saying, "It is not difficult to have a lot of children; we had to struggle a lot not to have them!"'

In Ana's memory-narrative, as in the vast majority of the stories collected during my research, the trauma of abortion is almost concealed. In their manner of remembering pronatalism, the women present and analyse themselves as the Other, a character in the story of their own past, utterly detached from the 'I' in the account. Thus, the accounts represent, in their own narrative composition, an implicit resource for self-awareness in either remembering a traumatic loss, or just leaving the past in the past. The passage from her own person (the author of the narrative text) to a persona (an actor of her own remembered past) makes possible the act of undergoing and verbalising not only the reconstruction of events but also the emotions, among which the despair over the lack of control over her own body and sexuality are among the strongest.

'We were seen as machines – I'm telling you – as perfect machines who were supposed to have as many children as possible!' is what one woman emphasised in her story about her youth in the last decade of Romanian communism. 'But how to raise them, and feed them, and educate them – especially in those times?!' (Maria, born 1955, mother of one child). Many of the women I interviewed began their family life in the early 1980s and repeatedly explained their reluctance to become mothers in a totalitarian regime. Most of them also spoke about the fact that they had to think primarily about the children they already had and, as life was hard enough, they were ready to accept any consequences in order to keep their family as small as possible, especially in the last decade of the communist regime – officially called the 'Golden Era' (*Epoca de Aur*) of Ceaușescu's Romania, when daily life became increasingly difficult. As a direct consequence of the regime's determination to pay off all the country's external debts, a plan of extreme rationing was put into place. Deprivation of heating, electricity and hot water, along with continuous struggles for basic necessities, became a daily reality. In these living conditions, having yet another family member was considered by most of the women I interviewed as unimaginable.

Nevertheless, no public protest against abortion restrictions occurred. The only notorious act of protest was the spread of anti-pronatalist black humour, which was one of the main (and only) tools for expressing one's discontent with the communist regime's politics and policies. Taking into account the multiple facets of daily life touched by the regime's political demography, the anti-pronatalist jokes were extremely popular in the private sphere. Thus, a joke like the following: 'A woman calls Radio Erevan, asking: "Is it true that one can use aspirin as a contraceptive method?"' – '"Yes, comrade!"' came the quick answer. After five minutes, the same woman calls again: "And how exactly can one use aspirin as contraception?" "By keeping it between the knees – that's how!"', can be understood only in its historical context. Along with the official banning of abortion on demand, the communist regime also restricted access to modern contraception, making it almost impossible to obtain. As explained above, couples were thus forced to turn to 'traditional methods', from the interruption of the sexual act to the use of a large number of surrogate substances and products, including the infamous aspirin. In many cases, along with being totally ineffective, the surrogate methods were extremely harmful to women's reproductive health. Consequently, the idea that the best contraceptive method was abstinence gained more and more currency.

In fact, as motherhood was presented as a 'wonder of nature' and 'a patriotic duty', publicly advocating for the possibility of not becoming a mother was as unimaginable as having as many children as the Party desired for its utopian demographic plans. In the State's discourse, Romanian women were not officially considered individual beings, but as 'socialist-mothers' *(femei-mame)* – that is to say they had an identity idealised by propaganda, with a major role in the construction of Romanian communism. The only way women could fight back was by fighting against their own (reproductive) body and imposing on it unimaginable methods of not getting pregnant or, once a pregnancy did occur, of interrupting it. Thus, illegal abortion became the only popular resistance strategy that could be effectively used to oppose the regime's pronatalist policies. During the twenty-three years of the abortion ban, and especially during the Golden Era, it is estimated that nearly 10,000 women died from the complications of illegal abortion (Trebici 1991). The actual statistics on post-abortion mortality do not exist, because the policy at that time encouraged healthcare providers to classify any maternal death due to the complications of an illegal abortion as anything else but this. Over the years, only bitter memories remained:

> You were forced to have four children, but maybe you didn't want to do that, as there was no future for the baby. Instead, you used every means available ... Women used to get pregnant a lot, as there were no contraceptives, nothing. But you couldn't have a baby every time you got pregnant. If you got pregnant ... you had to take the chance and suffer all pain! (Elena, born 1959, mother of three children)

Conclusion: Illegal Abortion as Common Practice, or Resisting through Inner Violence

In October 1966, when the State Council of RSR implemented the anti-abortion decree, the country's population was 19,140,783 socialist citizens *(Jurnalul Naţional* 2005). Within the next year, almost half a million new citizens were born. Known as 'people of the decree' *(decreţei)*, they remained the largest generation ever born during the communist regime. Ceauşescu's dream of being the leader of a big socialist nation, bigger than twenty-five million citizens, could have been possible – in theory – by the beginning of the 1990s. However, the counting officially 'stopped' in December 1989 at 23,151,564 (*Jurnalul Naţional* 2005).

The banning of abortion in the autumn of 1966, after almost a decade of a very permissive law permitting voluntary termination of pregnancy as the first available method of fertility control, was a political act imposed by the Party-State. Women's individual rights to control their own reproduction were dismissed, as the nation's needs were seen and praised as more important. This change in the country's abortion politics affected every Romanian woman by its abrupt and powerful implementation. As they could not publicly oppose the regime's abortion politics, women used their own bodies – the very bodies that were supposed to assure the strength of the socialist nation – in order to resist the regime. Thus, they opposed the violence of a totalitarian state with the violence against their own wombs. In time, as everyone had to find a private method of interrupting an unwanted pregnancy, illegal, often self-induced abortion became a modus vivendi – a real national 'abortion-culture' as Kligman explained (2000).

The case of Ceauşescu's Romania and its pronatalism is a classic example of how a state and its public policies can influence and ultimately harm its subjects, when their individual rights are not primarily taken into concern. Deeply interested in advancing 'Romania's way to communism', by the creation of a bigger and better socialist society, the regime proclaimed that fertility control was primarily the right of the state, and not the individual right of every socialist woman. Consequently, women's bodies were instrumentalised for the regime's demographic goals and human reproduction became a public, political affair. Even so, the banning of abortion on demand in the name of the collective (greater) good – the good of the nation – was never successful in completely eradicating the interruption of unwanted pregnancies. Instead, it inevitably managed to only eliminate the phenomenon from the public sphere, and to foster in private one continuous strategy of popular resistance thought inner violence: 'But you couldn't have a baby every time you got pregnant. If you got pregnant ... you had to take the chance and suffer all pain!'

Lorena Anton is a Marie Curie-CIG Fellow in Social Anthropology at the University of Bucharest (2013–2017), where she is developing a project on reproduction control in post-communist Romania. She completed a Ph.D. in Ethnology at the Universities of Bordeaux and Bucharest, then held a postdoctoral fellowship at ADES, CNRS and University of

Bordeaux. Recent publications include 'On n'en parlera jamais de tout ça! Ethnographier la mémoire de l'avortement en Roumanie de Ceauşescu', in *Ethnologie Française* (2014) and 'Cultural Memory', in *Protest Cultures: A Companion* (Fahlenbrach et al., Berghahn Books, 2016).

Notes

1. Country surveys on sexual and reproductive health (including one on 'young adults') were published only sporadically in the 1990s by the Romanian Ministry of Health in collaboration with different international organisations (see in Reference list: RRHS 1995 and 2001; YARHSR 1998; SSRR 2005). The last and only national report on abortion and contraception in Romania, developed in collaboration with the World Health Organization, was realised in 2004.

2. More detailed discussion of methodology is provided at the beginning of the first section of this chapter. Part of this fieldwork was supported by the CNCSIS (National Council for Scientific Research) grant no. 440/2007 during my Ph.D. research in ethnology (specialisation: social and cultural anthropology), a dual graduate programme *(cotutelle)* between the University of Bordeaux and University of Bucharest (2005–2010).

3. All translations from Romanian into English are mine.

4. Low fertility rates were nevertheless common to East European countries at that time, being correlated to socio-economic changes determined by the postwar period and the shift to a new political regime.

5. The 1957 law, considered one of the most liberal in Europe at that time, permitted abortion during the first trimester of pregnancy, on a simple request and for a very low fee, if performed by qualified personnel in medical facilities. As a result of the lack of modern contraception, and of almost any contraceptive education, repeated pregnancy terminations became the norm for fertility regulation for Romanian women.

6. When I started my research on the memory of 'abortion in communism' in 2004, I was aware of a very limited number of qualitative studies concerning this subject with the notable exception of Gail Kligman's ethnographic research captured in *The Politics of Duplicity* (1998) and translated into Romanian in 2000, along with quite a few quantitative studies done by foreign demographers. Another study, Raluca Maria Popa's *Women's Bodies, Men's power...* (2006), also influenced and guided my research on the internal archives of the Central Committee of PCR.

7. The files consulted were: file 101/1966, file 102/1966, file 127/1966 (from the Funds of the Central Committee of PCR – section 'Chancellery') and file 8/1966, file 10/1966, file 2/1967, file 7/1967, file 8/1972, file 10/1975, file 15/1985, file 10/1987 (from the Funds of the Central Committee of PCR – section 'Administration-Politics').

8. Kligman (2000) explains that this concession was perhaps made as a gesture to the international demographic convention to be held in Bucharest in 1974, thereby precluding any objections to Romania's current legislation about the higher age

limit, as in Western medical research positive correlations had been noted between a woman's advanced age and the probability of birth defects.

9. For the best implementation of the Party's demographic goals, a large number of institutions and state organisations were involved in the realisation of demographic directives: the Ministry of Health, the Red Cross, the National Women's Council, the Union of Communist Youth, the General Trade of Romanian Trade Unions, the Interior Ministry, the Attorney General Office, the Schools of Medicine, the Institute for Maternal and Child Welfare, the Ministry of Labour, the Ministry of Tourism, the Council for Socialist Culture and Education, the Ministry of Education and Teaching, the Ministry of Justice, the Ministry of the Food Industry, the (regional, municipal, city and community) Popular Councils, as well as important journals such as Scînteia (the Party's official paper), Femeia (The Woman, dedicated to women's readership) or Muncitorul sanitar (The Health Worker, dedicated to the medical profession). To efficiently coordinate their activities, a 'supra' organisation directly subordinated to the Grand National Assembly, namely Comisia Națională de Demografie (the National Demographic Commission), was created in 1971. This commission was the first national agency to implement and supervise the regime's political demography for twelve years, after which it was supplanted by another agency, Consiliul Sanitar Superior (the Higher Council of Health).

10. As with many other official public policies, the implementation of this measure varied significantly from one region to another. It did also vary in direct relation to a woman's profession – for example, many women who worked in state factories remembered this, but those who had high-skilled jobs did not.

11. According to the Official Bulletin of the Ministry of Health (cited in Keil and Andreescu 1999: 484), in 1966 Romania's TFR was 1.90 (slowly decreasing from 2.87 in 1957, the year when free abortion became legal). It rose considerably in the three years after the anti-abortion decree (3.65 in 1967, 3.63 in 1968 and 3.19 in 1969), but then it slowly decreased in the 1970s (2.88 in 1970 to 2.45 in 1980) and even more in the 1980s (2.37 in 1981 to 2.19 in 1989).

12. Except condoms (which were very rare, and thought by some to be purposely defective), what is known today as medical contraception was very hard to find in the 1970s (as communist Romania was neither producing nor importing them). It started to appear slowly in the 1980s on the black market, but was very expensive, and generally had no proper medical indications (or with indications only in foreign languages). Some women paid for illegal (and very expensive) intrauterine devices, and others for tubal ligations after their first or second child; however, doctors willing to perform these acts, harshly punished under the penal code, were hard to find and generally under the supervision of Securitatea.

13. This abortive method was used extensively in the 1980s when the Party's control over women's bodies became increasingly stricter. In addition to its effectiveness, the probe method had the advantage that, if properly used, it did not leave any 'external marks'. When complications occurred and the woman arrived at the local hospital haemorrhaging severely, she was able to explain that she was having 'a miscarriage'. Without visible proof of auto-induced acts, the doctors could officially

classify the problem as a miscarriage and then perform a real curettage. The problem was with the 'political commissions' – men of Securitatea, the Party's political police – who were supervising the gynaecological exam rooms in order to detect any illegal act against the regime's pronatalist politics. Doctors who were known to resolve 'miscarriages' too easily and frequently were supervised day and night during their shifts, and even outside the hospital.

References

Anton, L. 2008. 'Abortion and the Making of the Socialist Mother during Communist Romania', in L. Bernstein, L (ed.), *(M)Othering the Nation: Constructing and Resisting Regional and National Allegories Through the Maternal Body*. London: Cambridge Scholars Press, pp. 49–61.

Ceaușescu, N. 1969. *Romania on the Way of Completing Socialist Construction. Reports, Speeches, Articles*. Bucharest: Meridiane Publishing House.

David, H. and A. Băban. 1996. 'Women's Health and Reproductive Rights: Romanian Experience', *Patient Education and Counselling* 28: 235–45.

Ghețău, V. 2004. 'Declinul demografic al României: ce perspective?', *Sociologie românească* 2 (2): 5–41.

———. 2007. *Declinul demografic și viitorul populației României*. București: Alpha MDN.

Jurnalul național: Decrețeii, 14 februarie 2005.

Keil, T.J. and Andreescu, V. 1999. 'Fertility Policy in Ceaușescu's Romania', *Journal of Family History* 21(4): 478–92.

Kligman, G. 2000. *Politicile duplicității: Controlul reproducerii în România lui Ceaușescu*. București: Humanitas.

Leydesdorff, S., L. Passerini and P.R. Thompson. 2005. *Gender and Memory*. New Brunswick/New Jersey: Transaction Publishers.

Mureșan, C. 2008. 'Impact of Induced Abortion on Fertility in Romania', *European Journal of Population* 24: 425–46.

Nora, P. 1972. 'L'événement monstre', *Communications* 18(*L'événement*): 162–72.

Popa, R.M. 2006. 'Corpuri femeiești, putere bărbătească. Studiu de caz asupra adoptării reglementărilor legislative de interzicere a avortului în România comunistă (1966)', in O. Băluță (ed.), *Gen și putere. Partea leaului în politica românească*. Iași: Polirom, pp. 93–116.

Radstone, S. and K. Hodgkin. 2003. *Memory Cultures: Memory, Subjectivity and Recognition*. New York: Routledge.

RRHS. 1995. *Romania Reproductive Health Survey, 1993. Final Report*. Institute for Mother and Child Health Care, Bucharest, Romania & Centers for Disease Control and Prevention, Atlanta, Georgia, USA.

———. 2001. *Reproductive Health Survey Romania, 1999. Final Report*. Edited by F. Șerbănescu, L. Morris and M. Marin. Romanian Association of Public Health and Health Management (ARSPMS), School of Public Health, University of Medicine and Pharmacy Carol Davila, National Commission for Statistics, Bucharest, Romania; Division of Reproductive Health, Centers for Disease Control and Prevention, Atlanta, Georgia, USA; UNFPA, USAID and UNICEF.

Romanian Population Policy. 1984. *Population and Development Review* 10(3): 570–73.

SSRR. 2005. *Studiul Sănătăţii Reproducerii România 2004. Raport Sintetic.* Ministerul Sănătăţii, Banca Mondială, UNFPA, USAID, UNICEF. Buzău: Alpha MDN.

Trebici, V. 1991 *Genocid şi demografie.* Bucureşti: Humanitas.

WHO. 2004. 'Abortion and Contraception in Romania. A Strategic Assesment of Policy, Programme and Research Issues'. Geneva, Switzerland.

YARHSR. 1998. *Young Adults Reproductive Health Survey Romania, 1996. Final Report.* Prepared by F. Şerbănescu and L. Morris. International Foundation for Children and Families, National Institute for Mother and Child Health Care and National Commission for Statistics, Bucharest, Romania; Behavioral Epidemiology and Demographic Research Branch, Division of Reproductive Health, Centers for Disease Control and Prevention, Atlanta, Georgia, USA; United States Agency for International Development and Centre for Development and Population Activities, Washington D.C., USA.

Chapter 11

Quietly 'Beating the System'

The Logics of Protest and Resistance under the Polish Abortion Ban

by Joanna Mishtal

The collapse of state socialism in the Eastern European region in 1989 and the advent of democracy were accompanied, paradoxically, by deterioration in rights. Specifically, women's reproductive rights, as well as employment rights – in particular protection of women against discrimination in the labour market – have suffered. Nowhere has this regression of women's rights in a newly 'democratic' nation been more pronounced than in Poland, where the Catholic Church has been decisive in influencing a myriad of policies in nearly every aspect of post-socialist life. Therefore, the democratisation era in Poland has been marked by a deeply contentious politics of morality manifested in both political rhetoric as well as in laws (Mishtal 2015).[1] The politics of morality encompass particular 'moral' discussions and mechanisms used to enact individual surveillance and political intimidation to maintain legislative control over reproduction. This moral governance, promoted in the name of Catholic-nationalist state-building, also manifests in specific discourses used to shape health policy. However, moral governance does not fully succeed in Poland, as women routinely resist the church's strictures through various unsanctioned, individualised practices. This chapter examines and theorises such practices as forms of protest logics in the context of a post-socialist democratisation process.

The 'Return of God' in Post-socialist Politics

After 1989, Polish women experienced major changes in access to reproductive health services. When a Catholic-nationalist government led by Lech

Wałęsa – a former electrician in the Gdańsk shipyard and an activist hero of the Solidarity oppositional movement – came to power in 1989, a new era of political influence for the Catholic Church ensued. Wałęsa was a devout and overt Catholic – he always wore a lapel pin with a picture of the Black Madonna of Częstochowa pinned to his jacket, a practice he continues to this day. For Wałęsa, the Church, Solidarity, and the Polish nation were inseparable both symbolically and politically. Perhaps equally important, the church supported Solidarity through the tumultuous 1980s when the opposition suffered arrests and persecutions by the communist regime. After becoming Poland's president in the newly independent Poland in 1990, Wałęsa eagerly repaid the debt by heeding the church's agenda in the post-socialist health, education, and tax reforms during the critical regime transition. Wałęsa and the church successfully created a kind of Catholic political habitus wherein priests were ubiquitous during state events, and crucifixes were hung in both the upper and lower Houses of Parliament, as well as in numerous other government offices throughout the country.[2]

The religious agenda in Polish politics emerged as a form of 'reproductive governance' through which the de facto state-church merging in post-socialist Poland deployed not only legislative controls, but also economic hardships, and religio-political discourses targeting women's reproductive decisions and practices (Morgan and Roberts 2012: 243). The restrictions on reproductive rights that resulted from this emergent form of governance after 1989 included a ban on abortion (one of the harshest in Europe), limits on access to contraceptives, and the elimination of sex education from schools. The reproductive rights situation was decidedly different during the state socialist era. Briefly considering the scale of these changes in a comparison to pre-1989 policies is useful for understanding how women have responded to, and coped with, limited family planning options in the last two decades.

Under the communist regime (1947–1989), Polish women's rights were significantly bolstered by the church-state separation. In 1956, the state legalised and subsidised abortion for medical and socio-economic reasons (Fuszara 1991).[3] Polish women rapidly took advantage of the new law, and by 1965 158,000 women (at the rate of 33 per 1,000) pursued safe and legal abortion in state hospitals during that year alone. After this peak, abortion rate began to decline, which coincided with an increase in biomedical contraceptive use. In fact, despite the opposition from the church, there was a six-fold rise in sales of the birth control pill from 1969 to 1979 (Okólski 1983). The state openly endorsed family planning and sex education and established subsidies for both. In 1959, a law was passed requiring doctors to inform women who had just delivered a child or had an abortion about their contraceptive options, which included education about the newly available hormonal contraceptives. In addition, the national healthcare system began to cover 70 per cent of the cost of prescription contraceptives (ibid). Overall, state socialists not only made abortion care widely available and accessible in public healthcare facilities, but encouraged contraceptive use. This shift stood in clear conflict with the Catholic Church's position that vehemently forbids abortion, but also contraception, as a form of 'artificial' meddling with natural 'procreative' processes (John Paul II 1995: 10–11).

Yet, on the whole, Polish women were generally slower to start on the pill, as compared to women in the United States and Western Europe. This was due to the fact that the national supply of hormonal contraceptives in Poland was limited and, as was the experience in Russia (Rivkin-Fish 2005: 24–25), the high levels of hormones contained in the pill back then caused unpleasant side effects. Moreover, the pill was prescribed only in small amounts, requiring frequent medical visits (Okólski 1983: 269). Far more women and couples relied on non-biomedical methods, especially withdrawal and the so-called 'calendar' method (periodic abstinence), the latter of which the Catholic Church approved. The relatively low use of biomedical contraceptive methods might therefore have been the result of a combination of factors, including the opposition of the church, the strong side effects of the pills, and the cost and inconvenience of frequent clinical monitoring of its use. Condoms were the only modern contraception both popular and relatively widely used at the time. Given the slow adoption of more effective hormonal methods, abortion remained an important solution for unintended and unwanted pregnancies in Poland and elsewhere in the Soviet and East European region. Despite the inadequate quality and supply of contraceptives, state socialist policies nevertheless offered women new options in family planning. They also broke with the previously dominant discourse on the primacy of motherhood, opening up new ways of thinking about reproductive and sexual choices.

After the fall of the state socialist regime in 1989, the newly formed administration, which had a Catholic-nationalist character, working in tandem with the church, implemented several critical legal changes that virtually banned abortion and seriously affected access to contraceptive knowledge and services. In the early 1990s, school-based sex education was replaced with the religious 'Preparation for Life in a Family' courses, teaching periodic abstinence during marriage as the only church-sanctioned contraceptive method; condoms and the pill were depicted in the course textbooks as physically and psychologically harmful. In 1993, abortion was effectively banned, as compared to the pre-1989 provision. This critical legislative change took place without a referendum, and in spite of the widely publicised opinion polls showing that the majority of Poles opposed restrictions on abortion (Nowakowska and Korzeniowska 2000: 219–25). The current law makes abortion illegal in all but three cases: when the woman's life or health is in danger, when a prenatal test shows a serious incurable foetal deformity, or when the pregnancy is the result of rape or incest and has been reported to the police and the pregnancy is less than twelve weeks. Because of potential complications, all terminations in the first two cases can only be carried out in a hospital. Since 1956, on average only 3 per cent of all abortions have been performed for these reasons; hence, 97 per cent of abortions were likely to be driven underground (Johannisson and Kovács 1996). Contraceptive health insurance coverage was eliminated in 2002, making it difficult for many women to continue to stay on the pill (Mishtal 2010, 2015).

Simultaneously, the issue of conscientious objection used to refuse reproductive health services emerged in full force in Poland. The Conscience Clause, as it is now known in Poland, written into the post-socialist Medical Code of Ethics in 1991, allows physicians to refuse services that conflict with their conscience, but in such events providers must make a viable and realistic referral elsewhere for care. The church encouraged physicians, with escalating intensity, to utilise the Clause not only to refuse to provide those abortions that are still legally permissible, but also to refuse to prescribe contraceptives, and to decline to refer women elsewhere. The church rationalises encouraging doctors to refuse as a way to 'protect' women from what the Vatican commonly refers to as the 'culture of death' and 'contraceptive mentality'. As a result, the Conscience Clause has been used in a systemic way wherein a director declares a 'moratorium' on abortions for the entire hospital or clinic, rather than as legally intended for individual use, reducing access to remaining abortion services (in cases of rape, incest, life or health endangerment) or emergency contraceptive care in hospital facilities (Mishtal 2009).

From a broader sociocultural perspective, the immediate post-socialist decade has been marked by a multitude of efforts to regain control over women's reproduction and sexuality, after the presumably 'morally lax' communist era of access to abortion (Gal and Kligman 2000). Moreover, the nationalist resurgence of pronatalist discourses encouraging higher reproduction has also been evident in Poland. In 1995, Pope John Paul II took an active part in promoting biologised gender roles and arguing that women 'fulfill their deepest vocation' through motherhood (John Paul II 1995: 5–6). Because of this intensification of the traditional patriotic paradigm of the 'Polish Mother', problematising 'the maternal' in any way was generally off limits, although Polish feminists have sought to transgress and destabilise this dominant stereotype (Oleksy 2004). This discourse of 'familialism' also surfaced in other post-Soviet nations where the Catholic influence was not necessarily strong – a trend that has been understood as a way to re-masculinise the men whom state socialism disempowered vis-à-vis women by facilitating women's independence through reproductive rights, education, and employment (Haney 2003; Rivkin-Fish 2005: 12–13).

Given the multitude of ways in which Polish women's family planning options have been restricted, how do women respond to, and cope with, these highly charged circumstances? As is the case in this study, the body is often the key site targeted for surveillance and control (Foucault 1980), and it can also be the key site of resistance and dissent. Rather than complying with the abortion ban, the response of Polish women has been to develop their own coping strategies to control fertility, in particular circumventing the legislation by pursuing illegal abortions through newspaper advertisements, finding abortion services on the Internet, where illegal sales of abortion pills are offered, and by searching for doctors willing to provide desired services, in particular hormonal contraceptives. Therefore, the ban on abortion rapidly resulted in the 'privatisation' of abortion care in the widespread clandestine underground (Mishtal 2015).

In this chapter, I examine the extent to which women's strategies to 'beat the system' by circumventing the ban on abortion can be considered as a form of protest logics developed in response to reproductive rights restrictions in Poland after 1989 – a form of civic resistance that bypasses both structural constraints of the abortion ban policy and simultaneously challenges the hegemonic meta narrative of Polish motherhood as a patriotic imperative. In my analysis, I draw on fieldwork carried out in Poland in 2007, 2014, and 2015. In 2007, I conducted research into four medical clinics in Poland, in Gdańsk and the Tricity area, with women patients who came to the clinics for general care. I conducted semi-structured interviews with fifty-five women aged eighteen to forty on-site at the clinics in private rooms about clandestine abortion services. I also draw on an analysis of Polish online discussion groups and forums that I followed between 2013 and 2015 – in particular discussion vignettes that are about abortion knowledge, access, and services. I also draw on key informant semi-structured and unstructured interviews conducted in the summer of 2014 and 2015 in Warsaw.

'Beating the System', Quietly

Despite the Polish ban on abortion, which is one of the harshest in Europe, and despite the limited access to contraceptives because of a lack of subsidies as well as conscience-based refusals of services, the birth rate in Poland did not increase as a result of these limitations. Paradoxically in fact, fertility control in Poland has been highly successful. While a rise in teen pregnancies did take place in the early 1990s, the total fertility rate (TFR) actually declined markedly during the 1990s when reproductive rights restrictions were implemented (Makara-Studzińska, Kołodziej, and Turek 2005). In fact, Poland's TFR of only 1.3 children per woman per lifetime is one of the lowest in the world, and well below the replacement level of 2.1. This means that Poland has had negative population growth starting from the exact time in the early 1990s when access to abortion began to be restricted through unreasonable requirements of multiple doctors for abortion approval, refusals of care, and ultimately through the legislative ban in 1993.

Until the 1993 ban, Poland had a relatively high rate of abortion – typically well over 100,000 per year – similar to other Eastern European nations and Russia. After the 1993 ban, the numbers dropped well below 1,000 per year, reaching the all-time low of only 123 abortions in 2001.[4] For a nation of 38 million people with a historical record of high abortion utilisation, such extremely low numbers of abortions recorded by the state are clearly not reflective of the actual number of abortions taking place. The abortion ban fuelled the development of clandestine abortion underground, as physicians who previously provided the service in public hospitals began to offer abortions illegally in their private offices, creating a 'white coat' underground. Moreover, despite of the lack of subsidies and very high Catholic affiliation declared in Poland at 87 per cent, contraceptive use has grown over the last two decades, as Catholic women make pragmatic and deliberate choices to use methods explicitly forbidden by the church (Mishtal 2015; Mishtal and Dannefer 2010: 235). Pharmaceutical companies such as Bayer, Schering, and Organon promote contraceptives through elaborate websites and in popular press, thus offering extensive information as well as a counterpoint to the religious discourses found in the Catholic media and Sunday Masses.

Since the ban and the emergence of clandestine abortion provision, it has been difficult to estimate the number of illegal procedures that Polish women obtain annually, because the estimate would have to include not only underground abortion, but also abortion travel outside of Poland, and other less visible methods such as online purchases of misoprostol, a drug globally used to self-induce abortion. The Polish state has shown no interest in collecting statistics for illegal abortions and their health consequences, and therefore gathers no data about them. Until recently, some right-wing factions belittled the extent of underground abortion or even denied its existence.

The Polish Federation for Women and Family Planning estimates that 80,000–200,000 illegal abortions are performed annually – these include abortions in Poland and those obtained by Polish women who travel to neighbouring nations where abortion remains legal and records of utilisation are available (Nowicka 2001: 226–27; Stefańczyk 2004: 2). The challenges involved in research that directly pursues questions on threatening or illegal practices such as clandestine abortion have been assuaged to some degree through using the 'three-closest-friends' methodology (Sudman et al. 1977). In this approach, proxy questions pertaining to the informants' friends are used to explore the topic in depth, allowing research participants to withhold whether or not they have personally participated in illegal activities (Gipson et al. 2011: 61). In this research project, I explored the extent of women's familiarity with accessing clandestine abortion services, as well as their perceptions of difficulty (or ease) in pursuing abortion in a clandestine setting in Poland. If women possess the 'know-how', this could be a potential deterrent to political action to make abortion legal again. Therefore, I was further interested to understand whether or not women believed that the current law should be changed.

Extensive and Common Knowledge

The narratives revealed that nearly all the women I spoke to during my research had extensive knowledge about how underground abortion functions, including where to look for a provider, the cost and how it varies between different geographic locations, and the way clinics typically look. Some women, in response to my question about whether or not they have heard about illegal, underground abortion, began their answer by saying 'sure' *(pewnie)*, 'well of course' *(no oczywiście)* or 'most definitely' *(jak najbardziej)*, suggesting that this is common knowledge. For example, Natalia, a 21-year-old grocery store inventory clerk offered the following answer:

> Sure, everybody knows about abortions. You can read about it in teen magazines like *Bravo*. There are also ads that you can see in the newspapers – they always advertise by saying "inexpensive" or "discreet" and such. Everyone knows about this, but that's not something people will talk about. The prices are going down, I hear: it used to be 1,000 [złotych; equivalent to €240 or £198], but now you can get one for 500. If I had to recommend to someone where to go, I'd just say "check the paper", you can find all the ads there.

Interestingly, even though Natalia notes the taboo nature of the topic, she goes on to say that she 'hears' the prices are going down. Later in our conversation she explained that the topic is not so uncommon among close friends, but the tacit agreement is that these discussions are typically reserved for one-to-one moments. Most often, she added, conversations begin because of a real need for advice, a referral, a friend to accompany, or a need to borrow money for the procedure.

The sequence of events was also generally known, in particular the fact that abortions are performed by trained physicians in their private clinics, which are often located in the doctors' villas.[5] Here Marta, a 34-year-old nurse, recounts a friend's experience:

> All you need to do is just call one of the ads in the paper, like my friend did it. A car pulled up at a designated place and picked her up. They drove to a private office in the suburbs, and when they got there the driver pulled right into the garage at the doctor's villa. She got out and went straight upstairs to his office without having to go outside. The same driver took her back after it was over. She said she didn't have to travel far, it was fairly close to the centre of Gdańsk.

About half of the women personally knew of someone who had obtained an abortion clandestinely, and a few women also offered to discuss their own experiences. Celina, a 36-year-old border and customs officer described the following in response to my question as to whether or not she had heard about underground abortion:

> Well, I used it myself. At the time when I got pregnant my relationship with my husband wasn't going well, so both of us were favour of terminating. I decided I didn't trust the newspaper ads so I went to my gynaecologist and asked him. He told me he didn't do abortions, but that he knew another doctor who did and gave me his cell phone. This was a good method; I would highly recommend going through your own gynaecologist, because they all know each other. My abortion was 1,500 złotych [equivalent to €360 or £298], and was done in very good conditions, it was very professional. It was a nice private clinic and everything went well.

Some women I spoke to indicated that referrals to abortion providers can be obtained from their own physicians, and nearly every woman offered to tell me the price and some description of the setting. Below, Paulina, a 32-year-old store manager:

> A number of my friends had abortions in private offices – the offices are usually quite beautiful and it costs about 2,000. You can find out which doctors perform them in many ways. One of my friends recommended a doctor to another friend, and two sisters I know used the same doctor for their abortions. If I needed a doctor I would go to my gynaecologist and ask her first. She won't necessarily be the one who'll do it but she can refer me, since all abortions are done locally.

Overall, women's narratives show significant knowledge and consistency of understanding of underground abortion. In fact, 47 of 55 women in this study had extensive knowledge about it and the 'know-how' to pursue the service. This included the understanding of how the system functions in general, the cost, locations, and time involved, as well as ways of finding providers via newspaper ads or one's own obstetrician or gynaecologist. Furthermore, women generally believed that access to clandestine abortion is widespread, quick and uncomplicated, relatively safe, and services are performed in pleasant 'private' settings.

Striking in the women's narratives, however, is that knowledge and utilisation of underground abortion does not necessarily translate into a desire to loosen the restrictive abortion law, as almost half of the women I interviewed found the law to be fine in the present form.[6] Paulina (above), for example, argued that 'This is happening [illegal abortions] and will continue to take place. If restrictions on abortion become more severe, there will only be more illegal ones'. But when I asked her about the current law, she responded, 'I think the ban is fine the way it is. I'm worried that if the ban was eased, women would begin to use abortion as a method of contraception. At the same time we need to care about the women who are here, not about some future beings'. Other women said, 'The law is fine the way it is because abortions are really available – gynaecologists do it and it can be done quickly. You can get an appointment very fast; within a week it's all over. It's a good system because it allows women to get abortions if they need them', or 'I think the law is fine now. We don't need to rekindle the whole controversy, and you can still get an abortion if you need it'. Only one of the women in this study associated the ban with risks of unsafe abortions. None cited humiliating and stigmatising experiences, nor unequal access based on income as reasons to change the law. Interestingly, the majority of women who declared that the current restrictive law is fine were under thirty years of age, and women who saw the law as too restrictive were mainly over thirty, suggesting, perhaps, that younger women, who reached reproductive age after the 1993 abortion ban was already in place, cannot draw on the experiences of when abortion was legal and accessible. Additionally, they have been mainly exposed to the post-socialist neoliberal, anti-state discourses, which depict privatisation of any service as an avenue to higher quality products and care.

Yet, women who are poor, adolescents, unemployed, or migrants are likely to face serious challenges in accessing clandestine services. As many noted, prices in Warsaw, Krakow and Gdańsk typically range between 1,000–4,000 złotych (between €240 or £198 and €960 or £794).[7] The average monthly income per capita in Poland is approximately 1,200 złotych, which means that the least expensive procedure would still cost a month's income (GUS 2011: 1). Moreover, women's disposable income is likely to be smaller, as the economic woes in Poland affect women disproportionately. Scholars have documented the 'feminisation of poverty' in Eastern Europe and in Poland in particular, where women are fast becoming the new economic 'underclass': they are twice as likely to fall below the poverty line as men, and constitute the majority of the unemployed (Ciechocińska 1993; Pine 2002: 107). The combination of low income and the high cost of abortion mainly allows the better-off women to access these services, leaving the rest with few alternatives.

Virtual 'Hand Holding'

A non-surgical option for Polish women is to purchase pills online for an abortion via self-administered misoprostol medication, which is commonly available as treatment for ulcers, or via a mifepristone-misoprostol regimen, which is more effective. But not all sources of these pills are legitimate. Recently, the Federation for Women and Family Planning has been reporting a new wave of newspaper advertisements for medical-pharmacological abortions, but sales of fake, expired, improperly stored, or sub-standard pills have been reported in Poland. The pharmaceutical option is appealing because the pills, besides being less invasive, are also less expensive than a surgical procedure (200–400 złotych), but this method becomes far less effective after the twelfth week. To address these concerns, some international reproductive rights NGOs (non-governmental organisations) took up the provision of the pills on the Internet. Internationally known is the Dutch organisation Women on Waves (WoW), which reports being contacted primarily by Polish women, and therefore its website offers Polish language guidance, instructions about the purchase, and details about what to do and what to expect (Nowicka 2008: 25–27). While WoW is the most prominent international advocacy organisation, there are several linked feminist groups that are active on the Internet not only keeping women informed of their options but also arranging services. In particular, Women on Web, and its Polish version Kobiety w Sieci, operates an active website and forum with advice via the 'You Have a Choice' (www.MaszWybor.net) website. A newer organisation, rapidly becoming well-known in Poland, is Ciocia Basia ('Aunt Basia'), which describes itself as 'an activist group created to support women from Poland (where abortion is illegal) who want to come to Berlin to have an abortion'.[8] Online guidance is vital in the work of these groups, which are involved at multiple levels of healthcare provision, including counselling, referral, language translation, and coordinating accommodation. But rather than operating in total secrecy, media campaigns constitute an important part of their work to call attention to the restrictive laws in Poland. For example, in addition to the well-known actions of the Women on Waves sailing to nations where abortion is illegal, in June 2015, the Dutch, German, and Polish activists coordinated an 'abortion drone' delivery of abortion pills from Frankfurt an der Oder, Germany, across the border to the Polish town of Słubice, an event that was widely covered in the international media (Dutch Campaigners 2015).

In terms of the most tangible work of helping women in need of an abortion, local Polish online discussion forums have taken up, in an act of virtual hand-holding, the process of acquiring the two-pill mifepristone-misoprostol combination, sometimes referred to as 'M&Ms', referencing the popular candy (Podgórska 2009). It appears as though the women who provide online advice to others have gone through the experience themselves and now want to help those who visit the forum. For example, in response to an anxious inquiry from someone who wanted the pills but was concerned about being already in the tenth week of pregnancy, the answers offered were both reassuring and gave concrete information. One replied: 'Stay calm, I've conducted an action in the 11th week.[9] You can order a set from WoW (Women on Web), but you have to act. It's best if you order already today'; another replied: 'Make the payment as soon as possible. The pills arrive as soon as within five days, as was the case for me. Don't panic, we'll be with you' (Podgórska 2009).

Unlike on the forum where women are helped with a legitimate purchase from WoW (Women on Waves or Women on Web), on another discussion forum the following advice was offered: 'You're asking yourself whether it's possible to recover your period on your own? You can do it up to the 12th week using two medications Mifepristone … and Misoprostol. I myself have used such cure successfully'.[10] This forum's participants also offered sales: 'I get my supply from Germany. I'm attaching a flyer in Polish language. You want to take care of it quickly, honestly, and discreetly? Don't wait! In case of questions, please call – I'll answer everything, help, and offer advice! I give 100% guarantee. I'll help in conducting the entire cure! Price: 345zl'. Another seller offered in June 2011 '... a set from Women on Web. The set contains 1 pill RU-486 and 6 Misoprostol-200. Price for the set 400 zł, that's what we paid, but we didn't need to use them after all. Pick up is possible in person in Wrocław during the evening hours, after prior agreement'. When these sellers are asked for personal contact information by interested buyers, the forum's webmaster blocks the stream and requests that exchanges of personal information be done via a private messaging board. But in some cases the seller lists the phone number before a webmaster intervenes.

The danger of purchasing medication from a stranger is clear, but such offers are common and appear to constitute another underground market, if not a community of users and sellers. Just as Polish doctors who provide abortion illegally make significant profit, so can sellers of abortion pills online. It is not uncommon to also see a post from a concerned participant urging women to use the WoW website instead. For example, under a vignette titled 'Cytotec price', a post warns: [11] 'Ladies, I advise against unknown sources for this, but if you need help I recommend webpage: http://www.womenonweb.org/index.php?lang=pl'. As with euphemisms for abortion in the newspaper advertisements, the online sellers of pills have their own; the most common is 'original set' *(oryginalny zestaw)*, which indicates that the pills were bought from WoW, but for whatever reason they are no longer needed and are therefore for sale.

This virtual community that has emerged in recent years can be interpreted as a form of resistance practice mediated through technology (Cammaerts 2012: 127). It is both a site of critical information and advice, but also potentially misleading and unsafe. Yet, these public forums proliferate and streams of discussions on the topic of abortion are long, although some exchanges become little more than aggressive arguments between pro- and anti-abortion rights participant-observers.

Claiming The Right That Is Not?

Polish women are defying an increasingly radical state, as the October 2015 parliamentary elections resulted in the victory of the Law and Justice Party led by the surviving Kaczyński twin. It is a far-right administration (running on a nationalist, anti-immigrant, and pro-rural poor platform) that has already warned of plans to ban abortion altogether. Acting on their own, Polish women 'beat the system' using strategies that not only defy the abortion law, but also stand in defiance of the state and the church, both of which urgently call for more births as a way to 'boost morality' and stem the persistent demographic decline. But to what extent can these individualised and privatised strategies be considered a form of protest or resistance vis-à-vis the reproductive governance launched by the religious and nationalist politics of the post-socialist era? Surely, obtaining an illegal abortion or using contraceptives against the church's prohibitions accomplishes precisely what the women want – to shape their lives according to their wishes, plans, and possibilities. But I would also argue that this can be understood as a form of resistance, however limited politically, and a stopgap strategy for dealing with larger social and collective concerns about reproductive rights and health as well as gender inequality that should be addressed collectively and with policy solutions.

Anthropologists who have theorised resistance argue that intention is significant in interpreting whether a practice amounts to resistance, and that some scholars perhaps see resistance where none is present (Abu-Lughod 1990). Others, however, argue that resistance among the 'weak' and marginalised populations can manifest in limited and subtle ways (Scott 1985), like in the practice of gossip or pilfering to resist oppression (Scheper-Hughes 1992), or even the use of black humour as a way to cope with injustice and trauma (Goldstein 2003). The spectrum of what constitutes resistance has been extended to include deliberate inaction as an informed, strategic response to power (Halliburton 2011). Contestation can therefore assume a number of forms that are subtle and perhaps based on pragmatic sense, but which undoubtedly result in resistance-like practices and expression of dissent (Lock and Kaufert 1998: 13).

Most overt forms of resistance in Poland have been waged by feminist groups advocating for reproductive rights and attempting to bring about more collective action via policy channels. But these efforts have not had a major effect on the legislation, mainly due to widespread political passivity of the society at large, but also due to a political climate hostile to any contestations of the church. Significantly, the medical community and the public have generally abstained from joining the struggle. Doctors did little to stop the abortion policy restrictions of the early 1990s, yet trained gynaecologists and anaesthesiologists are fundamental to the functioning of underground abortion. The provision of illegal abortion by Polish doctors can be understood as both a form of resistance to the restrictive law and a way to capitalise financially, as doctors can earn far more in their private clinics, and they are able to shield themselves from the potential harassment by the church, leaving women to endure the secrecy and stigma as well as the cost of a clandestine procedure (De Zordo and Mishtal 2011).

Moreover, women's rights in Poland have been eclipsed by morality discourses about the 'rights of the family', 'foetal rights', and more recently 'embryonic rights' – a trend that has been observed in many geopolitical settings where reproductive governance, religion, and nationalism comingle (Morgan and Roberts 2012). Lessons from the HIV/AIDS activism in Poland offer another example that discourages political engagement, wherein the involvement of the Catholic Church in AIDS prevention campaigns led to the marginalisation of the voices of sexual minorities, as activists were eclipsed by the 'moral authority' of the church (Owczarzak 2009).

Women's non-governmental organisations – better understood in Poland as social or civic organisations because they are not service providers but maintain a political advocacy character – have been facing great challenges in trying to generate popular interest in issues that should in fact be addressed through political action (Nowicka 2010: 2). This is true not only of advocacy of abortion rights, which is a highly polarised arena, but also of areas where a widespread agreement exists, such as rights to infertility services or rights to sex education in schools – both of the latter are overwhelmingly supported by the Polish population, but opposed by the church and the conservatives (Mishtal 2015).

Yet, any kind of organising is difficult, and political involvement of Poles has been observed to be 'marginal', as a national opinion poll found that 52 per cent believed that involvement in social movements has no effect on what is happening in the nation (Wciórka 2000: 3–4).[12] More recently, a survey about the attitude of Poles towards different forms of protest indicates that a significant number (47 per cent) believe that protest 'doesn't do anything' *(nic nie daje)* (Pankowski 2013: 6). These findings are peculiar for a nation where the Solidarity oppositional movement has been the first political movement in the region and instrumental in toppling the communist regime. Likewise, in terms of social action and getting organised in Poland the figures are extremely low: according to eight polls taken between 1998 and 2012, less than 2 per cent was involved in any politically motivated organisation, or women's organisation, or involved in a specific political action around an issue (Boguszewski 2012: 3).

'Alternate strategies' were always an important part of Polish society's way of managing daily life under state socialism (Wedel 1986). What is interesting is that under the new democratic system, the same strategies of informal economies and reliance on extended kin and friend networks have proven more effective once again (Pine 2002). The same has been shown for present-day Russia, where 'individualised strategies' are preferred over collective action (Rivkin-Fish 2005). The preference for private 'alternate strategies' rather than political mobilisation is also obvious in the narratives of women in this study, who generally view both anti- and pro-abortion sides as satisfied in the current situation, since they perceive abortion as available and safe, and thus the restrictive law need not be changed. In other words, there is no need to 'rekindle controversies' when each side gets what it wants. This attitude mirrors rather closely the dominant political discourse that depicts the current abortion ban as a 'compromise' with the church, while in reality Poland's abortion law is one of the harshest in Europe.

In the end, women's strategies to bypass the abortion ban and curb fertility amidst what the state and the church see as a demographic 'crisis', establishes a contentious relationship to the religio-political hegemony. From the perspective of social movement theory, which identifies three kinds of protest logics: logic of numbers (mass demonstrations), logic of damage (destruction or disruption), and logic of bearing witness (public performance and civil disobedience) (Cammaerts 2012: 121). Polish women's own 'unofficial' biopolitics of controlling their reproduction might be interpreted as a fourth category: the logic of clandestine civic disobedience, wherein more than just bearing witness, they actively subvert established laws and controls. But Kligman (1998), who has written about Romanian women's experiences under Ceauşescu's abortion ban, might argue that while 'beating the system' is a mechanism to bypass the obstacles, it also encourages one to live with them, as the dissent is not in the public space. Indeed, thriving underground abortion in Poland – its existence more clearly acknowledged by the state in recent years – has had no impact on the larger structures. Therefore, quiet and individual dissent without the political act of visibility and public engagement is unlikely to produce the kind of real change for which feminist organisations in Poland continue to struggle.

Joanna Mishtal is an Associate Professor of Anthropology at the University of Central Florida. She received her Ph.D. in cultural anthropology from the University of Colorado at Boulder, and held a Postdoctoral Fellowship at Columbia University, Mailman School of Public Health. Her research examines reproductive rights, health, and policies in Poland in the context of EU governance. This long-term research is the subject of her ethnography, *The Politics of Morality: The Church, the State and Reproductive Rights in Postsocialist Poland* published by Ohio University Press in 2015.

Notes

The author would like to thank the women who agreed to participate in her research and the clinic directors and staff who facilitated this fieldwork.

1. For a detailed analysis of the consequences of the rise of religious power in Poland and resistance to the resulting restrictions in reproductive rights see ethnography *The Politics of Morality: The Church, the State and Reproductive Rights in Postsocialist Poland* (Mishtal 2015). A portion of this chapter utilises data about Polish underground abortion described in Chapter 5 of this ethnography.

2. Additionally, the 'International Religious Freedom Report 2003' released by the U.S. Department of State in 2003 observes that Polish priests 'receive salaries from the State for teaching religion in public schools, and Catholic Church representatives are included on a commission that determines whether books qualify for school use'. See: Bureau of Democracy, Human Rights and Labor, pp. 2–3: http://www.state.gov/g/drl/rls/irf/2003/24427.htm [retrieved 14 August 2016].

3. In the post-World War II era, abortion was legalised in the 1950s and 1960s by state socialist governments across the Soviet region. In addition to Poland, it was legalised in Czechoslovakia in 1958, in Romania in 1957, in Soviet Union in 1955, in Hungary in 1953, in Bulgaria in 1956, and in Yugoslavia in 1969. Abortion remained legal in these nations throughout the state socialist period with the notable exception of Romania during Nicolae Ceaușescu's regime, which banned abortion from 1966 to 1990.

4. There was a small temporary increase in 1997 when abortion was briefly legalised. In 1996 the Polish Parliament, temporarily holding a left-leaning majority, liberalised the 1993 law by including socio-economic reasons for abortion. But the following year the parliamentary power shifted once again in favour of the Catholic Solidarity Election Action (AWS), which promptly took the liberalised abortion law to the Constitutional Tribunal, where the law was changed back to its 1993 form, claiming socio-economic reasons for abortion to be unconstitutional (Zielińska 2000: 34).

5. The term villa used commonly in Poland can simply mean a single-family house, but generally it also implies a higher income of the residents.

6. Of the 55 women, 23 believed the law is fine, 24 said it was too restrictive, and 8 said it was too permissive.

7. Chełstowska argues (2011: 98) that Polish doctors are 'turning sin into gold', and estimates that illegal abortions in Poland generate around $95 million (€69,307,100 or £57,275,800) annually for doctors, tax- and record-free.

8. See: https://www.facebook.com/Ciocia-Basia-728670193835998/ [retrieved 14 August 2016].

9. To conduct an action *(przeprowadzałam akcję)* can also be translated in this case as 'to walk somebody through it'.

10. The quotes in this and the next paragraph are selected from the discussion forum Interia.pl. See: http://forum.interia.pl/orginalny-zestaw-wow-slask-tematy,dId,570753 [retrieved 14 August 2016].

11. Other feminist organisations have also warned women in Poland against abortion pills that might not be genuine, including http://www.maszwybor.net/blog/ [retrieved 14 August 2016].

12. Wciórka reports (2000: 3–4) that the reasons for political passivity in Poland are typically observed as cultural and seen as the effects of state socialism, including: lack of civic and democratic traditions, the discrediting of the concept of 'social work' or 'civic work', lack of organisational skills necessary to civic engagement, low civic awareness, lack of a sense of influence on national affairs and one's surroundings, lack of faith in the effectiveness of civic engagement augmented by the negative opinion of Polish politics, lack of a developed 'new middle class', and underfunding of education as well as minimal education about civic engagement. Wciórka also reports that grass-roots movements are not 'attractive' for mass media, therefore such movements are unable to become an element of mass culture or cultural 'imagination'.

References

Abu-Lughod, L. 1990. 'The Romance of Resistance: Tracing Transformations of Power through Bedouin Women', *American Ethnologist* 17(1): 41–55.

Boguszewski, R. 2012. 'Aktywność Polaków w organizacjach obywatelskich'. Retrieved 14 August 2016 from http://www.cbos.pl/SPISKOM.POL/2012/K_018_12.PDF

Cammaerts, B. 2012. 'Protest Logics and the Mediation Opportunity Structure', *European Journal of Communication* 27(2):117–34.

Chełstowska, A. 2011. 'Stigmatisation and Commercialisation of Abortion Services in Poland: Turning Sin into Gold', *Reproductive Health Matters* 19(37): 98–106.

Ciechocińska, M. 1993. 'Gender Aspects of Dismantling the Command Economy in Eastern Europe: The Case of Poland', in V.M. Moghadam (ed.), *Democratic Reform and the Position of Women in Transitional Economies*. Oxford: Oxford University Press.

De Zordo, S. and J. Mishtal. 2011. 'Physicians and Abortion: Provision, Political Participation and Conflicts on the Ground: The Cases of Brazil and Poland', *Women's Health Issues* 21(3S): 32–36.

'Dutch Campaigners Fly Abortion Pills into Poland'. 2015, *BBC News*, 27 June 2015. Retrieved 14 August 2016 from http://www.bbc.com/news/world-europe-33299660

Foucault, M. 1980. *The History of Sexuality*. New York: Vintage.

Fuszara, M. 1991. 'Legal Regulation of Abortion in Poland', *Signs: Journal of Women in Culture and Society* 17(1): 117–28.

Gal, S. and G. Kligman. 2000. *The Politics of Gender After Socialism*. Princeton: Princeton University Press.

Gipson, J., D. Becker, J. Mishtal and A. Norris. 2011. 'Conducting Collaborative Abortion Research in International Settings', *Women's Health Issues* 21(3S): 58–62.

Goldstein, D.M. 2003. *Laughter Out Of Place: Race, Class, Violence, and Sexuality in a Rio Shantytown*. Berkeley: University of California Press.

GUS (Główny Urząd Statystyczny). 2011. 'Sytuacja gospodarstw domowych w 2010 r. w świetle wyników badań budżetów gospodarstw'. Warsaw: Central Statistical Office, pp. 1–16.

Halliburton, M. 2011. 'Resistance or Inaction? Protecting Ayurvedic Medical Knowledge and Problems of Agency', *American Ethnologist* 38(1): 86–101.

Haney, L. 2003. 'Welfare Reform with a Familiar Face: Reconstituting State and Domestic Relations in Post-Socialist Eastern Europe', in L. Haney and L. Pollard (eds), *Families of a New World: Gender, Politics, and State Development in a Global Context.* Routledge: New York, pp. 159–78.

Johannisson E. and L. Kovács. 1996. *Assessment of Research and Service Needs in Reproductive Health in Eastern Europe – Concerns and Commitments.* New York: The Parthenon Publishing Group.

John Paul, II. 1995. 'Encyclical Evangelium Vitae: To the Bishops, Priests and Deacons, Men and Women Religious Lay Faithful and All People of Good Will on the Value and Inviolability of Human Life'. Vatican: Libreria Editrice Vaticana, pp. 1–90.

Kligman, G. 1998. *The Politics of Duplicity: Controlling Reproduction in Ceauşescu's Romania.* Berkeley: University of California Press.

Lock, M. and P.A. Kaufert. 1998. *Pragmatic Women and Body Politics.* Cambridge: Cambridge University Press.

Makara-Studzińska, M., S. Kołodziej and R. Turek. 2005. 'Nierozwiązany problem: nieletnie matki', *Annales Universitatis Mariae Curie-Skłodowska* LX(Supplement) 16: 297.

Mishtal, J. 2009. 'Matters of "Conscience": The Politics of Reproductive Health and Rights in Poland', *Medical Anthropology Quarterly* 23(2): 161–83.

———. 2010. 'The Challengers of Reproductive Healthcare: Neoliberal Reforms and Privatisation in Poland', *Reproductive Health Matters* 18(36): 56–66.

———. 2015. *Politics of Morality: The Church, The State, and Reproductive Rights in Postsocialist Poland.* Athens, OH: Ohio University Press.

Mishtal, J. and R. Dannefer. 2010. 'Reconciling Religious Identity and Reproductive Practices: The Church and Contraception in Poland', *European Journal of Contraception and Reproductive Health* 15(4): 232–42.

Morgan, L.M. and E.F. Roberts. 2012. 'Reproductive Governance in Latin America', *Anthropology & Medicine* 19(2): 241–54.

Nowakowska, U. and M. Korzeniowska. 2000. 'Women's Reproductive Rights', in U. Nowakowska (ed.), *Polish Women in the 90s.* Warsaw: Women's Rights Center Publication, pp. 219–48.

Nowicka, W. 2001. 'Struggles For and Against Legal Abortion in Poland', in B. Klugman and D. Budlender (eds), *Advocating for Abortion Access.* Johannesburg: Women's Health Project, pp. 226–27.

———. 2008. 'The Anti-Abortion Act in Poland – The Legal and Actual State', in *Reproductive Rights in Poland: The Effects of the Anti-Abortion Law in Poland, Report.* Warsaw: Federation for Women and Family Planning, pp. 17–44.

———. 2010. 'NGO-sy od wewnątrz. Społeczeństwo nie chce się organizować', *Gazeta Wyborcza.* Retrieved 14 August 2016 from http://nowicka-wanda.blog.onet.pl/2010/01/15/ngo-sy-od-wewnatrz-spoleczenstwo-nie-chce-sie-organizowac/

Okólski, M. 1983. 'Abortion and Contraception in Poland', *Studies in Family Planning* 14(11): 263–74.

Oleksy, E.H. 2004. 'Women's Pictures and the Politics of Resistance in Poland', *NORA* 12(3): 162–71.

Owczarzak, J. 2009. 'Defining Democracy and the Terms of Engagement with the Postsocialist Polish State: Insights from HIV/AIDS', *East European Politics and Society* 23(3): 421–45.

Pankowski, K. 2013. 'Potencjał niezadowolenia społecznego – stosunek do rożnych form protestu'. Retrieved 14 August 2016 from http://www.cbos.pl/SPISKOM. POL/2013/K_055_13.PDF

Pine, F. 2002. 'Retreat to Household? Gendered Domains in Postsocialist Poland', in C. Hann (ed.), *Postsocialism: Ideals, Ideologies and Practices in Eurasia*. New York: Routledge, pp. 95–113.

Podgórska, J. 2009. 'Aborcja on-line: Świeża krew prosi o pomoc'. *Polityka.Pl* 1. Retrieved 14 August 2016 from http://www.polityka.pl/tygodnikpolityka/ spoleczenstwo/1500423,1,aborcja-on-line.read

Rivkin-Fish, M. 2005. *Women's Health in Post-Soviet Russia: The Politics of Intervention.* Bloomington: Indiana University Press.

Scheper-Hughes, N. 1992. *Death Without Weeping: The Violence of Everyday Life in Brazil.* Berkeley: University of California Press.

Scott, J. 1985. *Weapons of the Weak: Everyday Forms of Peasant Resistance.* New Haven: Yale University Press.

Stefańczyk, I. 2004. 'Reproductive Health Services in Poland: Country Report'. ASTRA – Central and Eastern European Women's Network for Sexual and Reproductive Health and Rights. Retrieved 14 August 2016 from http://www.astra.org.pl/pdf/ publications/POLAND.pdf

Sudman, S., E. Blair, N. Bradburn and C. Stocking. 1977. 'Estimates of Threatening Behavior Based on Reports of Friends', *Public Opinion Quarterly* 41(2): 261–64.

Wciórka, B. 2000. '*Społeczeństwa obywatelskie? Między aktywnością społeczną a biernością*' BS/21/2000 Warsaw.

Wedel, J. 1986. *The Private Poland.* New York: Facts on File Publication.

Zielińska, E. 2000. 'Between Ideology, Politics and Common Sense: The Discourse of Reproductive Rights in Poland', in S. Gal and G. Kligman (eds), *Reproducing Gender: Politics, Publics, and Everyday Life after Socialism*. Princeton: Princeton University Press, pp. 23–57.

Chapter 12

Abortion Governance in the New Northern Ireland

by Robin Whitaker and Goretti Horgan

The 1998 Belfast Agreement was widely celebrated as a 'new beginning' for Northern Ireland: a solution to three decades of sectarian and political violence and the means to restore democratic government after nearly continuous direct rule by the British government during the Troubles. Unsurprisingly, the Agreement pivots on recognition of the 'communities' that defined the Northern Ireland conflict: ethnic Catholics, assumed mainly to be Irish nationalists, and ethnic Protestants, assumed mainly to be British-identified unionists.[1] This communalist focus is reflected in the Agreement's commitment to deliver 'parity of esteem' for the 'two communities' and in institutional arrangements and laws designed to protect them. Notably, the Agreement provides for power-sharing government but no official opposition. 'Key votes' must win cross-community consent in the Assembly. But the Agreement seems to point beyond a two-communities framework too, with detailed provisions for the protection and promotion of equality and human rights, including women's rights (Whitaker 1998).

From one perspective, democracy appears healthier than ever a decade and a half later. After a series of suspensions, devolved government has been continuously operative in Northern Ireland since 2007, with its remit expanding to include policing and justice issues in 2010. Those parties once viewed as the extremists of Northern Ireland politics now share power. Yet if the Agreement is a success at the level of 'elites and activists' – those most involved in prosecuting conflict and negotiating its settlement – the overall picture remains mixed at the everyday level (Todd 2010: 87–88). Voter turnout has decreased steadily since 1998, and has been under 55 per cent since 2011. In a 2012 opinion poll, fewer than one in ten respondents said the Assembly was an improvement on direct rule. Violence and killing has declined, but 'peace walls' – physical barriers separating working-class Catholics and Protestants – have proliferated in Belfast. Workplaces and public spaces are now more likely to be 'mixed', but public housing and education are almost completely segregated. Income inequality is rising and devolution has done nothing to mitigate social deprivation in Northern Ireland's most disadvantaged neighbourhoods (Finlay 2011; Gray and Horgan 2012; Nolan 2012, 2013). As for access to abortion, greater political autonomy has tightened an already restrictive regime, such that it is now virtually impossible to attain a legal termination in Northern Ireland. No major party supports a liberalised abortion law and the three largest – including the main partners in the power-sharing government – explicitly oppose abortion in all or most circumstances.

While this chapter is informed by long-standing involvement as activists and researchers in reproductive and gender politics in Northern Ireland (e.g., Horgan 2009; Horgan and O'Connor 2013; Whitaker 2008), we focus here on politicians' public statements and policymaking efforts. Together with their resistance to legal reform, these reveal politicians' commitment to consolidating a conservative 'moral regime' in post-Agreement Northern Ireland, Morgan and Roberts' (2012: 242) term for 'the privileged standards of morality that are used to govern intimate behaviours, ethical judgements, and their public manifestations'.

Efforts to contain women's sexuality during the Troubles were linked to the conceptual and practical policing of boundaries between antagonistic national 'communities' (Aretxaga 1997; Conrad 2004). In the post-conflict period, anti-choice politicians on both sides present opposition to abortion as the glue binding a fragmented 'Northern Ireland community'. Paradoxically then, the strength of the dominant moral regime requires the continued existence of ostensibly rival nationalisms that allow anti-choice politicians to cast opposition to abortion as a moral bond between (former) enemies and abortion as a foreign threat, against which the community's borders must be defended. In speeches and documents, they cast pregnant women as simultaneously vulnerable and threatening to the 'babies' in their wombs, reinforcing their own position as community protectors and regulators. While they vary in detail, the largest parties all have policies that allow abortion only where women are victims of circumstances beyond their control – in some cases, only if their lives are in clear danger. The prevailing perspective is exemplified by recent cases where women whose foetuses had fatal abnormalities were told either to carry the pregnancy to term or leave Northern Ireland for a termination. Widespread public dismay about their suffering has led government politicians to consider that 'marginal' legal changes may be necessary in such tragic cases (David Ford Says 2013).

Finally, we argue that, despite its rhetoric, Northern Ireland's anti-abortion regime is better characterised as pro-birth than pro-life when considered in the context of broader social policies.[2]

We focus in particular on the efforts of elected politicians for two main reasons. First, parties in many jurisdictions – including the rest of the United Kingdom and the Republic of Ireland – often address abortion only reluctantly (Halfmann 2011). In contrast, politicians in the new Northern Ireland have been enthusiastic participants in campaigns to restrict reproductive choice. Second, the power-sharing form of democracy endorsed by the Agreement is based on principles and mechanisms that have expanded both the rhetorical and technical resources available to anti-choice politicians. Attending to how elected politicians have activated the language of the peace process and worked through the new institutions and arrangements to restrict abortion rights highlights the disjunctive nature of post-Agreement democracy (Caldeira 2000; Holston 2008) and its relative failure to deliver on the more expansive aspirations for women's equality and human rights outlined in the Agreement. In short, we argue that the restoration of political democracy has contributed to an erosion of women's social and political agency – that is, their substantive citizenship.

Abortion before the Agreement

When the 1967 Abortion Act passed through Westminster, it gave doctors clear guidance on when abortions were legal and offered women ready access to safe, publicly funded terminations (Bloomer and Fegan 2014; Capper 2003). The new law also helped initiate an international wave of liberalised legislation (Francome 2004). However, it put Britain – England, Scotland and Wales – not the United Kingdom as a whole, at the forefront of abortion care. For the Act did not extend to Northern Ireland. There, abortion remained subject to the same (ambiguous) legislation that had previously applied throughout the United Kingdom: the Offences Against the Person Act (1861), the Infant Life (Preservation) Act (1929), and their interpretation in the 1939 Bourne judgment, in which Dr Alex Bourne was acquitted of 'unlawfully' procuring a miscarriage for performing an abortion on a 14 year-old, pregnant as a result of gang rape. The presiding judge reasoned that Bourne acted out of a sincere conviction that the termination was necessary to preserve the mother's life, which, the judge noted, might be difficult to distinguish from her health (Lee 1995a).

In 1967, Northern Ireland was unique among the countries of the United Kingdom in having its own devolved government, held by unionists continuously since the state's formation. The Northern Ireland regime discriminated systematically against Catholics and Irish nationalists, who in turn regarded the state as illegitimate. Yet, if Northern Ireland was divided, its very existence contested on national and sectarian grounds, the main parties and churches were quick to assert unity on matters of sexual morality.[3] Thus, when the rest of the United Kingdom liberalised divorce and abortion law and decriminalised homosexuality in the late 1960s, Northern Ireland politicians adamantly and successfully resisted reform (Conrad 2004; McCormick 2009). Strikingly, civil rights activism aimed at ending discrimination against Irish nationalists and Catholics during this period did not foreground discrimination against women as such, despite women's central role in grass-roots campaigns (Horgan 2009; Sales 1997).

In 1972, with the Northern Ireland government manifestly unable to deal with increasing civil unrest, the British government prorogued Northern Ireland's Parliament. Direct rule continued nearly unbroken for three decades. Yet, Britain continued to defer to local politicians' claims to Northern Ireland exceptionalism on sexual and reproductive rights. Homosexuality was decriminalised in Northern Ireland only in 1982, after the European Court of Human Rights ruled in Dudgeon v UK (1981) that the prevailing law contravened the European Convention on Human Rights. The situation for women facing unwanted pregnancies during this period was neatly conveyed by the Northern Ireland Abortion Campaign (NIAC), which in 1980 sent 600 coat hangers to British Members of Parliament (MPs). Affixed to each was a facsimile plane ticket and a note indicating that these represented 'the two ways in which Northern Ireland women get abortions' (Evason 1991: 27).

Court cases in the 1990s might have allowed for wider access to abortion, but these were never codified (Lee 1995b), leading the Standing Advisory Commission on Human Rights to remark: 'The law on abortion in Northern Ireland is so uncertain that it violates the standards of international human rights law' (Lee 1995a: 16). Without official guidelines, doctors were left to interpret the law themselves, risking prosecution if they got it wrong. Unsurprisingly, it was nearly impossible to get a termination in Northern Ireland throughout the Troubles.

None of this stopped women from getting abortions. Although the legal situation precludes accurate data on abortion rates for Northern Ireland, in the quarter century after the 1967 act was adopted, five women are known to have died in Northern Ireland from backstreet abortions and a 1994 survey found that 11 per cent of general practitioners (GPs) there had treated women for the effects of illegal abortions (Simpson 1995). Less dramatically, at the time of the Agreement, around 1,500 women giving Northern

Ireland addresses paid for the procedure at British clinics every year (others likely gave false addresses). From a pro-choice perspective, the costs were clear: a 2000/2001 survey (Rossiter and Sexton 2001) found that only a third of Northern Ireland abortion seekers had consulted their GPs, raising concerns about appropriate follow-up care. Northern Irish women had to pay for travel as well as clinic fees. These costs were compounded if the abortion was performed after the first trimester or if someone went along for support. Women reported that stress related to the logistics of the journey – sometimes a woman's first to a big city – and finances – nearly half of those surveyed had to borrow money – could be worse than the abortion itself (Rossiter and Sexton 2001). But as long as the Troubles continued, activists would struggle to move women's rights up the political agenda.

Abortion after the Agreement I: Westminster Bows to the 'Stormont Boys' Club'

In May 1998, 71 per cent of voters endorsed the Belfast Agreement. June elections decided the members of the new Northern Ireland Assembly (NIA). The inaugural plenary took place inside a week. But the parties remained divided on key provisions of the Agreement and did not form a power-sharing executive until late 1999. In February 2000, persistent disagreements over paramilitary decommissioning led Britain to reinstitute direct rule, not restoring devolution until 30 May 2000. Within three weeks, Democratic Unionist Party (DUP) Assembly Member (MLA) Jim Wells introduced a motion asking the Assembly to oppose 'the extension of the Abortion Act 1967 to Northern Ireland' (NIA Debate 20 June 2000: 36).

At the time, criminal justice was still reserved to Westminster, so power over abortion law lay with Britain, not Northern Ireland. The British government had stated clearly during debates on the Agreement's enabling legislation that it would not unilaterally extend the 1967 Act. Belying her pro-choice reputation, then Secretary of State for Northern Ireland Marjorie Mowlam reiterated this pledge in Parliament in January 1999 (Colthart 2009). Despite these assurances, Wells claimed: 'In Westminster there is a very active lobby group called Voice for Choice, which is seeking to impose the 1967 Abortion Act on this community'. Citing a 'leaked document', he urged:

> We must send out ... a very clear, cross-community message – supported by different parties with different viewpoints – that the people of Northern Ireland totally resist any extension of the 1967 Abortion Act to this community. ... In the time that this debate

has taken, 72 more children have been aborted in Great Britain under the terms of the 1967 Abortion Act. That must never happen in this part of the United Kingdom. (NIA Deb 20 June 2000: 103)

The Northern Ireland Women's Coalition responded with an amendment to Wells' motion, asking MLAs to refer the issue to the Assembly's Health Committee. Sinn Féin supported the Coalition's amendment but, when it fell, voted for the original motion – along with every other Irish nationalist MLA present. Only a handful of unionists and 'non-aligned' politicians dissented. Wells achieved his 'clear cross-community message' to British politicians: hands off Northern Ireland's abortion law.

Not that it was needed. Problems in the peace process led the British government to suspend the Assembly again in 2002. Yet, although direct rule lasted until 2007, Britain did nothing to advance abortion rights in Northern Ireland and, once devolution was restored, reiterated its intention to let the region chart its own course on abortion (Colthart 2009). However, in 2008, the British Labour government suggested amendments to the 1967 Abortion Act could be introduced through the Human Fertilisation and Embryology Bill. A cross-party group of MPs led by Emily Thornberry, a loyal Labour MP, announced a plan to introduce a motion to extend the Abortion Act to Northern Ireland. The leaders of Northern Ireland's main political parties – two unionist, two nationalist – responded with a joint letter to every Westminster MP, denouncing Thornberry's proposal (Abortion Costs 'Put Women in Debt' 2008). Within days, Northern Ireland's religious leaders followed suit (Irish Catholic Bishops' Conference 2008). Thornberry pulled the motion at the last minute, after the Prime Minister told her it 'would put the Stormont administration at risk' (McCann 2008; Rossiter 2009). However, her colleague, Diane Abbot MP, refused to bow to her party leaders and tabled the motion.

When the Bill was debated in October 2008, the government pushed the abortion amendments to the bottom of the order paper and set time limits that ensured the amendments would not reach debate. According to the *Guardian* (22 October 2008), this tactic was the outcome of backroom dealing. In June, many Labour MPs had rebelled against government plans to introduce 42-day detentions without charge for terror suspects. It was widely rumoured that Democratic Unionists had saved the government from defeat by trading their votes on the detention bill for assurances that the 1967 Act would not be extended (Brown Wins Crunch Vote 2008). Describing the government's actions as 'an egregious example of cheap political advantage', the *Guardian* (22 October 2008) concluded: 'It is bowing, it would seem, to what one blogger calls the Stormont Boys' Club'.

Abortion after the Agreement II: New Opportunities?

Within Northern Ireland, some pro-choice groups spotted opportunities in the Agreement's promises on equality and human rights. In 2001, the Family Planning Association (fpaNI) used the Agreement's obligations on gender equality to secure a judicial review of the failure of the Department of Health, Social Services and Public Safety (DHSSPS) to issue guidance clarifying when abortion is legal in Northern Ireland. In 2004, the Court of Appeal instructed the Department to issue such guidance and investigate barriers to obtaining legal terminations. In January 2007, Ulster Unionist Michael McGimpsey, then Health Minister in the Assembly's power-sharing executive, issued consultation guidelines stating that abortion was legal when a woman's mental or physical health is in 'grave' danger of 'serious and permanent damage' due to a pregnancy (DHSSPS 2007).

At the time, DUP MLA Iris Robinson was chair of the Assembly's multiparty Health Committee. In October 2007, Robinson challenged Minister McGimpsey's guidelines by moving:

> That this Assembly opposes the introduction of the proposed guidelines on the termination of pregnancy in Northern Ireland; believes that the guidelines are flawed; and calls on the Minister of Health, Social Services and Public Safety to abandon any attempt to make abortion more widely available in Northern Ireland. (NIA Debate 22 October 2007: 26)

The DUP, Sinn Féin and the Social Democratic and Labour Party (SDLP) supported the motion. Unsurprisingly, with McGimpsey as Health Minister the Ulster Unionist Party (UUP) opposed it, but emphasised that this position did not signal support for liberalised abortion access. Alliance, a non-aligned liberal party, had a free vote. Robinson's motion passed handily. She subsequently wrote to Minister McGimpsey that the Assembly's Health Committee 'fully endorsed' advice from the Association of Catholic Lawyers of Ireland that:

> The starting point of the Guidance should have been a clear statement of the illegality of abortion in Northern Ireland: that it is a crime punishable by a maximum of life imprisonment ... The Guidance should then have recalled the central if not sole purpose of this prohibition: the protection of the unborn child, a purpose which has informed the law against abortion for over 700 years. Only when the rule had been clearly stated should the scope of the

exception have been considered. (John Keown, quoted in Robinson 2008)

In March 2009, guidelines were finally issued for medical staff. These stated that abortion is lawful in Northern Ireland only where 'it is necessary to preserve the life of the woman' or where 'there is a risk of real and serious adverse effect on her physical or mental health, which is either long term or permanent' (DHSSPS 2009: 1.4). They also reminded medical practitioners that performing an abortion illegally or assisting in such a procedure carries a maximum penalty of life imprisonment (ibid.: 1.8). These, too, were withdrawn when the Society for the Protection of the Unborn Child won a court challenge in which they claimed the document lacked clear guidance on conscientious objection and counselling. However, the judicial review did uphold the guideline interpretation of the circumstances for legal abortion. Revised guidance with provisions on conscientious objection and abortion-related counselling was issued for consultation in 2010 (Bloomer and Fegan 2014; DHSSPS 2010).

After Assembly elections in May 2011, the Health Ministry was claimed by the DUP, a party founded by Ian Paisley, who also founded the fundamentalist, evangelical Free Presbyterian Church and was given an honorary doctorate by Bob Jones University, a private American college dedicated to Christian fundamentalism. To the delight of anti-abortionists, they appointed Edwin Poots, a creationist associated with the Caleb Foundation, an organisation set up in 2009 to promote law and government in line with biblical thinking, whose associates refer to themselves 'jokingly' as 'The Caleban'. In a 2012 interview, its chair said that on the question of abortion there should be no exceptions for rape or foetal impairment: 'I don't think the mother should be given the right to murder someone. Where do you draw the line? It is a living soul from conception' (quoted in Clarke 2012).

In 2012, it was becoming clear that Minister Poots would not issue the guidance on which his predecessor had consulted. The fpaNI went back to court. Finally, in April 2013, his office issued new guidelines. The very title – 'The Limited Circumstances for a Lawful Termination of Pregnancy in Northern Ireland' – along with advice to clinicians echoes the language the Association of Catholic Lawyers of Ireland used in their response ('Dedicated to God and his Holy Mother'). The opening clause reads:

> The aim of the health and social care system must be *protection of both the life of the mother and her unborn child.* The objective of interventions administered to a pregnant woman must be to save the mother's life or protect against real and serious long-term or

permanent injury to her health. *Intervention cannot have as its direct purpose the ending of the life of the unborn child.* (DHSSPS 2013: 1.1, our emphasis)

The final sentence of that clause upholds Roman Catholic teaching: only 'indirect' abortion is permissible: doctors may remove a fallopian tube or a uterus and in the process remove an embryo or foetus but may not remove the embryo or foetus and save the fallopian tube or uterus. Doctors are warned that the 'circumstances where a termination of pregnancy is lawful in Northern Ireland are highly exceptional' and the guidance is concerned with 'the application of the very strict and narrow criteria ... under which a termination of pregnancy may be lawful in Northern Ireland' (ibid.: 1.3).

If this guidance reflected the Northern Ireland government's attempt to secure a 'moral regime' in which sex cannot be detached from its reproductive consequence, the professional bodies representing nurses, midwives and doctors – the Royal Colleges – were equally clear that it was at odds with their own standards of care. The Royal College of Nursing (RCN) said 'we do not believe that it is fit for purpose' (RCN 2013: 4), adding that 'Guidance that seeks primarily to reinforce a particular viewpoint, rather than to explain and assist in a neutral tone, rarely constitutes good guidance. This document provides graphic illustration of this point' (ibid.: 5). The Royal College of Midwives (RCM) said: 'The document would appear to have been written in such a way as to create uncertainty and fear of possible criminal or legal repercussions amongst those working in this area of healthcare and thereby exert a "chilling" effect on the provision of abortion services for women in Northern Ireland' (RCM 2013: 2).

In short, fpaNI tried to use the courts to hold the Agreement to its promise to deliver on equality and human rights for women. It was repaid with increasingly restrictive interpretations of the existing abortion law, as successive health ministers responded to pressure from anti-choice activists inside and outside the Assembly, culminating in Edwin Poots's attempt to align the law with Catholic and evangelical Protestant fundamentalist teaching in terms that are evermore threatening to healthcare providers. As the RCN pointed out, the language describing the circumstances in which the Minister considers abortion should be legally available 'escalates from "limited" in the title of the document to "highly exceptional" in the first sentence of paragraph 1.3 to "very strict and very narrow" in the second sentence and then to "very limited" in the penultimate sentence of the same paragraph' (RCN 2013: 5). This draft also introduced a new threat, the possibility of ten years' imprisonment for any health professional who knows about the 'carrying out of a procedure which is not lawful in Northern Ireland' but does not report it to the police (DHSSPS 2013: 2.7.iii).

This last point is particularly concerning given the one meaningful material change for women seeking abortions in Northern Ireland fifteen years after the Agreement: the amateur abortions symbolised by NIAC's coat hangers have been replaced by pills bought on the Internet. The increasing popularity of this method, together with the availability of emergency contraception over the counter since 2002, is reflected in a decline in the numbers giving Northern Irish addresses at British clinics, although over a thousand still do so each year. Its appeal is obvious: no travel costs and no need to explain a sudden trip to England. But the dangers are clear too if women do not know about the safe women-run websites that provide the correct medication and advice. When BBC Northern Ireland ordered abortion drugs on the web, it found that some suppliers requested only credit card details and sent pills made mainly of a common painkiller (Garvan 2013). While other suppliers do provide the correct medication, only two – Women on Web and Women Help Women (womenhelp.org) – provide full information and support via telemedicine (Gomperts et al. 2008). If women taking the pills without medical supervision develop complications or are frightened by the blood and pain that surrounds any miscarriage and seek medical help, they risk prosecution for procuring an illegal abortion. Under Poots's proposed guidelines, any health professional they approach were asked to choose between breaking the law and breaking ethical codes of patient confidentiality.

Abortion after the Agreement III: Protecting the Vulnerable

In October 2012, Marie Stopes International (MSI) opened a clinic in Belfast. Alongside other sexual health services, the clinic offers pharmaceutically induced abortions up to nine weeks gestation – provided the legal criteria concerning risk to a woman's life or health are met. Given that narrow ground, the clinic is unlikely ever to perform more than a handful of terminations. Nevertheless, anti-abortion politicians subjected it to the parliamentary equivalent of the pickets that greet MSI staff and clients. In January 2013, clinic staff appeared before the Assembly justice committee to give evidence on its compliance with criminal law. In her introductory remarks, the clinic director explained the MSI's 'mission is children by choice not chance' (NIA Committee for Justice 10 January 2013: 3). When the committee chair, Paul Givan responded: 'Do you accept that the law in

Northern Ireland is very clear, and that we protect all children whether by choice or by chance?' the clinic director replied that MSI is 'clear about the law' and would not 'break the law to make the law' (ibid.: 32).

Three months later, Givan, a Democratic Unionist, joined forces with a unionist from another party and a member of the nationalist SDLP to move an amendment entitled 'Ending the life of an unborn child' to an otherwise unrelated Criminal Justice Bill (NIA Debate 12 March 2013). Making seven references to the 'unborn child' and none at all to women, the amendment called for a total ban on abortions outside National Health Service (NHS) facilities, even within the very narrow restrictions of Northern Ireland's law.

Givan's opening statement claimed moral force from the idea of a shared morality across national and sectarian boundaries:

> In bringing forward the amendment, I have been humbled and immensely gratified by the support that it has received from across the political and religious spectrums in Northern Ireland and in the Republic of Ireland. The protection of vulnerable women and unborn children is an issue that transcends normal politics and religious boundaries. ... Across the island of Ireland, we share a common bond in seeking to protect and provide the best care for mothers and unborn children. ... That this common political bond has been replicated across our religious communities is demonstrated by support from the Church of Ireland, the Presbyterian Church in Ireland and the Catholic Church. People ask what a shared future looks like, and I point to this moment of an SDLP, DUP and Ulster Unionist bringing forward proposed legislation related to the most basic of human rights; the right to life. (ibid.: 9)

The invocation of a 'shared future' gains force from the recent history of sectarian violence but also from the prominent role Givan's own party played in anti-nationalist and anti-Catholic politics in Northern Ireland, particularly when it was still led by the fundamentalist Protestant Minister, Ian Paisley. The amendment's real target was also clear in Givan's speech:

> The unborn child has no voice to alert the authorities that an offence may be taking place. That is particularly relevant in our context, in light of the known ideological position of Marie Stopes International, whose vision is – Members should listen to this – 'Children by choice not chance'. It opposes our criminal law [on abortion], which protects our children, whether it is by choice or chance. (ibid.: 15)

Every SDLP and DUP MLA present supported Givan, referring repeatedly to the need to protect 'vulnerable' women and 'children'. Coming from a power-sharing government that had contracted out £130 million in public funds to private healthcare providers over the previous three years (Connolly 2013), this construction helped justify the attempt to prevent a legal medical service from being offered outside the public system. Non-aligned and Sinn Féin MLAs spoke against the motion, although Sinn Féin was careful to say the party only supports access to abortion 'in the case of rape, sexual abuse or incest, or when a pregnant woman's life is in danger' – that is, where the woman is a victim of circumstances not in her control. In a debate lasting over five hours, only two MLAs, both 'non-aligned' in national terms, made unambiguously pro-choice speeches.[4] Ironically, given the proposal's cross-community genesis, it fell despite getting majority support because Sinn Féin deprived it of the nationalist votes it needed to pass the double majority test.

The strongest opposition took place outside the Assembly. Over 100 people challenged Givan's amendment in an open letter to the *Observer* sent on 8 March – International Women's Day. The signatories admitted to breaking the law by either taking the abortion pill or helping others to do so. Arguing that the amendment was 'aimed at closing down the debate on abortion here, as much as it is about closing down Marie Stopes', they hoped to 'force MLAs to stop pretending that "no one here wants abortion to be easily available". ... We represent just a small fraction of those who have used ... this method because it is almost impossible to get an NHS abortion here'. The letter concludes by referring to gaps and cuts in social spending: 'If our politicians showed as much zeal in protecting the lives of children who are already born, perhaps we would have fewer women seeking abortion because of poverty'.

Pro-birth Politics

As this last point suggests, for all their 'pro-life' rhetoric, the approach of the same politicians to children's issues adds up to a moral regime better characterised as 'pro-birth' than 'pro-life'. The Assembly rushed passage of the Welfare Reform Act 2008 in one day, with minimal debate. Yet, this legislation has detrimental impacts on children that include requiring lone parents whose youngest child is over three years of age to seek employment, and changes to the Local Housing Allowance so that the poorest families pay a large proportion of rent from social security payments intended for food and other essentials. More recently, the Assembly allowed the Health in Pregnancy Grant, which gave all pregnant women £190 towards a healthier diet, to be abolished, and the Surestart Maternity Grant of £500 to be limited to the first child only.

Further, the DUP Minister in charge of social security issues is pushed for limiting a benefit cap that will limit the total benefits available to families to £26,000 a year. This means that benefits will be paid only for the first four children in any family. There will be no family allowance, no tax credits, no account at all taken of the needs of the fifth or subsequent children – despite the fact that children experiencing persistent and severe poverty were more likely to come from large families (Adelman et al. 2003) and that one in ten families in Northern Ireland have four or more children, compared to just one in twenty in Scotland.

Evidence of a 'pro-birth' rather than 'pro-life' approach is further confirmed by levels of spending on children relative to regions of the United Kingdom where abortion is legal and free on the NHS. A report from the Northern Ireland Commissioner for Children and Young People (NICCY and ERINI 2007) found that while 27.3 per cent of the population of Northern Ireland are children, only 14.1 per cent of the budget for personal and social services is spent on children's services. The research also found that Northern Ireland has the lowest spending per child on children's services; Scotland spends 44, and England 35 per cent, more per child than Northern Ireland, despite higher need.

Democratic Disjunctures

For women seeking legal abortions, the new Northern Ireland is more restrictive than the Northern Ireland of the Troubles. The medical professionals who might care for them worked for several years in the shadow of draft guidelines that the Royal College of Nurses characterised as 'aggressive, patronising and unhelpful' (RCN 2013: 6). During the consultation phase, the Director of Family and Children Policy for the DHSSPS told the Assembly Health Committee that there may be some problems with 'the language or tone' in the draft guidelines, but the intention of the wording was to provide 'as much clarity as possible' on the law as it stands (NIA Committee for Health and Social Services 22 October 2013: 10). In the same session, the Head of the DHSSPS Family Policy Unit said that the guidance 'was cleared by the Executive' before it was issued (idem). Thus, however the language might get toned down, the power-sharing government indicated, it was prepared to support an interpretation of the law in which anyone performing an abortion outside the 'highly exceptional' circumstances in which it is legal is under threat of 'criminal prosecution with a maximum penalty of life imprisonment' (DHSSPS 2013: 1.3, 2.13). That includes women who attempt to self-induce and those who assist them (DHSSPS 2013: 2.5). Women, however, continue to get abortions, whether through the costly but safe and legal route of travelling to Britain, or the clandestine use of abortion pills bought online.

In this final section, we argue that, for all it is held up as proof that former enemies can share power, Northern Ireland's pro-birth moral regime abrogates women's citizenship rights (Horgan and O'Connor 2013; Side 2006) in ways that are diagnostic of wider democratic deficits and disjunctures. These are inseparable from the symbolic and material privilege of communal identification in Northern Ireland's political culture.

Northern Irish Women from every background seek abortions. However, no nationalist or unionist party in the power-sharing government represents them with a pro-choice policy, and the three largest explicitly oppose abortion in all or most circumstances. Irish nationalists do so in several idioms. One of these draws on historical connections between the Catholic Church and Irish nationalism on both sides of the Irish border: SDLP political representatives often use the vocabulary of Catholic 'vitapolitics' (Marchesi 2012). One MLA described his party's position as 'pro-life … It is our view that the unborn have the same civil right to life as anyone else' (Ramsey 2010). Speaking in the Assembly, he accounted for his position on abortion as follows: 'My culture, background and faith mean that I – not just politically, but personally – want to be a champion for the unborn child. I want to protect the unborn child' (NIA Debate 12 March 2013: 54). The SDLP also draws moral authority from the Northern Ireland civil rights movement. Thus, in a speech partly targeted at her party's nationalist rival Sinn Féin, with its connections to armed republicanism, Carmel Hanna said:

> As a party that was born out of the civil rights movement, the SDLP believes that the right to life is the most basic right of all. That includes the right to life of the unborn. My party has been consistently opposed to the taking of life, whether it be the life of Paul Quinn, who was so brutally murdered in Monaghan at the weekend; life that was lost during the civil conflict that society has endured for the past four decades; or life that is taken by the state through capital punishment. (NIA Debate 22 October 2007)

Sinn Féin's own position, reiterated repeatedly in Assembly debates, is to allow women access to abortions in circumstances of rape, incest, abuse or grave danger to their life or health – that is, if they are sexual victims, rather than sexual agents. Its representatives often mention the non-Irish provenance of the 1967 Abortion Act. Thus, Deputy First Minister for Northern Ireland, Martin McGuinness, explained in 2012: 'We've had a very consistent position down the years. Sinn Féin is not in favour of abortion and we resisted any attempt to bring the British 1967 Abortion Act to the north [of Ireland]'. At the same time, reflecting claims to be a party of the left, McGuinness insisted Sinn Féin's position has 'absolutely nothing to do with Catholic orthodoxy, it's about what we believe is good for our people' (Martin McGuinness Says Sinn Féin 2012).

Like the SDLP, Democratic Unionists readily personify foetuses and invoke religious grounds for their position. Thus: 'we give thanks to almighty God that, thus far, this Province has been spared from becoming home to such ungodly legislation, which legitimises the murder of the unborn child, on demand' [5] and 'in the West, we have destroyed more viable human life than Hitler ever put in a gas chamber. … I believe that those boys and girls who are in their mother's womb are being let down'.[6]

This framework reflects the party's close links to evangelical Protestantism. Less intuitively, given its staunch defence of Northern Ireland's position in the United Kingdom, the DUP presents Britain as an alien threat. In a statement directed at pro-Union rioters, First Minister Peter Robinson (2013: np) said: 'Let these so-called "leaders" set out their case as to how Direct Rule will get the flag back or aid the unionist cause. … are they content to have Westminster impose same sex marriages and abortion on demand on our community?' From one perspective, this speech is a matter of realpolitik, an attempt to maintain the DUP's position as the voice of hard-line unionism and a straightforward bid to hang on to ruling power. But Robinson invokes homosexuality and abortion – sex detached from reproduction – as special dangers to 'our community'.

Nancy Scheper-Hughes and Margaret Lock (1987) encourage anthropologists not only to attend to the individual body and its symbolic construction, but also to how these come together in struggles for the body politic. In polities of all kinds, they argue, 'the stability of the body politic rests on its ability to regulate populations (the social body) and to discipline individual bodies' (ibid.: 8). The nature of that regulation varies across time and space, but Scheper-Hughes and Lock suggest that perceived threats to social order, real or imagined, engender intensified concern with symbols of self- and social control: 'Boundaries between the individual and political bodies become blurred, and there is a strong concern with matters of ritual and sexual purity, often expressed in vigilance over social and bodily boundaries' (ibid.: 24).

In this sense, attempts to keep Northern Ireland safe from abortion turn individual women's bodies into a battleground for political and conceptual control in the face of threats from outside. But at the same time, they defend a hierarchical opposition between the political or public domain and that of domestic or private life within Northern Irish society. In classical liberalism, free adult males – citizens – exercised custody over those tied to social and biological reproduction: women, children, servants and workers. Paradoxically, the very encumbrances that disqualified the latter from citizenship enabled the supposed autonomy of citizens in public. Modern democracies, in contrast, produce persistent inequalities by working through 'legalized differences' among citizens with formal political equality (Holston 2008: 311–13; also see Brown 1995).

In Northern Ireland, politicians activate the privileges attached to communal identification to restrict women's reproductive rights. Against the background of violent conflict, opponents of liberalisation gain moral force by claiming to unite former enemies – but to do so they must simultaneously maintain ethno-national fragmentation; for these politics hinge on the privilege accorded to speaking as a unionist or as a nationalist, as a Catholic or as a Protestant. Cross-community consent safeguards such as weighted voting rules and power-sharing government give institutional force to the rhetoric, which helps explain the success of affirmative action policies aimed at communal inequities, relative, for example, to those targeting gender discrimination (Harvey 2012). One problem for women seeking abortions is that they embody the wrong kind of difference.

Of course, those who support the status quo argue that they represent the Northern Ireland majority. This claim has never been tested in a referendum and opinion poll evidence suggests that the majority would like abortion to be available under specified circumstances, if not 'on request' (Horgan and O'Connor 2013). But even assuming they are correct, insofar as 'the social conditions of citizenship are constitutive of its political possibilities' (Caldeira and Holston 1999: 719), this leaves a disjuncture between democracy in its guise as a numbers game and the ethos of democratic citizenship. Said otherwise, political democracy may coexist with significant gaps in the conditions needed for full citizenship: 'access to infrastructure … and the security of the body can no more be neglected in the analysis of democracy than the right to vote' (Holston 2008: 311).

The Agreement promises an expansive approach to rights and equality. On those terms, Northern Ireland's abortion regime exposes significant disjunctures in post-Agreement democracy; for the lack of civil and social rights to control their own bodies impairs women's right to full social and political participation. Women without ready means to organise and pay for travel to a private clinic are particularly vulnerable to having their personal, social and political autonomy attenuated due to an unwanted pregnancy (Horgan and O'Connor 2013).

In a moral regime dedicated to children by chance or by choice, where the 'unborn child' is imagined as an individuated person bearing rights in its own right, the human rights and the agency of women are suspended the moment they become pregnant. On the one hand, this suspension is accomplished by construing women as 'vulnerable' and in need of protection, a construction that always entails a relationship of subjection and inequality and, as such, is inherently at odds with full citizenship. On the other, it is justified by presenting them as threats: 'in our United Kingdom, the most dangerous place for a child is in its mother's womb'.[7] If the pregnancy is unwanted, women are left either to continue against their will or seek a privatised solution, legal or illegal but always illicit according to the ethos of the official moral regime. To the extent that these options make the situation liveable for such women, they allow the pro-birth regime to maintain the fantasy that 'there is no appetite for abortion in Northern Ireland'.[8] But that fantasy rests on a gamble in which the stakes are potentially huge.

Coda: Shortly before this chapter went to press, the Northern Ireland government issued new guidelines on abortion for health and social care professionals (DHSSPS 2016). The new guidance is more neutral in its tone than earlier drafts but reiterates that abortion is legal in Northern Ireland only where 'it is necessary to preserve the life of the woman' or where 'there is a risk of real and serious adverse effect on her physical or mental health, which is either long term or permanent'(ibid.: 2).

Robin Whitaker is Associate Professor of Anthropology at Memorial University of Newfoundland and sits on the board of Women Help Women (womenhelp.org), an international non-profit organisation dedicated to increasing women's reproductive health choices. Her research addresses gender and political culture in post-conflict Northern Ireland. Among others, her academic publications include a special issue of Anthropology in Action (co-edited with Pamela Downe) on 'Feminist Anthropology Confronts Disengagement' (Spring 2011). She also writes for the wider public as a columnist for TheIndependent.ca, and is currently developing new research on the politics of debt in Newfoundland and Labrador.

Goretti Horgan lectures in Social Policy at Ulster University, sits on the board of the Northern Ireland Anti-Poverty Network and is a founder-member of Alliance for Choice in N. Ireland. Her research explores reproductive rights, including child and women's poverty. She is currently working on a comparative study of women in Northern Ireland who have a medical abortion illegally using pills bought on the internet and women in Scotland who have it legally through the National Health Service.

Notes

1. As 'ethnic' labels, these often pertain – in scholarship, state policy and everyday life – to perceived backgrounds rather than religious belief or self-identification.
2. Thanks to Pamela Downe for the 'pro-birth' distinction.
3. McCormick (2009) suggests that the unionist government preferred to avoid reforms that might antagonise the Catholic Church, for fear of exacerbating potential instability.
4. Five unionists voted against the amendment but did not make speeches.
5. Speech by Thomas Buchanan in NIA Debate 22 October 2007; also see speech from Alex Easton in the same debate.
6. Jonathan Bell speech in NIA Debate 12 March 2013: 25.
7. Jonathan Bell speech in NIA Debate 12 March 2013: 23.
8. Pat Ramsey speech in NIA Debate 12 March 2013: 56.

References

'Abortion Costs "Put Women in Debt"'. 2008, *BBC News* 12 May. Retrieved 22 March 2014 from http://news.bbc.co.uk/2/hi/7396817.stm

Adelman, L., S. Middleton and K. Ashworth. 2003. *Britain's Poorest Children: Severe and Persistent Poverty and Social Exclusion*. London: Save the Children.

Aretxaga, B. 1997. *Shattering Silence: Women, Nationalism, and Political Subjectivity in Northern Ireland*. Princeton, NJ: Princeton University Press.

Bloomer, F and E. Fegan. 2014. 'Critiquing Recent Abortion Law and Policy in Northern Ireland', *Critical Social Policy* 34(1): 109–20.

Brown, W. 1995. *States of Injury: Power and Freedom in Late Modernity*. Princeton: Princeton University Press.

'Brown Wins Crunch Vote on 42 Days'. 2008, *BBC News* 11 June. Retrieved 25 March 2014 from http://news.bbc.co.uk/2/hi/uk_politics/7449268.stm

Caldeira, T. 2000. *City of Walls: Crime, Segregation and Citizenship in Sao Paulo*. Berkeley: University of California Press.

Caldeira, T and J. Holston. 1999. 'Democracy and Violence in Brazil', *Comparative Studies in Society and History* 41(4): 691–729.

Capper, D. 2003. 'The Condition of Abortion Law in Northern Ireland', *Northern Ireland Legal Quarterly* 54(3): 320–26.

Clarke, L. 2012. 'Creationist Bible Group and its Web of Influence at Stormont', *Belfast Telegraph* 1 September. Retrieved 5 April 2014 from http://www.belfasttelegraph.co.uk/news/politics/creationist-bible-group-and-its-web-of-influence-at-stormont-28787760.html

Colthart, G. 2009. *Abortion Law,* Parliamentary Briefing Note, SN/SES/4309. London: UK Parliament.

Connolly, M. 2013. 'Health Department Pays Private Healthcare Firms £130m', *BBC News Northern Ireland,* 25 February 2013. Retrieved 22 March 2014 from http://www.bbc.co.uk/news/uk-northern-ireland-21550443

Conrad, K. 2004. *Locked in the Family Cell: Gender, Sexuality, and Political Agency in Irish National Discourse.* Madison: Wisconsin University Press.

'David Ford Says Northern Ireland's Abortion Legislation Must Be Consulted On'. 2013, *BBC News Northern Ireland,* 12 October. Retrieved 22 March 2014 from http://www.bbc.com/news/uk-northern-ireland-24507940

Department of Health, Social Services and Public Safety (DHSSPS). 2007. *Guidance on the Termination of Pregnancy: The Law and Clinical Practice in Northern Ireland.* Belfast: DHSSPS.

———. 2009. *Guidance on the Termination of Pregnancy: The Law and Clinical Practice in Northern Ireland.* Belfast: DHSSPS.

———. 2010. *Guidance on the Termination of Pregnancy: The Law and Clinical Practice in Northern Ireland.* Belfast: DHSSPS.

———. 2013. *The Limited Circumstances for a Lawful Termination of Pregnancy in Northern Ireland: A Guidance Document for Health and Social Care Professionals on Law and Clinical Practice.* Belfast: DHSSPS.

———. 2016. *Guidance for Health and Social Care Professionals on Termination of Pregnancy in Northern Ireland.* Belfast: DHSSPS.

Dudgeon v. United Kingdom, Appl. No. 7525/76, Council of Europe: European Court of Human Rights, 22 October 1981.

Evason, E. 1991. *Against the Grain: The Contemporary Women's Movement in Northern Ireland.* Dublin: Attic Press.

Finlay, A. 2011. *Governing Ethnic Conflict.* London: Routledge.

Francome, C. 2004. *Abortion in the USA and the UK.* Aldershot: Ashgate.

Garvan, S. 2013. 'Concern Over Danger of Abortion Pills Bought online', *BBC Radio 1,* 11 February. Retrieved 22 March 2014 from http://www.bbc.co.uk/newsbeat/21403080

Gomperts, R., et al. 2008. 'Using Telemedicine for Termination of Pregnancy with Mifepristone and Misoprostol in Settings Where There is No Access to Safe Services', *British Journal of Obstetrics and Gynaecology* 115(9): 1171–78.

Gray, A.M. and G. Horgan. 2012. 'Devolution in Northern Ireland – A Missed Opportunity?' *Critical Social Policy* 32(3): 467–78.

Halfmann, D. 2011. *Doctors and Demonstrators: How Political Institutions Shape Abortion Law in the United States, Britain, and Canada.* Chicago: Chicago University Press.

Harvey, C. 2012. 'Contextualized Equality and the Politics of Legal Mobilisation: Affirmative Action in Northern Ireland', *Social and Legal Studies* 21(23): 23–50.

Holston, J. 2008. *Insurgent Citizenship: Disjunctions of Democracy and Modernity in Brazil.* Princeton: Princeton University Press.

Horgan, G. 2009. 'Women and Civil Rights in 1968 Derry', in P. McClenaghan (ed.), *Spirit of '68: Beyond the Barricades.* Derry: Guildhall Press, pp. 121–34.

Horgan, G. and J.S. O'Connor. 2013. 'Abortion and Citizenship Rights in a Devolved Region of the UK', *Social Policy and Society* 13(1): 39–49.

Irish Catholic Bishops' Conference. 2008. 'Church Leaders Back Politicians' Anti-Abortion Letter', media release, 16 May. Retrieved 25 March 2014 from http://www.catholicbishops.ie/2008/05/16/church-leaders-politicians'-anti-abortion-letter/

Lee, S. 1995a. 'Abortion Law in Northern Ireland: The Twilight Zone', in A. Furedi (ed.), *The Abortion Law in Northern Ireland: Human Rights and Reproductive Choice.* Belfast: Family Planning Association Northern Ireland, pp. 16–26.

———. 1995b. 'An A to K to Z of Abortion Law in Northern Ireland: Abortion on Remand', in A. Furedi (ed.), *The Abortion Law in Northern Ireland: Human Rights and Reproductive Choice.* Belfast: Family Planning Association Northern Ireland, pp. 27–45.

Marchesi, M. 2012. 'Reproducing Italians: Contested Biopolitics in the Age of "Replacement Anxiety"', *Anthropology & Medicine* 19(2): 171–88.

'Martin McGuinness Says Sinn Féin Remains Opposed to Abortion'. 2012, *BBC News Northern Ireland.* Retrieved 25 March 2014 from http://www.bbc.co.uk/news/uk-northern-ireland-19930422

McCann, E. 2008. 'Why Northern Ireland Women Need their own Abortion Act', *Belfast Telegraph*, 17 July. Retrieved 5 April 2014 from http://www.belfasttelegraph.co.uk/opinion/columnists/eamon-mccann/eamonn-mccann-why-northern-ireland-women-need-their-own-abortion-act-13910745.html#ixzz1unEnxlAA

McCormick, L. 2009. *Regulating Sexuality: Women in Twentieth Century Northern Ireland.* Manchester: Manchester University Press.

Morgan, L.M. and E. Roberts. 2012. 'Reproductive Governance in Latin America', *Anthropology & Medicine* 19(2): 241–54.

NICCY and ERINI. 2007. *An Analysis of Public Expenditure on Children in Northern Ireland.* Belfast: Northern Ireland Commissioner for Children and Young People.

Nolan, P. 2012. *The Northern Ireland Peace Monitoring Report, Number One.* Belfast: Community Relations Council.

———. 2013. *The Northern Ireland Peace Monitoring Report, Number Two.* Belfast: Community Relations Council.

Northern Ireland Assembly Committee for Health and Social Services (Official Report). 2013. *Guidance on the Termination of Pregnancy in Northern Ireland.* 22 October.

Northern Ireland Assembly Committee for Justice (Official Report). 2013. *Marie Stopes International: Compliance with Criminal Law on Abortion in Northern Ireland.* 10 January.

Northern Ireland Assembly Debate (Official Report). 20 June 2000.

Northern Ireland Assembly Debate (Official Report). 22 October 2007.

Northern Ireland Assembly Debate (Official Report). 12 March 2013.

Ramsey, P. 2010. 'Concern at Abortion Conference', media release, 8 October. Retrieved 5 April 2014 from http://www.sdlp.ie/newsroom/press-releases/2010/7826-ramsey_concern_at_abortion_conference/

Robinson, I. 2008. 'Letter to Michael McGimpsey MLA, on Behalf of the Committee for Health, Social Services and Public Safety'. Retrieved 23 February 2012 from Northern Ireland Assembly Archive Site.

Robinson, P. 2013. 'First Minister Comments on Flag Protests', media release, 4 January. Retrieved 11 August 2016 from http://cain.ulst.ac.uk/issues/politics/docs/dup/pr040113.htm

Rossiter, A. 2009. *Ireland's Hidden Diaspora: The Abortion Trail and the Making of a London-Irish Underground, 1980–2000*. London: IASC Publishing.

Rossiter, A. and A. Sexton. 2001. *The Other Irish Journey: A Survey Update of Northern Irish Women Attending British Abortion Clinics, 2000/2001* London: Voice for Choice and MSI.

Royal College of Midwives (RCM). 2013. *Response to DHSSPS on The Limited Circumstances For a Lawful Termination of Pregnancy in Northern Ireland*. Belfast: RCM.

Royal College of Nursing Northern Ireland (RCN). 2013. *Response of the Royal College of Nursing to a DHSSPS Consultation on The Limited Circumstances For a Lawful Termination of Pregnancy in Northern Ireland: A Guidance Document for Health and Social Care Professionals*. Belfast: RCN.

Sales, R. 1997. *Women Divided: Gender, Religion and Politics in Northern Ireland*. New York: Routledge.

Scheper-Hughes, N. and M. Lock. 1987. 'The Mindful Body: A Prolegomenon to Future Work in Medical Anthropology', *Medical Anthropology Quarterly* 1: 6–41.

Side, K. 2006. 'Contract, Charity, and Honorable Entitlement: Social Citizenship and the 1967 Abortion Act in Northern Ireland after the Good Friday Agreement', *Social Politics* 13(1): 89–116.

Simpson, A. 1995. 'Abortion in Northern Ireland: Victorian Law', in A. Furedi (ed.), *The Abortion Law in Northern Ireland: Human Rights and Reproductive Choice*. Belfast: Family Planning Association Northern Ireland, pp. 6–15.

Todd, J. 2010. 'Northern Ireland: From Multi-phased Conflict to Multilevelled Settlement', in J. Coakley (ed.), *Pathways from Ethnic Conflict: Institutional Redesign in Divided Societies*. London: Routledge, pp. 76–94.

Whitaker, R. 1998. 'What Do We Get?' *Fortnight* 370 (May): 17.

———. 2008. 'Gender and the Politics of Justice in the Northern Ireland Peace Process: Considering Roisin McAliskey', *Identities* 15(1): 1–30.

Reproductive Governance meets European Abortion Politics

The Challenge of Getting the Gaze Right

by Lynn M. Morgan

Introduction

As Elizabeth Roberts and I defined the concept of reproductive governance, it 'refers to the mechanisms through which different historical configurations of actors – such as state institutions, churches, donor agencies, and non-governmental organisations (NGOs) – use legislative controls, economic inducements, moral injunctions, direct coercion, and ethical incitements to produce, monitor and control reproductive behaviours and practices' (Morgan and Roberts 2012: 243). This perspective has proven useful in illuminating shifting state control over reproductive matters, and it has been especially valuable in showing why reproduction looms so large in recent social and political movements across the globe. In this afterword, I draw inspiration from the authors included in this volume to highlight three aspects of reproductive governance. First is the vexed and contradictory role of rights-talk in reproductive rights activism and scholarship. Second, I examine how powerful institutions create and authorise certain rights-bearing subjects while demoting or excluding others. Third, I briefly explore the relationship of neoliberal economic restructuring to reproductive governance. Throughout this short chapter, I offer suggestions for expanding the scope of abortion research by linking it to other dimensions of social analysis.

Abortion Rights Talk

'The right to abortion is fragile', says Mette Løkeland (this volume). All the chapters in this book spring from the conviction that abortion should be regarded as a woman's right, as affirmed within the United Nations human rights system (Zampas, this volume). Yet the right to abortion is still elusive for many women, even in liberal Western Europe where waiting periods are common and the procedure is quite often limited to the first twelve weeks of pregnancy. Even where abortion is legal, the right to abortion can prove wobbly and unstable – 'a right that isn't' – despite decades of sustained po- litical mobilisation on the part of women's health and feminist activists. Of course, the opponents of abortion rights claim that women's rights must be weighed against the competing rights of embryos, foetuses, and clinicians. The previous chapters invite us to examine not just whether abortion is or is not considered a right in a given country, but the practices through which abortion rights are continually made, revised, contested, and all-too-often unmade. Even where abortion is widely accepted, it seems destined to be a precarious right. Anton, De Zordo, and Mishtal (this volume) argue that politicians use abortion instrumentally as a bargaining chip when they are intent on 'political deal-making and nation-making'. Why has the project of establishing abortion rights unfolded so unevenly? How does a right be- come a right?

The assertion of a 'right' to abortion is relatively new. This idea was popularised on a global scale only after the 1994 International Conference on Population and Development (ICPD) in Cairo and the 1995 Fourth World Conference on Women in Beijing. In its standard iteration, sexual and reproductive rights are linked together under the rubric of human rights, because control over one's sexuality is obviously related to one's re- productive autonomy: 'Sexual and reproductive rights, including the right to choose if, when, and with whom to have children in a safe and secure manner, are integral to human rights' (*The Lancet* 2006b: 8). The framework of rights has been particularly appealing to feminist activists, as Bradshaw and colleagues note (2008), because 'some of the most effective organizing over the past twenty-five years has been around rights-based claims' (2008: 57). Undoubtedly, rights-talk has been wildly successful as rhetorical and political strategy. In the twenty-plus years since the Cairo and Beijing con- ferences, activists have used the language of reproductive rights to fight for expanded access to abortion (including medication abortion using mifepris- tone and misoprostol), contraception, sterilisation, and assisted reproduc- tion. As a result, many regions (including those traditionally considered Catholic – such as Spain, Italy, Uruguay, Argentina, and Mexico City) have eased criminal abortion laws; according to the Guttmacher Institute (2012: 3), 'Between 1997 and 2008, the grounds on which abortion may be legally performed were broadened in 17 countries'. In addition to liberalising abortion law, several countries have increased penalties against domestic and gender-based violence, implemented gender equitable sex education programmes, endorsed same-sex marriage (most notably in Argentina in 2010 and Ireland in 2015), provided financial support for families, and improved access to reproductive health services. This list of changes can give the impression that there is an inexorable march towards the decriminalisation of abortion in the name of gender equity and autonomy.

Yet the notion of a 'right' to abortion has not been uniformly adopted. When Zampas says of the Catholic Church and countries such as Saudi Arabia, Russia, and Egypt, 'Their aim is to prevent further progress on human rights', she is referring only to one definition of human rights. Clearly, her progressive definition of sexual and reproductive human rights is not universally shared. Social scientists have recently begun to take a dynamic, ethnographic, non-essentialist approach to understanding human rights; they know that human rights are not universally shared, and that tensions between the universal and the local are key to analysing how 'rights' are received in any given context. 'Human rights', several scholars agree, 'are an evolving, living body of ideas, not a static set of norms' (Corrêa, Petchesky and Parker 2008: 153). Stern and Straus point out that 'the fight for human rights is ... always local, political, and historical'. Human rights advocates always claim universality, they say, but rights-talk generates 'a more profound tension, one that persistently pulls human rights practice and understanding in twinned yet often countervailing directions simultaneously' (2014: 9). This explains why the backlash against reproductive rights seems to gather steam just when Zampas' 'progress' appears to be finally at hand.

Precisely because sexual and reproductive rights have gained such global political legitimacy, they are generating a significant, even ferocious, backlash. As a result, some abortion-rights advocates prefer to dispense with the language of abortion rights altogether, and to appeal instead to the need to safeguard women's health. This strategy has been effective, as two small examples demonstrate, but unfortunately does little to advance the abortion rights agenda. First, the 2000 Millennium Development Goals included a proposal to reduce maternal mortality but refrained from endorsing an explicit right to voluntary termination of pregnancy; indeed, abortion has been conspicuously absent from global public health conversations about maternal mortality (Barot 2011). Second, when the prestigious medical journal *The Lancet* took a stand on reproductive and sexual matters, it settled on language emphasising health rather than rights (2006a).

In addition to reiterating our collective commitment to reproductive rights advocacy, feminist scholars need to understand the power and limitations of the 'rights' framework when applied to abortion; this is what Sonia Corrêa, Rosalind Petchesky, and Richard Parker have labelled 'the indispensability and insufficiency of human rights' (2008: 152).

In the past twenty years, religious conservative activists have shed their theological framings and begun to adopt secular discourses to advance their 'pro-life' and 'pro-family' causes (Vaggione 2005, 2009). Abortion opponents now use the secular language of biomedical science and bioethics as well as human rights to couch their arguments. They can be heard arguing for 'natural' rights, foetal rights, parental rights, and the right to religious liberty. Much as liberals might argue that Muslims in the West or transgendered persons have rights to citizenship (see Corrêa, Petchesky and Parker 2008: 157), conservatives argue that foetuses should also be granted citizenship rights, fathers should be granted paternal rights, and clinicians should be granted the right to religious liberty. Throughout the 1980s and 1990s, conservative strategies focused on shifting attention from women's rights to foetal rights. This development coincided with what Wanda Nowicka terms the 'growing opposition to a progressive human rights agenda and the universality of human rights' (2011: abstract). When conservatives claim rights discourses for their own, it becomes clear that the march towards abortion rights is by no means assured. There is no teleological impulse propelling us forward. Nowicka writes, 'Human rights advocates must ... face the reality that the struggle for full recognition of sexual and reproductive rights, especially the right to abortion, will never be a linear process or lead to a final "victory"' (Nowicka 2011: 127). The chapters in this volume show precisely how the backlash takes shape on the ground as the aura of universal human rights hovers in the vicinity of Russian, Irish, or Polish wombs.

With 'foetal subjects' now well instantiated in many national conversations (see Morgan and Michaels 1999), these chapters show that the conservatives' emphasis is shifting again. Abortion opponents throughout the world are now arguing for expanding the 'right' to religious liberty and freedom of expression. In Spain, as Martín Aragón shows, 'the shift to a rights-based rhetoric' is now being applied to 'public health workers' rights to religious freedom' (this volume). Likewise in Italy, the right to religious liberty is invoked to justify conscientious objection on the part of obstetricians and gynaecologists (De Zordo, this volume). This approach is proving extremely productive and influential for abortion foes, who are honing secular law to achieve religiously motivated goals. This was seen in 2012 in the United States, when the U.S. Conference of Catholic Bishops issued a statement of concern about threats to 'religious freedom'. This argument won the day in the 2014 Burwell v. Hobby Lobby case, in which the U.S. Supreme Court cited religious freedom when it ruled that certain family-held corporations need not be required to cover contraceptive costs for their employees. The Hobby Lobby company (a U.S. chain of craft supply stores) was represented in that case by the Becket Fund for Religious Liberty, a legal firm that promotes a 'vision of a world where religious freedom is respected as a fundamental human right that all are entitled to enjoy and exercise'.[1] The right to religious freedom allows Catholic constituencies to find common cause with conservative and evangelical Protestants, Muslims, and Russian Orthodox. Religious liberty has already been invoked to justify the 'right' of health providers, adoption agencies, and businesses to claim conscientious objector status and therefore to refuse to participate in abortion, dispense emergency contraception (even to rape victims), permit same-sex couples to adopt children, or provide wedding services for same-sex couples. Throughout the world, activists are preparing a massive expansion of religious freedom arguments as the next wave of resistance to counteract progressive claims for sexual and reproductive rights.

Pitting the 'right' to abortion against the 'right' to religious freedom is just one way that the competition for rights is manifested. Several of the chapters in this book illustrate other forms of resistance to abortion as a right. Luehrmann explains that abortion was never understood as a 'right' in Russia; instead, it was an 'unpleasant duty and necessity'. Anton explains how Ceaușescu's pronatalist ideology in Romania ignored individual rights and denied women access to contraception, thereby creating a society in which motherhood was mandatory and entrepreneurs set up clandestine abortion operations. In Poland, Mishtal shows that the return of democracy led to a deterioration rather than an expansion of rights, specifically with respect to abortion; Whitaker and Horgan make a similar point about the new Northern Ireland, which 'is more restrictive than the Northern Ireland of the Troubles'. In Sweden, as Linders and Bessett show, abortion was legalised not to grant women reproductive autonomy but to prevent 'unsuitable' women from becoming mothers. Even in progressive Norway, Løkeland points out, the right to abortion is imperilled by proposals to limit second trimester abortion and expand conscientious objections for healthcare providers. The backlash is glaringly evident in the Americas, too. After abortion was completely banned in El Salvador in 1998, legislators changed the Constitution to protect life from conception; Salvadoran women are now convicted and jailed on the suspicion of having provoked an abortion (Oberman 2013). Although abortion was once legal in Chile, General Augusto Pinochet banned it in 1989 and Chile remains one of seven countries in the world where abortion is illegal under all circumstances. The therapeutic abortion option was eliminated in Nicaragua in 2006, and in the Dominican Republic from 2009–2014 (when the restriction was again eased). Abortion restrictions have mounted in the United States as Republican legislators use the issue to rally their supporters, thereby whittling away at access to abortion in many jurisdictions (Guttmacher Institute 2014). The right to abortion remains exceedingly tenuous.

Feminist social scientists face a conundrum: how to study reproductive rights ethnographically, in all its contested manifestations and complexities, while simultaneously insisting on a progressive (if not liberal, Western) definition of sexual and reproductive rights? Who owns the discourse of human rights or religious rights? Feminist social scientists such as those writing here want to cling to the claim for abortion as a fundamental human right, while at the same time acknowledging the appropriation of rights-talk by our political adversaries. They do this by documenting the dynamic and ever-changing processes through which abortion rights do and do not take hold, showing that religion functions hand in hand with politics, examining the consequences of abortion restrictions, and revealing strategies and 'protest logics' used by activists. Martín Aragón found that healthcare workers utilised a law designed to pay for prenatal care to justify financing abortions, and De Zordo shows that conscience provisions may be 'faked' by physicians trying to avoid an extra workload or discrimination. These authors show abortion politics to be wholly relational: conscientious refusal is a way to manage co-worker relationships and contain stigma and court promotions; clinicians are sometimes permitted to couch their job responsibilities in moral (rather than ideological) terms.

Rather than viewing the outcome of abortion rights' movements as preordained, these chapters emphasise the contingency, dynamism, and precariousness of abortion rights. Each author stresses the idiosyncratic national histories and sociopolitical configurations that are crucial to understanding specific policy outcomes; each emphasises the ongoing sense of commotion, tussle, and agency. All abortion politics are thick and local. Even within the Catholic Church hierarchy (so often discussed as a monolithic institution), there is constant debate about, for example, whether to distribute Catholic pastoral authority into secular realms such as bioethics, genetics, or human rights. One of the lessons of these chapters is that abortion policy is rarely, if ever, settled. This is true even where the 'abortion law seems to have installed a solid status quo', as in Belgium (Celis and Coene, this volume). Abortion rights do not suddenly spring into existence when the United Nations issues an authoritative policy document, any more than anti-abortion movements materialise with the publication of papal encyclicals. The social movements for and against abortion do not follows prescribed paths;

rather, they are mutually constituted and deeply affected by changing social relationships. Whether we like it or not, the rights framing is likely to continue to be intensely politicised, as long as 'rights' is the currency through which abortion is codified and negotiated.

Making Reproductive Subjects

Reproductive governance directs our attention to the discourse- and subject-making powers wielded by states and other powerful actors: corporations, courts, non-governmental organisations, and religious authorities. The power to make subjects is the power to promote certain kinds of procreation while impeding others. Who is authorised to parent, and by what means? Which 'children' merit protection by the state, and when do those lives begin? Anthropologist Shellee Colen coined the term 'stratified reproduction' to refer to 'arrangements by which some reproductive futures are valued while others are despised' (Ginsburg and Rapp 1995: 3). In this volume, Whitaker and Horgan, for example, show how embryos and foetuses are cast as vulnerable social subjects in Northern Ireland, while women who face unwanted pregnancies are ignored or vilified (see also Morgan and Michaels 1999; Paltrow and Flavin 2013). Martín Aragón develops a related concept of the 'hierarchy of deservingness' (this volume). This ideology facilitates access to medical care in Spain for certain categories of people: children, pregnant and postpartum women, and those with chronic illnesses. Meanwhile, politicians exclude whole categories of people, who then take matters into their own hands. In Spain, undocumented Latin American immigrants who are denied medical services resort to using misoprostol (Cytotec) without medical supervision, much as their compatriots do at home. This is happening in the United States as well, where the black-market use of misoprostol is on the rise among immigrant women who cannot get access to legal abortion because of the Hyde Amendment or because they are excluded from the Affordable Care Act or by the states in which they reside (Hellerstein 2014).

An example from my fieldwork in Chile shows how abortion politics is linked to subject-making. When I noticed the banner campaign in the capital city of Santiago featuring gigantic photographs of adorable children who have Down's syndrome, it seemed innocuous enough. My first impulse was to think, 'How sweet, a publicity campaign to foster awareness and fight discrimination'. The campaign had a dark side, however, when considered within the framework of reproductive governance. Abortion under all circumstances has been banned in Chile since the last days of the dictatorship in 1989. As a result, prenatal testing for genetic conditions like Down's syndrome is virtually non-existent, because there is no possibility of terminating an affected pregnancy. One sees many more Down's syndrome people on the streets in Santiago than where I live in the United States. Not coincidentally, the banner campaign took place in 2014 at the same time as a movement to decriminalise some abortions in Chile. In this context, the campaign to foster awareness of Down's syndrome could also be read as an anti-abortion campaign; what fiend would abort such foetus that would turn into such a beautiful child? The sponsors of the campaign had also produced a 2014 video that went viral in Chile, in which children with Down's syndrome explain to their imaginary pregnant mother that she should feel excited and happy, rather than scared, when she learns that her child will have Down's syndrome. In the United States, the video was received by those who emphasised the link to abortion policy. A blog sponsored by the ultra-conservative Heritage Foundation announced the video with a statement that read: 'In the United States, many unborn children with Down Syndrome have been aborted', and 'Abortion-on-demand has taken the lives of more than 55 million children in the U.S. – including large numbers of children diagnosed with Down syndrome and other disabilities' (Trinko 2014). When the Universidad Católica in Santiago mounted its own mini version of the same exhibition, it was simultaneously expressing its opposition to 'eugenic' abortion. Even if the two campaigns were not explicitly linked, the campaign to promote tolerance towards people with Down's syndrome in Chile needs to be understood also as an anti-abortion statement.

The construction of deservingness can also be seen in my current research in Costa Rica, where efforts are underway to legalise in vitro fertilisation (IVF) (which has been banned since 2000) in the wake of a decision by the Inter-American Court of Human Rights. Roman Catholicism is the state religion in Costa Rica. The Catholic hierarchy strongly opposes IVF, and part of its strategy is to elevate the status of pregnant women and mothers. Each year the Catholic Church holds a special mass honouring pregnant women, and Mother's Day in Costa Rica takes place on the Catholic Feast of the Assumption, the day that the Virgin Mary is said to have died and ascended to Heaven. While the Church sanctifies mothers, the state creates policies to promote the 'right kind' of reproduction involving heterosexual procreative sex, 'responsible' fatherhood, and mothers who are not too young, too old, or too fertile. Ideally, parents also should not be Nicaraguan migrants, nor should they cost the state money by requiring expensive infertility treatments. The ongoing debate over the legalisation of IVF has some constituents actively working to reshape the subjectivities of zygotes and embryos. IVF opponents argue that zygotes are 'persons' deserving of human rights and dignity, even prior to implantation in a woman's womb (Leal 2015). They view IVF not as a baby-making, pro-life technology (as it is viewed in Chile), but as a murderous practice that creates excess embryos and callously kills them. While IVF opponents work to naturalise embryos as 'persons', they denaturalise processes that create embryos outside of coitus. They talk about IVF as 'a process in which embryonic human beings are *artificially created* outside a mother's womb' (Kukla 2012, my emphasis). Although IVF is labelled as 'artificial', the 'natural-ness' of other things – celibacy, C-section birth, or infant formula, for example – is left unquestioned. In this sense, selfish would-be mothers, doomed embryos, and 'artificial' IVF emerge as central subjects in paternalistic narratives that privilege hetero-, sexual, procreative reproduction – and that position this ideal reproductive profile as the authentic repository of national identity.

The construction of national identities through reproductive biopolitics emerges in the chapter by Linders and Bessett, who show that Sweden's approach to abortion services is imagined, in part, as a humanitarian response to what is unfolding in neighbouring countries. Schulz and Schmitter show how discourses such as 'bodily autonomy' or 'pro-choice' affect the shape of abortion debates in the United Kingdom and Switzerland, while Luehrmann unpacks the concept of 'post-abortion syndrome' that made its way to Russia from the United States. In Russia, she shows, abortion stories 'become the unlikely place where questions of historical memory and national identity can be addressed' (this volume). These examples show that national identity is drawn from and dependent on reproductive politics in more ways than we might imagine; indeed, the relationship between national identity and reproductive governance may be one of the enduring lessons of this anthology.

Neoliberal Reproductive Governance

Although this volume does not emphasise the economic dimensions of abortion rights (except for Mishtal, this volume), the theoretical emphasis on subject-making power cannot be uncoupled from changes in neoliberal capitalism, socialism, and transitional economies. Viviana Zelizer gave us a brilliant demonstration of the relationship between reproduction and economics when she showed that children in the United States who were once valued for their contributions to household economies have gradually been transformed into 'priceless children' whose parents consume on their behalf (Roberts 2015: 452; Zelizer 1994). In Costa Rica, some people

I interviewed suggested that the impasse over reproductive politics might be the result of a quid pro quo between the government and the Catholic hierarchy. In the late 2000s, the government was pushing to pass a free trade agreement with the United States, but Church leaders were balking because they were concerned about the agreement's effects on the poor. Many voters saw the vote as a referendum on Costa Rica's future. Would the country retain its historic commitment to the welfare state or would it cave to corporate and political pressure to open markets and reduce trade tariffs? Eventually, the clerics chose to stand aside; they did not actively oppose the agreement. In a 2009 referendum, Costa Ricans approved the CAFTA-DR Free Trade Agreement by a slim margin. The rumour on the street was that the Catholic hierarchy cut a deal with the presidential administration then in power; the Church would support CAFTA (despite its reservations) if the president would agree not to loosen the laws against IVF, abortion, or same-sex marriage. There is no way to verify this story but even as rumour it shows how people understand the realpolitik of reproductive governance; free trade becomes ethical and desirable while sexual and reproductive rights movements become intolerable and offensive to the body politic.

One more anecdote from Costa Rica should suffice to demonstrate how the deadlock over in vitro fertilisation is complicated by the open markets of neoliberalism. IVF procedures tend to be little regulated around the world, at a time when fertility tourism and surrogacy are on the rise (Inhorn and Patrizio 2012; Pfeffer 2011). As a result, poor women are being exploited. Frozen ova and embryos created through IVF sometimes circulate on international black markets (Nahman 2011). In Costa Rica, these abuses provide fodder for IVF opponents, who argue that IVF should be prohibited entirely to prevent human ova or embryos from being objectified or sold. 'La vida humana no se negocia, human life should not be commodified', they say. Well-meaning Costa Rican lawmakers feel a moral obligation to both comply with international human rights law and offer the world an exemplary piece of legislation that will protect women and embryos from commercial exploitation. The framework of reproductive governance shows how Costa Ricans struggle with reproductive policy in deciding how to act as responsible global citizens in an era of neoliberalism and competing rights' claims.

Refocusing the Analytical Gaze

The enormous scope of global abortion politics presents a challenge for feminist social scientists – where to focus the analytic gaze? As we examine the changing landscapes of population politics in places such as Ireland or Italy, it is important to situate sexual and reproductive rights within larger frameworks including 'global capitalism, militarism, neocolonial and race-ethnic conflicts, and the gender hierarchies that persist everywhere' (Corrêa, Petchesky, and Parker 2008: 151). Too often, discussions of sexual and reproductive rights tend to be isolated from analyses of neoliberalism and global politics. When sexual and reproduction rights are analytically segregated from domains such as migration, health rights, humanitarianism, or poverty, it is too easy to assign reproduction to a private realm and to imagine women primarily in their embodied roles as reproducers rather than as other kinds of human rights aspirants, citizens, and subjects.

The chapters in this volume focus on abortion as the ultimate barometer of progress towards reproductive rights. Anthropologists of reproduction and human rights insist on the importance of considering context (Merry 2006; Merry and Levitt 2011; Willen 2011), and in this vein it could be argued that abortion is too narrowly individualistic and focused on 'choice' to capture the totality of women's reproductive experiences. Critics in the United States have argued that focusing on abortion leads us to neglect the governmental conditions and policies that make up the larger fight for reproductive justice, especially for women of colour. Reproductive justice can be understood to encompass the kind of contraception encouraged for black women, for example, or the racism inherent in adoption policy, or the popularity of baby safe haven laws (see Briggs 2012; Browner 2015; Luna and Luker 2013; Oaks 2015; Roberts 1998). In Europe, as some of the authors show, reproduction is always a subtext when right-wing politicians talk about immigration policy and the expansion of Islam; in these ways, xenophobia affects the parameters and shape of reproductive governance. Abortion is omnipresent in debates over ostensibly unrelated issues such as hospital conscientious objection protocols or mitochondrial DNA transfer. Even simple and widely accepted procedures to treat infertility can explode into proxy battles over abortion. Abortion may be the crucible of reproductive justice, but we should not lose sight of the fact that it is only one part of the story.

Many of these studies are set within national and regional boundaries, but there are limits to using country studies to understand the global dimensions of abortion. These limitations are especially pertinent in an age when women travel to find safe abortion services, as Irish women do, or when high-profile abortion cases can achieve instant international notoriety. This is what happened when Savita Halappanavar died in Ireland of septic shock after being denied treatment for a miscarriage-in-progress in 2012. Her case, like many others around the world, sparked international outrage and drew public attention to the consequences of draconian abortion laws. An emphasis on the legality and politics of abortion is vital to securing abortion rights, but sometimes deflects our attention from the policies that affect abortion behind the scenes; these include trade accords and visa requirements that affect the cross-border movement of people and patented drugs, the availability and distribution of technologies such as ultrasound machines and handheld plastic aspirators, and the corporate decisions of pharmaceutical and device manufacturers (see Erikson 2011). Who profits from the off-label use of misoprostol (and its counterfeits) to induce clandestine abortion? The cross-border economics and business of abortion remains understudied.

Movements for and against reproductive rights have become globalised. Chapters in this volume focus on Europe, yet many of the features of anti-abortion activism surface also in Latin America. Crisis pregnancy centres, the increase of conscience clauses, the marketing of post-abortion syndrome, March for Life (discussed by Celis and Coene in their chapter on Belgium), and the tactic of creating moral panics over sex education or second trimester abortion are not developed de novo in each country; they bear the hallmarks of well-organised transnational manoeuvres. We need social science analyses of conservative Catholic policymaking and anti-choice activism at a larger-than-national level (Buss and Herman 2003). When Pope Francis announced in April 2015 that he would send 'missionaries of mercy' around the world to absolve women of 'previously unpardonable sins, including abortion' (Miller 2015), he was rejecting the framework of reproductive rights; according to this comparatively progressive pope, abortion is not a right but a sin. Meanwhile, the Helms Amendment prevents United States funds from being used to provide abortion services, even for victims of sexualised violence in European locations including eastern Ukraine (Vikhrest 2015). These chapters contribute to the much-needed literature on transnational organising by abortion opponents, yet we still need ethnographic analyses of the role of superpowers (including the European Union) in steering abortion policy worldwide (Goldberg 2009).

The challenges of global ethnography require theories and methods that can capture the complexity of the phenomena we study, according to Susan Erikson (2011). We see such complexity exemplified in Mishtal's chapter about the effects of Polish pronatalism, the resurgence of conservative Catholicism, and the larger European preoccupation with demographic shifts manifested in massive immigration, widespread austerity and unemployment, and sharply declining birth rates. How and why do birth rates decline, and what conditions give rise to pronatalist statecraft? Carole Browner (2015) points out that declining fertility rates are not simply the result of women deciding to have fewer children; they are the result of neo-liberal economic policies that require women to work outside the home and manage childcare, therefore making large families 'less attractive and less feasible'. In this context of changing economics and gender relations, the chapter by Schulz and Schmitter shows that abortion policies can be a reflection of progress towards women's liberation and gender equality. But Linders and Bessett urge caution, because in Sweden relaxed abortion laws also reflect discrimination against certain women who are deemed unfit mothers and eugenic impulses that regard some children as unworthy. Seeing abortion in the context of reproductive governance allows us to analyse pregnancy termination as one dimension of other social shifts and global trends (see Rivkin-Fish 2010).

As we think critically about expanding the analytic gaze to understand abortion politics, each discipline has its strengths. Legal scholars keep tally of the ever-changing legal landscape while legal advocates search for high-impact litigation. Political scientists compare national level policies and transnational social movements (Alvarez 2000; Htun 2003). Clinicians and public health experts examine the epidemiological, demographic, and health consequences of abortion and anti-abortion legislation (Grossman et al. 2014). Historians show that efforts to regulate bodies have deep roots; in the late nineteenth century, for example, 'practices ... such as childhood masturbation, prostitution, homosexuality, abortion, and the use of birth control, were codified, managed, or outlawed' in an effort to control sexual expression and to foster favoured kinds of reproduction (Roberts 2015: 452). Anthropologists and sociologists – including several included in this volume – tend to work close to the ground, where they can talk to interlocutors, trace their movements, dissect their discourses, watch local media, and engage in proverbial thick description. In Argentina, for instance, colleagues and I have traced the secular professional activities of religiously motivated anti-abortion activists to examine their mark on national politics (Irrazábal 2010, 2011; Morán Faúndes and Peña Defago 2013; Morgan 2014). It is not easy to trace the global perambulations of abortion politics, but neither is it impossible.

Inspired by the chapters in this volume, future abortion research in Europe and elsewhere could expand in several directions. How do abortion rights fit into larger human rights movements? Why, for example, did Amnesty International broaden its scope to include sexual and reproductive rights in 2007, and what were the consequences of this decision? Why do so many mainstream human rights organisations continue to exclude reproductive rights from their mandates? What about religious alliances; how do Catholic theoreticians and political strategists form alliances with their evangelical Protestant and Russian Orthodox counterparts to regulate bodies and sexual morality? We need to follow the money; who profits from existing reproductive policies, and how do businesses profit from abortion or its alternatives? We need feminist science studies scholars to investigate the movement of the non-human 'actants' critical to abortion, such as miso-prostol pills ordered online, or manual vacuum aspiration or ultrasound devices (see Suh 2015). We need to know how abortion fits within systems of nationalised and privatised medical care. We could benefit from greater insights into the political calculus of legislators and judges forced to adjudi-cate abortion law and policy. If abortion is a political issue, one wonders, is it best studied in clinics? We need to know more about fathers as reproduc-tive subjects and as the covert beneficiaries of legal and illegal abortion (see Daniels 2008). We need further studies of the gendered impacts of labour conditions including those that facilitate or impede reproductive justice, including parental leave, childcare, and food and housing subsidies. Even in postwar Europe where abortion rights may seem relatively advanced, there is much to be done.

Lynn M. Morgan is Mary E. Woolley Professor of Anthropology at Mount Holyoke College. She is author of *Icons of Life: A Cultural History of Human Embryos* (University of California Press, 2009), *Community Participation in Health: The Politics of Primary Care in Costa Rica* (Cambridge University Press, 1993), *Fetal Subjects, Feminist Positions* (University of Pennsylvania Press, 1999) and over thirty articles. Her awards include the Rachel Carson Prize from 4S and fellowships from the National Science Foundation, National Endowment for Humanities, Social Science Research Council, and the School for Advanced Research. She is currently writing about the backlash against reproductive rights movements in Latin America.

Note

1. See website: http://www.becketfund.org/our-mission/ [retrieved 24 December 2015].

References

Alvarez, S.E. 2000. 'Translating the Global Effects of Transnational Organizing on Local Feminist Discourses and Practices in Latin America', *Meridians* 1(1): 29–67.

Barot, S. 2011. 'Unsafe Abortion: The Missing Link in Global Efforts to Improve Ma-ternal Health', *Guttmacher Policy Review* 14(2): 24–28.

Bradshaw, S., A. Criquillion, V.A. Castillo and G. Wilson. 2008. 'Talking Rights or What is Right? Understandings and Strategies around Sexual, Reproductive and Abortion

Rights in Nicaragua', in M. Mukhopadhyay and S. Meer (eds), *Gender, Rights, and Development: A Global Sourcebook*. Amsterdam: Royal Tropical Institute, pp. 57–68.

Briggs, L. 2012. *Somebody's Children: The Politics of Transracial and Transnational Adoption*. Durham: Duke University Press.

Browner, C. 2015. 'The Politics of Reproduction: From Reproductive Rights to Reproductive Justice', in L. Disch and M. Harkesworth (eds), *Oxford Handbook of Feminist Theory*. New York: Oxford University Press.

Buss, D. and D. Herman. 2003. *Globalising Family Values: The Christian Right in International Politics*. Minneapolis: University of Minnesota Press.

Colen, S. 1995. '"Like a Mother To Them": Stratified Reproduction and West Indian Childcare Workers and Employers in New York', in F. Ginsburg and R. Rapp (eds), *Conceiving the New World Order: The Global Politics of Reproduction*. Berkeley: University of California Press, pp. 78–102.

Corrêa, S., R. Petchesky and R. Parker. 2008. *Sexuality, Health, and Human Rights*. London: Routledge.

Daniels, C.R. 2008. *Exposing Men: The Science and Politics of Male Reproduction*. Oxford: Oxford University Press.

Erikson, S.L. 2011. 'Global Ethnography: Problems of Theory and Method', in C.H. Browner and C.F. Sargent (eds), *Reproduction, Globalization, and the State: New Theoretical and Ethnographic Perspectives*. Durham: Duke University Press, pp. 23–37.

Ginsburg, F.D. and R. Rapp. 1995. *Conceiving the New World Order: The Global Politics of Reproduction*. Berkeley: University of California Press.

Goldberg, M. 2009. *The Means of Reproduction: Sex, Power, and the Future of the World*. New York: Penguin.

Grossman, D., K. White, K. Hopkins and J.E. Potter. 2014. 'The Public Health Threat of Anti-abortion Legislation', *Contraception* 89(2): 73–74.

Guttmacher Institute. 2012. 'Facts on Induced Abortion Worldwide', Guttmacher Institute. Retrieved 27 May 2015 from http://www.guttmacher.org/pubs/fb_IAW.html

———. 2014. 'More State Abortion Restrictions Were Enacted in 2011–2013 Than in the Entire Previous Decade', Guttmacher Institute. Retrieved 27 May 2015 http://www.guttmacher.org/media/inthenews/2014/01/02/index.html

Hellerstein, E. 2014. 'The Rise of the DIY Abortion in Texas', *The Atlantic*, June 27. Retrieved 27 May 2015 http://www.theatlantic.com/health/archive/2014/06/the-rise-of-the-diy-abortion-in-texas/373240/

Htun, M. 2003. *Sex and the State: Abortion, Divorce, and the Family under Latin American Dictatorships and Democracies*. Cambridge: Cambridge University Press.

Inhorn, M.C. and P. Patrizio. 2012. 'The Global Landscape of Cross-border Reproductive Care: Twenty Key Findings for the New Millennium', *Current Opinion in Obstetrics & Gynecology* 24(3): 158–63.

Irrazábal, G. 2010. 'El derecho al aborto en discusión: La intervención de grupos católicos en la comisión de salud de la Legislatura de la Ciudad de Buenos Aires', *Sociologías* 12(24): 308–36.

———. 2011. 'La bioética como entrenamiento y facilitadora de la influencia de agentes católicos en el espacio público en Argentina', *Revista del Centro de Investigación* 9(36): 5–23.

Kukla, K. 2012. 'The Real Reason IVF is Facing Possible Legalization in Costa Rica', *Human Life International*, November 28. Retrieved 27 May 2015 from http://www.hli.org/2012/11/the-real-reason-ivf-is-facing-possible-legalization-in-costa-rica/

Leal, A. 2015. 'La dignidad humana del cigoto', *La Nación*, 19 May. Retrieved 26 May 2015 from http://www.nacion.com/opinion/foros/Alejandro-Leal-dignidad-humana-cigoto_0_1488451163.html

Luna, Z. and K. Luker. 2013. 'Reproductive Justice', *Annual Review of Law and Social Science* 9: 327–52.

Merry, S.E. 2006. *Human Rights and Gender Violence: Translating International Law into Local Justice*. Chicago: University of Chicago Press.

Merry, S.E. and P. Levitt. 2011. 'Making Women's Human Rights in the Vernacular: Navigating the Culture/Rights Divide', in D. Hodgson (ed.), *Gender and Culture at the Limit of Rights*. Philadelphia: University of Pennsylvania Press, pp. 81–100.

Miller, M.E. 2015. 'Pope Francis Will Send "Missionaries of Mercy" to Absolve Women of Abortion "Sin"', *Washington Post*, May 7. Retrieved 26 May 2015 http://www.washingtonpost.com/news/morning-mix/wp/2015/05/07/pope-francis-will-send-missionaries-of-mercy-to-absolve-women-of-abortion-sin/

Morán Faúndes, J.M. and M.A. Peñas Defago. 2013. '¿Defensores de la vida? ¿De cuál "vida"? Un análisis genealógico de la noción de "vida" sostenida por la jerarquía católica contra el aborto', *Sexualidad, Salud y Sociedad* 15:10–36.

Morgan, L.M. 2014. 'Claiming Rosa Parks: Conservative Catholic Bids for "Rights" in Contemporary Latin America', *Culture, Health and Sexuality* 19(2): 1–15.

Morgan, L.M. and M.W. Michaels (eds). 1999. *Foetal Subjects, Feminist Positions*. Philadelphia: University of Pennsylvania Press.

Morgan, L.M. and E.F.S. Roberts. 2012. 'Reproductive Governance in Latin America', *Anthropology and Medicine* 19(2): 241–254.

Nahman, M. 2011. 'Reverse Traffic: Intersecting Inequalities in Human Egg Donation', *Reproductive Biomedicine Online* 23(5): 626–33.

Nowicka, W. 2011. 'Sexual and Reproductive Rights and the Human Rights Agenda: Controversial and Contested', *Reproductive Health Matters* 19(38):119–28.

Oaks, L. 2015. *Giving Up Baby: Safe Haven Laws, Motherhood, and Reproductive Justice*. New York: New York University Press.

Oberman, M. 2013. 'Cristina's World: Lessons from El Salvador's Ban on Abortion', *Stanford Law & Policy Review* 24(271):1–38.

Paltrow, L.M. and J. Flavin. 2013. 'Arrests of and Forced Interventions on Pregnant Women in the United States, 1973–2005: Implications for Women's Legal Status and Public Health', *Journal of Health Politics, Policy and Law* 38(2): 299–43.

Pfeffer, N. 2011. 'Eggs-ploiting Women: A Critical Feminist Analysis of the Different Principles in Transplant and Fertility Tourism', *Reproductive Biomedicine Online* 23(5): 634–41.

Rivkin-Fish, M. 2010. 'Pronatalism, Gender Politics, and the Renewal of Family Support in Russia: Toward a Feminist Anthropology of "Maternity Capital"', *Slavic Review* 69(3): 701–24.

Roberts, D. 1998. *Killing the Black Body: Race, Reproduction, and the Meaning of Liberty*. New York: Vintage.

Roberts, E.F.S. 2015. 'Reproduction and Cultural Anthropology', in J.D. Wright (ed.), *International Encyclopedia of the Social & Behavioral Sciences*, 2nd edition, Vol 20. Oxford: Elsevier, pp. 450–56.

Sack, K. 2014. 'Transplant Brokers in Israel Lure Desperate Kidney Patients to Costa Rica', *New York Times*, August 17. Retrieved 26 May 2015 from http://www.nytimes.com/2014/08/17/world/middleeast/transplant-brokers-in-israel-lure-desperate-kidney-patients-to-costa-rica.html?_r=0

Stern, S.J. and S. Straus. 2014. 'Embracing Paradox: Human Rights in the Global Age', in S.J. Stern and S. Straus (eds), *The Human Rights Paradox: Universality and its Discontents*. Madison: University of Wisconsin Press, pp. 3–30.

Suh, S. 2015. '"Right Tool", Wrong "Job": Manual Vacuum Aspiration, Post-abortion Care and Transnational Population Politics in Senegal', *Social Science & Medicine* 135: 56–66.

The Lancet. 2006a. Sexual and Reproductive Health. October. Retrieved 27 May 2015 from http://www.thelancet.com/series/sexual-and-reproductive-health

The Lancet. 2006b. 'Executive Summary of Lancet Sexual and Reproductive Health Series'. Retrieved 27 May 2015 from http://www.who.int/reproductivehealth/publications/general/lancet_exec_summ.pdf

Trinko, K. 2014. 'Children with Down Syndrome Tell Pregnant Mom about the Happy Life Her Son with Down Syndrome Will Have', *The Daily Signal*, March 17. Retrieved 27 May 2015 from http://dailysignal.com/2014/03/17/watch-children-syndrome-tell-pregnant-mom-happy-life-son-syndrome-will/

Vaggione, J.M. 2005. 'Reactive Politicization and Religious Dissidence: The Political Mutations of the Religious', *Social Theory and Practice* 31(2):1–23.

Vaggione, J.M. (ed.). 2009. *El activismo religioso conservador en Latinoamérica*. Córdoba: Católicas por el Derecho a Decidir.

Vikhrest, A. 2015. 'All-enveloping Silence Persists around Rape in Ukraine Conflict', *Women Under Siege, Women's Media Center*. Retrieved 31 May 2015 from http://www.womenundersiegeproject.org/blog/entry/all-enveloping-silence-persists-around-rape-in-ukraine-conflict

Willen, S. 2011. 'Do "Illegal" Im/migrants Have a Right to Health? Engaging Ethical Theory as Social Practice at a Tel Aviv Open Clinic', *Medical Anthropology Quarterly* 25(3): 303–30.

Zelizer, V.A. 1994. *Pricing the Priceless Child: The Changing Social Value of Children*. Princeton: Princeton University Press.

Acknowledgements

We would like to thank first Dr Lorena Anton, who had the germinal idea of this book and launched us into this great adventure. By the time we had our initial Skype meeting with Lorena about this volume in 2011, we had already observed that a book about abortion politics in Europe was sorely needed, in particular since many significant scholars are conducting researchers in this area. Therefore, we would like to thank all the authors, who gave their unique and valuable contribution to this volume with high quality chapters based on thorough anthropological, sociological, historical and legal analyses of the complex debates on reproductive governance, abortion rights, women's rights and the status of the embryo/foetus in different times and geopolitical and social contexts in Europe. We appreciate their commitment to the long-term process of publishing an edited book.

We are grateful to the anonymous external reviewers of this book for their perceptive comments and suggestions and for the support they gave to this book's publication. We would also like to thank Berghahn Books for their early expression of interest in this volume and our editor that patiently accompanied us throughout the editing process. We also thank Eileen Quam for her excellent work on this book's index.

Finally, Dr Mishtal and Dr De Zordo would like to thank the Charlotte Ellertson Postdoctoral Fellowship in Abortion and Reproductive Health (US-Ibis Reproductive Health & Columbia University), which nourished and advanced their passion and interest in the area of abortion research, and linked them to the wider interdisciplinary community of reproductive rights scholars and advocates in the United States and elsewhere around the world. Dr De Zordo is also grateful to the Beatriu de Pinós Postdoctoral Fellowship (Spain, Catalunya-Universitat de Barcelona), which provided her with the space and time she needed to work on this challenging book. Finally, she would like to thank her family for their support during the large process of this book's edition, and particularly her son Leo, who was born when the first idea for this book germinated.

Dr Anton would like to express her gratitude to her co-editors Dr De Zordo and Dr Mishtal for their openness to the initial idea of this book, their work during the entire editing process and especially their constant support during the final steps of this great adventure. Also, she would like to thank the Marie Curie-Career Integration Grants programme (European

Comission-FP7), which provided her with the resources to work on this book. Last but not least, Dr Anton would like to thank her family for their support during the entire adventure of this book.

Index

Protest, Culture and Society

General editors:
Kathrin Fahlenbrach, Institute for Media and Communication, University of University of Hamburg, Germany.
Martin Klimke, New York University Abu Dhabi.
Joachim Scharloth, Technical University Dresden, Germany.

Protest movements have been recognized as significant contributors to processes of political participation and transformations of culture and value systems, as well as to the development of both a national and transnational civil society.

This series brings together the various innovative approaches to phenomena of social change, protest and dissent which have emerged in recent years, from an interdisciplinary perspective. It contextualizes social protest and cultures of dissent in larger political processes and socio-cultural transformations by examining the influence of historical trajectories and the response of various segments of society, political and legal institutions on a national and international level. In doing so, the series offers a more comprehensive and multi-dimensional view of historical and cultural change in the twentieth and twenty-first century.

Lightning Source UK Ltd.
Milton Keynes UK
UKHW04f1000101018
330262UK00003B/68/P